CONTESTING MARKETS

Contesting Markets

Analyses of Ideology, Discourse and Practice

edited by
ROY DILLEY

EDINBURGH UNIVERSITY PRESS

© Edinburgh University Press, 1992

Edinburgh University Press
22 George Square, Edinburgh

Typeset in Linotron Garamond
by Koinonia Ltd, Bury, and
printed in Great Britain by
Hartnolls Ltd, Bodmin

A CIP record for this book is available from
British Library

ISBN 07486 0371 9

Contents

Notes on the Contributors

Paul Alexander is Associate Professor in the Department of Anthropology, University of Sidney.

John Davis is Professor of Social Anthropology, All Souls College, Oxford.

Roy Dilley is Lecturer in Social Anthropology at the University of St Andrews.

Peter Geschiere is Professor of African Anthropology and Chairman of the African Studies Centre, Leiden University, The Netherlands.

Stephen Gudeman is Professor of Anthropology, Department of Anthropology, University of Minnesota.

Christopher Hann is Professor of Social Anthropology, University of Kent.

Keith Hart is Lecturer in Social Anthropology and Director, African Studies Centre, Cambridge University.

Ladislav Holy is Professor of Social Anthropology at the University of St Andrews.

Heinz Lubasz is Reader in the History of Ideas, Department of History, University of Essex.

Joanna Overing is Senior Lecturer in Social Anthropology at the London School of Economics and Political Science.

Tristan Platt is Director of the Institute of Amerindian Studies and Lecturer in Social Anthropology at the University of St Andrews.

Peter Preston is Lecturer in Sociology, Department of Government, Strathclyde University.

Michael Stewart was until recently Junior Research Fellow at Corpus Christi College, Cambridge. He is about to take up an ESRC Research Fellowship at the London School of Economics and Political Science to work on Romanian peasant economics.

Jock Stirrat is Lecturer in Social Anthropology and a part-time development consultant based at the School of African and Asian Studies, University of Sussex.

Norman Stockman is Lecturer in Sociology, Department of Sociology, University of Aberdeen.

Preface

This edited collection of essays is based on a selection of papers presented at a conference entitled 'The Notion of the Market in Social Anthropological and Sociological Perspective' held at the University of St Andrews in early January 1991. This meeting was the fifth in a series of occasional conferences organised by members of the University's Social Anthropology unit. While most of those attending this conference were social anthropologists, also included were sociologists, political scientists, historians and economists. Given the significance and scope of the subject it seemed appropriate to include other disciplines at the meeting, and this collection of essays broadly encompasses that interdisciplinary intent. Whilst over twenty papers were read at the conference, unfortunately only a selection of these are published here due to the constraints of space. The success of the conference as a whole rests with all the participants, the excellence of their many contributions, and the convivial and relaxed atmosphere they helped to create.

As convenor, it falls to me to thank, on behalf of the participants, the University of St Andrews and its Principal for providing facilities to host the conference, as well as the University's Arts and Divinity Research Committee for providing initial financial support in the form of a conference guarantee. I also gratefully acknowledge the generous financial support given to the conference by the British Academy, Economic and Social Research Council (Award No. Y318263003), Nuffield Foundation, Royal Anthropological Institute and Fritz Thyssen Foundation (Germany), all of which provided grants to attract a distinguished and international group of scholars.

The conference focused on the subject of 'the market' – that key term of political and economic debate in Europe and America during the 1980s. This debate crystallised not just around the market concept in itself, but also concerned its scope of application to increasing areas of the lives of all the members of a globalising world economic system. Indeed, the scope of its application was extended to non-western societies by international agencies and development policies under the control of western interests. The encompassing power of market discourse – its pretensions to encompass the totality of social processes – lies at the heart of the matter. The ideological charge that the market carries is obvious to anyone who has an opinion on current affairs. Thus, the conference called for an examination of the historical and sociological contexts in which market discourses emerge and the ways in which those discourses are deployed. For if the market as a concept is a product of European and

American history, then its application to societies other than those of the First World needs most urgently to be investigated.

This collection of essays is concerned with market discourse and with the significance of the concept of the market. As an exploratory exercise this volume opens up a series of questions about the status of the concept in numerous areas of social and economic analysis. The contributors to the volume do not subscribe to one particular theoretical position, nor do they necessarily agree on what status should be attributed to the concept of the market. All of them, however, do agree that an inspection of the market concept is long overdue, and that this inspection throws up important implications for social and economic theory, comparative analysis, development policy and more.

The question of the status of the concept of the market is central to all the analyses presented here. The concept can be addressed on at least three different levels of abstraction: as an abstract model in theoretical discourse; as a folk model of actors' conceptions that is related to practice in some way; as a descriptive term of real world events. Debate over the issue can be split along lines crudely characterised in the following way: *market realists* wish to retain the term as a description of the flows of material things, services, information and so on, and as an analytical concept with some explanatory power; *market modellers* and discourse analysts question the market as an objective scientific entity by claiming that as a folk model its construction has to be contextualised with reference to particular cultures and political strategies; finally, *market comparativists* elucidate by a piecemeal approach not only forms of socio-economic behaviour in non-western settings, but also, through a comparative framework which these studies generate, the nature of market models and practice in western societies. Despite the range of theoretical stances presented here, one consequence arising from this volume as a whole is that greater reflexivity, clarity and specificity must henceforth be sought in any attempt to utilise concepts of the market in future analysis.

This collection starts with an inspection of historical and contemporary aspects of western economic discourse (Part I) and moves, via a consideration of the relationship between the ethnography of economic practices and the models used in their interpretation (Part II), to the issue of the articulation of modes of discourse by which indigenous cultural constructs and western notions are assimilated, 'hybridised' and juxtaposed with regard to forms of external trade and exchange (Part III). The influence of market rhetoric within development discourse is next considered in Part IV, followed by case studies of the way the market features as a symbol and cultural construct in contemporary national-level political discourse. A conclusion and overview of the whole volume draws the collection to a close.

There is a history and intellectual debt which lies behind the organisation of the 1991 markets conference. I warmly acknowledge the perseverance of members of the ESRC team, with whom I worked in Aberdeen in 1985-6, in the face of my increasing sense of unease over concepts of the market; Professor Bahram Tavakolian, Peter Preston and David Oldman for intellectual stimulation and good company in the bars of Old Aberdeen; Keith Hart for his encouragement of the project early on and

Mark Hobart for his kind help and advice. More recently, my thanks go to Stephen Gudeman for contributing much to the shape of this volume and, in particular, in his role of conference summariser, for his many valuable and constructive comments on the conference proceedings. To Mrs. S. Davis and William Singleton go my appreciative thanks for their efforts in typing and preparing the manuscript for press.

ROY DILLEY
St Andrews, 1992

I

Contesting Markets

A General Introduction to Market Ideology, Imagery and Discourse[1]

ROY DILLEY

I worked out a theory of how a free people can take its economic
decisions without interference from politicians, who know nothing
about it anyhow, by using that extraordinarily sensitive and automatic
mechanism – the market. (Enoch Powell, on *Talking to Myself,* BBC2)

The apparent triumph of the ideology of free-market economics in the west during
the 1980s has paradoxically spawned an increasing sense of unease about the status of
the concept of the market. Whilst the concept has become hegemonic, it is also in
crisis. This crisis arises as part of a broader challenge to the metanarratives of
modernity in general, and to the master concepts of social science in particular. The
functioning of markets in western societies is now recognised as underinvestigated.
Quite how, or whether, the market concept should be deployed as a term of
translation that applies to societies other than those of the west is yet more complex.

This collection of essays addresses the ways in which market discourses are
constructed and invoked in particular settings. The volume has three broad aims:
first, to highlight the specificities of market discourse in *our* local discussions of social
processes; second, to return to the root of our market metaphor – that is, aspects of
trade and those places in which it is conducted – and ask what part market thinking
plays in western representations of social practices, the agents of which may understand them differently; third, and most significantly, to grasp the implications of the
gap that opens between the limitations of market discourse and the alternative
understandings of trade and exchange that can be recognised if we attend to the
particularity of other times and other places. The normative terms and dominant
narratives of market discourse all too easily engulf these alternative models of practice
and cultural understanding. Part of our project, then, requires a willingness to locate
and listen to the diversity of voices and conversations that may fall outside market
discourse. But, this is not all.

A central concern of the contributors to this volume involves the articulation of
economic discourses. This might be seen as the discursive counterpart to the articulation of economic processes, and in common with these processes this articulation is
the site of unequal power. The specific conjunctures of discourses are many and

complex. For example, particular interest groups in western and non-western societies have avidly assimilated market theory, rhetoric and imagery. The case studies presented here show how this culturally constructed discourse articulates with other available social discourses, and how through this process of assimilation the market concept becomes transformed, mediated and translated within its new cultural environment (see the chapters by Hann, Holy, Stewart and Stockman on eastern/central Europe and China). This is not just an issue merely for the once state-planned economies of communist countries, but articulation also occurs within those cultures on the periphery of the 'world market' (see Geschiere on Cameroon, Platt on Bolivia, Overing on the Amazon Basin).[2]

Whilst some of the contributors to this volume point to the articulation of discourses between cultures, others point to modes of articulation within western culture (see Preston and Lubasz on the elevation and dominance of economic narratives over various dissenting western voices; also Hart on cold-war rhetoric, and Stirrat on development discourse). The articulation of yet other modes of market discourse has important implications for social theory, for economic anthropology (see Alexander, Davis and Stewart), and for those wishing to understand development policy prescriptions (see Hart and Stirrat). First, if what we understand as market processes are culturally mediated and differently construed on the periphery of the world market, and if cultural understandings relate to social practice, then the way in which other cultures model market processes and forces is critical to a more complete understanding of the 'impact of the market' on the periphery, as well as to directives aimed at economic development (see Geschiere, Hart and Stirrat). Second, economic concepts and market-derived notions within economic anthropology must also be inspected both in terms of their applicability to other cultures and of their adequacy as descriptions of the systems which generated them (see Alexander, Davis and Stewart). The politics of privileged representation, and the claims of certain voices to scientific status, are crucial issues in economic anthropology. Third, the implications of market discourse for social theory need to be traced. Dominant representations of the social totality frequently draw on diverse images and metaphors of the market and on notions of exchange. The ability of market-based images to represent social totalities must be problematised, and the possibility of other forms of cultural representation must be investigated ethnographically (see Overing). Representations of exchange are predicated on the recognition of particular forms of personhood and types of social agency. Thus, the analysis of the construction of these representations must precede sociological explanations of sociality or exchange.[3]

1.1 A MASTER CONCEPT OF WESTERN DISCOURSE: THE ESSENTIALISATION OF THE MARKET

1.1.1 On the Word 'Market'

> What is a market? Is it a place, is it a process, a principle, a power? History though yields no definitive answers to the questions. (Agnew 1986:17)

> Indeed, what is usually referred to as 'the market' is no more than a blank
> space occupied by a diversity of changing social relations. (Tribe 1981:94)

If the market is indeed a 'blank space', then we have certainly inscribed indelibly on it all of Agnew's properties. This process of inscription within our own understandings can be recognised in the etymological development of the term in English. Indeed, the possibility of erasing our own inscriptions must be entertained if we are to attend to the ways other cultures inscribe the field of exchange.

The English word 'market' derives from the Latin terms *mercatus* meaning 'trade' or 'a market', and its cognate forms *merx*, 'merchandise', and *mercor*, 'to buy (*OED*). A history of this usage reveals a complex development of ideas and social practices. Progressive elaborations of the meaning of the term 'market' have established a variety of referents which today constitute its range of meanings [4], and these accretions can be seen in three stages. From its early use, whose principal concrete referent was a social gathering at a particular place, the term became progressively abstract through the sixteenth century in reference to the *processes* of buying and selling, doing business and seizing opportunities. Finally in the seventeenth and eighteenth centuries, the definite article frequently precedes the noun that now denotes an abstract aggregate geographical form ('the French market') and a vector of turnover and rates of exchange. This progressive abstraction from a particular type of striking physical form and locale, produces a model to which is attributed abstract properties. It also becomes the subject of metaphorical elaboration. Thus the market as a physical locale is the point of departure for the construction of a metaphor which once dissociated from its original inspiration becomes the subject of displacement (Parkin 1982). As a displaced metaphor detached from its concrete referent, the term 'market' has become a 'pocket' whose contents are defined in relation to the uses to which it is put. [5]

These broad changes in usage and referent parallel shifts in social practice and ways of modelling the economy. In very broad strokes, what is connoted here are transitions from the seventeenth century (and earlier) doctrine of fair price and the moral economy of provision coming under attack by mercantilists and political economists in the eighteenth century, who deployed increasingly abstract conceptions of market processes in the struggle for a new economic order. The wedge driven between market as physical location and market as principle becomes particularly incisive as the sphere of the economic is increasingly modelled as a distinctive domain.

1.1.2 Of Morality and Markets

Market and commercial activities often attract cultural evaluations cast in moral terms. Such constructions in western societies are seen as resulting from a distinction between the spheres of morality and of markets. That this ideological opposition between markets and morality is at all possible relates to the 'emancipation' in western thought of the economic sphere from the political and religious ones (Dumont 1977 and 1986) and, once the separation is made, the constitution of mutual relationships between these two domains of life becomes an ideological possibility which can take a variety of forms. [6] Yet condemnations of marketing and commerce are articulated in a variety of ways in diverse historical and cultural contexts, and the ideological separations of western thought may not be relevant in explaining them. My contention is that moral evaluations of trade and commerce must be viewed empirically as arising from a context of changing politico-economic relationships. The market represents a contested field of power, and the moral evaluations attached to the agents and relations of exchange are a consequence of the processes of contestation. Many of the chapters below discuss attributions of morality to commercial exchange, and these attributions are moral responses on the part of market agents to the potential imbalances of power engendered through exchange relations. Moreover, these studies show that prices – that key to understanding the market in orthodox economics – are morally and culturally construed in terms of a just, fair or right price.

Parry suggests that Aristotle's distinction between householding (*oikonomia*) and commerce (*kapelike*), based on a separation between 'natural' and 'unnatural trade', is a form of moral condemnation of commerce which must be seen in terms of an 'ideological commitment to a traditional householding economy oriented towards self-sufficiency' (1989:85); that is, moral condemnation is drawn from an ideology of peasant autarky.[7] This idea is seen also to lie behind medieval theories on the morality of trade and exchange (Parry 1989:84). Whilst no doubt giving currency to Aristotelean ideas, the Schoolmen's concern with the 'just price' focused their attention on the problems of price setting (see de Roover 1968, Southern 1968). Thomas Aquinas, for example, held that prices, though they may vary according to the conditions of different markets, should correspond with the labour and costs of the producer (Tawney 1961:52).[8] A producer charging more than would maintain himself suitably in his social station committed the sin of covetousness and avarice: 'It is right for a man to seek such wealth as is necessary for a livelihood in his station. To seek more is not enterprise, but avarice, and avarice is a deadly sin' (Tawney 1961:44). Markets were thus places where one realised through exchange, set within a moral universe of provision, one's daily bread as a right divinely sanctioned by the Gospels. Price-fixing by public officials or the strictures of the Schoolmen were attempts to articulate a view of man who was in need of protection from vice, cupidity and avarice to which he or she may succumb in the domain of the market-place. Moral condemnation here belongs to a Christian ethic, trying in part to resolve the dilemmas posed by a division between the activities of this world and the promise of the next (Dumont 1986). This radical opposition between the out-worldly and the in-worldly demands on an individual can be seen also as a feature of 'religious ethicisation' of a salvation religion from which develops a *contemptus mundi* (Parry 1986). Yet, these theocratic doctrines were also part of a political ideology which was systematised by a particular section of medieval society, the 'thin upper crust' (Morris 1977).

The changing nature of the politics of exchange relations is apparent from Thompson's work on the eighteenth century (Thompson 1971). The eighteenth century saw the death of the 'moral economy' of provision as a model of social practice and the emergence at the end of the century of a new political economy of the 'free market'. Until the early eighteenth century, exchanges in corn took place directly between consumer and farmer at pitch sales conducted in market-places. Millers and bakers were still conceived in the 'paternalist' provisioning model as working not for profit but for a fair allowance suitable to their station. However, the developing role of such middlemen and dealers came increasingly under legal scrutiny and moral opprobrium. The rise of 'economic' pricing was encouraged by millers, bakers and other dealers who diverted the flow of corn from open pitch-market gatherings to sale by sample. Supplies of corn were hoarded and their release manipulated in order to engineer price levels. These hoarders were described by the Pamphleteers – 'moralists first and economists second' – as 'enemies both to God and man, opposite both to Grace and nature' (Thompson 1971:131). Gentlemen farmers and rural labourers alike complained that the new market procedures amounted to what could be called a loss of 'market transparency'.

That the direct, 'transparent' sale between farmer and consumer competing in local and regional open pitch-markets was transformed by the opaque, indirect practices of middlemen and dealers is ironic, since 'free-market' theory later legitimised such practices in terms of those very characteristics of market transparency and self-regulation. Platt describes similar paradoxes in the Bolivian debate over what really represented free-market trade. Indeed, more generally, the question of market transparency and rationality is raised by many contributors. Clearly, the question of market transparency, like rationality, is relative: the vision of the market as giving a clearer view of the workings of exchange (and by extension of political systems, see Stirrat) may be propagated by development policy-makers, Eastern European liberals and so on. By contrast, however, ordinary folk often see through the workings of the market and find something other than transparent rational choice. For them, the workings of 'market forces' are opaque, mysterious and beyond their control (see Geschiere, Hann, Holy and Stewart).

The breakdown of the 'bread nexus', although apparently effected at the hands of 'the market mechanism' is perhaps better seen in terms of the undermining of the 'moral economy' by powerful, vested trading interests which represented themselves and were represented as agents of the 'free market'. [9] Their increasing power over exchange relations allowed middlemen and dealers to divert the flow of provisions from the old channels into the new. The moral evaluations of the new forms of corn trading and of their agents do not seem to be informed by a progressive subversion of a 'closed estate economy', the root cause of many evaluations for Parry (1989). Instead, the moral representations of changing trade practices involve the disempowerment of particular trading groups within what were previously local and regional networks of corn distribution. The rising demands of an increasingly urban-based population for basic subsistence items, and the new forms of circulation of agricultural produce, appeared to engulf the world of known networks for corn distribution. The moral outcry was a response to the sense of uncertainty and opaqueness triggered by the activities of high-profile middlemen who redefined the politics of exchange relations.

Negative moral evaluations of market activities are noted by a number of contributors (see Hann, Holy and Stockman on the Confucian and Maoist stigmatisation of commerce and the idea of commercial wealth as a danger to social order, and Stewart on the moral aspects of peasant–Gypsy relations). By contrast, Platt's analysis of local Bolivian trade casts middlemen/women in a more positive role as they facilitated trade relations between indian peasants and market-towns, the organisation of which along lines of 'free trade' the indians resisted. At issue in these cases is the way that the relative positions of exchange partners or interest groups are affected by the politics of commerce and trade; that is, moral evaluations are the consequence of changing political relations resulting from trading activities. [10] More particularly, these evaluations often involve the labelling of specific identifiable agents of trade (entrepreneurs, engrossers, middlemen and so on), whose economic activities constitute a redefinition of power relations; it is the very 'visibility' of these market agents which attracts some sort of moral response. Hart and Geschiere, on the other hand, discuss contrasting cases in which the agents of trade on the 'world market' are 'invisible' to local communities, yet the consequences of trade are also assimilated in moral terms. The response of certain Cameroonian peoples, for instance, is to represent changing politico-economic relations as the result of spiritual agents endowed with a particularly aberrant form of morality. The relationship between morality and commerce cannot simply be derived from the structure of a peasant ideology. Moral evaluations, whose forms are always culture specific, result from the processes of contestation within, and over, exchange relations. In the hands of exchange partners – perhaps for the lack of any other means – morality is a weapon in the attempt to address potential imbalances of power relations which arise from and are articulated through the extension and development of 'market' relations.

The identification and moral evaluation of the hand of invisible agents of trade among some Cameroonian peoples takes the form of witches. Yet eighteenth century political economy and modern economics also identify the hand of invisible agents of exchange as Providence (see Lubasz on Adam Smith) or as the market itself. Moreover, this form of agency is similarly attributed a moral dimension. [11] Dumont notes that whilst the ideological emergence of the category of the economy in western thought liberated it from politics, religion and morality, at the same time economic action itself came to be seen as oriented to the common good, and thus had a special, though limited, moral character of its own (Dumont 1977). A 'natural harmony of interests', by which apparent discords are automatically harmonised to the public good, is present in Mandeville's *Fable of the Bees* (1723) and later in Adam Smith's *The Wealth of Nations* (1776), and this conceptualisation contrasts with the Hobbesian world of an 'artificial' harmony of interests in which man is protected from the consequences of his natural state by a Sovereign. The mechanism for harmonising interests and contributing to the commonweal in Smith's *The Wealth of Nations* is taken by subsequent commentators to be the 'invisible hand of the market', which is self-regulating and co-ordinates the activities of its participants (see Lubasz's critique of this misrepresentation of Smith). [12] In the absence, then, of Hobbes's sovereign to tame and control human nature, the market tames and controls all by itself, policing society like 'Leviathan in sheep's clothing' (Jameson 1990/91:273).

The moral character of the market results from a change in basic 'ideologeme' (Dumont 1986:109), for now exchange is seen as advantageous to all parties to a transaction (compare the view held by members of Thompson's eighteenth-century 'crowd' who saw the gain of one party as a *loss* to the other). It was the mercantilists who adopted this view of exchange as advantageous to all in the home market, but who nevertheless remained attached to the idea that international trade was a zero-sum game. Indeed, it was also the expansion of mercantilist and free-trade interests and discourse in the seventeenth and eighteenth centuries which extended the word 'market' to cover the trade in a commodity over an aggregated geographical area. Moreover, with the identification of the centrality of the market as a self-regulating system with a role in establishing a natural harmony of interests, the market concept became further abstracted to the level of a principle and social agent.

Contemporary views about the morality of the market are divided between those who hold the market to be amoral, and those who hold the market to be a vehicle of morality. In social anthropology, the view that market principles have undermined the moral universes of peasant and tribal societies is illustrated by Bohannan and Dalton's reference to the way the brides and the cults of Africa have been sullied with market morality (1962:7; see also Scott 1976). The opposite view is perhaps less often proposed in social anthropology [13], although in general this view is particularly characteristic of liberal economists who associate free-market co-ordination with political freedom and the common good (see note 11).

Whatever moral construction is put on the market, a potential negation is necessarily implied. For liberal economists, the moral order produced by the beneficial market is threatened by state intervention which endangers freedom. [14] Yet, when the market mechanism is seen not to produce the proclaimed common good then a claim on morality is reasserted by populist demands for political intervention in the name of equity (Dumont 1977:79). For state socialists, the state attempts to define a complete field of morality for the building of a just society, and again, once the system fails to deliver its promised ends, the moral code is reconstructed to privilege the market as a new potential form of morality. While each formula appears to be the solution to the other's failures, the moral constructions of state and market are products of the politics of a contested domain. (See Hart, and the chapters by Hann, Holy and Stockman which consider the cultural constructions of the morality of the market and the state in central Europe and China.)

Anthropologists have often worked among peoples whose moral universes are conceived as *sui generis*. Their modes of social organisation occupy a different order of organisation from that of the state and the market. Both market and state are seen as factors external to the mode of social organisation of their subjects, and these factors constitute agents of moral disintegration and outside interference. If 'cold-war rhetoric' of the west saw market and state as representations of social totalities which were in moral opposition (Hart)[15], then the anthropologist produced a moral opposition between his or her 'community' and the amoral external forces of both the market and the state. Hart argues that his idea of an intermediate 'informal economy' became assimilated and progressively transformed by the moral oppositions of cold-war rhetoric about state and market.

1.1.3 Modelling the Market

All real markets are in a sense local ones, and that the only non-local
market is a model of perfection, a moral and economic goal of a
particular segment of the population. (Davis 1985:511)

A challenge to market discourse can be located in the increasing sense of unease about
theory and methods in economics,[16] and to this can be added specific anthropological
and sociological criticisms of aspects of economics and market theory. [17] In this
volume Preston reviews a range of critiques of orthodox economics, Lubasz argues for
a reinspection of one of economics' canonical texts as a vehicle for contemporary
theory, and Alexander, Davis and Stewart question many of the economic assumptions deployed in the analysis of price, the organisation of business and the role of the
entrepreneur. In all, it would seem that the constituent features of market models of
economics are susceptible to repeated contextualisations which reveal their cultural
underpinnings. Other problems can also be pointed out.

Identifying Markets

If the market model of price equilibrium has only extremely limited application in
western economies (Block 1990:65), and if the price mechanism is not always a firm
determinant of demand, it is because demand is not a transparent concept and refers
to both desire (seen as a transcultural passion whose forms may vary) and need (seen
in terms of nature). Indeed, many of the so-called proofs of the law of demand invoke
the 'law of false necessity' (Block 1990:28). Thus, 'real' examples of institutions with
'high marketness' (Block 1990:59) are elusive, and even contemporary examples of
spot markets – such as stock, commodity and foreign-exchange markets – are highly
specialised institutional arenas not unlike 'speculative tournaments' in which the
construction of the fame and reputation of market-makers and players is built around
the manipulation of special tokens of value (Appadurai 1988:49). It would seem that
the search for examples of real markets which conform to the model resembles
Strathern's search for the 'real Elmdoners', most of whom 'vanish under scrutiny'
(1984).

The 1973–4 oil price rises represent one of the 'biggest triumphs' for the laws of
supply and demand, in that petrol consumption declined markedly on a world-wide
basis (McCloskey 1986:59). Yet to offer this case as scientific proof of the operation of
market mechanisms is problematic, as McCloskey points out. The plausibility of the
attempt is encouraged because the complex processes involved in a sense 'simulate'
the market. That this oil crisis was precipitated as part of a political strategy on behalf
of certain oil-producing countries to redefine geo-political relationships as well as to
engineer a price rise suggests that the strategic political use of the 'market' actually
constituted these resources as 'scarce'. Thus, the rendering of this political crisis as an
economic formula is not only partial, it is also little more than tautology (Tribe
1981:94). And this 'simulation' of the market through political strategy produces, if
you like, 'true symptoms' (as movements of price) but yet feigns the presence of the
real – namely, proof of self-regulating market mechanisms (Baudrillard 1990:167–8).

Market Aggregation and Integration

Attempts to circumscribe and define a market as a geographical aggregation of localised exchanges embrace a number of issues. First, an aggregate market is in part a consequence of the development of communications, transport and the like. But it is more than just an aspect of infrastructure. A market is, secondly, a description of the trajectory or flow of a single item, thing, service and so on as it passes from hand to hand, from place to place. Status as a commodity is, however, just one moment in the intricate flow of items through specifiable social settings. As Appadurai shows, things have complex 'biographies' and their status changes according to social context (1986; see also Werbner 1989:66–9 on decommoditisation and 'semantic conversion'). An aggregate market, then, when circumscribed with reference to the geographical spread of an item, at best refers to only a very brief moment in the life of that thing. More problematic though, is the extent to which market as a description can subsume different sorts of trajectories of a thing without regard for its social setting. Thus, the geographical spread of an item or the regional mapping of desire for a thing provides only a very rudimentary circumscribing feature of an aggregate market. [18]

A third feature circumscribing a market is its description as an aggregation of processes involved in exchange. This is market integration through the price mechanism. If we consider the items exchanged to be the *commodities* of political economy, then exchange creates objective relations between things which are alienable from persons; whereas if we consider the items to be the *goods* of economics, then exchange creates subjective relations between individuals and objects of desire (see Gregory 1982). Whether market relationships are seen in terms of links between persons represented as an aspect of things or in terms of a person and an object of desire, both regard price (an aspect of the thing or the reflection of desire) as part of the *process* of market integration. Integration is, then, a consequence of the millions of separate local transactions being mediated by the price mechanism. But the price index as an index of market integration is problematic for economics (see McCloskey 1986:144). The suggested seamlessness of the web through which markets are connected appears unmediated by variations in culture, varieties of knowledge or folk representations of what price might mean or how it is articulated. Furthermore, as Alexander points out here, little empirical evidence is ever summoned to show how in any particular case supply and demand do actually determine prices; instead, many empirical economic studies suggest that the cultural notion of 'fairness' is often associated with price; indeed, many prices in the west are based on costs plus mark-up, and those based purely on demand are often considered as unfair profiteering. Since price alone, then, is not always a good determinant of market behaviour, nor does it necessarily equilibriate supply and demand, the extent to which the price mechanism operates within any form of market must also be seen as a function of the social, cultural and political matrices through which the index of price must pass, as well as a function of the bodies of culturally specific knowledge through which notions of price are apprehended.

Integration as a defining feature of a market depends 'on agreeing to the rules of a language in which "integration" means something' (McCloskey 1986:144). Integration is obviously minimally conceived in terms of a price nexus of some sort, such that integration rests on the rudimentary issue that a drastic price change in one location may provoke consequences elsewhere – and at times these may be catastrophic for Third World nations. But in these cases, integration through price is played out on a pitch tilted by the politics of Third World production and First World consumption – not an image reminiscent of those flat, level playing-fields portrayed in economistic market models.

The definition of markets as related either to the geographical spread of one particular item or to the processes of integration must be seen as attempts to capture a market essence in a static or synchronic manner. A means of resolving the problem is to incorporate a historical dimension which provides 'genealogical' definitions of particular, socially situated markets (McCloskey 1986). [19] One measure of market integration could also be how socially situated actors see themselves in relation to any particular market. (See Howe 1990 on the cultural construction of Northern Ireland labour markets). The degree to which they view a market as aggregated is a form of cultural knowledge which informs their social and economic behaviour – as does their construction of concepts of price.

Systems of Accounting

Systems of accounting, particularly double-entry bookkeeping, as a means of plotting profit and loss are generally taken as an indispensable part of the scientific, rational conduct of business for the calculation and maximisation of returns. Yet, the basic categories of economic analysis – such as profit, loss, revenue, capital, investments, current expenditure – are not transparent in meaning, for what costs fall into which category depends on the system of accounting in use and on the reasons for accounting (for example, assets stripping, taxation and so on). The notion of profit, therefore, is not unambiguous since its meaning derives from the accounting practices by which it is calculated (Hindess 1988:83). Block points to the cognitive functions that systems of accounting may perform (1990:33), but they are also linked to state fiscal policy, particularly to taxation. Thus they derive part of their form from the institutional structure of a national economy. Alexander adds that western systems of pricing setting should be discussed not in terms of efficiency or rational conduct but in terms of the forms of control they imply for the organisation of business. In the absence of double-entry bookkeeping, and of a state fiscal policy of taxation, not only are definitions of profit and profit maximisation problematised, but any methods of bookkeeping that may exist in different cultures reproduce the cultural rationalities of the particular forms of trade. In Davis's chapter, accounting procedures plot the dispersal of social and economic capital and not profit as defined as a rate of return.

Rationality and Unintended Consequence

Instrumental rationality of market behaviour and the maximisation of preferences on the market are impoverished as explanatory concepts of social action (see Foster 1984, Hargreaves Heap 1989 and Hindess 1988). Processes of 'deliberation' (Hindess 1988) about preferences, metapreferences or the 'styles of reasoning' adopted by actors in specific social situations are equally important. Numerous chapters in this collection illustrate that social actors deliberate over various styles of reasoning available to them, and that specialised ways of thinking are employed in different social situations. Moreover, Stewart argues that Gypsies' horse-trading practices are better understood in terms of the underlying intentionality rather than their instrumental rationality relating to price.

Orthodox market models suggest that rationality is both the predicator of behaviour as well as the outcome of behaviour: it is action and context. The market is a constantly repeated game sufficient only unto itself. It is a dynamic structure that goes nowhere, and only a *deus ex machina* can initiate change (Dahrendorf 1973). The market is a game whose rules are defined by rationality, a game in which rational actors obey the rules. Yet, the rational pursuit of self-interest alone cannot of itself rule out the possibilities of opportunism, embezzlement, sharp practice and other rule violations (Williamson 1975:253). That actors *do obey* the rules of the economic game, even when the chances of detecting rule violations are slight, suggests that they are not acting instrumentally. That actors *should not obey* the rules of the game defined by economic models is only logically consistent with the assumption of self-interest. The logical consequence of the rational pursuit of self-interest is chaos and not order. The self-referential terms of the market game must, therefore, be set within its broader social context, in which actors deliberate and choose between styles of reasoning. The problem, then, with the notion in orthodox economics of the 'invisible hand of the market'[20] – the harmonious, co-ordination of unintended consequences – is that if chaos is the only logical conclusion of the market game, then the order which is said to result from the invisible hand can only be achieved by the surreptious introduction of a form of social determinism by social location of the behaviour of actors. Otherwise, 'the idea that an aggregation of unintended consequences could explain anything about social structure would be an absurdity' (Hindess 1988:25) – unless, of course, guided by a 'Providentially-designed nature' (see Lubasz on Adam Smith's invisible hand of *nature in the market*).

1.2 MARKET AS CIPHER OF SOCIAL PRACTICE

Models of the market occupy a central position in numerous branches of sociological theory (see Preston on the failure of modern social theory to address the market issue, and his proposals for modes of engagement). Hindess concludes that 'for all the striking difference between them, Marxism and liberalism both tend to analyse the market in terms of an essence or inner principle that produces necessary effects simply by virtue of its presence' (1986:8). If markets, then, are constituted through the particularities of systems of production, reproduction and so on in any given cultural milieu, just how 'the market' as the essence of economic activity can also act as a transhistorical, acultural, disembodied agent which disrupts, individualises and de-moralises other cultures is problematic. Brenner calls the essentialist aspect of Marx's writings 'neo-Smithian', and this line of thought is developed by later Marxists who identify a 'special dynamic ... as a function of the imperatives of exchange on the market' (1977:38); thus, the formation of capitalist relations of production are the result of market-determined forces. [21] Markets therefore count, they are accorded primacy, they are agents of social transformation. [22] Yet Lenin argued that the presence of markets was not sufficient to produce capitalist classes; instead, relations of production and the expansion of markets should be seen as a 'single, living and organic process of development of commodity economy and the growth of capitalism' (1960:I:124).

There is an 'essentialist fallacy' over the issue of markets, a fallacy which predisposes the observer to classify types of exchange on the basis of apparent similarities with what we know as the market and to attribute them market-like properties. Godelier pointed to something similar when he stated:

> despite an apparent similarity between forms of marketing and circulating goods, the very mechanisms of this circulation ... are different, and this difference is based on the necessity for the various forms ... being compatible, functionally and structurally, with the dominant condition of production and ... of reproducing these modes of production. (1977:22)

This insight into the specificity of forms of marketing is important in order to grasp the processes of production, reproduction, consumption and forms of exchange as mutually constitutive (Gregory 1982, Strathern 1985), or as a 'single organic process' (Lenin). [23] Markets are cultural constructs, as Alexander argues below, and not essences with revolutionary possibilities for social transformation.

1.2.1 The Substantivist Legacy

The notion of the market appears as a central issue in the formalist–substantivist debate of the 1960s. The concern of the protagonists was in a large measure centred around the two referents of the term 'market'. First, as place, the market is the physical location of a set of human activities and practices involving exchange of material items. Second, as principle, the market now becomes not the physical location but instead the theoretical abstraction from a set of human activities and practices. Much debate revolved around the issue of whether the former should or could be analysed in terms of the latter.

The substantivists still recognised, however, the integrity of the market as principle (Polanyi 1968 and Dalton 1968). The typologies constructed by Bohannan and Dalton to distinguish between systems of exchange confined the operation of market principles to specific arenas or types of society, such as the national economies of western nations (1962). Taking their lead from Polanyi, the substantivists pursued the idea that the market had become 'disembedded' from western social and cultural systems. [24] The Great Transformation which had taken place in European society involved 'the rise of the market to the ruling force in the economy' (Polanyi 1968:132). Morality was substituted by the market.

Polanyi's position over market systems is somewhat ambivalent and contradictory, and it appears he was addressing a complex political agenda (see Halperin 1988). Yet he none the less admitted that 'the formal method of approach offers a *total description* of the economy as determined by choices induced by an insufficiency of means'

(1968:125, my emphasis). These admissions, the legacy of the substantivists, have had a profound effect in social anthropology, since they conceded an area of analysis exclusively to economics. That is, they gave credence to, and maintained the integrity of, neo-classical and marginalist economic theory as regards the analysis of western market systems. What could be called 'Polanyi's paradox' can be noted here: that the western notion of a market economy is historically situated, but yet as an object it is susceptible to analysis only in terms of an economic theory which is itself a historical product of that social context. This legacy left anthropological and sociological analysis unable to rise to the challenge of complexities already encapsulated by economics. (See Preston's chapter on the emergence in the nineteenth century of an intellectual division of labour). Whilst the early substantivists did not seriously challenge the status of market theory or the conceptual basis of market principles, their discussions of typologies of exchange and the like had the effect of suspending anthropology's disbelief in the concept of the market.

Later critiques in the 1970s by substantivist and Marxist anthropologists have effectively questioned neo-classical and orthodox economic theory, but it is surprising how little of this has stuck when it comes to the concept of the market and the way it is deployed in social analysis.[25] A partial answer to this problem of the continuing dominance of economic discourse, even in social anthropology, lies in the appearance of a disembedded market operating on a world-wide basis. Bohannan and Dalton were convinced that sectors dominated by the market principle were becoming enlarged or expanded on the world stage at the expense of reciprocity and redistribution. The irresistible force of economic processes and of market forces seemed to be confirmed: 'It seems safe to predict that the process will continue, and that African economies are becoming like our own in the sense that the sectors dominated by the market principle are being enlarged' (1962:25). Cook was quick to pounce on the obvious paradox in the substantivist's position by pointing out that the authors were 'concocting tortured arguments in defense of a theory... for the analysis of... moribund types of economies' (1968:210). This seemed to confirm the futility of the fight they were conducting against the inevitable in world history. It seemed that if the substantivists had won certain theoretical battles, apparent victory in the war went to the formalists, who were aided by a real world that hit back by becoming a market system.

The world economy, seen in terms of a market metaphor, embraces the idea that trading relations have been extended over time and space (see Braudel 1982) and that diverse parts of the world are now interconnected and interdependent. This is the 'externalist approach' to the development of markets which are seen to arise as the consequence of external influences (Blanton 1983). Yet this encompassment of the globe is a product of the growth of western industrial capitalism, and to gloss such complex historical processes in terms of the development of the fetishised market concept is to say very little at best, and can be thoroughly misleading at worst. Taussig's analysis of the terror on the Putumayo – an extreme example of the violence and political control involved in the extraction of rubber for western industrial consumption – shows how these realities were squeezed uncomfortably into a model of market economics for the purposes of representation (Taussig 1986).

By contrast, what can be described as an 'internalist' explanation (see Blanton 1983) of the development of markets posits the notion of a human propensity to truck, barter and exchange. On the basis of these natural propensities, markets emerge only when conditions are appropriate: thus the uncivilised realise their full human potential and eventually join the ranks of free-marketing civilised individuals (see Platt on the ideological implications of importing Adam Smith's ideas into nineteenth-century Bolivia by free-traders). This approach calls on natural and essentialist notions to explain market development (see Preston's critique of naturalism within economics).

Whether construed in terms of internalist or externalist approaches, conceiving of the market as a transhistorical and acultural agent derives from our conception of a disembedded economy, seemingly stripped of the cultural knowledge that generates it. If the market cannot be disembedded from the bodies of knowledge which generate it, and if the way the market is modelled and deployed in discourse is informed by culturally specific bodies of knowledge, then the theoretical claims suggested by the deployment of the marker metaphor for the world economy have to be questioned. These claims privilege a dominant economic discourse that presumes a similarity between the constructions through which we make sense of the world and those of other cultures located in different parts of the global networks of politics and trade. In other words, the world as market is one particular representation of the various networks which stretch around the globe. This is but one cultural articulation which must be accommodated within the chorus of other voices at present muted by the models and metaphors of economic discourse.

1.2.2 The Social Agency of the Market

Social anthropologists have often taken the notion of the market as given from orthodox economic theory and adopted it uncritically into social analysis. Market notions are used unreflexively in anthropological literature; rarely has the status of the market concept been inspected in analyses and surprisingly we have been theoretically silent on the notion. [26] For the anthropologist too the market counts, it brings about an effect, it is an agent in social affairs. [27] Yet, 'the market' as such can only have an effect if those we are describing also share in this conception; that is, if it is part of their body of knowledge which forms the grounds for their social action. If they do not, then we have to be very specific about *what is* having an effect. Plattner talks of the 'obvious local effects of market activities' (1985:vii) but then goes on to specify *objects* which were traded – 'steel tools, manufactured cloth, and such'. Undoubtedly, the introduction of these objects may have an effect on social organisation and indigenous production – just as the social uses of income and wealth derived from trade may also have an effect. But these issues should not be equated with the fetishised object which the market has become in analysis.

The sub-discipline of economic anthropology grew as an offshoot of economics. [28] Economic anthropologists concerned with promoting formalist positions have increased the sophistication of their economic models as part of a positivistic social scientific enterprise. [29] And as free-market liberal economics appeared to triumph in the 1980s, so has the notion of the market become the centre-piece of contemporary economic anthropology. Plattner's recent collection *Markets and Marketing* proclaims that 'the pretense that theories of market and marketing were irrelevant became less viable' as economic activities were seen increasingly in a market context (1985:vii–ix). If Plattner's charge that substantivism was a 'natural history of tribal and band economies', then what he proposes can only be described as a 'natural history of the market'. This natural history assumes the identity of its preconstructed object of study, and is only another form of Leach's 'butterfly collecting'. That economic anthropology has resisted a redefinition of its method bears witness to the force of our naturalistic assumptions which define 'economy' as an object which can be apprehended only in terms of 'objective science'. [30] (See Alexander's call for a refocusing of concerns in economic anthropology.)

Central-place theory, another type of formal analysis which focuses on market notions, features market-places as various nested units which are arranged in complex regional systems (see Smith 1974). It focuses on specific physical locales as a means by which a circumscribed analytical object – a regional system – can be achieved. Once this analytical object is defined it is then susceptible to investigation. As formal analysis, central-place theory is a powerful tool for organising the complex reality of observed market activities. But description and analysis in terms of the model then lead to the problem of reaccommodating real world events as deviations from the model.

In all these types of analysis, formalism relies on the definition of an axiomatic core and a set of derivational propositions (Gudeman and Penn 1982), and in the pursuit of universal applicability formalism only uncovers its own assumptions. Moreover, as Halperin suggests, a comparative science of economics should not rely on native folk knowledge for its units of analysis and analytic categories (1988:176). Yet presumably the units and categories that are used derive from our own folk knowledge, and it is within this body of knowledge that the market concept is so central. Thus, the force of the market as a social agent is not only assumed but it is also uncovered through the very process of analysis. Any study of markets, then, must recognise the participant's understanding and conception of their own social and economic activity. [31]

1.2.3 *Images of the Market in Social Anthropology*

> ... the market cannot be superseded as a general frame of reference
> unless the social sciences succeed in developing a wider frame of
> reference to which the market is itself referable. (Polanyi 1968:143)

The invocation of the market image and metaphor as part of an analytical strategy in social anthropological investigation is a more subtle aspect of the dominance of economic discourse. Barth's transactional analysis (1965) encapsulates a market model (see Asad 1972) – this is nothing new. The market model of transactionalism embodies a latent theory of structure and agency. The individual is the constitutive agent of the market, but at the same time he or she is also subject to it. A freely competitive market tends towards a state of equilibrium; that is, in Barth's terms social order is the unintended consequence of individual transactions. The market is thus the cumulative outcome of the actions of atomistic individuals, yet is itself also a transcendent, active agent to which the individual actor responds.[32] The analogy in transactionalism is made between the market-place and society itself, which conveniently leaves the notion of market as principle (its so-called 'invisible hand') to operate as the structuring agency bringing about social order.

P. Bourdieu's *Outline of a Theory of Practice* represents a complex body of ideas in which, nevertheless, the market metaphor is also present. Despite its explicit concerns drawn from structuralism and Marxism, the work conceals a sub-text which can be read as neo-formalist, and draws quite conspicuously on a market metaphor. This is particularly evident in his discussion on Kabyle marriages, for which he defines 'objective structures' or 'laws of the matrimonial market'. Types of marriage are conceived as constituting sorts of more or less privileged sub-markets ranging from extra-ordinary, distant marriages arranged by men between members of different lineages, clans or tribes to 'ordinary marriages' which are the responsibility of women, who are 'less concerned with the symbolic profits accruing from political unity' (1977:62). In the former there is a common interest in raising the 'indisputable index of the symbolic value of their products [women] in the matrimonial exchange market' (ibid. :56); whereas in the latter, women, unconcerned with symbolic capital, are 'structurally disposed to devote themselves more readily to strictly economic practices and pursue material profits' (ibid. :62). Their dealings are seen as closer to the 'economic truth of exchange' than those of men.

These two sub-markets, among others, comprise the matrimonial market, the 'economic truth' of which, Bourdieu claims, is closer to the surface in female exchanges than in men's transactions. The truth of these latter is buried beneath layers of symbolic construction. Alongside this explicit analogy with the market (including its laws which are related to 'economic truth') there is also introduced the concept of human capital (in Bourdieu's hands now in expanded form), which is taken direct from the Chicago economists and labour-markets theorists to account for an individual's position in a labour market (Douglas 1982:129).

The 'spirit of economic calculation', the 'economic truth' of transactions, the laws of the matrimonial market and the exchanges of human capital all form for Bourdieu 'the structure of objective relations'. The embroidering in symbolic form of male exchanges is a type of *méconnaissance* (misrecognition) designed to prevent 'a system governed by the law of interested calculation, competition' and so on from being apprehended as such (ibid. :172). Thus it would appear that if we peel back the layers of ideological construction of those 'naively idyllic representations' (ibid. :171) of an *un*disenchanted world, then we find something akin to *homo economicus* operating in a market and maximising material and symbolic profit (ibid. :183). This is the 'economic truth' closer to the surface in female exchanges; a truth also identical to economic theory now generalised and construed as the economics of practice.

This market metaphor, along with its connection to economically rational man, is employed by Bourdieu as an analytical strategy in pursuit of a model of Kabyle structure and practice. It should be noted that Bourdieu's discussion of marriage practices is part of a broader theoretical debate sparked off by Lévi-Strauss's *The*

Elementary Structures of Kinship. Bourdieu is concerned to restore the subjective experience of actors' interests in order to account for strategy, as well as, more intricately, showing how those interests and dispositions coincide so that 'those who are the product of the same conditions of production... recognise and pursue the same goals' (ibid.:63–4). This he accomplishes via the concept of 'habitus'.

These remarks are perhaps suggestive of a broader framework of debate in social science to which Bourdieu responds, albeit with a good measure of sophistication. The conditions of possibility for this debate revolve around a series of oppositions which western social theory tries to resolve or make compatible. The oppositions implied are variously rendered as structure versus strategy, objective properties versus subjective experience, social order and social change, closure and openness, fixed network and individual mobility, constraint and practice. This is a 'double image' (Strathern in press)[33] or what Foucault calls the 'duplication of man', by which he refers to the way that human sciences have constituted man as their object as well as their subject; man was detached as a cause as well as construed as a consequence in social science (1989). This double image, this duplication of man is seen, as I have pointed out earlier, in the model of the market: the agency of the individual constitutes the market; the market itself constitutes an agent over and above the individual.

Social theorists, it would appear, often draw on the metaphor of the market and its axiomatic assumptions about the individual and so on in order to introduce into the analysis issues such as strategy, change, openness, mobility and the like. In short, the notion of the market is attractive, compelling and irresistible as a metaphor since it offers a ready-made analytical device to suggest flux in the face of structural constraint and closure. Not only that, but because of its double image, it can itself be construed as an agent of structure, collectivity and equilibrium. Bourdieu drew precisely on this metaphor as soon as his analysis confronted the issues of individual interest, strategy and structure.

The relationship between the naturally given, maximising individual and the market should also be problematised, for the market is so often taken as the paradigmatic case of individual self-interest in social scientific discourse. The linkage, or the 'locus of simultaneity' (Foucault 1989), between the private, self-interested individual and the market might be traced back to Adam Smith, or to the later work of neo-classical and marginalist economics. Yet, it would appear that the arena of the individual has not always been associated with the market. The Physiocrats and Ricardo's 'early' work modelled the economy as a cycle pinned securely to the 'natural' fertility of the land (Gudeman 1986). The source of all wealth and surplus was modelled as the result of natural fecundity; human actors lacked intentionality, they were not considered as economic makers or creators; tastes and desires were not part of the image of man and there was no creative role for the individual in a material sense. In Ricardo's early work, man had an active role only in relation to the polity (Gudeman 1986:51–2; see also Foucault 1989 on the Physiocrats). Thus, the 'locus of simultaneity' between man the rational, competitive, autonomous individual and the notion of the market should not be taken as a self-evident truth. Rather, conceived of as a representational model of the world, it would appear to be associated with a relatively contemporary constellation of ideas in western analysis. But in a perverse moment one may wonder, had world history been different and other discourses become dominant, then the Cameroonian metaphor of the funeral might have come to stand in place of the market as the representation of the arena of competitive, individualistic exchange (see Geschiere).

I have put forward a case for the inspection of the notion of the market and its associated metaphors in social scientific discourse. Why, if the market model has been so successfully exposed in all its weaknesses and contradictions, does the image reoccur so obviously as a disembodied agent and, more intriguingly, as a subtle metaphor organising theoretical discourse? Part of the answer lies in the properties of the market model as it is construed by social science, in particular its characteristic double image. Moreover, the strategies of deployment of the market metaphor have to be set within the wider framework of social scientific debate itself. Thus, the way in which Bourdieu claims that agents' practice in Kabylia becomes intelligible to us says perhaps more about the power of the market metaphor, by means of which he locates his analysis within a familiar idiom, than it does about the production of local models by Kabyle peasants of their own social practice. To turn Bourdieu's terminology back upon himself: the dispositions and interests defined by the conditions of possibility of social scientific debates predispose analysts and theorists to pursue similar goals, strategies and metaphors in their attempts to conceptualise social worlds.

1.3 IDEOLOGIES, METAPHORS AND PRACTICE

1.3.1 The Power of Market Ideology

> The market is not an invention of capitalism. Is has existed for centu-
> ries. It is an invention of civilisation. (M. Gorbachev quoted in *The
> Guardian*, 11. 6. 1990)

Ideological discourse about the market is powerful for it is constructed around ideas of an essential human nature and natural law theory of the individual, of a naturalisation of economics and historically created trading relations, and of the 'eternal truths' of economic and political freedom (see N. Lawson [1983] 1989). Moreover, the fetishisation of exchange and the market creates the illusion that the social world is made to appear to be purely a matter of transactions and exchanges (compare transactionalism and exchange theory). Thus, as the 'totalising structure' the market affords a model of the social totality (Jameson 1990/91:272). The historical and epistemological precedence, over other forms of representation, of a model of market exchange as the means by which the totality of social life is grasped was pointed out by Marx.[34] This may be true for a particular historical moment of capitalism, but as Overing argues here, it is production and not exchange which represents the totality of Piaroa social life. Indeed, market-place activities ('shopping') are assimilated as production and not exchange in Piaroa thought. Furthermore, Overing's critique of Lévi-Strauss's theory of exchange, which predicates social life on the exchange of women, goods and symbols, points to theoretical implications for a social anthropology that has taken circulation as the ideological representation of the totality of social life.[35]

The contemporary image of the market stresses features not captured by Marx's original formulation. Like Marx, Bloch states that the 'quite other world' of the economy can appear to reproduce through non-human agency – by the fetishes' (1989:174); that is, the collisions of individuals give rise to an alien social power standing above them. Yet the power of encompassment of market discourse as a form of dominant ideology is that it is represented *both* as a *non-human agent* as well as being constituted by *individual human agency*, that is, the *double image* of market agency. The market model thus appeals to individuals as a means of achieving social empowerment – the realisation of their own abilities by taking responsibility on themselves; yet, the market also imposes its own disciplines and is an agent empowered to transform social contexts.

The market as a form of dominant ideology relies on this combination of contradictory themes, on its ability to embrace inconsistency. By virtue of this combination the market becomes a powerful *generalising* concept, since these loosely interrelated features are advantageous in that they allow it to function as an ideological concept in many situations and in relation to diverse problems. Ideology does not have to be consistent, logically coherent or neatly systematic to be dominant or functional (Asad 1979); for the generalising nature of the market concept draws it strength as ideology from this contradictory combination.

If there has been a collapse of the double image within English constructions of kinship (Strathern, in press), then what Jameson points out about the market is perhaps indicative of a similar shift: 'the market has become a substitute for itself, and fully as much a commodity as any of the items it includes within itself' (1990/91:x). The marketing of the market is certainly apparent in the attempts to export the concept to the countries of central and eastern Europe. It is also a commodity which takes with it its own discipline (a form of 'secular theology', Hart 1986), a discipline conceived as an alternative to the ill-discipline, corrupt morality and ill-conceived rationality of planned state socialism. But like all items with social biographies, the commodity status of the market depends on its context, and once the concept is transplanted into new contexts it takes on new constructions, different symbolic aspects, and is located into different social discourses that change its meanings (see chapters by Geschiere, Hann, Holy, Platt, Stewart and Stockman).

1.3.2 Market Metaphors

> [Pythagoras] sayde that this world was nothing but a very mercate, where there meete three sortes of men, the one to buy, the other to sell, and the thirde to looke on, who (he sayde) were the Philosophers, whom hee counted the happiest of them all. (S. Guazzo, *The Civile Conversation* [1581] quoted in Agnew 1986:17)

The role of market-place based metaphors has been indicated in numerous types of social anthropological analysis. Dahrendorf recognised in 1968 the metaphorical possibilities of the market ('this may well be its noblest application' [1973:502]), and went on to suggest that this metaphor could even guarantee freedom. The metaphorical elaborations of markets suggest that its 'essential nature ... is that it juxtaposes elements of a concrete image [the market-place] in order to formulate some set of more abstract relationships [market principles]' (Beck 1978:83). These abstract relations, say in the form of market mechanisms, become further displaced through applications of the metaphor to represent social totalities and so on. Thus one particular 'mission of metaphor' is to provide identity for 'inchoate' subjects (Fernandez 1974), in this case the social whole or collectivity to which individuals belong.

Bourdieu's Kabyle ethnography suggests that the image and metaphor of the market-place (*suq*) are articulated for purposes different from those of our market-based elaborations. Aspects of personhood, strategies of honour and men's reputations are associated with the market-place: 'men can go to the market with only their faces, their names and their honour for money' says the Kabyle adage (Bourdieu 1977:185). That 'the market will judge' refers not to the laws of the market or to ruthless undertakings in investment, but to the collective judgment that is shaped and manifest in the market-place (ibid.:186). The market here refers to that public domain of men in which assessments of a man's personhood are made on the basis of his trading activities. Individuals and market are brought into a specific relationship among the Kabyle, for men are made or unmade in Kabyle markets; for us individuals and their choices are its foundations.

Kabyle market discourse suggests that a man is considered a 'market-man' on the basis of the conduct of his affairs. A man who does not meet the requirements of market conduct, however, is not a 'market-man' but a 'house-man' or a 'fireside-man', derogatory epithets that put a person in his place. These invocations of market images are located in a discourse which opposes market to house, public domain to private domain, male world to female world. Indeed they are reminiscent of a set of oppositions, although different, which we draw on in our own market discourse: market versus state, freedom versus constraint, capitalism versus communism and so on (see Holy on the symbolic elaborations of the market in Czech culture). As a feature of Kabyle discourse though, the market metaphor here articulates aspects of gender relations and a mapping of gender-specific social space.

Keenan (1987) notes that free marketeers in the west have reduced their ideas to a few fairly simple concepts which make sense to the man in the street. To see how they make sense one can consider M. Thatcher's pronouncement that: 'There is no such thing as society. There are only men and women and there are families'. This declaration not only substitutes one abstract entity – society – for another – the family – but it creates an ambiguity around the term 'family' which allows it to be read on two levels. Family is both an abstract entity as well as a physical grouping of individuals thought to be contained in one household or which can be gathered together for 'family photographs'. The popular appeal of this declaration can be found in its multivocality, for it purports to substitute concrete for abstract images. This same polysemic quality is present in articulations about the market since the term conflates three referents: market principles, aggregate markets and market-places. Market as a self-regulating mechanism may not be readily apprehended by people in general, but the image of the world made up of market stalls or the analogy between the national coffers and a housewife's purse can. Moreover, our experience of haggling and our introspections on consumer choice in market-places is the foundation upon which confirmation that abstract forces of the market operate at large. The conflation of these referents, the abstract and the concrete, produces powerful and persuasive images of market rhetoric in which the term 'market' becomes a polysemic symbol. Thus, the formulation of a set of abstract relationships by means of a concrete image is not just a means of grasping 'inchoate' subjects but, through a process of slippage between referents, the image performs ideological functions by standing for various forms of abstract relationship at one and the same time.

1.3.3 Models and Action

> The ideas of economists and political philosophers, both when they are
> right and when they are wrong, are more powerful than is commonly
> understood. (M. Keynes, quoted in McCloskey 1986:xviv)

Besides the symbolic and metaphorical role the market plays in specific cultural discourses, market theories can also become 'metaphors for living' (Hargreaves Heap 1989), an idea which raises the issue of the relationship between the 'non-ornamental metaphors' (McCloskey 1986) of the market and social action.

To state that the market is a fiction (Dahrendorf 1973) or that the market is as much a utopian dream as socialism (Jameson 1990/91) does not negate the possibility that such a model can be a guide for particular types of social action. Market ideology cannot be simply dismissed as a floating epiphenomenon which plays no part in the cognitive realms or the interpretative schemata of social actors. It can stand as a 'model of' and as well as a 'model for' social reality (Geertz 1966). As Jameson notes: 'The ideology of the market is unfortunately not some ideational or representational luxury or embellishment that can be removed from the economic problem… it is somehow generated by the thing itself' (1990/91:260). Ideology and reality are 'semi-autonomous', for ideology is brought into a relationship with social institutions and practices through the interpretative processes of social actors.

As a description of empirical processes and events the model of the market is neither adequate nor satisfactory. It is not an accurate representation of social and economic processes in either western or non-western cultures. None the less the model is invoked and reproduced within western discourse with repeated regularity. If people can be imagined and even imagine themselves to be operating under a pure market model, it is because choice takes place in a pre-given environment. The environment for competitive exchange of a market-like setting is conditioned by its political context (Hart 1986), but that context is not an outcome of the market itself. In the absence of political institutions the consequences of market exchanges would be chaos.

Because the representational model of the market is so divergent from reality, however, it is difficult to see how it could assist in actors' interpretations and understandings of the world (Holy and Stuchlik 1983:102), and also why it should be repeatedly reproduced in social discourse. Isolated aspects of behaviour can be made meaningful by the invocation of the model, and its degree of generality can be functionally advantageous as a broad interpretative device. In certain respects too the model provides a sense of empowerment for those who invoke it: the power of their own agency in social affairs is thus proclaimed (see Stirrat on 'empowerment' in development rhetoric). By contrast, the model can also explain people's lack of power as the passive victims of market mechanisms.

A similar problem has, however, confronted social anthropology over representations of segmentary lineage systems. And like the lineage model, the market model operates not necessarily as a framework for a common-sense understanding of the world but as a sort of 'social structure in reserve' (Salzman 1978, quoted in ibid. :102), that is as part of a cultural repertoire which can be drawn on or mobilised under special circumstances. It is a 'shadow form of organisation' (Salzman 1981:236) which, although seemingly illusory, has a potential for activation: it is a possible world but not a probable one.

It is these cognitive and interpretative aspects of the market model which account for its reproduction as a representational model in western discourse. In particular, this social structure in reserve comes to the fore under conditions of social disruption and uncertainty. Just as Weber's charismatics come to prominence in times of psychic, physical, economic, ethical, religious and political distress, so this social structure in reserve, this metaphor of the social totality, is deployed under such conditions of socio-economic and political change. The paradox here is that the market is elevated to the touchstone of certainty in a world in which changes were wrought under the very banner of the market. As Block says of the response to the turmoil of the late 1960s and 1970s: 'we may no longer know what kind of society this is, but we know that it is a market economy' (1990:3).

Periods of social disruption and change do not just create conditions of uncertainty which have to be managed and assimilated by members of society, but these conditions produce a sense of the inchoate in human experience of the world. As Fernandez argues (1986), these conditions are conducive to the creation of metaphor, in this case the non-ornamental metaphor of the market. Indeed, the concrete image of the market provides the metaphor for making sense of the world, and as an abstract process it offers a solution to current crises. The market model mediates between experience and reality by offering itself as a new interpretative schema, which in due course becomes a routinised form of understanding ourselves and others. Following Block's suggestion, the market model offers a defence against uncertainty and ambiguity, and protects people from having to consider a broader range of human possibilities (1990:31–2).

The routinisation and adoption of this metaphor are achieved through what can be called 'maintenance mechanisms' (see Salzman 1981). 'Literary validation' of the market model is derived from authoritative texts such as those of Smith, Hayek and Friedman (see Platt on the scriptural authority of Smith in nineteenth-century Bolivia, and Lubasz on the [mis]use of Adam Smith). The 'ritual enactment' of the model is represented as the activities of the stock and commodity markets, and the operational generalisation of the model means that the model can be applied to a wide range of social situations. Market principles, forcefully articulated by prominent individuals, politicians and government, become part of an 'asserted ideology'; that is, they become a dominant discourse by 'the repeated verbal expression among the populace at large that a particular social pattern is in general practice in society, although in fact practice differs markedly from the expressed pattern' (ibid. :237). One particular source of validation of the discourse comes from the day-to-day practice of successful business ventures. Repeated assertions that success derives from practising ideal market behaviour lends strong confirmation to others about the validity of the model. Yet the success of business as an index of proof belies the shadow which falls between the model and practice. Rather than as proofs of a scientific theory, the repeated assertions of the market model provide business with a purchase on reality, a means of *anticipating* possible outcomes in a world in which certainty is never given. Whether those outcomes are as predicted or not, the model at least offers fixed points of anticipation around which activity and potential strategies can be organised.

Market ideology does not provide a transparent perspective on social truth, nor is it merely a construction promoted by conservative tendencies, which, fearful of the passions of human nature, need to impose taming and controlling mechanisms in the form of sovereigns or invisible hands (Jameson 1990/91:273). Market ideology also filters down to the repertoire of interpretative schemata held by social actors. As such, it offers them a means of coming to terms with changing practical everyday experience, as well as offering an explanatory device for their failures and successes – no matter how flawed it may be.

1.3.4 Modes of Accountability

> There will be no science of man unless we examine the way in which individuals or groups represent to themselves the partners with whom they produce or exchange, the mode in which they clarify or ignore or mark this function and the position they occupy in it, the manner in which it takes place, the way in which they feel themselves integrated with it or isolated from it, dependent, subject or free; the object of the human sciences... is that being who, from within forms of production by which his whole existence is governed, forms the representation of those needs, of the society by which and with which or against which he satisfies them, so that upon that basis he can provide himself with a representation of economics itself. (Foucault 1989:352–3)

In order to investigate these representations more fully we must move beyond the elementary dichotomies of gift versus commodity (Gregory 1982), moral economy versus political economy (Cheal 1988), market versus non-market and so on.[36] Tambiah himself has made initial steps in this direction by plotting the 'semiotics of the fetishism of objects' in three different cases (1984). Rather than focus on object fetishism here, I wish to develop the idea of the fetishism of agency as a form of 'accountability' (Douglas 1982). Accountability here refers to the way a culture attributes and holds responsible specific forms of agency or aspects of social persons in their representations of exchange. These representations, of which the market is one, are predicated on specific constructions of personhood and notions of individual agency. [37] (Note the importance of 'fellow-feeling' in Smith's *The Theory of Moral Sentiments* and see Lubasz's references to Smith on the 'uncertain elements' in dealing with men in distant countries.) The market model implies a form of accountability in which human agency and *naturally* constituted persons are represented in exchange. [38] Yet, the image of the market in contemporary western society can also be seen to provide a new arena for the social construction of personhood through consumer choice: I shop therefore I am. By contrast, Czech personhood is constructed in the market as a capacity to produce rather than to consume, a distinction which relates to the nature of Czech political economy (see Holy). From my own fieldwork among the Tukulor of Senegal, personhood is an aspect of a commercial exchange relationship which is inseparable from the commodity transacted. It is neither the individual's ability to produce or to consume which defines personhood, but rather that commercial exchange recognises the personhood of transactors in terms of 'a spirit of the contract' (*hake*) through which both parties are defined as mutually interdependent social persons, and attempts to renege on a deal are likely to bring misfortune to the offending party. Other chapters in the volume suggest a relationship between constructions of social personhood and representations of exchange. Trade networks between Zuwaya traders constitute worlds of socially recognised individuals, and beyond them stand only strangers and outsiders who are held in a different regard from trusted insiders. Similarly, Alexander discusses how notions of strangerhood and gaps in cultural knowledge have implications for Javanese exchange relations, and Geschiere shows how some Cameroonian representations of market agency take a particular form of social personhood in the figure of the *nyongo* who is endowed with spiritual potency. Also, while the objects and relationships of market exchange among the Piaroa appear safe and innocent, the potency of powerful Piaroa leaders involved in dangerous indigenous exchange is represented in the fetishised objects transacted (see Overing).

It would appear that the greater the alienability from the items traded, the greater the extent to which notions of individual agency and aspects of the person are seen as instrumental in informing the ideology of exchange. Modes of accountability of exchange embrace, then, at least three different variables: the nature and extent of object fetishism, the bases of control which exchange hides, the forms of agency and personhood represented in exchange. In Stewart's chapter all three features come together. Gypsies celebrate through the game of horse-trading their own social identity, which individually is articulated in terms of personal luck (*baxt*). If their own agency is not represented as such in trade it is because exchange masks a form of control over Gypsy women – figured symbolically in horse-swaps – from whom men appropriate the value of female labour in pig production in order to fund their own horse-trading activities.

I.4 CONCLUSIONS: POLITICISING MARKET DISCOURSE

> The fundamental level on which political struggle is waged is that of
> the struggle over the legitimacy of concepts and ideologies. (Jameson
> 1990/91:263)

The debate about the market must be politicised in a number of respects. First, from the critique of power, the market logo is an ideological representation of western capitalism in which market exchange is represented as the sole generator of value[39]; thus production is represented as exchange and consumption. The market model of perfect competition also neglects considerations of power either in terms of inequalities of individual exchange relationships or in terms of market structures being conditioned by the institutions of the state and polity in which they are located. As many chapters in this volume show, the establishment of new forms of marketing are frequently the result of political struggle, as indeed is the channelling of market idioms into indigenous discourse that takes place around crucial contradictions within local modes of production (Geschiere). In addition, the notion of the market can also be seen as a gloss on the complex global political and economic relationships which span the world.

Second, the market is not a politically neutral concept within western discourse but is part and parcel of political debate. The terms deployed within this debate are highly ideological, revolving around the paired negations of market and state and so on (see Hart). That the perspective of political economy exposes a number of inherent weaknesses in market theory should not detract from the recognition of the ideological foundations and the essentialist and naturalistic elements in *both* liberalism and Marxism (see also Hindess 1986). Debates about the nature of western economic systems carry a political load, and in order to step beyond the confines of this political debate – and hence move beyond the opposition between political economy and liberal economics – it is necessary to pay attention to the *cultural* representations that we and other cultures construct about trading activities.

Thus, whilst an important critique of the market comes from political economic approaches which emphasise relationships of power, the terms of this critique remain set within the limits of western discourse about the nature of economic systems. That is, not only has the application of the market concept to be recognised as a gloss on the politics of exchange, but the construction of the market must also be recognised as a culture-specific model of contemporary economic discourse. The scope of western discourse can be broadened to include the western origins of anti-economistic critiques (see Kahn 1990) as well as the conversations and voices which can be heard throughout the history of European social thought (see Gudeman and Rivera 1990). To those must also be added the voices of non-western cultures, whose experience and models of market exchange have yet to be fully articulated, and whose voices have so far remained generally muted (Gudeman 1986, Gudeman and Rivera 1990 are, however, important contributions in this area). [40] As McCloskey states: 'the way out of the modernist maze is to pick up the thread of rhetoric. Rhetoric does not deal with truth directly: it deals with conversation' (1986:28). And it is an invitation to widen this conversation to include other voices that must be achieved.

Third, the political posturing of economic anthropology is all too plain to see. The recurrent wish to prove that natives are rational is both limited and too easy, in one sense (Douglas 1982); yet such an endeavour brings with it formal modelling and the neo-classical hand-luggage of instrumental rationality and market models. By contrast, the substantivist emphasis on difference led to the construction of sometimes misleading typologies – an exercise, in the eyes of some commentators, that is fired by romanticism and a discontent with western systems (see LeClair 1968). Economic anthropological discourse of claim and counter-claim produces its own political dynamic. But as A. MacIntyre notes: 'There is an error in supposing we can identify economic or social factors independently from ideological or theoretical items; (quoted in Halperin 1988); and besides the motives of exchange are almost always over-determined. Moreover, economic anthropology privileges *our* models and interpretations of economic processes, and again it must be noted that it gives little credence to indigenous model-making activities.

Fourth, the power of market discourse derives from its seemingly solid foundations of naturalism and essentialism, the locus of its persuasiveness in western discourse. But the hegemony of market discourse reveals itself in the 'power to name' (Parkin 1982) other people's trading activities in market terms, the ability to intervene in others' discourses and to impose its own metaphors. The problem of the articulation of modes of cultural discourse about exchange and markets is taken up here (see, for instance, Geschiere, Overing and Platt) and is an attempt to redress the balance of power between different discourses. Appadurai (1986:48), discussing the problem of knowledge and commodities, suggests that as the institutional distance and spatial journeys of commodities grow more complex so culturally formed mythologies, constructed stories and ideologies are likely to emerge. But to treat *our* stories and interpretative models as in some way less constructed or ideological than theirs (for example Bolivian tin miners and cargo cult members) is also an exercise of power. Whilst we may appropriate their worlds and forms of trading practice by assimilation with market models, there is also a form of counter-appropriation of aspects of our worlds through their cultural categories, such as the Bolivian tin-miners' devil or the Bakweri's *nyongo* zombies (see Geschiere). These are attempts to bridge the gulf between the known, bounded social worlds inhabited by particular peoples and the unbounded, unknown networks of relationships spawned by increasing world trade (see Hart). In addition, consideration of these native models of market processes is crucial for an informed understanding of issues involved in development policy. Indeed, development initiatives predicated on liberal economics' notion of 'the market' defines a model unrepresentative of culturally informed practice in the west, let alone what goes on among the rest.

If truths are produced within discourses, and if the effects of truth are power, then the effective power of market discourse does not simply rest on its essentialist claims to truth. It is also related to the problem of locating and constructing a counter-discourse (see Taussig 1986). In a not dissimilar way from the Chinese official who, having trouble defining his social system after a number of policy experiments, said 'those that work we call socialism, and those that don't work we call capitalism'

(Shinn 1985); the defining power of market discourse is likewise hegemonic. The challenge taken up by the contributors to this volume goes beyond the contemporary moment of political fad and fashion. For this collection attempts to contest the hegemony of market discourse within social anthropology and social science generally, and invites analysts to attend to the possibility of other voices within the 'world market'. Furthermore, the examination of the historical and sociological contexts in which market discourse emerges refines a sense of the specificity of the market as an idea and its relationship to practice.

NOTES

1. This chapter is based on ideas set out in an initial position paper circulated to conference participants prior to the meeting in January 1991. These ideas were later elaborated in a more extended version presented to the conference, and I wish to thank participants for their helpful comments, criticism and advice. Much inspiration has been gained in the writing of this introduction from the works of S. Gudeman, in particular Gudeman and Penn 1982, Gudeman 1986, Gudeman and Rivera 1990 on models, metaphors and cultural modelling. I warmly acknowledge this debt, which is no doubt apparent at numerous points in the text. I would also like to thank the members of the Social Anthropology Departmental Seminar at Manchester, where a version of this paper was read, for the many constructive points they raised. In the preparation of this introduction I have also benefited particularly from discussions with members of the Social Anthropology Unit at St Andrews, especially Ladislav Holy and Tristan Platt. To Richard Fardon, a supportive ex-St Andrews hand, also goes a special note of thanks for commenting in detail on an early draft. This introduction is provocative: as an exercise in theoretical slash and burn methods it attempts to clear an analytical ground on which market notions can be considered. Responsibility for any remaining excesses and errors in argument or detail rest, however, solely with the author.

2. The regional scope of this volume is not intended to be exhaustive or complete, but simply represents the area interests of conference participants who were able and willing to address this topic. Greater regional coverage of these issues is a project requiring further investigation. Note also that references to chapters included here are made by simply citing the name of the author. All other references to published works include the date of publication.

3. See Jackson 1982 on the related point that emphatic understanding precedes acts of alliance.

4. The following discussion is based on entries in *The Compact English Dictionary*.

5. See Fardon's reference (1987:170) to 'Neitzche's pocket problem': that a word, like a pocket, can contain a variety of things and those contents reflect the habits of the user.

6. Economics as a discipline negates morality (see Novak 1985). The bracketing of morality by economics is linked to the claims of the discipline to be a positive science which sustains the distinction between fact and value.

7. Compare Hindu India where 'the innocence of commerce' is a function of a division of labour between castes whose mutual interdependence does not give rise to an ideology of autarky from which moral condemnation can be drawn (Parry 1989).

8. Price, then, became a social phenomenon determined either by the community in the form of the *communis estimatio*, the 'natural' or 'vulgar' price, which was reached spontaneously by chaffering in markets, or by public regulation whereby 'legal' prices were fixed by public authorities (de Roover 1968).

9. As Tribe argues, as a shorthand form of argument, the notion of the 'penetration of market relations' represents an obstacle to analysis, since once the processes effecting change are sufficiently elaborated then 'such terms are both redundant and pitifully insufficient, being revealed for the teleological and rhetorical devices that they are' (Tribe 1981:99).

10. See also Appadurai (1986) who discusses the 'fundamental antagonism' between merchants and political elites in terms of a politics of taste.

11. Boulding claims: 'The case for the market is certainly the moral and economic inadequacy of its alternatives' (W. Block et al. [eds.] 1985:254). Also, despite the idea in economics that autonomous choice implies nothing about its moral content – thus it attempts to be a universal science – efficiency has come to stand for the common good. See ibid. for a discussion of the virtues and vices of a free-market order by ecclesiastics (among whom an anti-market mentality predominates) and economists. Friedman's *Free to Choose* (1980) and Hayek's *The Hand of Serfdom* (1944) and *The Constitution of Liberty* (1960) are also examples of moralising economics (see Hindess's discussion [1986]).

12. The oft-quoted passage in defence of this claim is Smith's assertion that: 'It is not from the benevolence of the butcher, the brewer, or the baker that we expect our dinner, but from their regard to their own interest' (1904:I:16).

13. See, however, Blanton (1983) on the evolution of market efficiency and the 'civilisational processes' brought by the market system. Also, modernisation theorists suggest that the integration of countries into a world market offers greatest opportunity for prosperity by the greatest number of people. By contrast, world-systems and dependency theories suggest that the supposed effects of the world market in extending benefit and common good to a greater number turn out to be the extraction of common goods for the enrichment of the few.

14. The state's role in relation to freedom is sometimes paradoxical: 'the state may have to intervene in the market to restore competition and thus *force it to be free*' (Johnson 1989:2, my emphasis). Platt also describes the attempts in Bolivia to force buyers and sellers into 'free agreements'.

15, Blanton (1983) reproduces a similar ideological opposition between market and state in his proposals for the 'long-term evolution of civilization'.

16. See for examples of recent work: F. Block 1990, Harvey 1989, Hargreaves Heap 1989, Hindess 1986 and 1988, Jameson 1990/91, McCloskey 1986, Marsden 1986, Tribe 1981 and Williamson 1975.

17. See for instance: Appadurai (1986) on demand as a politicised issue and the economic expression of the logics of consumption; Baudrillard (1990) on how needs and use values are socially constructed (*the system of needs* is *the product of the system of production'* [1990:42]; Douglas and Isherwood (1979) on consumption as a process of sending and receiving messages; Parry and Bloch (1989) on money symbolism and aspects of market exchange; Sahlins (1976) on the cultural construction of demand and consumption.

18. The economist Novak states: 'In practice, a market is an aggregation of all those who want to purchase [items]... and those who want to manufacture and distribute them for sale' (1985:572).

19. The economist's dilemma is nicely articulated by McCloskey, for on the one hand he holds out hope for a broad enough definition of a market that can be applied 'to whole nations or whole worlds', yet on the other he admits that 'it would be nice to avoid having separate models for each isolated New England farm or modern nation' 1986:146). But this is precisely the problem that the niceties of a universal, positivistic economics privileges its own disciplinary concerns about the constitution and definition of markets.

20. Doubts have been expressed recently among free marketeers about this idea. Johnson, editor of the Lloyds Bank Review, recently suggested that the invisible hand amounts to no more than the 'law of large numbers' 1989:4).

21. See *Capital* III: 210–25 for a discussion of value and market price. Godelier argues that Marx offered a version of the market not dissimilar from that of neo-classical economics (1972:44). See the *Communist Manifesto* for an illustration of Marx's market essentialism: 'The cheap prices of its commodities are the heavy artillery with which it [the bourgeoisie] batters down all Chinese walls ... It compels all nations, on pain of extinction, to adopt the Bourgeois mode of production; it compels them to introduce what it calls civilization into their midst.'

22. In Weber's view classes are also linked to markets. Life chances are created in the market through people meeting competitively for the purpose of exchange; and: 'The kind of chance in the market is a decisive moment which presents a common condition for the individual's fate. Class situation is, in this sense, ultimately market situation' (1985:181–2).

    Durkheim, by contrast, distanced himself from the idea of markets as primary social agents, especially in his conception of the division of labour in society (see Durkheim 1984 [1893], also Giddens 1971). His social theory is informed by a biological and not an economic metaphor. The rise of individualism associated with an expanded division of labour is not the fetishised, abstracted construct from a 'natural order' upon which orthodox economic theory is predicated, but a social representation of the 'cult of the individual' located within the moral order.

    Durkheim's work links us back not only to issues of morality but his *The Division of Labour in Society*, as a polemical attack on the prevailing utilitarian individualism, tackles an issue with which Smith himself opens *The Wealth of Nations*. Smith argued that the division of labour arises from 'a certain propensity in human nature ...; the propensity to truck, barter, and exchange one thing for another' (1904:I:15). The rise of trade, and hence the market, is predicated on the division of labour. For Durkheim, however, the division of labour is not purely utilitarian, the individual is not defined in terms of a theory of natural law and the form of exchange between segments is the product of a particular moral order.

23. Godelier's approach substitutes one form of primacy for another – that of exchange for the primacy of the production and reproduction. Whereas atomistic naturalism and the assumption of self-interest are central to orthodox economic theory, Marxism substitutes man-the-maximiser by man-the-producer and thus two competing forms of naturalism emerge. (Compare this with Baudrillard's claim that Marxism is the highest form of ideological justification of capitalism [1990].) Within social scientific debate claims to naturalism are powerful tropes.

24. The process of disembedding is more ideological than real (Dumont 1977): it justifies an intellectual division of labour into domains of expertise and confuses the emergence of the discipline of economics with its object, the economy (see Meillassoux 1981:6 and Godelier 1972:268). Recent work suggests that economic processes are indeed 'embedded' and the economy has been 're-substantivised' within the social, institutional and industrial contexts of western society (see, for example, Marsden 1986, Roberts et al. 1985, Williamson 1975).

25. See for instance, Douglas and Isherwood 1979, Dumont 1977, Godelier 1972 and 1977, Sahlins 1976; more recent works include Appadurai 1986, Gregory 1982 and, more broadly, Baudrillard 1990, Foucault 1989.

26. Gregory and Altman, in a research methods handbook, deal with the 'myth of the Marché', although in an enigmatic and opaque manner (1989:212–5). While entertaining, the piece offers more in way of hope than of theoretical substance.

27. A few examples picked at random from the literature, drawn not from hard-core formalists but from a range of theoretical approaches, suggest this unreflexive usage of the term: 'apprenticeship emerges as an institution through these very market forces' (Goody 1989:255); 'The *double labour market* sets out to divide the proletariat into two categories corresponding to the forms of exploitation which are experienced' (Meillassoux 1981:120); 'We know that "the market", in the sense of the macro-economic interactions between the European capitalist economies and other societies, was an active determinant of many features of "native" life' (Plattner 1985:vii).

28. Anthropologists were advised: 'If he [the anthropologist] has had no economic training, he is recommended to study the fundamental principles expounded in one of the recognised economic textbooks' in order to acquire what is described as 'ordinary economic theory' (*Notes and Queries*, 1960).

29. For example, formalist methodology advocates a method of 'successive approximations' of reality in the construction of models (Cook 1968) and Halperin considers the aim of defining formal models as the 'promotion of prediction and simulation' (1988).

30. See Gudeman (1990) on the relationship between socio-historical context and economic theory. Clammer views the future of 'economic anthropology' as a closer alliance with history, symbolism, linguistics and so on and not as a movement towards an increasingly sophisticated economics (1987).

31. N. S. B. Gras in 1927 coined this enterprise 'anthropological economics', in contradistinction to economic anthropology. 'We may speak of anthropological economics, meaning by that term a study of the ideas that primitive peoples held about economic matters. Such ideas would doubtless be found to be vague, unformulated and greatly confused with other matters. Such a subject is quite undeveloped, and the interests involved, though of great significance, are but little noted' (Gras 1927:10). MacIntyre also suggests that: 'It is only when we understand and categorise the social and economic phenomena in such a way as to recognise the agent's and participant's understanding of social and economic activity ... that we provide characterisations that enable us to write rationally defensible explanatory narratives' (quoted in Halperin 1988).

32. A similar paradox exists in marginalism whereby prices are determined by individual preference, yet the individual consumer is determined by and subject to those prices (see Godelier 1972:40). M. Strathern points up a similar apparent contradiction in relation to transactionalism's reliance on the natural individual as an axiomatic assumption, by asking how the individual could be both a product of society and culture, and yet act *qua* an individual in terms of interests that were not defined by that culture or society (In press). This statement can be read with equal sense if the term market is substituted for culture and society.

33. Strathern points out that there is a similar type of 'double image' deployed in the mid-twentieth century social anthropology of Fortes and Radcliffe-Brown, which was concerned with the construction of the person. This double image here comprised the ideas of the person as a social construction of society on the one hand, and society seen as constructed by persons on the other (see Morgan Lectures, in which she also notes that over the last decade, this double image has collapsed).

34. See *Grundrisse*, a quotation from which appears in Jameson (1990/91:272).

35. Jameson (1990/91) goes on to suggest that the social totality of western capitalism is moving towards a second form of mapping which can be seen through analogies that are drawn between the market and media. These two are becoming cemented through notions of 'free choice', 'symbiosis' and the 'interpenetration of content', and through similarities of form and image.

36. Tambiah makes a similar point: 'We must chart more ideologies of exchange than the simple binary division between primitive and modern, status and contract ...' (Tambiah 1984:340).
37. The types of 'individuality' or social personhood which Tambiah attributes to various ideologies of exchange could be developed. For instance, the players of Kula control beauty magic, and whether they win or lose at the game depends on personal magnetism. This is a different form of 'individuality' from that represented in market exchange. Also, the types of intentionality behind the various 'loops' of amulet exchange refer to differing conceptions of social personhood. Priests raise levels of spiritual consciousness through exchange conceived as detached action removed from the immediacy of desire, whereas laymen operating in market-places are immersed in materiality and the gratification of human desire (Tambiah 1984).
38. Compare this with Parry on Maori gift exchange in which the agency of gifting partners is represented as the fertility of the gift itself; fecundity and increase stem from reciprocity rather than from human agency (1986:465).
39. Note Appadurai's claim that 'economic exchange creates value' (1986:3).
40. Such a project cannot be located 'outside the culture and intellectual traditions of the anthropologist who produces them' (Kahn 1990:232) any more than accounts of histories of European social thought are untainted by the historical moment of their production. All projects are open to an 'infinite regression of deconstruction and reconstruction' (Kahn 1990), since no account can adopt a historically and culturally neutral standpoint. While one should be aware of such limitations, the partiality of the attempts to be attentive to other voices must be acknowledged.

REFERENCES

Agnew, J. –C. 1986. *Worlds Apart: The Market and the Theater in Anglo-American Thought 1550–1750*. Cambridge: Cambridge University Press.

Appadurai, A. (ed.), 1986. 'Introduction: Commodities and the Politics of Value', in *The Social Life of Things: Commodities in Cultural Perspective*. Cambridge: Cambridge University Press.

Asad, T. 1979. 'Anthropology and the Analysis of Ideology', *Man* (N. S.), 14: 607–27.

Asad, T. 1972. 'Market Model, Class Structure and Consent: A Reconsideration of Swat Political Organisation', *Man* (N. S.), 7 (1): 74–94.

Barth, F. 1965. *Political Leadership among Swat Pathans*. London: Athlone Press.

Baudrillard, J. 1990. *Selected Writings*. Cambridge: Polity Press.

Beck, B. 1978. 'The Metaphor as Mediator between Semantic and Analogic Modes of Thought', *Current Anthropology*, 19 (1): 83–8.

Blanton, R. E. 1983. 'Factors underlying the Origin and Evolution of Market Systems', in S. Ortiz (ed.), *Economic Anthropology: Topics and Theories*. New York and London: University Press of America. pp. 51–66.

Bloch, M. 1989. 'The Symbolism of Money in Imerina', in J. Parry and M. Bloch (eds.), *op. cit.* pp. 165–90.

Block, F. 1990. *Postindustrial Possibilities: A Critique of Economic Discourse*. Berkeley: University of California Press.

Block, W., G. Brennan and K. Elzinga (eds.), 1985. *Morality of the Market*. Vancouver, B. C. : The Fraser Institute.

Bohannan, P. and G. Dalton (eds.), 1962. *Markets in Africa*. Evanstone: Northwestern University Press.

Boulding, K. 1981. *Evolutionary Economics*. London: Sage Publications.

Bourdieu, P. 1977. *Outline of a Theory of Practice*. Cambridge: Cambridge University Press.

Braudel, F. 1982. *The Wheels of Commerce*. London: Collins.

Brenner, R. 1977. 'The Origins of Capitalist Development: A Critique of Neo-Smithian Marxism', *New Left Review*, 104: 26–92.

Cheal, D. 1988. *The Gift Economy*. London: Routledge.

Clammer, J. (ed.), 1987. *Beyond the New Economic Anthropology*. London: Macmillan.

Cook, S. 1968. 'The Obsolete Anti-Market Mentality', in E. LeClair and H. Schneider (eds.), *op. cit.*

Dahrendorf, R. 1973 [1968]. 'Market and Plan', in *Essays in the Theory of Society*. Stanford: Stanford University Press. pp. 217–31. Excerpts reprinted in E. Etzioni-Halevy and A. Etzioni (eds.), *Social Change: Sources, Patterns and Consequences* (2nd edn.) New York: Basic Books, pp. 500–4.

Dalton, G. 1968. 'Economic Theory and Primitive Society', in E. LeClair and H. Schneider (eds.), *op. cit.*

Davis, J. 1985. 'Rules and Laws: Outline of an Ethnographic Approach to Economics', in B. Roberts et al. (eds.), *op. cit.*

Douglas, M. 1982. *In the Active Voice*. London: Routledge.

Douglas, M. and B. Isherwood. 1979. *The World of Goods: Towards an Anthropology of Consumption*. London: Allen Lane.

Dumont, L. 1977. *From Mandeville to Marx: The Genesis and Triumph of Economic Ideology*. Chicago and London: University of Chicago Press.

Dumont, L. 1986. *Essays on Individualism: Modern Ideology in Anthropological Perspective*. Chicago and London: University of Chicago Press.

Durkheim, E. 1984 [1893]. *The Division of Labour in Society*. London: Macmillan.

Fardon, R. 1987. '"African Ethnogenesis": Limits to the Comparability of Ethnic Phenomena', in L. Holy (ed.), *Comparative Anthropology*. Oxford: Blackwell. pp. 168–88.

Ferguson, J. 1988. 'Cultural Exchange: New Developments in the Anthropology of Commodities', *Current Anthropology*, 3(4): 488–513.

Fernandez, J. 1974. 'The Mission of Metaphor in Expressive Culture', *Current Anthropology*, 15(2): 119–33.

Fernandez, J. 1986. *Persuasions and Performances: The Play of Tropes in Culture*. Bloomington: Indiana University Press.

Forster, J. J. H. 1984, 'Donham's Formalism', *Man* (N. S.), 19(2): 322–5.

Foucault, M. 1989. *The Order of Things*. London: Routledge.

Geertz, C. 1966. 'Religion as a Cultural System', in M. Banton (ed.), *Anthropological Approaches to the Study of Religion*. London: Tavistock.

Gell, A. 1982. 'The Market Wheel: Symbolic Aspects of an Indian Tribal Market', *Man* (N. S.), 17(3): 470–91.

Giddens, A. 1971. *Capitalism and Modern Social Theory: An Analysis of the Writings of Marx, Durkheim and Weber*. Cambridge: Cambridge University Press.

Godelier, M. 1972. *Rationality and Irrationality in Economics*. London: New Left Books.

Godelier, M. 1977. *Perspectives in Marxist Anthropology*. Cambridge: Cambridge University Press.

Goody, E. 1989. 'Learning, Apprenticeship and the Division of Labour', in M. Coy (ed.), *Apprenticeship: From Theory to Method and Back Again*. New York: State University of New York. pp. 233–56.

Gras, N. S. B. 1927. 'Anthropology and Economics', in W. Ogburn (ed.), *The Social Sciences and their Interrelations*. Boston, N. Y. : Houghton Mifflin & Co. pp. 10–23.

Gregory, C. 1982. *Gifts and Commodities*. London: Academic Press.

Gregory, C. and J. C. Altman (eds.), 1989. *Observing the Economy*. London: Routledge.

Gudeman, S. 1986. *Economics as Culture: Models and Metaphors of Livelihood*. London: Routledge and Kegan Paul.

Gudeman, S. and M. Penn, 1982. 'Models, Meaning and Reflexivity', in D. Parkin (ed.), *op. cit.*

Gudeman, S. and A. Rivera, 1990. *Conversations in Columbia: The Domestic Economy in Life and Text.* Cambridge: Cambridge University Press.

Halperin, R. H. 1988. *Economies across Cultures: Towards a Comparative Science of the Economy.* London: Macmillan.

Hargreaves Heap, S. 1989. *Rationality in Economics.* Oxford: Basil Blackwell.

Hart, K. 1986. 'Heads or Tails? Two Sides of the Coin', *Man* (N. S.), 21(4): 637–56.

Harvey, D. 1989. *The Condition of Postmodernity: An Enquiry into the Origins of Cultural Change.* Oxford: Blackwell.

Hindess, B. 1986. *Freedom, Equality and the Market.* London: Tavistock.

Hindess, B. 1988. *Choice, Rationality and Social Theory.* London: Unwin Hyman.

Holy, L. and M. Stuchlik (eds.), 1981. *The Structure of Folk Models.* London: Academic Press.

Holy, L. and M. Stucklik. 1983. *Actions, Norms and Representations: Foundations of Anthropological Enquiry.* Cambridge: Cambridge University Press.

Howe, L. 1990. *Being Unemployed in Northern Ireland: An Ethnographic Study.* Cambridge: Cambridge University Press.

Jackson, M. 1982. *Allegories of the Wilderness: Ethics and Ambiguity in Kuranko Narratives.* Bloomington: Indiana University Press.

Jameson, F. 1990/91. *Post Modernism, or, The Cultural Logic of Late Capitalism.* London and New York: Verso.

Johnson, C. (ed.), 1989. *The Market on Trial* (Lloyds Bank Annual Review, Vol. 2). London and New York: Pinter.

Kahn, J. 1990. 'Towards a History of the Critique of Economism: The 19th Century German Origins of the Ethnographer's Dilemma', *Man.* (N. S.), 25(2): 230–49.

Keenan, 1987. 'Free Markets, Ideology and Control: the South African Case', in J. Clammer (ed.) *op. cit.* pp. 142–87.

Lawson, N. 1989. 'The State of the Market', in C. Johnson (ed.), *op. cit.* pp. 26–36.

LeClair, E. and H. Schneider (eds.), 1968. *Economic Anthropology: Readings in Theory and Analysis.* New York: Holt, Rinehart and Winston.

Lenin, V. I. 1960 [1893–4]. 'On the So-Called Market Question', *Collected Works.* Vol. I. London: Lawrence and Wishart.

Marsden, D. 1986. *The End of Economic Man? Custom and Competition in Labour Markets.* Brighton: Wheatsheaf Books.

Marx, K. 1909 [1873–94]. *Capital: A Critique of Political Economy,* Vols. I–III. Chicago: Charles H. Kerr.

Mauss, M. 1969. *The Gift: Forms and Functions of Exchange in Archaic Societies.* London: Cohen and West.

McCloskey, D. N. 1986. *The Rhetoric of Economics.* Brighton: Wheatsheaf Books.

Meillassoux, C. 1981. *Maidens, Meal and Money: Capitalism and the Domestic Economy.* Cambridge: Cambridge University Press.

Morris, B. 1977. 'Are there any Individuals in India? A Critique of Dumont's theory of the Individual', *The Eastern Anthropologist,* 31(4): 365–77.

Novak, M. 1985. 'Overview', in W. Block et al. (eds.), *op. cit.* pp. 567–87.

Parkin, D. (ed.), 1982. 'Introduction', *Semantic Anthropology.* London: Academic Press.

Parry, J. 1986. 'The Gift, the Indian Gift and the "Indian Gift"', *Man* (N. S.), 21(3), 453–73.

Parry, J. 1989. 'On the Moral Perils of Exchange', in J. Parry and M. Bloch (eds.) *op. cit.* pp. 64–93.

Parry, J. and M. Bloch, 1989. 'Introduction: Money and the Morality of Exchange', in J. Parry and M. Bloch (eds.), *Money and the Morality of Exchange.* Cambridge: Cambridge University Press.

Plattner, S. (ed.), 1985. *Markets and Marketing: Monographs in Economic Anthropology, No. 4,* Lanham: University Press of America.

Polanyi, K. 1957. *The Great Transformation: The Political and Economic Origins of Our Time.* Boston, Mass. : Beacon Press.

Polanyi, K. 1968. 'The Economy as Instituted Process', in E. Leclair and H. Schneider (eds.), *op. cit.*

Polanyi, K. 1971. *Primitive, Archaic and Modern Economies: Essays of Karl Polanyi,* (ed. G. Dalton). Boston: Beacon Press.

Roberts, B. , R. Finnegan and D. Gallie (eds.), 1985. *New Approaches to Economic Life. Economic Restructuring: Unemployment and the Social Division of Labour.* Manchester: Manchester University Press.

Roover, R. de, 1968. 'Economic Thought: Ancient and Medieval Thought', in *International Encyclopedia of the Social Sciences,* Vol IV. London: Macmillan and Free Press. pp. 430–5.

Sahlins, M. 1976. *Culture and Practical Reason.* Chicago: University of Chicago Press.

Salzman, P. C. 1981. 'Culture as Enhabilmentis', in L. Holy and M. Stuchlik (eds.), *op. cit.* pp. 233–56.

Scott, J. C. 1976. *The Moral Economy of the Peasant: Rebellion and Subsistence in Southeast Asia.* New Haven and London: Yale University Press.

Shinn, R. L. 1985. 'From Theology to Social Decisions – and Return', in W. Block et al. (eds.), *op. cit.* pp. 175–95.

Smith, A. 1904 [1776]. *An Inquiry into the Nature and Causes of the Wealth of Nations,* Vols I & II. London: Methuen.

Smith, A. 1976 [1759]. *The Theory of Moral Sentiments.* Oxford: Clarendon.

Smith, C. 1974. 'Economics of Marketing Systems: Models from Economic Geography', *Annual Review of Anthropology,* 3: 167–201.

Southern, R. W. 1968. 'Aquinas, Thomas', in *International Encyclopedia of the Social Sciences,* Vol I. London: Macmillan and Free Press. pp. 375–7.

Strathern, M. 1984. 'The Social Meanings of Localism', in T. Bradley and P. Lowe (eds.), *Locality and Rurality: Economy and Society in Rural Regions.* Norwich: Geo Books. pp. 181–97.

Strathern, M. 1985. 'Kinship and Economy: Constitutive Orders of a Provisional Kind', *American Ethnologist,* 12: 191–209.

Strathern, M. in press. *After Nature: English Kinship in the Late Twentieth Century. Notes for the Lewis Henry Morgan Lectures 1989.* University of Rochester, Rochester, New York.

Tambiah, S. J. 1984. *The Buddhist Saints of the Forest and the Cult of Amulets.* Cambridge: Cambridge University Press.

Taussig, M. 1986. *Shamanism, Colonialism and the Wild Man: A Study in Terror and Healing.* Chicago and London: University of Chicago Press.

Tawney, R. 1961. *Religion and the Rise of Capitalism.* Harmondsworth: Penguin.

Thompson, E. P. 1971. 'The Moral Economy of the 18th-Century English Crowd', *Past and Present,* 50: 76–136.

Tribe, K. 1981. *Genealogies of Capitalism.* London: Macmillan.

Weber, M. 1985. *From Max Weber: Essays in Sociology* (Translated, Edited and with Introduction by H. H. Gerth and C. Wright Mills). London: Routledge and Keagan Paul.

Werbner, R. 1989. *Ritual Passage, Sacred Journey: The Process of Organisation of Religious Movement.* Washington D. C. and Manchester: Smithsonian and Manchester University Press.

Williamson, O. 1975. *Markets and Hierarchies.* New York: Free Press.

Part 1

Economic Thought and
Western Discourse

2

Adam Smith and the Invisible Hand – of the Market?

HEINZ LUBASZ

There has been a lot of talk recently about the invisible hand of the market, brought on no doubt by the resurgence of *laissez-faire* ideology in the US and Britain and reinforced by what one can only call the outbreak of free-market mania elsewhere. The market in question is, of course, not the local or the weekly market, or even the long-term world-wide market for this or that commodity. The market in question here is the economy as a whole in a commercial or market society, that is, an economy so completely permeated by exchange relations that the 'services' of land (which includes raw materials), labour and capital (the 'factors of production') are just as readily available to any entrepreneur – individual or firm – who can raise the money to pay for them as the goods produced by means of these factors of production are available to any consumer who can afford to buy them. These consumers – again, individuals and firms – are the 'effectual demanders': people not just as they have needs and wants but as they can turn these needs and wants into effective demand in the market by means of money. What then is meant by 'the invisible hand of the market' is broadly this, that material good is done to others in the entire absence of benevolence and altruism: the market itself brings it about that the private pursuit by individuals and firms of their own greatest profit makes 'everyone' as well off as possible – at least 'on balance and over time'. As it is less than self-evident how such purely self-interested activity can bring about so wholly beneficial an outcome, reference is made to the market's invisible hand. But as this reference does not explain much, theories are put forward to show just how the market functions as an invisible hand. And that is where our troubles begin: many theories, no agreement.

This chapter has three main parts. The first part compares the view of modern economists that the invisible hand is the hand of the market itself with Adam Smith's view that it is the hand of *nature* – in 'the market', and goes on to elaborate Smith's conception of nature. The second addresses the providentialist dimension of the concept, and deals with the highly providentialist 'invisible hand' passage in Smith's The *Theory of Moral Sentiments* (1759), a passage often – and mistakenly – cited in support of the present-day proposition that 'the market' somehow yields an equitable distribution of income. The third part shows in detail how in *The Wealth of Nations* (1776) the invisible hand of *nature* works so as to promote the interest of the society.

2.1

It is not easy to believe how great the muddle is that surrounds the phrase 'the invisible hand of the market' and the piece of economic reasoning for which it stands. To begin with, the phrase itself, which is reliably said to be 'the most famous metaphor in economics,' is firmly attributed to Adam Smith.[1] Yet it occurs nowhere in Smith's writings. All one can find there is mention of 'an invisible hand' – without any addendum. The precise identity of this hand, which is in any case mentioned just once in *The Theory of Moral Sentiments* (1976b:184–5) and once in *The Wealth of Nations*,[2] has to be construed from the context(s). It turns out to be the invisible hand not of the market but of providentially designed nature. At first glance this difference may seem trivial: one can readily imagine that Smith might have meant by the invisible hand (of nature) much the same as modern economists mean by the invisible hand of the market. But, as we shall see, the difference between these two expressions is considerable, and the reasoning which underlies the one is quite different from the reasoning which underlies the other. The invisible hand is one thing to Smith and another to modern economists.

To compound the confusion, modern economists agree among themselves that the invisible hand is the hand of the market, but mean quite different things by it. Neo-classical economists identify it with perfect market balance, while so-called 'Austrian' economists identify it with perfect market freedom; Keynesians for their part think the whole idea a lot of rubbish (see for example Keynes [1972] and Robinson [1962]). To elaborate briefly: neo-classical economists tend to identify the invisible hand with a purely hypothetical condition, the condition of perfectly competitive equilibrium. According to two of their leading lights, Kenneth Arrow and Frank Hahn, Adam Smith's invisible hand is 'a poetic expression of the most fundamental of balance relations, equalisation of rates of return, as enforced by the tendency of factors [of production] to move from low to high returns.' (Cited in Ingrao and Israel 1990:ix.) So the neo-classical invisible hand functions as a merely notional ideal condition of resource allocation. 'Austrian' economists, *per contra*, identify the invisible hand with the real, actually existing market, to the extent that this market is a free nexus of impersonal communication and exchange. The most eminent of the 'Austrians', Friedrich von Hayek, brings out what he takes to be the salient feature of the market by contrasting it with the redistributive economy of the tribe (an atavistic longing for which he thinks is deeply rooted in our emotions and thus constitutes a perennial threat to the 'free market' – and to its counterpart, the 'open society').

> We still esteem doing good [he writes,] only if it is done to benefit specific known needs of known people…but in fact we generally are doing most good by pursuing gain…[The modern entrepreneur] is led to benefit more people by aiming at the largest gain than he could if he concentrated on the satisfaction of the needs of known persons. He is led by the invisible hand of the market to bring the succour of modern conveniences to the poorest homes he does not even know. (Hayek 1976:145.)

So the 'Austrian' invisible hand is simply the market as efficient supplier of effectual demand.

None of this is true to the spirit of Adam Smith, let alone to the letter. Smith did not demand total market freedom à la Hayek, nor did he hold with perfect market balance in the manner of Arrow and Hahn.[3] Moreover, in sharp contrast to both neo-classicals and 'Austrians', he certainly did *not* believe that the interest of the society was automatically promoted by the private pursuit of the greatest possible profits. The sad fact is that Adam Smith's concept of an 'invisible hand' of nature has been seriously distorted by being turned into 'the invisible hand of the market' in whatever version, neo-classical or 'Austrian'; and the piece of Smithian economic reasoning the concept of the invisible hand originally stood for has been not so much refined and superseded as simply lost. In my view that reasoning is sufficiently interesting, and the contrast between it and modern free-market ideas is sufficiently illuminating, to make it well worth recovering.[4]

The one fundamental point on which Smith and the moderns fully agree is that what Smith calls 'commercial society' and what moderns call 'the market' is neither an interpersonal pattern of reciprocities nor an arranged order of redistribution: it is an impersonal order governed by impersonal forces. It is these forces, whatever their nature, which are responsible for bringing about the favourable though unintended collective outcome of intentional individual activity. But at this point agreement ends.

Modern economists hold with the sovereignty of market forces – the forces of supply and demand – and the supremacy of the profit motive. In their view it is market prices which steer entrepreneurial activity in the 'right' direction: prices guide individuals and firms by pointing them towards whatever pursuits appear most profitable. In this way total entrepreneurial activity maximises aggregate wealth – and for modern economists the maximising of aggregate wealth is essentially what the interest of society consists of. How that wealth is distributed is to these same economists either a quite separate question or an illegitimate one; to neo-classicals it is a 'normative' question in welfare economics, separate from the purely scientific issues of 'positive' economics (Blaug 1980:146–8); to Hayek it is a question that cannot even properly be put, since there simply is no distribution apart from production (Hayek 1976:72 and 178 n. 12). Most modern economists seem to understand Adam Smith – whom many of them tend to read cursorily or not at all – in the light of such assumptions as these and consequently they confuse his conception of the invisible hand with their own, the invisible hand of the market.

Adam Smith's vision differs from the modern vision in every important respect. In the first place he does not hold with the sovereignty of market forces. Much like his French contemporaries, the Physiocrats, he held with the sovereignty of providentially designed nature (including human nature). In keeping with this assumption he believed that it was 'the natural inclinations of man' (377; 357) – indeed a combination of such inclinations, including the desire for gain – that steered the individual in the 'right' direction. Second, Smith's 'invisible hand' directly links the *production* of maximal national wealth with its more or less equitable (but of course not equal) *distribution*:[5] as maximal wealth production requires the maximal employment of productive labour, the invisible hand brings it about that there is maximal employment, and that consequently some share of the wealth produced finds its way into the pockets of the workers. Even though there be no distribution apart from production, the very conditions of production in pre-technological society are such as to secure adequate sustenance to industrious labour. Thanks to the way the invisible hand operates in Adam Smith's scheme of things, the socially advantageous production of wealth and its more or less equitable distribution among 'the three great orders' of commercial society – land, capital and labour – go hand in hand.

The point is this. In Smith's vision the self-interested individuals do not pursue in any and all directions whatever happens to be most profitable; they are led by their natural inclinations to *channel* their investments so as to do the country as a whole the most good. In contrast to modern economists who hold that society benefits no matter how private capital is invested – as long as it is profitably invested – Smith is quite clear and specific as to how private capital must be invested if it is to promote the interest of the society: 'The most advantageous employment of any capital to the country to which it belongs, is that which maintains there the greatest quantity of productive labour, and increases the most the annual product of the land and labour of that country' (600; 566).

This idea, that their naturally balanced natural inclinations (for gain, for security, for ease and for independence) direct individuals to invest their capitals in such a way as to employ as much of the country's productive labour as possible and so as to render the annual produce of the country's land and labour as large as possible – this seems to me the most remarkable of Smith's economic inventions, and we shall be considering it in detail. It holds the key to the meaning of the 'invisible hand' of – nature.

To get a firmer grip on Adam Smith's idea of the invisible hand of nature we need to know a little more about how he thought of nature altogether and of its role in economic life. This will take us some way towards understanding why he was convinced that nature should in the main be allowed to have full and untrammelled sway in economic affairs. It will also allow us to set aside a second, closely related misconception about Smithian theory. For, just as the invisible hand is the hand not of the market but of nature, so the force that obstructs nature is not the state as such but human institutions and human scheming generally.

Adam Smith is often dragged into twentieth-century debates on the issue of the state versus the market as though he had definitively pronounced on it. But for Smith the state was an obstacle to the system of natural liberty not in its own right, as rival entrepreneur, planner or policy-maker, but rather as the vehicle used – and abused – by schemers of all kinds seeking privileges against their fellow-citizens. As Smith saw it, the issue was not: the market versus the state but: nature versus privilege. In his eyes it was projectors, vested interests and privilege-seekers – foremost among them the manufacturers and merchants who were 'the contrivers of [the] whole mercantile system' (661; 626) – who were the miscreants, rather than the government they managed to bend to their will. As early as 1749 Smith said in a lecture: 'projectors disturb nature in the course of her operations on human affairs, and it requires no more than to leave her alone and give her fair play in the pursuit of her ends that she may establish her own designs' (cited in Viner 1927). (As Jacob Viner pointed out long ago, 'to leave her alone' is the English equivalent of that *'laissez-faire'* which the French Physiocrats were just then on the verge of introducing into economic discourse (ibid.) It is worth stressing, however, that the idea is not that *we* should be left to do as we please; it is not a matter of *'laissez nous faire'*, as later partisans of *laissez-faire* had it. It is rather that *nature* should be left alone – or, in other words, that we should be left alone only to the extent that we follow our natural inclinations.)

One way of learning what Smith meant by allowing nature to take its course is to look at a prime example of the privileges which he thought interfered with the natural order. Prominent among the institutions which in Smith's view disturbed 'the natural course of things' (380; 360) were the laws of primogeniture and entail which made the eldest son of a landowner sole heir. Smith believed these laws, instituted in the early medieval period, to have been largely responsible for the slow progress of agriculture, 'the industry of the countryside', compared with the splendid progress made by trade, 'the industry of the towns', not just during the Middle Ages but down to his own day (377; 363); primogeniture and entail do great harm by preventing large estates from 'being broke up into small parcels by alienation' (382; 361) and so coming under intense cultivation. Since Smith held agriculture to be *by nature* the most efficiently productive of human occupations and so the most apt to make the nation as a whole more prosperous, he counted the comparative neglect of agriculture a great material loss, a loss which would not have occurred in the first place if the human institutions of primogeniture and entail – as well as slavery (serfdom) and share-cropping – had not interfered with 'the natural order of things. ' (380; 360).

Smith's vision of the natural order was not confined to the economy. Having elaborated on the theme of the natural course of economic development and how it was thwarted by the intervention of human institutions he went on to note that the human laws of primogeniture and entail also offend against other features of the natural order, namely natural or rational law, and natural justice. '[Those laws] are founded upon the most absurd of all suppositions, the supposition that every successive generation of men have not an equal right to the earth, and to all that it possesses'(384; 363). Besides, the very manner of their institution was contrary to natural justice: those laws serve only to maintain the exclusive privileges of one order of men over others, 'that order having usurped [an] unjust advantage over the rest of their fellow-citizens' (385; 363). To notice how many kinds of damage he thought were done by institutional interference with the natural order is to realise that the great Adam was not just an economist but a philosopher writing on political economy in broad perspective.

Since Adam Smith's ideas on the natural order play so fundamental a role in his economic thinking and yet are little known, it makes sense to quote at least a few of them at some length.

First of all, why the 'natural' precedence of agriculture? I quote:

> As subsistence is, in the nature of things, prior to conveniency and luxury, so the industry which procures the former, must necessarily be prior to that which ministers to the latter. The cultivation and improvement of the country, therefore, which affords subsistence, must, necessarily, be prior to the increase

of the town, which furnishes only the means of conveniency and luxury…

That order of things which necessity imposes in general, though not in every particular country, is, in every particular country promoted by the natural inclinations of man. If human institutions had never thwarted those natural inclinations, the towns could no-where have increased beyond what the improvement and cultivation of the territory in which they were situated could support… Upon equal, or nearly equal profits, most men will chuse to employ their capitals rather in the improvement and cultivation of land, than either in manufacturers of in foreign trade. (377; 357–8)

Notice particularly that Smith implicitly but very firmly rejects the notion that investment decisions are made solely in terms of relative profitability, and expressly and just as firmly asserts that, given the prospect of equal or even somewhat less than equal profitability, it is the natural inclinations of man (which of course *include* the desire for gain but are not confined to it) that are the deciding factor.

Taking a look at the elaborate list Smith produces of the 'natural' attractions of agriculture will give us a graphic sense of what he has in mind in contending that the desire for gain is but one among several human passions and interests to be taken into account.

The man who employs his capital in land, has it more under his view and command, and his fortune is much less liable to accidents, than that of the trader, who is obliged frequently to commit it, not only to the winds and the waves, but to the more uncertain elements of human folly and injustice, by giving great credits in distant countries to men, with whose character and situation he can seldom be thoroughly acquainted. The capital of the landlord, on the contrary, which is fixed in the improvement of his land, seems to be as well secured as the nature of human affairs can admit of. The beauty of the country besides, the pleasures of a country life, the tranquility of mind which it promises, and wherever the injustice of human laws does not disturb it, the independency which it really affords, have charms that more or less attract everybody; and as to cultivate the ground was the original destination of man, so in every stage of his existence he seems to retain a predilection for this primitive employment. (377–8; 358)

Indeed, where, as in Britain's North American colonies, the price of land is not yet prohibitive, agriculture is widely preferred to manufacture, not for any greater profit it might yield but for the independence it affords. Every artificer who has accumulated a little more capital than he needs in order to continue in his trade will use it, not to enlarge his business but to buy and cultivate land.

From artificer he becomes planter… He feels that an artificer is the servant of his customers, from whom he derives his subsistence; but that a planter who cultivates his own land, and derives his necessary subsistence from the labour of his own family, is really a master, and independent of the whole world. (378–9; 359)

To be sure, these are more eloquent and elaborate reasons why men naturally prefer agriculture to manufacture than any Smith can offer in support of his parallel claim that 'for the same reason that agriculture is naturally preferred to manufactures,… manufactures are, upon equal or nearly equal profits, naturally preferred to foreign commerce'(379; 359). But we get the idea. Smith makes it plain enough that in his scheme of things the crucial role in investment decisions is never played by the bare interest in profit alone. It is played by a range of those natural inclinations of man which promote the natural order of things.

2.2

A natural order which is not a morally neutral, merely physical cosmos but actually directs individuals' activities towards a common or a 'higher' good which none of them intentionally seeks smacks to us of the providential. And providential of course it is. Talk of Providence and its invisible hand is no longer part of ordinary discourse. But in Adam Smith's day it was, and as he was a deist such talk probably came to him 'naturally'. Yet even in his day it made a world of difference whether one thought of Providence as intervening directly or only indirectly in human affairs. Providence could be imagined as thrusting its invisible hand *directly* into the universe from time to time in near-miraculous ways. So, for instance, 'when the warship *Prince George* survived a great storm which wrecked several other ships of the Royal Navy in 1703, Flag Captain Martin wrote in the ship's log that "the invisible hand of Providence relieved us"' (Raphael 1985:72). But Providence could also be thought of as intervening in the world only *indirectly*, availing itself of the regular features of the natural universe – space, time, geography, climate, natural resources, the facts of life and the sanction of death – and operating through the normal attributes of human nature. In the latter case it was specifically the invisible hand of Nature that was at work – the hand of a Nature which was itself thought of as being of Providential design.

When he writes on moral philosophy, as he does in *The Theory of Moral Sentiments*, Adam Smith is not above attributing the pattern of the human social order to the direct dispensation of Providence with a capital P, though even in that work the triumph of Providence's aim is secured, as we shall see, by the less obtrusive and indirect operation of an invisible hand availing itself of an aspect of human nature. In *The Wealth of Nations*, however, with its wholly worldly subject-matter, Providence does not intervene directly at all; apart from a fleeting reference to 'the wisdom of nature'(674; 638), its existence is not even hinted at. Its good work is left entirely to the invisible hand of nature, which simply guides individual human action by using the 'natural inclinations'(377; 357) of individuals to propel them towards a beneficent outcome which they do not intend. (Needless to say, the latter arrangement requires that humans allow themselves to be so guided; they must be willing, as Smith had earlier insisted, to 'leave [nature] alone and give her fair play in the pursuit of her [NB!] ends.') The important point for us post-providentialists to bear in mind is this, that it is the invariably beneficent nature of the outcome which betrays the providential character of the Smithian scheme of things. That scheme of things is on no account to be confused with the morally neutral modern conception of the unintended collective consequences of intentional individual action – consequences which need not be beneficent at all and may be disastrous.

What distinguishes Smith's conception of the invisible hand in *The Wealth of Nations* is that, in contrast to what he does in *The Theory of Moral Sentiments*, he dissociates it completely from all direct intervention of Providence in human affairs. Instead, he assimilates it to the regular workings of that most magnificent of all mechanical systems, the providentially designed Newtonian world-machine: the universal, law-governed, constant operation of Nature, which he understands to include human nature. The result is striking: the term 'invisible hand' as it appears in *The Wealth of Nations* is and remains inescapably providential in tone and overtone, as does the role it plays; and yet, because the operations of this invisible hand are always and only inscribed in certain familiar natural human attributes, the analysis in which *The Wealth of Nations*'s invisible hand plays so important a part appears totally 'scientific'. In sharp contrast to modern theories of the invisible hand of the market which separate the positive from the normative, separate what is from what ought to be, Smith's theory of the invisible hand of nature unites them; what analysis shows to be true can also be seen to be good. It follows that, in turning the Smithian invisible hand into the hand of 'the market', modern economists – unwittingly? – bestow on their scientific analyses an aura of Smithian providentiality.

If nevertheless the 'pre-scientific' *The Theory of Moral Sentiments*'s invisible hand passage is well worth a closer look this is not because it gives us additional insight into how Smith conceived the invisible hand to operate in commercial society – that is precisely what it fails to do – but because it helps us to see just how far modern commentators are prepared to go in their search for the invisible hand of the market – even where there is no market (as in *The Theory of Moral Sentiments* there is none.)

The Theory of Moral Sentiments's 'invisible hand' occurs in a chapter entitled 'Of the beauty which the appearance of UTILITY bestows upon all the productions of art, and of the extensive influence of this species of Beauty' – not at first glance a likely place to look for, for example, a theory of income distribution. Smith argues that we take pleasure in useful things because they are so *beautifully* – efficiently, systematically, elegantly – fitted to attain their end, no matter how worthless the end might be in itself (179–87). According to him we are, for example, likely to be 'charmed with the beauty of that accommodation which reigns in the palaces and œconomy of the great; and admire how every thing is adapted to promote their ease, to prevent their wants, to gratify their wishes, and to amuse and entertain their most frivolous desires. If we consider the real satisfaction which all these things are capable of affording, by itself and separated from *the beauty of that arrangement* which is fitted to promote it, it will always appear in the highest degree contemptible and trifling' (183). For 'in what constitutes the real happiness of human life… ease of body and peace of mind… [the poor] are in no respect inferior to those who would seem so much above them' (185). But Smith also finds that this, our appreciation of the beauty of utility, is itself beneficial:

> And it is well that nature imposes upon us in this manner. It is this deception which arouses and keeps in continual motion the industry of mankind… The earth by these labours of mankind has been obliged to redouble her natural fertility, and to maintain a greater multitude of inhabitants. (183–4)

A fine homily by an eighteenth-century professsor of moral philosophy on the vanity of riches, the fitness of the social order, and the power of Providence to secure her own 'darling end', the multiplication of the species – thanks to the hold which the beauty of utility has on us.

So far Smith has been arguing that men are tricked by Nature into being industrious, by their admiration and emulation of the beauty of the way the rich live. But there is a problem. If, as Smith supposes, Providence has divided the earth among a few lordly masters, what is to prevent these lords of the land from consuming the extra harvest themselves, thus to make it impossible, for lack of sustenance, for the people to be fruitful and multiply, and so to frustrate the plan of Providence? Here is his 'reply'.

> It is to no purpose, that the proud and unfeeling landlord views his extensive fields, and without a thought for the wants of his brethen, in imagination consumes himself the whole harvest that grows upon them. The homely and vulgar proverb, that the eye is larger than the belly, never was more fully verified than with regard to him. The capacity of his stomach bears no proportion to the immensity of his desires, and will receive no more than that of the meanest peasant. The rest he is obliged to distribute among those, who prepare, in the nicest manner, that little which he himself makes use of, among those who fit up the palace in which this little is to be consumed, among those who provide and keep in order all the different baubles and trinkets, which are employed in the oeconomy of greatness; all of whom thus derive from his luxury and caprice, that share of the necessaries of life, which they would in vain have expected from his humanity or his justice. The produce of the soil maintains at all times nearly that number of inhabitants which it is capable of maintaining. The rich only select from the heap what is most precious and agreeable. They consume little more than the poor, and in spite of their natural selfishness and rapacity, though they mean only their own conveniency, though the sole end which they propose from the labours of all the thousands whom they employ, be the gratification of their own vain and insatiable desires, they divide with the poor the produce of all their improvements. They are led by an invisible hand to make nearly the same distribution of the necessaries of life, which would have been made, had the earth been divided into equal portions among all its inhabitants, and thus without intending it, without knowing it, advance the interest of the society, and afford means to the multiplication of the species. When Providence divided the earth among a few lordly masters, it neither forgot nor abandoned those who seemed to have been left out in the partition. These last too enjoy their share of all that it produces. In what constitutes the real happiness of human life, they are in no respect inferior to those who would seem so much above them. In ease of body and peace of mind, all the different ranks of life are nearly upon a level, and the beggar, who suns himself by the side of the highway, possesses that security which kings are fighting for. (184–5)

This is Smith at his most pollyanna-ish, and at his least politico-economic. To place the king and the beggar 'nearly upon a level' may be good moral philosophy, but it is hardly good economics. To have Providence aboriginally divide the earth among a few lordly masters would have been pretty feeble as an account of the origins of private property in land even by eighteenth-century standards; but then Smith was here writing neither economics nor political theory. And to have Providence take care of the landless by making 'nearly the same distribution of the [bare] necessaries of life, which would have been made, had the earth been divided into equal portions among all its inhabitants' looks better as an alternative to the natural law proviso that all have access to the means of life than it does as a theory of income distribution. What is really at issue here is only that the great should be forced to share with those who serve them just enough to allow them to pursue Providence's favourite end, the multiplication of the species. That and nothing more.

The intervention of Providence which we encounter here may be less dramatic than the one recorded by Flag Captain Martin, but it is equally direct and much more fundamental. If Providence really did divide the earth among a few lordly masters, then private property in land and radical social and economic inequality are of Providential institution. That may account for the great and their grandeur being there from the beginning, providing something for the mass of men to emulate. But, as already noted, the landowners' entitlement to the whole produce of their servants' labour threatens the very end for which Nature has tricked the poor into working so hard: making the earth capable of supporting a larger population and enlarging that population as well. And that is where the invisible hand comes in – in the shape of the human stomach! It is a sort of inverse-Malthusian preventative check on the greed of the rich, required so that Providence's aim be not foiled. What the landowner cannot eat himself, he is obliged (why? why not let it rot?) to distribute among those who serve him. There is our 'theory of income distribution' vouchsafed by the invisible hand!

Amazing things have been read into this passage. Some read into it a 'more or less egalitarian' conception of income distribution,[6] apparently overlooking the fact that the rich already have all the land, get all that is most precious, while also getting the labour of the poor, plus the palaces built by the labour of the poor, and so on – while the poor get 'the necessaries of life'. Others insert a cash nexus, talking about what is 'paid' the servants [7], as though money had been mentioned, and despite the fact that for all we know (and for all Smith cares) these servants might be slaves, serfs, indentured servants or share-croppers, rather than people who are paid wages. Some overheated free-market enthusiasts [8] even profess to find in this pastoral morality-and-Providence tale some profound insight of Smith's into 'the paradox of commercial society' – even though the existence of commerce, capital, markets, profits, rents, wages, commodities, prices and so on is nowhere mentioned or even implied. All in all, it seems pretty obvious that Smith is here not concerned with the production, distribution, exchange and consumption of wealth. Quite the contrary, he is, among other things, preaching the vanity of the riches!

When he does come to consider the wealth of nations, Adam Smith leaves moral instruction behind and turns to political economy. And writes rather differently about the division of the earth and the distribution of surplus crops! *The Wealth of Nations* shows inequality of wealth to have arisen gradually and relatively late, in the age of shepherds (715; 674); shows the vast tracts of land owned by the great since the fall of the Roman Empire to have been seized by them, amid 'rapine and violence', via engrossment and usurpation (381–2; 361); and shows these lands to have remained in the hands of the same families not by any dispensation of Providence but thanks to the nefarious laws of primogeniture and entail (382–4; 361–3). As for the landowners being obliged to share what they could not consume, Smith points out quite sharply that it didn't take them very long to figure out how to keep everything and share nothing (418–9; 388–9). It surely says something about the real subject-matter of *The Theory of Moral Sentiments* passage that when he came to prepare a new edition of the book in 1790, long after he had published *The Theory of Moral Sentiments*, it doesn't seem to have occurred to Adam Smith that the 'economics' of the *The Theory of Moral Sentiments* passage needed revising.

2.3

The paragraph of *The Wealth of Nations* in which the invisible hand is mentioned reads as follows:

> But the annual revenue of every society is always precisely equal to the exchangeable value of the whole annual produce of its industry, or rather is precisely the same thing with that exchangeable value. As every individual, therefore, endeavours as much as he can both to employ his capital in support of domestic industry, and so to direct that industry that its produce may be of the greatest value; every individual necessarily labours to render the annual revenue of the society as great as he can. He generally, indeed, neither intends to promote the public interest, nor knows how much he is promoting it. By preferring the support of domestic to that of foreign industry, he intends only his own security; and by directing that industry in such a manner as its produce may be of the greatest value, he intends only his own gain, and he is in this, as in many other cases, led by an invisible hand to promote an end which was no part of his intention. Nor is it always the worse for the society that it was no part of it. By pursuing his own interest he frequently promotes that of the society more effectually than when he really intends to promote it. I have never known much good done by those who affected to trade for the public good. It is an affectation, indeed, not very common among merchants, and very few words need be employed in dissuading them from it. (455–6; 423)

Notice that preferring to support domestic rather than foreign industry is, as a motive, fully on a par with directing that industry so as to produce goods of the greatest value; that the route to the greatest gain is via the production of the most valuable product; and that the public interest is the interest not of society but of *the* society.

The above quotation stands at the centre of a protracted argument concerning capital investment and the systems of political economy which affect it. It is much easier to get an adequate grasp of the piece of economic reasoning which underlies Adam Smith's conception of the invisible hand if one takes in the broad sweep of that argument, which extends from Book II, chapter v ('Of the different Employment of Capitals') through Book III ('Of the different Progress of Opulence in different Nations') to Book IV ('Of Systems of political Oeconomy').

Three basic questions regarding *The Wealth of Nations*'s 'invisible hand' passage need to be raised at once, if only because modern interpretations of that passage tend to take the answers to these questions for granted – and get them wrong. The questions are: How does Smith conceive of the individual's interest? How does he conceive of the interest of the society? How does he conceive of the link between the two? Modern economists and others generally agree that by the individual's 'own interest' Adam Smith means the individual's interest in gain alone; that by 'the interest of the society' he means aggregate social revenue; and that for Smith the link between private profit and public interest is direct and automatic: as the sum total of private profit increases, so the aggregate revenue of the society increases. If all this is so, it follows that pursuing one's own profit is tantamount to promoting the society's interest. It also follows that the market in which relative prices indicate what invest-ment is most profitable is the absolute arbiter of economic life. The market itself thus becomes the invisible hand. One can even quote Adam Smith in support of this view – if only one selects the quotation carefully enough. For instance: 'every individual necessarily labours to render the annual revenue of the society as great as he can'. In short, it is not too difficult to read Smith in the light of modern preconceptions.

Reading the passage itself without such preconceptions, and in its wider context, yields rather different answers to our three questions.

First, Smith conceives the individual's 'own interest' to include more than just the interest in gain: there is also the interest in security and ease and the passion for independence. More often than not Smith speaks broadly of men seeking their 'advantage', and refers to 'the passions and the interests' as the motivating forces. So far as he is concerned, the quest for profit alone will not account for the way 'the market' works.

Second, Smith has a different view of how society's interest is promoted. He writes quite specifically:

> The most advantageous employment of any capital to the country to which it belongs, is that which maintains there the greatest quantity of productive labour, and increases the most the annual produce of the land and labour of that country. (600; 566)

The interest of the society is not promoted by just any profitable private investment; it is promoted by investments of capital by which, though that is not the investor's aim, the country's productive labour is maintained and the produce of the land and labour of the country is increased.

Third, Smith makes clear in the sequel that the individual's advantage and the society's interest may diverge:

> In a trade of which the returns are very distant, the profit of the merchant may be as great or greater than in one in which they are very frequent and near; but the advantage of the country in which he resides, the quantity of productive labour constantly maintained there, the annual produce of the land and labour must always be much less. (602; 568)

For Smith, therefore, the link between private profit and public interest is neither direct nor automatic: it is indirect and strictly conditional.

It is important to notice that the promotion of the society's interest is a matter of degree: the greater the quantity of the country's industrious labour employed and the greater the quantity (or the value) of the country's product, the greater the benefit to the society. This consideration is reflected in what has come to be known in the secondary literature as Adam Smith's hierarchy of investment priorities. [9] It is to a consideration of this hierarchy that we now turn.

In the chapter on the different employments of stock (Book II, chapter v) Smith deals with the various ways a capital can be invested. The outstanding feature of the chapter is Smith's ranking of these various ways in a hierarchy of investment priorities. As we would by now expect, he ranks them, not according to their respective degree of profitability to the investor, but according to the extent to which each of these ways adds to the quantity of domestic productive labour employed and to the quantity of the total annual product of the land and labour of the country, that is, to the extent to which they promote the interest of the society.

Let us take a closer look. Smith ranks the possible employments of stock in two overlapping series, the first of which lists branches of domestic investment while the second lists sub-forms of wholesale trade. The first series begins with the local retail merchant who employs no productive labour but his own, and whose capital augments the annual produce of the society by just his own profits. It continues with the wholesale merchant who employs more domestic labour and adds proportionately more per unit of capital to the society's revenue, followed by the manfacturer who does better still on both counts. It ends with the farmer who, together with the productive labour of his farm-hands, his cattle and his land, employs the greatest amount of labour and increases the most, per unit of capital invested, the annual produce of the land and labour of the society. The second series is presented in reverse order, beginning with the employment most advantageous to the society and ending with the least. It lists three sub-forms of wholesale trade in terms of the quantity of domestic labour employed and the frequency of returns to capital invested: the home trade, the foreign trade of consumption and the carrying trade. This last is the one which employs the least domestic labour (perhaps none: all the labour employed might be foreign labour) and in which the returns are least frequent, so that whatever capital and profits are involved are rarely available at home. Notice that these lists run in terms of the advantage *not* of the investor but of the country. The Smithian hierarchy of investment priorities is cast in terms of the degree to which the interest of the society is promoted.

We have, then, a linked hierarchy of what we might fairly call national investment priorities which, beginning with the one which is the most advantageous to the society, runs as follows: agriculture, manufacture, wholesale trade, retail trade and, for the sub-forms of the wholesale trade: the home trade, the foreign trade of consumption and the carrying trade.

Recall now our discussion of Adam Smith's conception of the natural order of things and of the natural inclinations of man which promote that order. We there encountered a Smithian scale of natural preferences: given equal or somewhat less than equal profits, every individual prefers greater security to less, greater ease to less, greater independence to less. That scale, as subsequently amplified, runs: agriculture, manufacture, foreign commerce; the home trade, the foreign trade of consumption and the carrying trade.

Making allowances for imperfect fit, the striking fact surely is that Smith's hierarchy of investment priorities to all intents and purposes runs parallel with his scale of natural preferences. And the fact that the hierarchy of investment priorities coincides with the scale of natural preferences is precisely the 'secret' of Adam Smith's 'invisible hand'.

The wider significance of this, the inner structure of Smith's vision of an economy free of all institutional interference, should now be evident: natural forces can safely be allowed more or less untrammelled sway precisely because the natural preferences of investors are really such as will, without their intending it, in fact promote the interest of the society. In advocating that all interferences be dropped in favour of 'the obvious and simple system of natural liberty', Smith was not advocating a free-market free-for-all. He was advocating a natural system in which the natural preferences of men meshed with the equally natural hierarchy of investment priorities. So far the invisible hand is the hand of nature. But because the balance among the natural inclinations of men is affected in some measure by the market balance, by large – though not by small – changes in profitability, the Smithian invisible hand is the hand of nature-in-the-market.

We should now be in a position to give an adequate interpretation of the 'invisible hand' passage cited at the beginning of this section, treating it as a test case for the general theory.

In the lengthy Book IV we get the famous, protracted criticism of the mercantile system (plus a brief one of the agricultural systems). And, early on in chapter ii, which deals with restraints of trade, we at last get the specific argument which culminates in the personal appearance of the invisible hand that has been plaguing us all along. It helps to follow Smith's argument from almost the beginning of the chapter.

> The general industry of the society can never exceed what the capital of the society can employ... No regulation of commerce can increase the quantity of industry in any society beyond what its capital can maintain. It can only divert a part of it into a direction into which it might not otherwise have gone; and it is by no means certain that this artificial direction is likely to be more advantageous to the society than that into which it would have gone of its own accord.
>
> Every individual is continually exerting himself to find out the most advantageous employment for whatever capital he can command. It is his own advantage, indeed, and not that of the society, which he has in view. But *the study of his own advantage naturally, or rather necessarily leads him to prefer that employment which is most advantageous to the society.* (453–4; 421. Italics added)

Well, here is the acid test. Does Smith, as modern writers claim, now argue that 'the study of his own advantage' leads the individual to invest his capital in what brings him the greatest profit? I think not. And is 'that employment which is most advantageous to the society' measured only in terms of the total annual revenue of the society? Again, I think not.

Smith argues as follows.

First, every individual endeavours to employ his capital as near home as he can, and consequently as much as he can in support of domestic industry; provided always that he can thereby obtain the ordinary, or not a great deal less than the ordinary profits of stock.

Thus, upon equal or nearly equal profits, every wholesale merchant naturally prefers the home-trade to the foreign trade of consumption, and the foreign trade of consumption to the carrying trade. [Recall here that each of these branches of trade is more advantageous to the society than the preceding one. The natural preference, given more or less ordinary profits, is for greater security and less toil and trouble.] *Home is in this manner the centre, if I may say so, round which the capitals of the inhabitants of every country are continually circulating, and towards which they are always tending,* though by particular causes they may sometimes be driven off and repelled from it towards more distant employment. (454–5; 421–2. Italics added)

This 'homing' tendency of capital has twin advantages of the greatest importance to the home country: first, in that it 'puts into motion a greater quantity of domestic industry'; second – and by the same token – as it 'gives revenue and employment to a greater number of the inhabitants of the country, than an equal capital employed in the foreign trade of consumption', and greater still, of course, than is the case with the carrying trade. It would be difficult to exaggerate how important this twin consequence of the natural preference for domestic investment really is. Its significance is that it bears both on production and on distribution. By stipulating the 'homing' tendency of capital, Adam Smith is 'securing' – so to speak – not only the maximisation of domestic production but also the maximal distribution of part of the nation's capital, in the form of wages, to those inhabitants who have no other source of income (the vast majority of them no longer being independent artisans and nearly all of them having long since lost the wherewithal of self-support: access to land).

It is simply not true then that, as some distinguished scholars claim, *The Wealth of Nations*'s invisible hand is concerned only with maximising production, and that one must look to the – weak and woolly – *The Theory of Moral Sentiments*'s invisible hand for a concept of income distribution. [10] And this fact has a further significance. For it is by no means the case that Smith imagines distribution in commercial society to be generally equitable (as those who refer to *The Theory of Moral Sentiments* passage like to claim for it). When he writes in *The Wealth of Nations* (96; 79) that 'it is but equity…that they who feed, cloath and lodge the whole body of the people, should have such a share of the produce of their own labour as to be themselves tolerably well fed, cloathed and lodged', he is not stating a general truth about income distribution in commercial society: he is arguing against the writers – and they were many – who advocated that wages be deliberately kept low. Besides, Smith is here addressing the special circumstance of an increase, during the economically progressive eighteenth century, in workers' well-being due to rising national prosperity. He is under no illusion that workers get an equitable share of the national wealth in times of economic stagnation, let alone in times of decline.

We can now follow Smith's argument to its close. We have seen that the individual's natural preference for security and ease, and the society's interest in maximal domestic production and distribution, go hand in hand. That was his first point. He now goes on: 'Secondly, every individual who employs his capital in the support of domestic industry, necessarily endeavours so to direct that industry, that its produce may be of the greatest possible value' (455; 422–3). The individual wants a maximally valuable product because he wants as large a profit as possible. But here another shock awaits those who hold with profit-maximisation as the supreme objective: Smith ties the size of the profit to the value of the produce! Instead of advocating, in the modern fashion, that entrepreneurs make the largest possible profit by keeping down wages and charging what they can get away with ('what the market will bear')[11] and by these means increasing their *rate* of profit, Smith stipulates an average rate of profit throughout the economy, ties profit to product, and in this way once again makes the society the beneficiary of individual inclinations. For, as he says elsewhere, cheapness is plenty (240; 222): if the investor of capital makes his profit by contributing to the production of plenty, he gains to the degree that the society also benefits – in lower prices, increased affordability, a better living-standard for all.

This leaves us with a final point to consider. What has so far been said applies in what Smith himself calls 'ordinary cases', that is, in cases where the ordinary rate of profit obtains throughout the economy. In these ordinary cases a natural balance among the desires for gain, for security, for ease and for independence will see to it that the invisible hand does its job (always provided that natural liberty prevails in the main).

But there are also extraordinary cases. These are cases in which the natural balance among the natural preferences is temporarily upset by a temporary but substantial change in the prospects for profit. After rehearsing once more the pattern with which by now we are amply familiar: 'The mercantile stock of every country naturally courts…the near, and shuns the distant employment…' and so on, Smith allows that the whole apple-cart may be upset. He writes,

> But if in any of those distant employments, which in ordinary cases are less advantageous to the country, the profit should happen to rise somewhat higher than what is sufficient *to balance the natural preference* which is given to nearer employments, this superiority of profit will draw stock from those nearer employments, till the profits of all return to their proper level. ' (628–9; 593–4. Italics added)

Yet so far from seeing this extraordinary case as one in which the pure pursuit of profit at last emerges triumphant,[12] Smith the eighteenth-century optimist sees the rise in profits as

> proof that… the stock of the society is not distributed in the properest manner among all the different employments carried on in it. It is a proof that something is either bought cheaper or sold dearer than it ought to be, and that some particular class of citizens is more or less oppressed either by paying more or by getting less than what is suitable to that equality, which ought to take place, and which naturally does take place among all the different classes of them. (629; 594)

The remedy, at any rate, is simple, and installs itself of its own accord:

> In this extraordinary case, the public interest requires that some stock should be
> withdrawn from those employments which in ordinary cases are more advan-
> tageous, and turned towards one which in ordinary cases is less advantageous to
> the public; and in this extraordinary case, the natural interests and inclinations
> of men coincide as exactly with the public interest as in all other ordinary cases,
> and lead them to withdraw stock from the near, and to turn it towards the
> distant employment.

By now we can anticipate the conclusion:

> Without any intervention of law, therefore, the private interests and passions of
> men naturally lead them to divide and distribute the stock of every society,
> among all the different employments carried on in it, as nearly as possible in the
> proportion which is most agreeable to the interest of the whole society. (630;
> 594–5)

I hope I have succeeded in making clear that the 'invisible hand' as Adam Smith
conceived it is not the hand of the market, propelled by market forces and the quest
for the greatest possible profit, but the hand of (providentially designed) nature – in
the market; that this hand operates through the natural inclinations of man; and that
it guides men via their *several* natural interests and passions so to invest whatever
capital they can command as in fact, though without their intending it, to promote
the interest of the society.

But I hope also to have made clear how precariously conditional the all-important
link between Smith's scale of natural preferences and his hierarchy of investment
priorities really is. If human beings should turn out *not* to be motivated as Adam
Smith takes them to be motivated – if, for example, there were no reliable natural
preference for security, ease and independence strong enough to outweigh the
desire for making the largest possible profit; or if it should turn out that foreign
direct investment, the existence of multinational corporations, and the virtually
instant transferability of capital from, say, London to Hongkong, should render
Adam Smith's essentially national vision obsolete; or if, finally, the advance of
technology and organisation were to make the massive demand for industrial labour
a thing of the past – if any or all of these were to be the case, Smith's reasoning
would fall to the ground and the invisible hand would be out of a job.

NOTES

1. Galbraith (1987:64), with plain reference to the market, calls the 'invisible hand'
   'the most famous metaphor in economics'. Hayek (1976:145), with plain reference
   to Adam Smith, speaks of 'the invisible hand of the market'. The usage is firmly
   entrenched.
2. Smith (1976a) 455–6; Smith (1937) 423. Because both these editions contain superb,
   but different, editorial material, and because both are widely used, all page references will be to both texts, citing the 1976 edition first.
3. Viner (1927), far and away the single best piece on Smith ever written – balanced,
   scholarly, perceptive and grinding no axes – makes amply clear that Smith was no

absolutist with respect to either competition or market 'freedom'. The big difference between Adam Smith and today's free-marketeers is that Smith realised, as they do not, that what people actually live in is countries, communities of sorts, not markets, and what they do in those countries is live, not just buy and sell.

4. So, for example, Smith's student Dugald Stewart understood well enough, at the end of the eighteenth century, that 'the great and lasting object of [Smith's] speculations [was] to illustrate the provision made by nature in the human mind, and in the circumstances of man's external situation, for a gradual and progressive augmentation in the means of national wealth. ' See his 'Accounts of the Life and Writings of Adam Smith L. L. D. ' in Smith (1980: 265–351, at 315). Viner, of course, still understood 'Smith's doctrine that economic phenomena were manifestations of an underlying order in nature, governed by natural forces' Viner (1927). But since then comprehension has yielded to doctrine.

5. 'It is but equity, besides, that they who feed, cloath and lodge the whole body of the people, should have such a share of the produce of their own labour as to be themselves tolerably well fed, cloathed and lodged. ' (96; 79).

6. The phase is Hollander's (1973:248); compare Raphael's notion that wealth is distributed 'so as to approach equality' (1985:72).

7. Karen I. Vaughn in Eatwell (1989:168).

8. I. Hont and M. Ignatieff, in the 'Introduction' to *Wealth and Virtue* find that in this passage Smith has unravelled 'the paradox of commercial society':

> The invisible hand passage in the *Theory of Moral Sentiments* explained the paradox of commercial [sic] society as an outcome of unintended consequences – the subsistence needs of the poor being served through a machine kept in motion by the blind cupidity of the rich (1983:10–11).

Quite apart from the fact that 'commercial society' has nothing whatever to do with what Smith is explaining, it is not clear, either, that there is a paradox. Presumably, if the subsistence needs of the poor were served by themselves working on land they had access to, there would be no need of the vaunted 'machine', even less of the rich who keep it in motion, and none at all of the paradox. It does seem a bit extravagant to start from the proposition that the few have exclusive right to the land which all need in order to secure a livelihood, and then to conclude that the exclusive owners are somehow the benefactors of the excluded. But this is not the first time in history that such a line of argument has been popular, or the first time it has proved profitable to those who were willing to peddle it.

9. Different accounts from mine of the hierarchy of investment priorities are offered by Hollander (1973: 277–300), Stigler (1976) and in a forthcoming article by Vivienne Brown in *Economics and Philosophy.*

10. For example, Macfie and Raphael in Smith (1976:184 n. 7).

11. Letwin (1965: 242) finds that this tying of profit to product is just a silly mistake of Smith's:

> If the entrepreneur is in a position to force down the cost of capital, labour or materials, or to force up the price of the product, then he can raise his profits without simultaneously and to the same degree raising his firm's contribution to national income.

There are two instructive lessons in that kind of uncomprehending comment, which is not uncommon among modern writers on Smith. The first is that, not understanding what Smith is driving at – namely, that a balance among natural inclinations would lead to private investment unwittingly promoting the public interest – writers who take profit maximisation as canonical cannot but conclude that Smith was naïve. Whatever is incomprehensible to them counts as a 'mistake' on Smith's part. The second is that the modern attitude, with all its 'realistic' brutality, exposes the Pollyanna in Adam Smith – an Adam Smith who, when all is said and done, is pretty close to the common Enlightenment dream that all *would* be for the best in this best of all possible worlds – if only...

12. Moss (1976) congratulates Hollander (1973) on 'discovering' the passage which seems at last to express Smith's 'approval' of the profit motive – without noticing that Smith is talking here about the extraordinary case, not the usual situation.

REFERENCES

Blaug, M. 1968. *Economic Theory in Retrospect* (2nd edn). London: Heineman.

Blaug, M. 1980. *The Methodology of Economics.* Cambridge: Cambridge University Press.

Eatwell, J. et al., (eds.), 1989. *The Invisible Hand* (articles from *The New Palgrave Dictionary of Economics*). London: Macmillan.

Galbraith, J. K. 1987. *Economics in Perspective: A Critical History.* Boston: Houghton Mifflin.

Hahn, F. 1982. 'Reflections on the Invisible Hand', *Lloyds Bank Review*, 144: 1–21.

Hayek, F. von, 1976. *The Mirage of Social Justice* (Vol. 2 of *Law, Legislation and Liberty, 3 Vols.*). London: Routledge and Keagan Paul (1973-9).

Hirschman, A. O. 1977. *The Passions and the Interests.* Princeton: Princeton University Press.

Hollander, S. 1973. *The Economics of Adam Smith.* Toronto and London: Heineman.

Hont, I. & M. Ignatieff (eds.), 1983. *Wealth and Virtue: The Shaping of Political Economy in the Scottish Enlightenment.* Cambridge: Cambridge University Press.

Ingrao, B. & Israel, G. 1990. *The Invisible Hand.* Cambridge, Mass. : M. I. T. Press.

Kaufmann, F. X. et al. (eds.), 1984. *Market, Staat und Solidarität bei Adam Smith.* Frankfurt am Main: Campus.

Keynes, J. M. 1926. *The End of Laissez Faire*, in *The Collected Works of John Maynard Keynes*, Vol. 9. London: Macmillan.

Letwin, W. 1965. *The Origins of Scientific Economics.* Garden City, N. Y. : Doubleday.

Moss, L. S. 1976. 'The Economics of Adam Smith: Professor Hollander's reappraisal', *History of Political Economy*, 8: 564–74.

O'Driscoll, G. P. Jr. 1976. *Adam Smith and Modern Political Economy.* Ames, Iowa: Iowa State University Press.

Raphael, D. D. 1985. *Adam Smith.* Oxford: Oxford University Press.

Robinson, J. 1962. *Economic Philosophy.* London: Watts.

Smith, A. 1980. *Essays on Philosophical Subjects*, (ed. W. P. D. Wightman). Oxford: Oxford University Press.

Smith, A. 1976a. *The Wealth of Nations*, (ed. R. H. Campbell and A. S. Skinner). Oxford: Oxford University Press.

Smith, A. 1976b. *The Theory of Moral Sentiments*, (ed. A. L. Macfie & D. D. Raphael). Oxford: Oxford University Press.

Smith, A. 1937. *The Wealth of Nations*, (ed. E. Cannan). New York: Modern Library.

Stigler, G. 1976. 'The Successes and Failures of Professor Smith', *Journal of Political Economy*, 84: 1199–213.

Teichgraeber, R. F. III, 1986. *'Free Trade' and Moral Philosophy.* Durham N. C. : Duke University Press.

Viner, Jacob, 1927. 'Adam Smith and Laissez Faire', *Journal of Political Economy*, 35: 198–232.

Viner, Jacob, 1958. *The Long View and the Short.* Glencoe, Ill. : The Free Press.

Viner, Jacob, 1991. *Essays in the Intellectual History of Economics*, (ed. D. A. Irwin). Princeton, . N. J. : Princeton University Press.

Wilson, T. & A. S. Skinner (eds.), 1976. *The Market and the State: Essays in Honour of Adam Smith*, Oxford: Oxford University Press.

3

Modes of Economic-Theoretical Engagement

PETER PRESTON

At the present time in Western Europe there is considerable debate in respect of the completion of the single market. Relatedly within Eastern Europe in the wake of the political changes of late 1989 there is much discussion about the construction of market economies. Within the domestic UK context we have experienced some ten years of relentless pressure/propaganda in favour of the market. It seems to me that it is an appropriate time to re-enter what is a long-established area of scholarly social scientific debate, namely, how ought we to theorise the market?

I will begin by taking note of some of the available scholarly material which addresses this matter, and will continue by looking at the work of the neo-classical theorists of *laissez-faire*. I will argue that the material of neo-classical economics both dominates and degrades social scientific analysis and that it must be set aside if we are to fashion a scholarly approach to analysing matters of human economic activity.

3.1 THE GENERAL CONTEXT

Within the history of ideas orthodox neo-classical economics is taken to be a late nineteenth-century tradition, usually associated with the names of Jevons, Menger, Walras and Alfred Marshall (Deane 1978). It was constructed, reports Dasgupta, in reaction to the perceived socialistic implications of the political economic approach; thus he observes:

> There is reason to believe that the marginalist's quest for an alternative approach to economic theory, ostensibly a scientific quest, had inherently a political purpose...An anti-capitalist critique indeed grew up...based on the implications of classical political economy...It seems clear that marginalism is a reaction to this. Marginalists not only repudiate the classical theories of value and distribution; they also repudiate the social and political implications of these theories. The marginalist system marks a revival of economic liberalism as against its socialist critique. (1985:95)

Marginalism came to dominate economics. For these theorists the market system exists as a given, largely independent of human kind whose multiple individual efforts generate it as a kind of all embracing epiphenomena. A measure of economic knowledge can be accumulated but its extent is limited to the knowledge necessary to guide the accommodation of individual actions to the trans-individual logic of the market system. Analysis aiming to inform planned economic activity is unavailable a priori, and the political model of state action implied by the theory is that of the liberal minimum state.

Deane records how marginalism *consciously narrowed its attention*: where the classical economists had considered economic growth over time, the distribution of material resources through society – that is class – and the central notion of value, the seeming core of economic activity, the marginalists merely abandoned these questions. The upshot was that philosophical, social scientific and political questions were simply defined away. As Deane notes: 'The focus of the marginal analysis was the market and the neo-classical theorists accordingly narrowed the scope of their subject so as to be almost exclusively confined to a study of market processes' (1978:99). That this suited entirely the ideological predelictions of the economists concerned is also noted; but where Dasgupta saw a conscious reaction, Deane presents a more dissimulating retreat into the pseudo-neutrality of positive scientificity (Deane 1978:110).

On this Pollard comments that around

> 1870 political economy was transformed into marginalist economics, and with it a key social science became a mathematics, irrefutable as long as it was internally consistent, but utterly lacking in a historical dimension, increasingly divorced from the other social sciences and unable to escape from its assumptions that capitalist categories, values, and mores are alone eternally valid...by making economics a-historical, the economists made social conservatism orthodox. To advocate further progress by basic social change, as had occurred in the past, was not only politically deplorable, but economically nonsensical. (1971:138–9).

Against all this we can contrast the tradition of political economy: holistic structural analysis coupled to culture-critical work. It is system-tendential analysis.

We can characterise political economic analysis as a holistic and engaged intellectual strategy which aims, as Marx put it (1973:100–8), at the intellectual reconstruction of the real, which as an intellectual procedure has as its objective the promulgation of a delimited–formal ideology which can serve to illuminate dynamics of change in such a way as to render them amenable to human knowledgeable intervention. We can best briefly unpack this summary statement by comparing it with the material it rejects: the professionally subdivided social sciences generally, and neo-classical argument on behalf of the status quo in particular.

Thus political economic analysis is problem centred: by this I mean that it focuses on extant socio-historical problems as they are identified in public discourse. One could think of C. Wright Mills (1959) on what constitutes the sociological imagination. It is not bound by the received objects of extant disciplines where typically these are conceived in positivistic terms as having in some way an extra-disciplinary referent which provides the base for the discipline's intellectual and professional independence. Political economy draws routinely on the full range of concepts and data within the social sciences. The familiar UK division of intellectual resources and labour into professional spheres is seen to be just that – a concern of professional groups anxious to differentiate themselves in the extant market-place.

Political economic enquiry is reflexive, which is to say it routinely examines its own intellectual machineries and attempts to display their origins within the very socio-historical processes which it aims to grasp. Relatedly, the sphere of ethics is drawn into the analysis rather than being denied as is the case with the orthodoxy who either make ethics emotional spasms or appeals to common sense; both strategies are blocking devices. Political economy investigates the ethical aspect of socio-historical states of affairs and builds ethical concerns into its prospective analyses. Such analysis feeds into the production of delimited–formal ideology where this is diagnostic and prescriptive with regard to central socio-historical dynamics of change. In contrast the orthodoxy argues on behalf of the planner-technocrats of a *status quo* misleadingly characterised as essentially a static equilibrium.

Political economic analysis thus characterised represents the central tradition of European social theory oriented to displaying the dynamics of change in the expectation of thereby effectively freeing deeply lodged impulses to democracy. The school of political economy in the UK includes figures such as Smith, Malthus, Ricardo, Marx and, a little later, J. S. Mill. On Abrams's (1968) reading, rather contradicting Dasgupta and Deane, this tradition declined in the UK through the nineteenth century into a non-theoretical empiricism which expired of its own irrelevance (see also Brewer 1980). Social theorists must recover the marginalised tradition in social theory by attempting to detoxify the pervasive informal ideology of the market.

The procedures of political economic analysis have been more widely discussed: see Hollis and Nell (1975) in economics and philosophy, Terrel Carver (1975) in political philosophy/science or again John Clammer (1985) working from an anthropological background and referring to the work of French theorists of modes of production. And in the sphere of development theorising it is strongly represented. Staniland (1985) takes the notion to be presently fashionable but, on examination, to be valuable. My own reading of the nature of political economy was influenced initially by Cardoso and Faletto (1979) who offered political economic analysis as a holistic and engaged mode of social scientific analysis which was more useful than either orthodox economics or Latin American structuralism in illuminating the circumstances of dependent economies and societies.[1]

There is also the dissenting tradition of institutional economics, which is recently discussed in a magisterial text by Hodgson (1988). In the sphere of development theory this type of work has been exemplified by Myrdal (See Preston 1982). In essence, 'sociologised economics' takes economic systems to be parts of social systems and requires therefore an appropriately 'sociological' treatment. In this vein a broader use of sociology is advocated by Swedberg (1987), whose work re-examines 'economic sociology'.

Swedberg argues that the classical tradition of economic sociology is in the process of re-establishment. Furthermore, he shows how the nascent disciplines of economics and sociology divided the intellectual and more especially the institutional cake, with economics taking the lion's share. In the late nineteenth and early twentieth centuries Swedberg recalls a trio of conflicts – methodological, political and institutional – which were conducted in a series of European and American centres, between proponents of what were to emerge as economics and sociology. Over methodology, Comte launched a series of attacks on contemporary political economists, who were empiricist, comparative and on Abrams's characterisation aimless (1968). A sharp reaction amongst economists in the UK ensued and contributed to the formation of neo-classicism. Second, sociology was seen as collectivist minded, and around the turn of the twentieth century this individualist–collectivist debate between economics and sociology was important and had both intellectual and political implications (Collini 1979).

Finally, sociology became established in the USA and UK after economics, and it had to defer to extant disciplinary spheres. This is a matter of the historical accident of institutionalisation of early social sciences but the upshot was that in the Anglo-Saxon world economics became the 'hard' social science and sociology became a vague, soft, study of left-overs. In brief, today's division of labour within the social sciences is significantly shaped by the squabbles of the late nineteenth century.

The early generation of sociologists established themselves and their disciplines, in which economic sociology was sketched out as a distinct sub-field. It is this legacy that Swedberg would argue is in process of re-establishment. [2] This early work was never developed, for in the period 1930–60 it was overshadowed by the dissenting economics associated with, in particular, Keynes: apparently there was no need, or intellectual space for, economic sociology despite the important work done by Schumpeter, Polanyi, Mannheim, Mauss, Tonnies, Sombart and Parsons.

The gist of all this can be summarised:

- The present pre-eminence of orthodox neo-classical economics, with its central idea of the self-regulating market, is the result of a quite specific episode which sees the establishment of an economics which is quite clearly both intellectually limited and politically biased.
- Against orthodox economics, which takes market as naturally-given, it can be shown that markets are social constructs.
- There is a wealth of available material with which to construct a 'scholarly economics'.

3.2 THE MARKET

The neo-classical theorists of the market offer a complex intellectual package. The central claim that *laissez-faire* capitalist systems maximise human welfare unpacks as a series of specific claims:

- Economically, the claim is that as free markets act efficiently to distribute knowledge and resources around the economic system, material welfare will be maximised;
- Socially, the claim is that as action and responsibility for action reside with the person of the individual, the liberal, individualist, social systems will ensure that moral worth is maximised.
- Politically, the claim is that as liberalism, ancient or modern, offers a balanced solution to problems of deploying, distributing and controlling power, such systems maximise political freedom.

- Epistemologically, the whole package is supplemented and buttressed by the claim to genuine positive scientific knowledge thus we have a claim to maximise knowledge and thus effective action.

Evidently this delimited–formal ideological package admits of attack from a number of directions: it is, however, probably safe to suggest that the intellectual longevity of the package owes more than a little to the notion of the market. With the notion of the market we find that a set of ideas are woven together in order to fashion a totalising discourse of some considerable power. I will begin by looking at the idea of the market and the burden of my argument will be that when the notion is examined, and made subject to the usual criteria of intellectual adequacy current within received European intellectual traditions, it will be found to be meaningless. I will then consider the remaining three, closely related, elements of the package.

3.2.1 Maximising Material Welfare

On Todaro's argument (1982) the core model around which economic debate has turned is the pure-market model: the notion of a self-regulating system which tends to equilibrium. The pure-market economic system is characterised by private owner-ship backed by legal guarantees; by pervasive perfect competition amongst suppliers to meet the demands of sovereign consumers; by an extensive division of labour into specialist firms with production for sale in the market place, all subject to the aims of profit and satisfaction maximisation. The system is driven by the fact of naturally given scarcity. The role of price is as an index of this scarcity. Supply and demand in the competitive market-place determine price. The market mechanism, or price mechanism, brings supply and demand into efficient balance: transmitting inform-ation through the system and distributing income to its members.

Scarcity

The pure-market model requires that there be a naturally given scarcity of desired goods and services. The market-controlled production system acts to meet with maximum productive and allocative efficiency the myriad wants of consumers exist-ing in a situation of scarcity. Scarcity moves the consumers to lodge demands and thus underpins the role of the market.

There is a series of problems with the notion of natural scarcity, which I term historical, relational, developmental and moral. All have in common that they ask that the notion of scarcity be contextualised .

Marshall Sahlins (1972) has argued that the notion of scarcity is absent in pre-modern societies. The notion of scarcity is cultural: it has to be made. Thus regarded it is clear that the notion of scarcity cannot plausibly be taken as a natural and given starting point for the analysis of economic behaviour read, consequently, as naturally determined. Human wants are generated along with the means to satisfy them – a point picked up in the relational criticism.

In the early years of what has now matured into the Green Movement, it was suggested that conservation of resources was necessary because these resources were finite. Against this view it was pointed out that resources were a function of knowledge. Crudely, there were no finite resources of, say, coal until someone (a) discovered the stuff could burn and (b) invented coal mines. Natural science, the associated technology and the capitalist industrial system that is its environment, all continue to progress. The paradoxical situation thus exists that scarcity is the cultural construct of a massively productive form of life. Scarcity is thus relative to the cultural capacities of any particular system.

A related point was made, famously, by Galbraith (1958) who argued that whilst scarcity, ordinarily understood, may indeed have been a problem in the past it certainly is not now, and moreover it is demonstrably the case that scarcity is generated by the industries purportedly satisfying it via techniques like advertising and planned obsolescence. In today's developed economies the problem is not scarcity, argues Galbraith, but abundance. An extension of this line of argument has addressed problems of Third World poverty: again, it is suggested, the problem is not so much productive incapacity in the face of unlimited naturally given scarcity, but rather the fact of inappropriate schedules of production in the light of contemporary public knowledge of 'interdependence' coupled to liberal-reformist ethics. Identifying scarcity requires that a judgement be made about the circumstances of an extant form of life. Even in those areas where scarcity begins to look to be an absolute, for example the area of food and starvation, the problem, as Susan George (1984) pointed out, is not underproduction. It is rather newly contrived patterns of wrong production maldistributed.

Of the ethical aspect to this notion of scarcity the philosophers Passmore (1970) and Macpherson (1964 and 1973) have both indicated how the notion of natural scarcity depends on the social, political and philosophical invention of classical liberal man. This model of humankind is a product of what we might call the English Enlightenment, the earliest of the political philosophical contributions to the rise of the modern world. The prime characteristics of this model of man are: first the ownership of self, and thus the possibility of selling labour in a market-place, which opens the way for the commodification of labour; and second the idea of the unlimited nature of human wants and the propriety of attempting to secure such wants, which opens the way to the accumulative dynamic of capitalism. Such a notion of ownership-of-self is ethically unprecedented; so too is the affirmation of the propriety of the attempt to satisfy consumption desires, taken as given and unlimited.

Thus when examined, and here I have looked at only four lines of commentary, scarcity, taken by the pure-market model as a natural given, turns out to be a complex cultural construct that can be dated to the early part of the mercantile capitalist period. To treat scarcity as a natural given, as does the economic orthodoxy, is both implausible and, evidently, it rules out a whole series of fascinating social scientific questions.

Competition and Specialisation

Competition to supply the market-place generates specialisation and lower cost, which aid the maximisation of material benefits. In the formal discourse of economics, and in the public sphere operating with our 'folk model' of the economy, both these ideas are taken to be technical expressions of truths about the naturally given system. But this technical discourse is wildly misleading. [3]

Pervasive perfect competition is necessary for the pure-market system to perform effectively. There must be a large number of more or less equal-sized suppliers offering goods in the market-place to an equivalent spread of consumers who have full knowledge of market prices. Any interruption of this situation will be regarded as a market imperfection and the system will, inevitably, be taken to be operating at less than optimum. The problem here is simple: market imperfections, so called, are the norm and, if this is the case, what value a theory that depends on perfect competition?

In a market system there is specialisation of production within a complex division of labour. Reading this notion narrowly, as do the neo-classical theorists, we have an idea of the market-led innovative refinement of the division of labour. Competition amongst private producers for advantage in the market-place puts a premium on price reduction, and technologically based specialisation aids price reduction. Overall, as the economic system develops it becomes ever more complex in the division of tasks into specialised areas. Such specialisation aids economic efficiency.

To reply briefly at this point. The neo-classical theorists posit a natural division of labour: as new technology becomes available new possibilities for specialisation are opened up and the competitive search for market advantage ensures such opportunities for specialisation are taken up. The division of labour is thus technologically led, and thereafter this neutral impulse feeds directly into the market system. In reality, however, any particular extant division of labour will reflect patterns of social power as well as technological advance. This point is picked up by Rueschemeyer (1986) who considers the division of labour or specialisation not as some sort of technical-market system given, but as dependent upon patterns of power in society.

Following Rueschemeyer, we can point to a habit of social theorists who look at the consequences rather than the causes of the increasing division of labour. He cites the classic causal argument of Adam Smith which links up the increasing division of labour with efficiency: market driven efficiency within capitalism powers the increasing division of labour. Thus the system develops. Rueschemeyer is not impressed by Smith's argument and he goes on to call attention to the notion of efficiency. This notion needs criteria: efficient for what or better for whom? And the answers given here are evidently not technical-neutral, they are socio-political. If efficiency is read as criterial then any discussion of efficiency has to be contextualised and this introduces the notion of power. What counts as economic efficiency depends on the socio-economic and political system within which economic activity takes place. As regards the division of labour it is clear that it develops and changes for a wide variety of socio-political reasons and that the state is a key player in defining the division of labour.

Efficiency

Suppliers and consumers aim at efficiency; the model of economically rational behaviour underpins the pure-market system. It is because every actor in the system

seeks to maximise rewards and minimise inputs that such a premium on competitively generated efficiency arises and is secured. Against the implicit claim of this
notion of efficiency to be technical and context free we can assert that the reverse is
the case; the received notion can only be read within the cultural frame of the modern
world. Like any other notion within social science it is context bound: thus we must
ask, as Rueschemeyer made clear, efficient according to what/whose criteria?

Susan George (1984) addresses the issue of what counts as efficient agriculture. She
points out that in developed countries with abundant land, labour shortage and
available high-tech inputs, efficiency means maximum output per unit of labour. In
contrast in the less developed contries (LDCs) where there is labour surplus, land
shortage and few available high-tech inputs, efficiency means maximum output per
unit of land. To judge the agricultural systems of the LDCs in terms of First World
notions of efficiency is an intellectual error; it also leads to policies productive of
hunger in the Third World. The World Bank, based in Washington and wedded
to market ideas, has pressed for agricultural policies in LDCs which stress cash-
cropping, and thus the marketisation of peasant subsistence-type agriculture. Yet,
while LDC hunger has increased along with involvement in the world food-product
trade, the market-oriented US farming community is in debt to the tune of some
$200 billion.

Relatedly, the notion of competitive striving for efficiency seems to be controlled
by other social conventions: it is a subsidiary goal, not a central one. For example, in
factories stability seems just as important and, between firms, quiet deals are struck
behind the scenes. In huge areas of human endeavour, health and personal care or
education it simply does not seem relevant at all: we make our evaluative judgements
in these areas on very different grounds.

Distribution

The market acts to distribute knowledge, information and resources. Besides problems of market imperfection, and of resource distribution (which would seem to be a
function of knowledge), we can bring two lines of reflection to bear directly on the
notion of market as knowledge and information distributor: namely, claims and
alternatives.

First, the extent to which the market is able to act as distributor hinges on the
nature of the distribution requirements of suppliers and demanders. Suppliers need to
have product specification, product market-introduction time scales, likely con-
sumer-groups and projected and monitored revenue systems and accounts. On the
other hand, consumers in the market-place need to fit their own needs with the
complex array of products available. The information and knowledge requirements
are enormous: the neo-classical orthodoxy would have us believe that all requisite
flows of information and knowledge are reduced to a simple single index – price.
Upon this index both suppliers and demanders are to base all their decisions, and by
implication all other, non-indexical, flows of information and knowledge within the
social system are downgraded: they can only be secondary to the system's satisfaction-
maximising function of the scarcity index of market price.

The question here is thus to what extent can the market function as an information and knowledge carrier? The claim of the free marketeers that price is a sufficient index seems implausible. Indeed, Keynes erected the directive role of the state on the inability of the market to transmit information in conditions of depression equilibrium, with idle plant, idle money and idle men. Also, in view of market imperfections, it would seem that information transmission would be a first casualty. On narrow economics grounds, knowledge counts as a resource and its flow will thus be controlled. More broadly, meanings, and thus knowledge claims, are widely distributed throughout society. Such a distribution is not smooth: it is structured in a whole series of ways.

The second line of reply to the stated role of the market as distributor of knowledge and information would be to ask if any other mechanism could be envisaged. Napoleoni (1972) states that the Walrasian model of the market economy, an area of neo-classical theory, can be manipulated so as to obviate the need for a market: thus from within the terms of the orthodoxy, rational economic planning is possible.

In sum: the notion of the market when examined, as it has been within the critical literature of economics, turns out to comprise a tissue of interrelated definitions which severally and in total collapse under scrutiny. As regards the continuing intellectual attraction of neo-classicism, Joan Robinson (1962), invoking Freud, has suggested that it all expresses a deep-seated desire for the security of the womb.

3.2.2 Free Markets Maximise Moral Worth

Within the intellectual ambit of the delimited–formal ideological package of the free marketeers there is a strong claim made with regard to the moral superiority of their schemes. Alternatives such as 'socialism' are taken to be productive of a morally debilitating collectivism. In brief, within this purportedly technical, neutral, scientific economics there is lodged a very clear and strong ethic.

Model and Ethic of Humankind

All social theories have within them a model of humankind; around this model are ordered the theory's wider statements about how the world is and might become (see, for example, Hollis 1977 and Hawthorn 1976). This sphere of reflection is termed 'philosophical anthropology' and orthodox economists deploy a quite particular philosophical anthropology: rational economic man is deployed as the route to rendering coherent the subjective meaning states of persons whose behaviour is then amenable to scientific treatment and evaluation via the notion of efficiency. This model presents humankind as centrally rational and calculative, and thereafter to be understood only in less reliable or subjective ways. This view of the extent to which human meanings can be rendered intelligible in a reliable manner flows directly from positivistic prejudices in natural science. In contrast, hermeneutic interpretive strategies do not reduce intelligibility to one axis but are much richer. The final step, for the neo-classicists, is to conjoin this rational calculating behaviour, the axis of intelligibility, with economic efficiency and thus produce the result that the ideal pure market most clearly expresses human rationality. And thereafter, empirical reality can be measured as divergent: not economically efficient, not fully expressing the rational economic axis of human thought.

The entire package from its model of man down to stategy of analysing behaviour as more or less rational, does indeed hang together. Presumably, it derives what plausibility it has from this logical elegance: however, whilst it is easy to reject, (the philosophical anthropology is impoverished, the model of science useless, the notion of efficiency culture-bound and the whole serves an ideological position), the notion of economic maximising does retain a certain power. In the common culture of the capitalist world the notion of economic-maximising behaviour on the part of discrete individuals is a totalising discourse: it can be applied to any behaviour and if the premise is accepted it is convincing with regard to any specified behaviour.

MacIntyre's distinctive contribution (1981)to this discussion lodges three broad claims about liberal democracy, individualism and contemporary moral discourse. MacIntyre takes the view that the consequences of the invention of 'the individual' are manifold. First, the key moral experience of the present is to see ourselves as morally autonomous agents (Kant or Kierkegaard) confronting others; self-responsi-bility and manipulative competition are conjoined in a social realm now lacking any notion of shared community. Second, the social world of individuals with 'rights' has come to face the role of bureaucratic managerialism that is concerned with 'utility'; disputes over decisions affecting the community collapse into assertions of rights, utilities and protest – thus, an emotivist moral culture. Third, the claims of bureau-cratic managers to technical expertise require: (i) a realm of morally neutral facts and (ii) law-like generalisation about this realm. It turns out that autonomous facts, the disjunction of facts and values, and notions of social laws are all products of the rise of the modern world and none are as self-evidently plausible as our common culture supposes. Thus the contemporary claims of the bureaucrat-managers are false.

On MacIntyre's argument contemporary moral discourse is thus a hotch-potch of fragments from the era preceeding liberal-individualism plus various modern bits of nonsense (rights, utility, protest, bureaucratic expertise, aesthetic consumerism and so on). The claim is made that the reconstitution of moral discourse requires reaching back to pre-liberal thinking where notions of community, tradition, the practicality of moral discourse and the project of self/community development were available: a sketch of this ethic is available in eighteenth-century republicanism.

3.2.3 Free Market Maximizes Human Freedom

The model of man affirmed by the neo-classical tradition, and savaged by MacIntyre, finds one line of expression in the notion of the sovereign power of the consumer in the market. On the basis of this idea the broader frame of a political system is built.

Consumer Sovereignty

The pure-market model is predicated upon the philosophical priority of the atomistic individual in pursuit of private satisfaction. Competition between suppliers within the market-place is competition to meet the private wants of the consumers. The sovereign consumer is thus required by the theory both as an assumption to get the system working (if no demands are being made then how could the market act to satisfy them?) and as a goal of the system. The whole business is thus supposed to be about satisfying the desires of these consumers.

In the atomistic individual we meet directly the liberal theory of humankind; one which Marx satirised through the image of Robinson Crusoe: the Robinsonades supposed that persons were first individual and thereafter social (Marx 1973). In addition, the notion of the sovereign consumer has been attacked by Galbraith (1958) who points to the existence of an entire industry geared to want creation. If the productive system is creating the wants it is satisfying, then consumer sovereignty drops out of sight.

A further argument against the notion of consumer sovereignty might look at technological advance: how can one demand products that have not been invented? It would seem to be bizarre to deny that technological advance opens up new possibilities; and it is no good to say, 'Well, now consumer sovereignty operates because it is no longer proactive but reactive to otherwise generated possibilities. ' One might also add that the exchange between consumers and producers is asymmetric: little consumers and giant business backed by science and technology.

The Politics attached to Neo-classical Economics

The practitioners of neo-classicism claim, and affect to believe, that their strategy of analysis is a value-neutral, technical and positive scientific endeavour. But, as must by now be all too clear, we have to see the theorums as the core element of a package deal of ideas which have in recent years presented themselves under the label 'The Free World'.

With neo-classicism we meet a central element of the delimited–formal ideology which celebrates the extant pattern of world capitalist development. Macpherson (1964 and 1973) has shown that the political philosophy of capitalism is liberal, or liberal democratic and has indicated convincingly the incoherent nature of both positions. In place of what he characterises as outmoded political theories, he advances the claims of a view centred upon formal and substantive democracy. [4]

3.2.4 Claims to Knowledge

The model of science affirmed by orthodox neo-classical economics is positivistic: the whole model of the market system is seen as an exercise in positive science and thus as generating value free and context independent statements.

Hollis and Nell (1975) argue that neo-classicism depends upon positivistic notions of scientificity and, having demolished these, they say that neo-classicism's pretensions to scientificity fall also. A condition of scholarship, on my view of social theory, is that it be reflexively embedded in the processes it offers to elucidate. The neo-classical theorists lay claim to a position outside the system they consider: it is a limited engagement and protestations of their own scientificity in the face of others ideology-mongering merely serve to complete, to the exent that any of them actually believe this, their own intellectual self-binding.

The matter of economics and methodology has been reviewed by Pheby (1988), who considers the empiricist's focus on method as the key to grasping the nature of (natural) science. He also reviews the influential 1953 paper by Milton Friedman. Conceived as a defence of neo-classicism, the author argues for an instrumentalist view of theories in science (and economics). On this view what matters is not the realism of the theory, but its success in making predictions. If Friedman's position is correct, then all the criticisms of the neo-classical model to the effect that it rests upon unrealistic premises are of no avail. On Friedman's position it does not matter whether the premises of neo-classicism are realistic or not, because what does matter is the theories' success in making good predictions which serve our purposes and which are borne out by subsequent experience. The problem for Friedman, and all those who stress the (natural) scientificity of neo-classicism, is precisely that it has not generated any useful results.

Looking at the broad approach taken by Friedman, it must be acknowledged that there is much that is attractive in such a position with its mixture of instrumentalism and pragmatism. I would agree that social theorising is about making practical sense. But where I would wish to talk about a delimited–formal ideology which is designed to address problems, with its intellectual machineries given by tradition, and would want the whole procedure/result subject to discursive examination; Friedman claims his work is naturalistic and technical. Broadly, the argument strategy which I affirm has a procedural requirement of reflexive self-embedding (strategic, in regard to the historical process addressed and technical in regard to argument procedures) whereas Friedman acknowledges no such received requirement. The technical moment of delimited–formal ideology making, as I understand it, is Habermasian 'free conversation' where the power of the argument holds sway: this regulative discipline affirms a consensus/coherence theory of truth. But in Friedman's case the technical moment, what must be the core and ground of his arguments, is a variation of correspondence theory: the descriptive value-neutral accommodation to the given. Pheby comments that if one is looking for a coherent philosophy of science then it cannot be found in Friedman's essay.[5] The problem of evaluating Friedman's disconnected empiricism is that the author's claims are contradicted by his practice: Friedman, an adherent of a complex delimited–formal ideological scheme oriented to the cause of the political right in modern capitalism, simultaneously presents himself as a neutral technical scientist.

3.2.5 Resumé of the Critique of the Neo-classical Scheme of Market

I take the view that the cumulative attack on neo-classicism is overwhelming. Any pretension by proponents of neo-classicism to the status of social scientificity, where this must, at a minimum, involve reflexive self-embedding in those processes which enquiry would grasp, has to be denied. The claims of the economic orthodoxy to a position of intellectual centrality within the European social theoretic tradition must also be denied. Finally, and more specifically, the notion of the market is now returned to the broad realm of scholarly concern.

3.3 THE MARKET IN SOCIAL SCIENTIFIC DISCOURSE

Within the sphere of the social sciences in the UK there seems to be a disposition to take the notion of the market entirely for granted. It would seem to be the case both that an intellectual division of labour, institutionalised in the separation of the social sciences into discrete professionalised spheres, has produced a situation whereby notions of the market are taken to be the province of economists and that the notion of market which is affirmed is that produced by the neo-classical theorists: the market is a natural given.

As a consequence there has been a huge intellectual void in the centre of our social science: in recent years the New Right colonised this space with a *mélange* of warmed-over middle European conservatism and bastardised Adam Smith. Faced with this efflorescence of market-nonsense, the general community of social scientists have had little or nothing available with which to make effective reply. And as enthusiasm for this market-nonsense has swept through post-cold war Eastern Europe it has been left to dissenting figures to lodge appropriate complaint: Galbraith states that

> those who speak, as so many do so glibly, even mindlessly, of a return to the Smithian free market are wrong to the point of a mental vacuity of clinical proportions. It is something we in the West do not have, would not tolerate, could not survive. (1990)

Within the UK we could speak of an intellectual, professional and political failure-via-neglect. The intellectual failure has been to neglect the scholarly study of a centrally important social scientific concept and that sphere of human social life so designated. With regard to the efforts of the economists, commentators are critical: Hodgson notes that whilst the

> study of market behaviour is a major theme, if not the major theme, of economic science as we know it... Remarkably, however, definitions of the market in the economic literature are not easy to find, and analytical discussions of the institutional concepts involved are extremely rare. Mathematical models of market phenomena abound...yet if we ask the elementary question – 'What is a market?' – we are given short shrift. (1988:172)

Professionally the failure has been one of responsibility: in place of a rationally secured discourse, which in my view would have moved outside and beyond received professional boundaries, arbitrary disciplinary territories and traditions of enquiry have been preferred, one consequence of which has been that the sphere of the economic has been subject only to a narrowly professional and technical treatment. Politically the failure is clear: the New Right marched gleefully into the resultant social scientific void.

Recent events in Europe, however, and the relative eclipse of the New Right do open an intellectual and political space in which a reaffirmation of the long established scholarly interest in the notion of the market might be made.

3.4 AN AGENDA FOR NEW RESEARCH

In order to move the debate forward one step, it seems to me that we need to do three things. First, we must ask a series of questions about our received thinking so as to set in train a process whereby the taken-for-granted vocabulary of orthodox economics is made clear, as well as that process by which *their* delimited–formal ideology finds pervasive–informal extension in *our* social scientific theorising. Second, we must contribute both to this critical work and to create new agendas by setting down in terms of a sociology of knowledge just what sorts of material are available within the sphere of orthodox economics. (Here I have in mind little more than a series of terminological maneouvres which might help discussants keep the various issues clear – in Confucian terms, a programme of the 'rectification of names'. Third, we must ask after a new framework for handling scholarly enquiry in the sphere of the economic.

3.4.1 Detoxification

The first area of concern must be with our received thinking in the area of economics. I argued earlier that it is possible to identify a triple failure through neglect in respect of the notion of the market. UK social science has typically left it up to the orthodox economists to handle matters relating to the human sphere of economic life. A key step in rectifying this error is the detoxification of our thinking: to purge it of the routine and tainted (or, indeed, meaningless) vocabulary of orthodox neo-classical economics. There seem to be four areas of criticism.

First, to address the general business of humankind making things and exchanging things and consuming things (material and non-material), the first issue to confront is contextualisation: how to pick these processes out of the totality of things which humans do, and show how they relate to one another. Our received, common-sense way of doing it is to speak of economic activity or the market. But this received discourse is both unsatisfactory as scholarship and, of course, it is the vocabulary of a quite specific delimited–formal ideology.

We can also report on how received thinking is taken up within social science: that is the distinction between economic social science and the rest – social studies. The historical, intellectual and institutional occasion of this division was noted earlier following Swedberg (1987). The informal expression of this judgement about the proper division of responsibility within the social sciences and the actual scientific status of the component elements must be addressed.

In brief, it seems to me that the received notion of the market is not merely unsatisfactory scholarship but it also evidently serves ideological ends. Following the example of the Frankfurt School, the attack on the cultural articulation of delimited–formal ideologies has to be a prerequisite of change. And as social theorists are also citizens, the *pre*-pre-requisite is the detoxification of scholarly social scientific thinking.

We have then the problem of detoxifying our own habits of thinking: that is, a *reflexive critique of the pervasive informal ideology of the market as it runs through our thought and work.*

Second, the problem of how to theorise the sphere of the economic, and the market, relates to the received division of labour. Here one might want to argue that we can reject the division of labour in so far as it is taken to legislate for an actually existing intellectual division, so to say. Maybe, however, we are obliged to run with it procedurally: thus the totality of scholarly social scientific concern is split – social, economic and political so as to facilitate enquiry. We are stuck with this division as a result of professionalisation of social science, even if intellectually it can only be a rough and ready strategy of keeping problems manageable.

However, there is another way of coming at this issue and that is to identify discrete modes of social theoretic engagement within social science work. Thus it seems to me to be clear that theorists typically argue on behalf of particular audiences. Most obviously UK social scientists argue on behalf of the policy planners. This view I have presented elsewhere (Preston 1987) and it carries the implication that the familiar professional division of social scientific labour should not be permitted to bind scholarly work. In sum, we have the detoxification task of *identifying received disciplinary boundaries and getting over them.*

Third, the task of political economy within western social scientific tradition, as discussed earlier, has been centrally concerned with grasping the nature of the social change in the modern world in a holistic and engaged fashion. (We wanted to know what was going on and what we could do about it.) The key intellectual machinery has been political economy which was engaged and intellectually catholic. In the work of those critics of the present state of intellectual and social and political affairs, such as Pollard and Macpherson, whom we met above, it is clear that we have to consider the broader package of ideas attached to political economy as well as the package deals these theorists attempted to combat, seemingly unsuccessfully on the whole. The return to the classical tradition of European social theory thus has more than 'methodological' implications. We have the task of *the recovery of relatively submerged traditions of enquiry:* namely, the political economic analysis of patterns of socio-economic change with a view to maximising democracy and, at the same time, the critique of the essentially liberal political philosophy which displaced it, a philosophy which is routinely taken for granted within lay and social scientific common sense.

Fourth, thus we inhabit a tradition of enquiry, leaving aside neo-classical distortions, that focuses on the shift to the modern world and the extent to which all this can be grasped and made subject to human will. In this tradition, rightly or wrongly, the economic (material) was made central, and our interest has been activist: we seek understanding in order to control. Our interest in the sphere of the economic is culture specific. We have to unpack and display these 'specifics': that is, we have to ask where our concentration on matters economic originated and what set of assumptions, about humankind and human society, were then adumbrated and how these ideas have subsequently been extended and revised. Thus we must move beyond the contextualising critique of neo-classical material to the rather more difficult task of *reflexively appreciating the sets of assumptions made by that European tradition of social theorising that perforce we inhabit.*

3.4.2 A Sociology of Knowledge Approach to Economic Theorising

To help underscore these points about the necessity of purging our habits of thought from economic ideas taken from orthodox neo-classical schemes that centre on the 'market-mechanism', it may be useful to sketch out in terms of a sociology of knowledge the variety of economics presently on offer. A rough sketch can be made by considering the sorts of work to which economic concepts are put. Thus we may identify the following varieties:

- business economics, which is designed with a view to ordering the behaviour of the private firm which operates within a relatively competitive market-institutional environment (neo-classicism plus management science);
- accountant economics, which is designed to offer formal summaries of the firm-in-the-market-institution performance (measurements of throughputs, outputs, performances and so on);
- state-planning economics, which is designed to offer macro-measures of the overall performance of the national economy taken as a unit within the state's control (thus, the familiar spread of measures found in any newspaper);
- dissenting economics, which offers critical reflection upon the economy-understood-as-social (thus, matters of social welfare would be routinely considered);
- economics-as-ideology, whereby ostensibly scientific ideas are deployed in contexts where they operate as ideological or even symbolic notions (rather obviously, the New Right's celebration of the market over the Thatcher period in the UK);
- political economy, which seeks to analyse complex patterns of change so as to inform the construction, criticism and comparative ranking of delimited–formal ideologies;
- scholarly economics, which looks to elucidate the nature of the sphere of the economic.

Evidently, this little sketch cannot take us very far. It may be, however, that the development of such a line of analysis will let us better understand the limited and restricted scope of the conceptual apparatus of orthodox economics. Relatedly, of course, the contrast with a fully articulated scholarly economics is implied.

3.4.3 Towards a New Framework for Scholarship

Assuming that the above noted set of questions can be answered we can move forward one step and offer a broad statement of a new, detoxified, verson of how to apprehend that which was previously grasped via ideas of the market. We can now offer a proximate statement that the economic is the sphere of making, exchanging and consuming things (material and non-material).

First, when we deploy the notion of making in order to offer a reading of a given form of life then we must note that our interest is suffused with received ideas. Since any process of making will be context-specific, ethnographic reports on an episode of making will thus be very complex. Simplifying these accounts must be seen in the light of particular interests that we have: thus the questions, what simplifications and to what end? Such an analysis would have us ask: what is made, by whom, with what objective in view and within which specifiable set of life contexts – and the whole tale is shaped by the particular interest of the enquirer. Second, when we deploy the notion of consuming we have the same questions: what, by whom, why and in what circumstances – and again all reports are shaped by the interests of the enquirer. Third, when we deploy the notion of exchanging, in the market, we again have the issues of what, who, where and why plus the skew given by the particular interest of the enquirer. In addition, a scholarly enquiry of exchange would ask: which individuals and groups, which objects (extant or ideal), which places, which social contexts (moral, political, institutional and representational). Fourth, this roughly characterised approach to deploying the notions of making, exchanging and consuming has the effect of making any question about the 'market' subject to an immediate triple contextualisation:

- as one element of production, exchange and consumption activities;
- in terms of a complex network of local social–political–cultural contexts for each of these three elements of economic activity;
- in terms of the totality of a form of life in which the sphere of the economic as encompassing the market is essentially arbitrarily designated.

Furthermore, any enquiry should be contextualised in terms of the particular interests of the enquirer. This element is introduced in line with my above announced interest in social theorising: I take it to be diverse and practical. Where scholarship orders extant examples according to the received classical European tradition (of endeavouring to grasp change and render it subject to human will) other modes of engagement will have their own interests shaping the enquiry. Thus if we wished to grasp, academically, the sphere of the economic it would not be very sensible to begin by asking, for example, a chartered accountant or businessman.

3.5 EXPECTATIONS

Earlier in this chapter I referred to what seemed to me to be an intellectual failure on the part of UK scholarship in respect to the notion of the market. It is certainly clear to me that the dominance of social scientific discourse by received ideas of neoclassicism is unjustifiable. I rather think that the changes in Eastern Europe plus the move towards unity within the European Community will demonstrate clearly that markets are not spontaneous constructions of liberal economic actors, but instead are complex social constructs which, if they are to be understood (and maybe specific patterns of change argued for), needs must be addressed by scholars working in the broad classical European tradition.

NOTES

1. Development theory has generated many objections to orthodox economics. For instance, Boeke (1953), a colonial administrator-scholar who argued for the inapplicability of orthodox western economics to the analysis of South-east Asia, posited a dual economy in which eastern and western systems were brought into relationships. Furnivall (1939), who deploys political economic analysis to plural societies, notes that economic activity is lodged within culture and that what might be tagged pure market behaviour is manifest only when there is an absence of common cultural rules. In plural societies colonial administration is necessary, for without it pure economic behaviour is *asocial*. Also, Streeten and Myrdal (See Preston 1982) offer a sophisticated institutional analysis of matters developmental and Wallerstein (1974) although using an orthodox idea of markets, lodges them in history and into the extensive networks of world systems. (See also Schiel 1987.)

   Dependency theory has thus routinely followed lines critical to orthodox economics. One figure who might stand for the whole 'school' is Celso Furtado whose work travels a familiar path: from the attempt to deploy the neo-classical paradigm, on to doubt about its usefulness in the Third World, through to complete disbelief in its scientific status anywhere. (See Preston 1982.)

2. The German Historical School of List, Roscher, Hildebrand, Knies and Schmoller lost out to the proponents of the Austrian School, a variant of emergent neo-classicism. However, argues Swedberg, their empirical, historical, comparative and evolutionary approach fed into the first generation of economic sociology; the names to note being: Weber (most importantly), Simmel, Pareto and Durkheim.

3. On this idea generally, see J. Habermas (1971).

4. There is now a large body of material addressing this point: see for example Ted Honderich (1990), C. Pateman (1979), and A. MacIntyre (1981 and 1988).

5. Pheby reviews some of the debate sparked by this essay: it moves within the sphere of 'philosophy of science'. This is not, so far as I can see, a helpful area of reflections: Feyerabend's point to the effect that Popper has occasioned the misdevelopment of the whole debate seems to be correct (1978). Once we enter the confused realms of empiricism, positivism, mitigated positivism and the varieties of post-empiricism, any plausible claims about natural science and social science will become obscure and lost.

REFERENCES

Abrams, P. 1968. *The Origins of British Sociology.* Chicago: Chicago University Press.

Boeke, J. H. 1953. *Economics and Economic Policy of Dual Societies.* New York: Institute of Pacific Relations.

Brewer, A. 1980. *Marxist Theories of Imperialism.* London: Routledge and Kegan Paul.

Callinicos, A. 1991. *The Revenge of History.* Oxford: Polity.

Cardoso, F. H. and E. Faletto 1979. *Dependency and Development.* Los Angeles: California University Press.

Carver, T. (ed. , transl.), 1975. *Karl Marx: Texts on Method.* Oxford: Basil Blackwell.

Clammer, J. 1985. *Anthropology and Political Economy.* London: Macmillan.

Collini, S. 1979. *Liberalism and Sociology.* Cambridge: Cambridge University Press.

Dasgupta, A. K. 1985. *Epochs of Economic Theory.* Blackwell.

Deane, P. 1978. *The Evolution of Economic Ideas.* Cambridge: Cambridge University Press.

Feyerabend, P. 1978. *Science in a Free Society.* London: Verso.

Friedman, M. 1953. *Essays in Positive Economics.* Chicago: Chicago University Press.

Furnivall, J. S. 1939. *Netherlands India: A Study in Plural Economy*. Cambridge: Cambridge University Press.

Galbraith, J. K. 1958. *The Affluent Society*. London: Hamish Hamilton.

Galbraith, J. K. 26 January 1990. *The Guardian*. Guardian Newspapers.

Glenny, M. 1990. *The Rebirth of History*. Harmondsworth: Penguin.

George, S. 1984. *Ill Fares the Land*. Washington: Institute for Policy Studies.

Habermas, J. 1971. *Towards a Rational Society*. London: Heinman.

Hawthorn, G. 1976. *Enlightenment and Despair*. Cambridge: Cambridge University Press.

Hindess, B. 1977. *Philosophy and Methodology in the Social Sciences*. Hassocks: Harvester.

Hodgson, G. 1988. *Economics and Institutions*. Oxford: Polity.

Hollis, M. 1977. *Models of Man*. Cambridge: Cambridge University Press.

Hollis, M. and E. J. Nell, 1975. *Rational Economic Man*. Cambridge: Cambridge University Press.

Honderich, T. 1990. *Conservatism*. London: Hamish Hamilton.

MacIntyre, A. 1981. *After Virtue*. London: Duckworth.

MacIntyre, A. 1988. *Whose Justice Which Rationality?* London: Duckworth.

Macpherson, C. B. 1964. *The Political Theory of Possessive Individualism*. Oxford: Oxford University Press.

Macpherson, C. B. 1973. *Democratic Theory*. Oxford: Oxford University Press.

Marquand, D. 1988. *The Unprincipled Society*. London: Jonathan Cape.

Marx, K. 1973. *Grundrisse*. (Tr Martin Nicolaus). Harmondsworth: Penguin.

Mills, C. W. 1959. *The Sociological Imagination*. New York: Oxford University Press.

Napoleoni, C. 1972. *Economic Thought in the Twentieth Century*. London: Martin Robertson.

Palmer, J. 1989. *1992 And Beyond*. Luxembourg: Office for Official Publications of the European Communities.

Passmore, J. 1970. *The Perfectibility of Man*. London: Duckworth.

Pateman, C. 1979. *The Problem of Political Obligation*. London: John Wiley.

Pheby, J. 1988. *Methodology and Economics: A Critical Introduction*. London: Macmillan.

Polanyi, K. 1944. *The Great Transformation*. Boston: Beacon Press.

Pollard, S. 1971. *The Idea of Progress*. Harmondsworth: Penguin.

Preston, P. W. 1982. *Theories of Development*. London: Routledge and Kegan Paul.

Preston, P. W. 1987. *Rethinking Development*. London: Routledge and Kegan Paul.

Robinson, J. 1962. *Economic Philosophy*. London: C. A. Watts.

Rueschemeyer, D. 1986. *Power and the Division of Labour*. Oxford: Polity.

Sahlins, M. 1972. *Stoneage Economics*. London: Tavistock.

Scheil, T. 1987. 'Wallerstein's Concept of a Modern World System: Another Marxist Critique', *Sociology of Development Research Center Working Papers 89*. Bielefeld: University of Bielefeld.

Staniland, M. 1985. *What is Political Economy?* London: Yale University Press.

Swedberg, R. 1987. 'Economic Sociology: Past and Present', *Current Sociology*, 35 (1): 1–221.

Todaro, M. P. 1982. *Economics for a Developing World*. London: Longmans.

Wallerstein, I. 1974. *The Modern World System*. London: Academic Press.

Part II

Economic Models and
the Ethnography of Practice

4

What's in a Price?

Trading Practices in Peasant (and other) Markets

PAUL ALEXANDER

The conventional view in most social sciences is that whereas economic behaviour in non-market societies is deeply 'embedded' in social relations, with the advent of the market the economy becomes progressively more autonomous. In modern societies the economy is represented as a separate and highly differentiated sphere in which transactions are no longer governed by social and kinship obligations but by the rational calculation of individuals. Indeed, some scholars would go further, arguing that in such societies social relations are themselves constituted by the market. In this chorus the economists are the discordant voices for most would deny that the extent of social embeddedness in earlier societies was significantly greater than the low levels they discern in our own. The 'propensity in human nature . . . to truck, barter and exchange' (Smith 1776:1:2) entails that economic behaviour in all societies is sufficiently detached from social relations to make economic analysis appropriate, and there is now a substantial literature in which the economic behaviour previously attributed to 'traditional' culture, society or personality is shown to be congruent with the rational pursuit of self-interest by essentially atomised individuals.

When applied to non-market societies this line of analysis is not so much wrong as vacuous; to characterise everything – from bride-price, through the size of kinship groups, to the value placed on certain personality traits – as adaptations to the 'pervasive uncertainty and high information costs of primitive life which create a demand for insurance' (Poser 1980:52) is to say nothing more than that societies with these institutions survive. The facility with which the functionalist accounts of an earlier anthropology can be translated into the terminology of rational expectations (Landa 1981; Posner 1980; compare Barnes 1990) says more about the models than about the phenomena they purport to explain.

Analysis couched in terms of rational choice are more plausible, however, when they are directed to what are variously termed rural economies, peasant economies, or bazaar economies.[1] These are economies characterised by recognisable markets for commodities, land, labour or finance, but where the observed behaviour in these markets appears incongruent with the trading practices of industrialised economies; or at least with our common-sense understanding of these practices in our own economy.

4. I TRADING PRACTICES

Although the significance of individual practices varies from case to case and none is diacritical, a set of trading practices appears broadly to differentiate peasant markets from markets, especially consumer markets, in industrialised economies.[2] In peasant markets commodities are seldom standardised or pre-packaged and are often subject to marked fluctuations in supply or demand. Production or overhead costs are not calculated and most traders do not keep written records after a transaction is completed. Vendors of particular commodities cluster together in one section of the market-place, rather than distribute themselves throughout it, and do not overtly compete to make a sale. Advertising, other than sales patter, is almost unknown and although many transactions are between persons previously unknown to one another, the market as a whole is structured by enduring trading partnerships which channel credit and supplies. As prices are seldom marked on goods or on the stall, except when required by the state, bargaining is the usual means of setting prices. Consequently there is a range of prices for most goods or services and while the price range for cheap, often-purchased, commodities or for transactions between traders is narrow, the top price for expensive, infrequently purchased consumer items may be twice the bottom price. Nor is there a clear distinction between wholesale and retail prices because, although purchases intended for resale will usually be in the bottom half of the range, skilled consumers can and do obtain the same price.

These social institutions which I have grouped together under the rubric of trading practices are ignored or marginalised in studies which treat markets as systems of material flows or as social systems; at best practices such as enduring trading partnerships are attributed to elements of culture or personality, or interpreted as adaptations to social structure or the environment. But trading practices become central concerns when markets are conceptualised as systems of communication or information (Geertz 1979; Plattner 1985): when the focus is on trading, rather than trade or traders (Alexander 1987:2). The most convincing explanations of trading practices from this perspective have begun with the postulate that the diacritical feature of peasant markets is that information is discontinuous, differentially allocated and difficult to acquire. Typical trading practices in such economies – the 'institutionalised peculiarities' of 'bazaar economies' as Geertz (1978) calls them – are analysed as ways of ameliorating inefficiencies in the flow of information. Bargaining, for example, is interpreted as a method of negotiating prices where conditions of supply are irregular, commodities vary in quality and time has a low value (Cassady 1974; compare Alexander and Alexander 1987). The concentration of vendors of similar commodities in one place is said to facilitate search in the absence of advertising and posted prices (Geertz 1978). The prevalence of stable trading partnerships is deemed a solution to high search and transaction costs; while repetitive deals rule out 'opportunism' or windfall profits in individual transactions, they are more profitable in the long term because they reduce the costs of finding reliable suppliers or distributors (Acheson 1985; Dannhaeuser 1983; Plattner 1985). One reason why such relationships are often personalised is the lack of formal legal sanctions against non-completion of contracts; trust becomes a substitute for the law. An indication of the scope of this style of analysis is that even the emergence of ethnic monopolies of economic functions, such as the Chinese domination of wholesaling in colonial Java (Alexander and Alexander 1991a), can be accounted for in these terms: 'Ethnically homogeneous middleman groups' are 'alternatives to contract law and the vertically integrated firm which emerged to economise on contract enforcement and information costs' (Landa 1981:361 and compare Rudner 1989).

A major hurdle in appraising this line of interpretation is that most accounts offer very little direct evidence about the distribution of information, let alone about the ways in which information is acquired and controlled.[3] For example, the best of these studies seldom report such apparently simple data as transaction prices at various points in the marketing system, although they often indicate a considerable range of prices, which throws some doubt on the later use of inferred averages (Acheson 1985; Plattner 1983; Finan 1988). One reason for the absence of this information is that it is difficult and very time consuming for ethnographers to obtain systematic and reliable data on transaction prices; another is that the economics literature on which this approach is based has also been content with averages or indices until very recently (Carlton 1986).

In the absence of reliable empirical data, the force of the interpretation therefore depends upon a series of implicit inferences which are grounded in anecdotes and flavoured by a common-sense understanding of our own economy. It seems reasonable to infer, for example, that in the absence of advertising and independent market reports, the presence of large numbers of traders dealing in small quantities of unstandardised, variable-supply commodities, inhibits the flow of price information through the system. But this does not in itself entail the proposition that obtaining such information is a major, or a particular, problem for bazaar traders. And while it is usually true that transactions between established trading partners result in lower than average prices, this does not necessarily mean that either partner relinquishes profit, let alone that they do so voluntarily to secure the longer term economic benefits of maintaining the partnership.

4. 2 TWO TYPES OF MARKET?

Whether we accept these inferences and thus whether we are persuaded by the 'information' interpretation of trading practices in peasant societies, turns on the aptness of a comparison, explicit or implicit, between peasant and industrialised economies.[4] For the purpose of the comparison, markets in industrialised economies are constituted by 'rational', 'impersonal' transactions which are individual and discrete, and where any particular transaction carries few implications for the future. Transactions are openly – indeed should be morally – strictly instrumental, with each actor attempting to maximise self-interest. Because information about prices, credit and commodity qualities is publicly available and widely distributed through a variety of media, the presence of numerous buyers and sellers shifts prices towards an equilibrium price which clears the market and distributes the commodities efficiently from producers to consumers.[5]

Whereas an earlier anthropology saw peasant markets as the closest empirical approximation to the idealised market (for example Tax 1953), they are now more commonly treated as underdeveloped variants of markets in industrialised economies.[6] The argument is that although peasant market-places contain numerous buyers and sellers who compete with one another, and although the primary goal of each actor is economic self-interest,[7] economic exchanges are often transacted in the context of long-term trading partnerships. While the transactions are conducted in recognisably commercial terms, parallel social relationships support the commercial relationships. These relationships – 'equilibrating relationships' (Plattner 1985) – which in most studies[8] are represented as emblematic of the entire gamut of bazaar trading practices listed above, are explained as adaptations to the pervasive uncertainty concerning the three major components of an economic exchange: goods, transactions and actors. The uncertainty is in turn sourced to the underdeveloped infrastructure: inadequate transport, storage and communications; a lack of legal sanctions; and cheap labour and scarce capital which gives time a low value (Plattner 1985).

Both descriptions are, of course, ideal types but the ways in which they were constructed are significantly different. The account of trading practices in peasant markets is an empirical generalisation from numerous case studies, leavened by the desire to defend peasants against charges of irrationality. The account of trading practices in industrialised markets, however, is derived from explicitly theoretical and reductionist models, which are not grounded, except by way of experimental simulation or anecdote, in empirical evidence. It was only with the growth of management studies in the 1970s that economists attempted to develop models whose axioms might more closely approximate trading practices in industrialised societies. Their methods, however, remain deductive, elegance is a more important criterion for evaluation than empirical fit, and the congruence between the assumptions and predictions of the models and observations about trading practices in industrialised economies remains low.

This comparison determines the interpretation in at least three significant respects. First, it constitutes the salient features of peasant markets which require explanation: practices which are 'irrational' in that they appear incompatible with our common-sense understanding of trading practices in industrialised economies and the universal axioms of human behaviour which we intuit as underlying these practices. Such features range from structures which do not appear to facilitate economies of scale or capital accumulation, through actions which do not appear to maximise self-interest, to a tendency to personalise economic relationships. Second, the comparison provides the criteria with which to evaluate interpretations. A successful explanation is one which demonstrates that apparently anomalous features are situationally rational: it describes (or infers) contexts in which the actions or structures are not incompatible with the universal assumptions. Thus the apparent divergence between the universal model of central-place theory and the observed distribution of peasant market-places is explained by describing deficiencies in transport, storage or political integration. And when placed in context, apparently altruistic acts are seen as compatible with self-interest because of the insurance benefits of maintaining social relationships or because they reduce risks. Third, and most importantly in the present context, it is the comparison which legitimates those inferences which cannot be directly supported by empirical evidence. As was noted above, there are very few empirical accounts of the way in which information concerning prices and supply conditions is distributed and controlled in any economy, not only in peasant economies. [9]

In sum, the explanatory authority of the interpretation does not rest on the empirical evidence presented in the course of the analysis but on the rhetorical weight of the comparison. My objection is not to the comparison *per se*: my objection is that the comparison is not used heuristically to suggest possible lines of analysis of independently gathered material. Rather it constrains the analysis: strictly determining what data is gathered, how this data is represented and what inferences may legitimately be drawn from it. The result, as Gudeman (1986:34) points out, is that such analyses 'continually reproduce and rediscover their own assumptions in the exotic materials'.

There are at least two distinct paths out of this impasse, although with any luck they might eventually converge. One is to recognise the centrality of the concept of culture for the comparative analysis of economies. A major theoretical problem with rational choice models in general is that culture is set to one side and the alternatives presented as rational choice versus unthinking adherence to social norms. In both cases 'rational choice' is a misnomer because, while both the totally socialised and the totally unsocialised human calculate, neither need choose between alternative courses of action. Economic cost–benefit analysis entails neither more nor less choice than calculations couched in kinship or religious terms (Barnes 1990).

A more fruitful comparison, therefore, might begin with the recognition that trading practices in all markets, not simply peasant markets, are culturally consti- tuted. Actors in any market are linked by commodity exchanges and by social relationships, but they are also linked by shared, common-sense, taken-for-granted understandings about the ways in which transactions should be conducted and the ways in which they are conducted. To explain why market participants act in the way they do requires an understanding of the concepts they use to plan, execute and justify economic actions in their day-to-day activities. These understandings cannot be captured by simply glossing indigenous concepts with terms which are assumed to be universally applicable, such as debt, commodity or price. As is increasingly recognised, such terms and their indigenous equivalents do not denote unproblematic brute facts, but are cultural constructs requiring detailed analysis. [10] It should be stressed that to acknowledge that social change cannot be understood 'in the absence of an understanding of the passions and imaginings that provoke and inform it' (Geertz 1984:523) is not to retreat to the substantivist rather than the formalist bunker; nor is it to assert the hegemony of culture over economics, let alone to claim that 'rational calculation based on perceived self-interest is limited to indi- viduals in capitalist societies. The intention is an analysis which simultaneously recognises the complexity and cultural specificity of a particular economy and facilitates comparison. This goal, commonplace in other areas of anthropology, cannot be approached by counterposing the economic to the cultural as separate 'things'; or by metaphors which portray a bounded economy 'embedded' in social relations like peanuts in a cake.

A second, complementary approach is to essay a more comprehensive, and dialectical, process of comparison. Rather than use an idealised model of industrialised markets as a benchmark against which peasant markets can be measured – and not surprisingly found wanting – we might attempt to tack backwards and forwards between descriptions of the two social forms without privileging either. In other words, we should try to treat peasant and industrialised economies less as the poles of a reified dualistic model and more as a preliminary classification which will be refined, or even dissolved, in the course of analysis. It is in this spirit that I want to use studies of price-setting in Javanese markets to suggest some questions which might bear investigation in our own economy.

4. 3 THE ECONOMICS OF INFORMATION

Our earlier accounts of price-setting in Javanese markets followed the lead of anthropologists such as Geertz and Plattner in drawing on some literature in the economics of information. Although we attempted to describe the Javanese economy 'in its own terms' and concluded that some of the assumptions of the information interpretation were untenable, the problems investigated and the structure of our explanations were heavily influenced by the early work in this area of economics. Before briefly referring to some of the findings, therefore, I want to draw attention to some aspects of this literature which have been embraced by anthropologists.

It should be emphasised at the outset that the main thrust of the analysis within economics is towards the consequences of asymmetrically distributed information for the efficient operation of ideal markets. The ostensible concern of these studies is with what can be deduced from mathematical models based on precisely specified axioms, not with the realism of the axioms or with how economic actors cope with these difficulties. Even most economists, however, seem unhappy with Friedman's well-known claim that the realism of the economic axioms is an irrelevant consideration, for most papers are prefixed by a series of anecdotes which are apparently intended to anchor the axioms in the 'real world'.[11] It was these anecdotes, not the mathematical analysis which followed them, which inspired anthropologists.

Although it now encompasses a wide range of topics,[12] the pioneer studies in the economics of imperfect information concentrated on two discrete areas: imperfect information concerning prices and imperfect information concerning the quality of durable goods. The classic case of asymmetry in product quality is the used car market where, it is assumed, one can only discover the quality of a car by using it. The seller thus has perfect information; the buyer very little. Akerlof's initial formulation (1970) argued that this should inhibit the formation of a market because rational buyers, unable to discern the quality of any particular car, would pay only the lowest price; consequently above average cars would find no buyers at their appropriate price. In practice, firms operating in such markets cope with this problem by providing warranties or by establishing a good reputation and thus encouraging repeat purchases. Lacking facilities for establishing warranties, bazaar traders, who are seen as facing similar difficulties with most products they sell, are limited to the latter measure.

A second line of argument which has influenced anthropological analyses, most notably Geertz's (1979) marvellously intricate account of the Moroccan *suq*, was also originally illustrated by a comparison between the used car and new car markets (Rees 1971). In the latter, where all new cars are assumed to be identical, the rational buyer searches extensively: comparing a wide range of offers and taking the lowest. But in the used car market the rational buyer searches intensively: finding out as much as possible about a single car and negotiating the best price she can. While both patterns are found in both types of market, extensive search is supposedly the dominant pattern in industrialised societies and intensive search characteristic of bazaars.

The final example to which I want to draw attention is also concerned with search. Investigations of asymmetry in price information assume that, while prices are public knowledge, market imperfections mean that it takes time to discover them (Stigler 1971; Phlips 1988:39–56). The paradigm case is the cost of hotel rooms where buyers are assumed to know the range of prices but not which hotels charge which price. Analysis therefore concentrates on search costs: how many hotels should you contact before accepting the lowest price? As search costs – as well as other transaction costs – are supposedly much higher in bazaar economies, it becomes plausible to interpret some bazaar trading practices, especially 'clientalization' (Geertz 1979:260), as attempts to reduce them.

4. 4 PRICE-SETTING IN JAVANESE MARKETS

This literature, used at about this level of sophistication, was the stimulus for our attempts to understand the processes of price-setting in Javanese markets. The first of these papers (Alexander 1986) set out to explain how some vegetable traders were able to flourish and expand, despite numerous well-attested reports of relatively narrow differences between average wholesale and retail prices, and despite ethnographic observations that mark-ups in most transactions were small. The conclusion was that the successful traders had located themselves at strategic points in the marketing structure and were thus able to reconstruct prices in the system as a whole two or three days before this information became generally available. At times when prices were fluctuating, the traders used this information edge in negotiations with their suppliers or distributors and it was on these 'windfall profits', rather than the meagre returns from most transactions, that the business depended. [13]

Generalising this finding, we then argued that the extent of bargaining and the prices in individual transactions were functions of the extent to which the two parties recognised that they shared price information (Alexander and Alexander 1987). When they recognised that the level of shared information was high, in such cases as the purchase of everyday commodities or in many transactions between professional traders, bargaining was muted and produced a narrow price range which fed back to subsequent transactions. But when a trader suspected that her customer might be ill-informed – because she was a stranger, for example, or was seeking an infrequently purchased commodity – bargaining was protracted and the price range was wide.

This analysis of bargaining was in its turn used to contest the common view that the long-term trading partnerships reported for most peasant markets are essentially adaptations to information uncertainties which sacrifice short-term gains in the interests of long-term benefits (Alexander and Alexander 1991b). We suggested that trading partnerships are established in two quite different circumstances. In the first – most commonly involving farmers and middlemen or wholesalers and retailers – one partner had the power to set the price. The extent of the other's information was thus irrelevant for they were powerless to act on it.[14] In the second case, where neither party was forced to complete an individual transaction, stable trading relationships were predicated upon the recognition that both had accurate price information: it was this recognition which muted bargaining and produced low prices, not altruism or a calculus of long-term gains. Moreover, far from being adaptations to information deficiencies, it was the existence of such relationships at strategic points in the marketing structure which inhibited the flow of information through the system, giving both partners the advantage in other transactions on which their profits depended.

The conclusion to this third paper remarked, not entirely seriously, that as bargaining was a more economically efficient method of price-setting than posted prices, the salient, 'irrational' phenomenon which required explanation was not bargaining in bazaar economies, but the simultaneous presence in industrial economies of a dominant ideology of market efficiency and a pricing system which inhibits the efficient operation of the market. Suspecting that many a good social theory begins life as a joke, I want to push this argument a little further using Javanese markets, or at least our accounts of a Javanese market, to suggest some aspects of industrialised markets which might bear further examination. The first of these is the role of price competition in consumer markets.

4. 5 INFORMATION IN CONSUMER MARKETS

In the paradigmatic market of liberal economic theory, a large number of autonomous and equally well-informed buyers and sellers compete so that the agreed prices accurately reflect the relative strength of supply and demand. As I have noted above, Javanese markets only rarely approach this ideal. In many markets buyers and sellers are not autonomous actors but are linked by power relationships which make one partner only a passive participant in price-setting, forced to take (within broad limits) whatever price is offered. Even in those markets, perhaps the majority, where buyers and sellers are free to act as they wish and where both are reasonable judges of product quality, there are often significant asymmetries in price information. Although bargaining is usual in these cases and the resultant price ranges might be said to reflect the relative force of supply and demand more directly than in the first instance, prices within this range are skewed in favour of the more knowledgeable person.

But we should not move immediately to the conclusion that Javanese markets are less efficient than consumer markets in industrialised economies or that consumers are better placed to obtain accurate information about prices or quality than Javanese buyers. Although it is true that prices are public knowledge in consumer markets, this does not mean that they are easy to discover; marketing textbooks are full of devices which enable firms to blur price profiles. In fact, while prices are generally public, a general feature of consumer markets is that relatively uninformed buyers confront sellers who possess an expert's knowledge of product quality. The main reason for this information asymmetry is structural: the wide range of commodities for sale and high level of division of labour in their production and distribution ensure that manufacturers and retailers know far more about the cost, quality and supply of the range of commodities in which they deal than do their customers. Consumers are additionally handicapped because they must acquire information about each of the numerous commodities which they purchase. It is this asymmetry in information, as well as the large numbers of buyers relative to sellers, which gives sellers the power to set prices. This is one of the reasons why prices posted on a take-them or leave-them basis are characteristic of consumer markets. In very few transactions can an individual consumer adjust the price in her favour, and in such cases the lower price usually takes the form of a discount from the posted price – 'a special price for you, madam' – not the consumer offering to pay what she thinks the item is worth. Although there are potentially a number of different pricing systems which might be used in consumer markets, it is the sellers who both determine the general use of posted prices and set the individual prices. Sellers also have the upper hand in deciding the quality and quantity of goods to be sold in each transaction. Given modern packaging, it is difficult for even the most tenacious and skilful consumer to establish the relative quality of two differently-branded cans of tomatoes [15], or to purchase three batteries rather than two or four; let alone decide which insurance policy gives the better coverage or which bank account gives the higher yield.

With this in mind, I suggest that the salient feature of the used car market and the reason why it epitomises unethical trading practices in all societies (except apparently in the Netherlands) is less that the quality of the commodity can only be established after it is purchased, than that repeat purchases are infrequent and therefore the seller is seen to have little incentive to ensure value for money. It is one of the few occasions in which the consumer is made directly aware of her lack of power *vis-à-vis* the seller. But contrary to the assumptions of models constructed in the economically innocent age of the 1970s, most individuals purchasing new cars or other 'durable' consumer goods are faced with the same problem of product quality and deal with it in the same ways: by researching the dealer's reputation and by demanding a warranty or a money-back guarantee. In 'real life', purchasers of used cars do not act rationally: they do not, as micro-economic theory would suggest, assume that the car they buy will be a 'lemon' and demand an appropriately low price. Why they do not is no great mystery: it is the same reason why my Javanese friend, who supported his request for a substantial discount on a particular brand of new car by quoting media reports that they were defective, is still walking to work. To anticipate a later point, this concentration on product consistency, usually termed value-for-money, rather than price, seems deeply embedded in our economic culture.

I suggest therefore that consumer markets differ from Javanese markets both in the relative lack of shared information between buyer and seller and in the inability of even a well-informed buyer to affect the price in individual transactions. These two characteristics are analytically connected. By concentrating on information asymmetries between buyers and sellers in peasant markets, anthropologists have inadvertently obscured the point that a considerable degree of shared information concerning both quality and price is required if bargaining is to proceed at all. The common assumption that bargaining prevails in peasant markets primarily because commodities are 'physically heterogeneous and therefore non-substitutable' (Faneslow 1990:250) is difficult to reconcile with the observation that in our economy it is precisely those commodities which are most freely substitutable – stocks, currencies, bonds, futures and, to a lesser extent, precisely graded bulk commodities – that are usually traded in this manner. Far from eliminating bargaining, precise grading of commodities facilitates price discrimination as long as both negotiators are experts. In situations where buyers might be expected to lack the minimum knowledge required to sustain a negotiated-prices market, some form of indicative pricing is common. Javanese traders selling craftware to tourists post prices as an indication of where negotiations might begin. For similar reasons, trade associations of physicians or vehicle repairers dealing with customers generally unable to evaluate their services, issue price guidelines 'which serve not necessarily as the agreed-upon price the firm should charge, but as a pronouncement of the just price' (Glazer 1984:1095).

4. 6 SEARCH

Another way of exploring this question is in terms of the locus of competition. In Javanese markets, competition pits an individual buyer against an individual seller. The rational buyer searches for the item she requires and then negotiates an agreeable price. If negotiations fail, she begins again with another vendor. In other words, she engages in intensive rather than extensive search, although this distinction is more useful in ordering data than explaining it.

In consumer markets, however, the locus of competition is between sellers who compete to attract individual buyers. But the corollary that consumers do, or even should, search extensively for the best price is difficult to accept. One reason is that sellers in consumer markets do not normally engage in price competition. Instead they concentrate on non-price competition, attempting to increase their market share by offering potential customers a wide range of services including attractive surroundings and convenient locations, rapid delivery, credit, after-sales service, even a smiling staff. Despite the ideology of numerous suppliers competing to offer similar goods at different prices, the individual consumer is seldom able to find identical goods at dissimilar prices, for even if she suspects that identical commodities are being sold elsewhere at lower prices, the dispersal of sales points increases the monopoly power of the seller by increasing the customer's search costs.

This is not to argue that sellers do not purport to compete over price – the benefits of price competition are after all the moral justification for our economy – merely to argue that, at least from the point of view of an individual consumer seeking to purchase a particular item, such competition is mainly illusory, for the influence of supply and demand on prices is delayed and indirect. There are, of course, numerous examples which are advertised in ways which appear directly to contradict this assertion. But 'sales' or selling widely recognised branded items at below the usual price – 'loss leading' – are methods of establishing a reputation for low prices or blurring price profiles, not a mechanism for clearing goods for which demand is low.[16] Ironically, the few examples of genuine price competition – the identical product selling for significantly different prices at accessible outlets – are often seen as unfair and to require state intervention: gasoline retailing is the paradigm case (Shepard 1990).

This comparison of the role of price competition in Javanese markets with its role in consumer markets in industrialised economies does accord with one prediction of the information model: price competition is most important in those markets with numerous well-informed buyers and sellers. It is in these, peasant, markets, not consumer markets, that price is the main weapon of competition.[17]

4. 7 PRICE-SETTING IN CONSUMER MARKETS

'Bargaining is at once the most obvious, and the most elusive, activity in the peasant market-place' (Alexander 1987:162). Gathering empirical data on the bargaining process in individual transactions is certainly a difficult ethnographic task, for the techniques used by the participants, such as switching currency units or rapidly diverting attention from one item to another, are intended to confuse or mislead their opponent. But despite these difficulties, we now have a range of fine-grained information from a number of peasant economies which illustrates how prices were negotiated in individual transactions.

By comparison, it is the process of price-setting in industrialised economies which remains opaque. The difference between 'command' and 'market' economies, or more precisely, between administered prices which are unresponsive to forces of supply and demand, and prices set by the market which are – by definition – completely responsive, has more than a little contemporary political significance. Yet an important paper published in 1986 begins as follows: 'an important unanswered question is, just how rigid are prices? Despite the great interest in this question, there have been virtually no attempts to answer it with data on individual transaction prices' (Carlton 1986:637).

The findings in this and other studies (Okun 1981; Williamson 1975), however, suggest that the usual practices of price-setting in industrialised economies bear little relationship to those assumed by market models. Carlton (1986:638), for example, remarks that although the costs of changing prices appear to be small, 'it is not unusual in some industries for prices to individual buyers to be unchanged for several years'. Moreover, prices do not change in the same way at the same time for all buyers: where buyer and seller have only a short association, prices are more likely to be rigid but also change in greater jumps; longer established trading partnerships result in smaller, but more frequent changes. If similar data were reported by an anthropologist studying a peasant market, we would surely infer that there was a social component to these ostensibly economic relationships and expect a careful and systematic account of the ways in which these transactions were carried out.[18]

For this innocent reader, the most striking aspect of the economics literature about price-setting is the overwhelming concentration on auctions,[19] although most trades are not conducted in this way. In a recent survey, Milgrom (1989) remarks that because of this lack of research, only informed guesses are possible concerning the circumstances which make one or another trading institution appropriate. When he is explaining why auctions – the most economically efficient form – are not used more often, his guesses seem plausible. They are less so with respect to the widespread preference for posted prices rather than the more economically efficient bargaining (he, like other economists, slips easily into the pejorative term, haggling). Milgrom's main point, that bargaining is costly in societies where time has a high value,[20] begs a number of issues, the most important of which is the relationship between the cost of time and the cost of the item. In situations 'where the opportunity to gain from price discrimination is low' (1989:18), Javanese, if not western tourists, spend little time haggling; but why don't consumers not bargain strongly when buying expensive items? His second point, that the 'lack of a fixed price makes it easy for the salesman to steal or take kickbacks from the buyer' (1989:18; compare Lazear 1986: 30) is initially more compelling. It does, however, force the conclusion that South-east Asian employees are unusually honest, for many South-east Asian firms do not fix prices for their products.[21] In my view, both points skirt the main issue: fixed, posted prices increase managerial control at the cost of reducing the firm's profits. The critical feature of this form of pricing is that it can be systematised; the calculation of prices delegated to clerks and audited by managers. Such pricing may also lower costs by deskilling sales staff; reducing their function to giving change.

Managerial control is further facilitated by the ways in which fixed prices are calculated. In his important book *Prices and Quantities*, Okun concludes, somewhat despairingly, 'It is much easier to document empirically the widespread nature of cost-orientated pricing practices *and their acceptance as inherently fair* than it is to provide an analytical foundation for these practices and attitudes' (1981:154, emphasis added). He shows that firms establish precise methods for defining and measuring costs, the operation of which is delegated to clerks. Once this system of cost-accounting is routinised, the firm need only decide on the markup to be applied to the unit cost in setting the price of their products. It is at this point, the determination of the magnitude of the markup, that the firm estimates the level of demand for its product and sets markups accordingly. Okun emphasises that generally speaking, markups change infrequently and are not heavily influenced upwards by perceived levels of demand: manufacturers with a long waiting list for their products do not increase markups for this reason.[22] Consequently prices are much more responsive to changes in costs than to changes in demand, and therefore prices may increase when demand is falling.

At root, as the emphasised phrase in the quotation suggests, Okun's explanation for the prevalence of cost-plus pricing is cultural: 'price increases based on cost increases are generally accepted as fair, but many that might be based on demand increases are ruled out as unfair' (1981:170). This sounds intuitively right to me: it seems reasonable for the cinemas to charge $5 less on Tuesdays because demand is less; it would be a 'rip-off' if they charged $5 more on Saturdays when demand was greater. Put in more general terms: discounts are OK because you appear to be getting a bargain.

4. 8 WHAT'S IN A PRICE ?

The conclusion I wish to draw from this is that understanding our economy requires an understanding of our notion of price, not in the technical sense it is used in economics, but the way it is used in everyday life to plan, execute and justify economic decisions. To do this properly requires detailed ethnographic fieldwork but some preliminary remarks are possible. [23]

When compared to Javanese concepts, the most remarkable feature of our view of price is our stubborn belief, despite all evidence, that there is a close relationship between price and value. Deep down inside, we all know that commodities and services have an appropriate price – a fair price – and should normally be traded at this price, although in special conditions prices may be lower. One reason for the robustness of this view, is the continuing stress in advertisements on value for money, another is the observation that prices seldom fluctuate (perishable foodstuffs are one important exception) and that the gradual increases are always justified in terms of increasing costs. 'Firms not only behave that way, but also condition their customers to expect them to behave that way' (Okun 1981:153). We recognise, of course, that a fair price may be difficult to calculate, in part because the notion of 'costs' is also culturally constituted: how much should be added by an exclusive dress-maker, for example, as the cost of producing only one or two of each item. Inherent in this notion, and one of the reasons why we often find bargaining abhorrent, is that prices should be the same for all.

This belief is central to the process by which our economy is reproduced. Whereas in Java price-setting is a public event in which the buyer actively participates, price-setting in our economy always takes place behind the scenes. If these practices are to be sustained, therefore, consumers must have some confidence in the justice of this process, for they are seldom privy to details and are thus unable to intervene in it. The philosophically inclined may speak of competition among firms as 'keeping the bastards honest', but I think that most people expect that even in the absence of direct competition, firms will, in broad terms, act fairly. This is presumably the source of what is surely the most unrealistic assumption of modern economic theory, at least until the past decade: the assumption that persons or firms only pursue their self-interest by relatively honest means, instead of by force or fraud. The supposedly atomised actors in our markets have so thoroughly internalised the rules of the game that fraud is inconceivable, and much of the ideological appeal of the image of the self-regulating market is the notion that force or fraud is suppressed by competitive forces (Granovetter 1985:483–7). It has often been claimed that traders in inefficient peasant markets have particular problems in establishing trust: it would truly be ironic if systemic trust should prove central to the operation of our own economy.

This chapter has only a genealogical relationship to the paper I presented at the conference, but draws heavily on the discussions. The research was funded by the Australian Research Council and by the Netherlands Institute for Advanced Studies in the Humanities and Social Sciences.

NOTES

1. To avoid sinking in a definitional swamp, I use these terms interchangeably to refer to non-industrialised market economies.
2. It is the combination of practices which constitutes the bazaar, examples of each of the individual practices can be found in industrial markets. There is now a very large literature on this topic, some representative studies not cited elsewhere in this chapter include: Beals (1975), Dewey (1962) Geertz (1963) Smart (1989).
3. There are, of course, several very good descriptions of the structure of information in peasant economies (eg. Szanton 1972, Davis 1973) as well as a number of detailed analyses of transaction prices (see note 9). But with the exception of Geertz (1979) and Alexander (1987), the ethnographically rich studies do not interpret their data in terms of access to information. For an excellent ethnographic account (by an economist) of the control of information in an industrial market see Wilson (1980).
4. Much of this section is taken from Alexander and Alexander (1991b).
5. For examples of these assumptions see any current textbook in micro-economics (compare Plattner 1985:134–6). For a demonstration that the assumption of an equilibrium price is untenable see Salop & Stiglitz (1982).
6. For those scholars strongly influenced by economics, the most convincing evidence that peasant markets are inefficient and therefore underdeveloped is the lack of a single price for similar commodities (for example Fanselow 1990:254 and Finan 1988: 704). For economists, 'Price dispersion is a manifestation – and indeed, it is a measure – of ignorance in the market' (Stigler 1971:62). But, as is discussed below, a lack of price dispersal is not necessarily an indication of efficiency.
7. While there remain considerable differences of opinion concerning the extent to which traders in peasant markets pursue their own self-interest, there is now a well established line of analysis which explains apparently altruistic actions in terms of long-term insurance goals (Scott 1976). Part of the problem is the use of the notion of self-interest as if it was unambiguous and culture free: as Granovetter (1985:483–5) points out, the atomised, single-mindedly self-interested agent is a caricature of economic actors in a market economy.
8. Geertz (1979) and Alexander (1987) are notable exceptions.
9. A recent study is Okun (1981), but Dalton (1959) remains among the most comprehensive discussion of this topic in the United States economy. Accounts of price-setting in peasant markets are, by comparison, plentiful. They include Firth (1942:189–202), Davis (1973:158–67), Geertz (1979), Issacs (1981), P. Alexander (1982:170–5), Cook (1982:261–78), J. Alexander (1986), and Alexander and Alexander (1987). Cassady (1974) and Modjeska (1985) are among the few explicitly comparative analyses.
10. Accounts of 'debt' include Gregory (1988) and Rudner (1989); 'commodity' Appadurai (1986); 'price' Cook (1982) and Alexander (1987).
11. For an interesting discussion of the role of narrative and mathematical metaphor in economics see McCloskey (1986:69-86, 138–52).
12. A recent comprehensive review is Phlips (1988).
13. This seems to be a very common pattern in produce markets, see Wilson (1980:500)
14. For a detailed and compelling account of such relationships in a Philippine market, see Russell (1987). In two of the best documented studies of 'equilibrating' relation-

ships, one partner sets the price (Acheson 1985; Finan 1988). Note also that in one of these examples it is the buyer who is most powerful, in the other the seller. Fanselow's assertion (1990:251) that there is a general information asymmetry in bazaar economies 'between the seller, who passes on something uncertain in return for something certain [money] and the buyer, who does the reverse' is ethnographically unsound for other reasons as well: in many situations goods are not traded for cash but for a promise to pay.

15. Compare Fanselow (1990:253): 'The introduction of brand names ... moves competition from the relationship between buyer and seller to the relationship between sellers, because buyers are consistently able to identify the provenance and quality of a good and therefore exercise choice between different products'.

16 'Since consumers learn by experience, they will discover, as time elapses, which shops persistently have low prices. For price dispersion to persist, it is necessary that the price image of a shop be blurred over time' (Phlips 1988:14).

17. Societies in which hierarchically organised firms, of whatever size, operate alongside peasant traders, confirm this point. In Sierra Leone, Issacs (1981:361) found
    'a pronounced difference between shopkeepers and hawkers. Price competition among the latter takes the form of retail price differentials, whereas among the former it is evidenced in the very strong tendency toward retail price equalisation, even among firms that obtain a commodity at widely varying wholesale prices. '
Similar findings have been reported for Java (Geertz 1963) and the Philippines (Dannhaeuser 1983).

18.   Their most striking features are the absence of bargaining, lack of apparent competition among sellers and uniform and largely inflexible prices. . . . In their demeanour both buyers and sellers assume that the advantage lies with the seller – buyers are free to purchase or not at the seller's set terms of trade. (Modjeska 1985:156)
This is not a description of a Western shopping mall, but a producer market in Papua New Guinea.

19. At least one of the contributors to this literature is sceptical of its value: 'Too much recent research effort in auctions has been simply applying the latest techniques ... to ever more complicated models; too little has been devoted to the very real and important economic questions that auctions raise (Milgrom 1985:261). Five years later there had evidently been no progress on one of the questions he raises: the comparison of alternative modes of transaction. See also Ashenfelter (1989).

20. As Geertz (1979:263) points out, 'the notion that supply elasticities of time are very high in the bazaar ... could hardly be more wrong'.

21. Nor do the larger firms permit true bargaining; price-setting usually involves negotiations within a graded series of discounts.

22. For a convincing demonstration that the rational strategy for a firm is to set prices high and adjust them downwards, see Lazear (1986).

23. For a social-psychological discussion of attitudes to the pricing system which mainly indicates how little is known, see Frey (1986). For a discussion of some of the problems in writing an ethnography of economic systems see Marcus and Fischer (1986:90–95).

REFERENCES

Acheson, J. 1985. 'Social Organisation of the Maine Lobster Market', in S. Plattner (ed.), *op cit.*, pp. 105–132.

Akerlof, G. A. 1970. '"The Market for Lemons": Quality Uncertainty and the Market Mechanism', *Quarterly Journal of Economics,* 84:488–500.

Alexander, J. 1986. 'Information and Price-setting in a Rural Javanese Market', *Bulletin of Indonesian Economic Studies*, 22: 88–112.

Alexander, J. 1987. *Trade Traders and Trading in Rural Java.* Singapore: Oxford University Press.

Alexander, J. and P. Alexander, 1987. 'Striking a Bargain in Javanese Markets', *Man*, 22: 42–68.

Alexander, J. and P. Alexander, 1991a. 'Protecting Peasants From Capitalism: The Subordination of Javanese Traders by the Colonial State', *Comparative Studies in Society and History*, 33(2):370–94.

Alexander, J. and P. Alexander, 1991b. 'What's a Fair Price? Price-setting and Trading Partnerships in Javanese Markets', *Man*, 26(3): 493–512.

Alexander, P. 1982. *Sri Lankan Fishermen: Rural Capitalism and Peasant Society.* Canberra: Australian National University Press.

Appadurai, A. (ed.), 1986. *The Social Life of Things: Commodities in Cultural Perspective.* London: Cambridge University Press.

Ashenfelter, O. 1989. 'How Auctions Work for Wine and Art', *Journal of Economic Perspectives*, 3 (3):23–35.

Barnes, B. 1990. 'Macro-economics and Infant Behaviour: a Sociological Treatment of the Free-Rider Problem', *Sociological Review*, 38(2):272–92.

Beals, R. L. 1975. *The Peasant Marketing System of Oaxaca, Mexico.* Berkeley: University of California Press.

Carlton, D. W. 1986. 'The Rigidity of Prices', *American Economic Review*, 76 (3):637–58.

Cassady, R. 1974. *Exchange by Private Treaty.* Austin: University of Texas Press.

Cook, S. 1982. *Zapotec Stonecutters: the Dynamics of Rural Simple Commodity Production in Modern Mexican Capitalism.* Lanham: University Press of America.

Dannhaeuser, N. 1983. *Contemporary Trade Strategies in the Philippines: A Study of Marketing Anthropology.* New Brunswick, N. J.: Rutgers University Press.

Dalton, M. 1959. *Men Who Manage.* New York: Wiley.

Davis, W. G. 1973. *Social Relations in a Philippines Market: Self-Interest and Subjectivity.* Berkeley: University of California Press.

Dewey, A. G. 1962. *Peasant Marketing in Java.* Glencoe, Illinois: The Free Press.

Fanselow, F. S. 1990. 'The Bazaar Economy Or How Bizarre is the Bazaar Really?', *Man*, 25:250–65.

Finan, F. J. 1988. 'Market Relationships and Market Performance in North-east Brazil', *American Ethnologist*, 15 (4): 694–709.

Firth, R. 1942. *Malay Fishermen.* London: Routledge.

Frey, B. S. 1986. 'Economists Favour the Price System – Who else Does?', *Kylos*, 39(4): 537–63.

Geertz, C. 1963. *Peddlers and Princes: Social Change and Economic Modernisation in Two Indonesian Towns.* Chicago: University of Chicago Press.

Geertz, C. 1978. 'The Bazaar Economy: Information and Search in Peasant Marketing', *American Economic Review*, 68: 28–32.

Geertz, C. 1979. 'Suq: The Bazaar Economy in Sefrou', in C. Geertz, H. Geertz and L. Rosen, *Meaning and Order in Moroccan Society: Three Essays in Cultural Analysis.* Cambridge: Cambridge University Press. pp. 123–313.

Geertz, C. 1984. 'Culture and Social Change: The Indonesian Case', *Man*, 19 (4): 511–32.

Glazer, A. 1984. 'The Client Relationship and a "Just" Price', *American Economic Review*, 74:1089–95.

Granovetter, M. 1985. 'Economic Action and Social Structure: the Problem of Embeddedness', *American Journal of Sociology*, 91:481–510.

Gregory, C. A. 1988. 'Village Moneylending, The World Bank and Landlessness in Village India', *Journal of Contemporary Asia*, 18:47–58.

Gudeman, S. 1986. *Economics as Culture: Models and Metaphors of Livelihood.* London: Routledge and Kegan Paul.

Issacs, B. L. 1981. 'Price, Competition, and Profits among Hawkers and Shopkeepers in Pendembu, Sierra Leone: An Inventory Approach', *Economic Development and Cultural Change,* 29 (2):353–73.

Landa, J. T. 1981. 'A Theory of the Ethnically Homogeneous Middleman Group: A Institutional Alternative to Contract Law', *Journal of Legal Studies,* 10:349–63.

Lazear, E. P. 1986. 'Retail Pricing and Clearance Sales', *American Economic Review,* 76 (1): 14–32.

McCloskey, D. N. 1985. *The Rhetoric of Economics.* Madison: University of Wisconsin Press.

Marcus, G. E. and M. Fischer (eds.), 1986. *Anthropology as Cultural Critique. An Experimental Moment in the Human Sciences.* Chicago: University of Chicago Press.

Milgrom, P. R. 1985. 'The Economics of Competitive Bidding: A Selective Survey', in L. Harwicz *et al.* (eds.), *Social Goals and Social Organisation.* New York: Cambridge University Press.

Milgrom, P. R. 1989. 'Auctions and Bidding: A Primer', *Journal of Economic Perspectives,* 3:3–36.

Mintz, S. W. 1964. 'The Employment of Capital by Market Women in Haiti', in R. Firth & B. Yamey (eds.), *Capital, Saving and Credit in Peasant Societies.* Chicago: Aldine Press.

Modjeska, D. N. 1985. 'Exchange Value and Melanesian Trade Reconsidered', *Mankind,* 15 (2):145–62.

Okun, A. M. 1981. *Prices and Quantities. A Macroeconomic Analysis.* Oxford: Basil Blackwell.

Phlips, L. 1988. *The Economics of Imperfect Information.* Cambridge: Cambridge University Press.

Plattner, S. 1983. 'Economic Custom in a Competitive Marketplace', *American Anthropologist,* 85:848–58.

Plattner, S. 1985. 'Equilibrating Market Relationships', S. Plattner (ed.), *op cit.*, pp. 133–152.

Plattner, S. (ed.), 1985. *Markets and Marketing.* Monographs in Economic Anthropology No. 4. Lanham: University Press of America.

Posner, R. A. 1980. 'A Theory of Primitive Society, with Special Reference to Law', *Journal of Law and Economics,* 33:1–53.

Rees, A. 1971. 'Information Networks in Labour Markets', in D. M. Lammerton (ed.), *The Economics of Information and Knowledge.* Harmondsworth: Penguin. pp. 109–18.

Rudner, O. 1989. 'Banker's Trust and the Culture of Banking among the Nattukottai Chettiars of Colonial South India', *Modern Asian Studies,* 23 (3) 417–58.

Russell, S. D. 1987. 'Middlemen and Moneylending: Relations of Exchange in a Highland Philippines Economy', *Journal of Anthropological Research,* 139–61.

Salop, S. C. and J. E. Stiglitz, 1982. 'The Theory of Sales: A Simple Model of Equilibrium Price Dispersion with Identical Agents', *American Economic Review,* 72: 1121–30.

Scott, J. S. 1976. *The Moral Economy of the Peasant.* New York: Yale University Press.

Shepard, A. 1990. 'Pricing Behavior and Vertical Contracts in Retail Markets', *American Economic Review,* 80(2):427–31.

Smart, J. 1989. *The Political Economy of Street Hawkers in Hong Kong.* Hong Kong: University of Hong Kong.

Smith, A. 1776 [1979]. *The Wealth of Nations.* Harmondsworth: Penguin.

Stigler, G. J. 1971. 'The Economics of Information and Knowledge', in D. M.

Lammerton (ed.), *The Economics of Information and Knowledge.* Harmondsworth: Penguin. pp. 61–82.

Szanton, M. C. B. 1972. *A Right to Survive: Subsistence Marketing In a Lowland Philippines Town.* Pennsylvania: Pennsylvania State University Press.

Tax, S. 1953. *Penny Capitalism: A Guatamalan Indian Economy.* Washington: Smithsonian Institution.

Trager, L. 1981. 'Customers and Creditors: Variations in Economic Personalism in a Nigerian Marketplace', *Ethnology,* 20:133–45.

Uchendu, V. C. 1967. 'Some Principles of Haggling in Peasant Markets', *Economic Development and Cultural Change,* 16:37–50.

Williamson, O. 1975. *Markets and Hierarchies.* New York: Free Press.

Wilson, J. A. 1980. 'Adaptation to Uncertainty and Small Numbers Exchange: the New England Fresh Fish Market', *The Bell Journal of Economics,* 11: 491–504.

5

Gypsies at the Horse-Fair

A Non-Market Model of Trade

MICHAEL STEWART

Romany-speaking Gypsies are the main movers of horses in the weekly fairs that are held across the Hungarian countryside throughout the annual agricultural cycle. Unlike Hungarian peasant workers who both breed and raise horses and use them productively (for carting and in agriculture) Gypsies acquire horses in order to sell them at a profit: they are traders between peasant users of these noble animals. Gypsies moreover are both seen by peasants and see themselves as people supremely suited to the role of horse-trader. A Hungarian ethnologist echoed a common assertion among his rural countrymen when he said of this profession that the Gypsies especially have a predilection for [it] …because for this no more is needed than a good whip' [Kiss 1939: 277] and, he might have added, a loud voice. Gypsies are as happy to accept this role, referring to themselves as 'boys of the "market"' (*forroske save*)

I have put the word 'market' in inverted commas here because in Romany there is no term for market; *forro*, also means 'town'. For Gypsies the *forro* is the location of generalised possibilities of dealing, of those appeals to other people's, especially non-Gypsies' (*gazos'*) needs which form the basis of the Gypsy trader's activity. The implication that there is not a distinct part of Gypsy life devoted to market behaviour is significant but can be left to one side at the moment. Passing over questions of terminology, to an outside observer there would be no hesitation in seeing the horse-fairs as markets in the classic sense of the term: there are numerous buyers and sellers in competition with one another; prices are freely agreed as a result of bargaining; more formally speaking, these prices fluctuate in co-ordination across these fairs at least within Hungary. Horse-trading was also, when research was conducted in 1985–6, integrated into a partial market economy in that horse-prices fluctuated in line with other prices in a more or less co-ordinated fashion despite the socialist planning of the overall Hungarian economy.[1]

It would seem reasonable then to try to analyse Gypsy behaviour in markets using the procedures devised by economic analysis which were explicitly formulated in response to the development of market exchange in north-western Europe some three centuries ago. Western economic theory is above all a theory of the economy as a market: it ought therefore at the least to be able to account for behaviour in 'actually existing' markets. Indeed the received wisdom in much economic anthropology has been that whatever the limitations of market analysis for 'gift' or 'redistributive' economies its analytic power was proven in explaining market institutions. Polanyi's work provides a classic illustration of this point of view. The flip side of Polanyi's renowned rejection of market economics in the analysis of primitive, so-called embedded economies was his barely critical acceptance of formalist economics for 'self-regulating market economies'.

Polanyi's position had disastrous consequences for the anthropological analysis of real-life markets. In their introduction to the volume *Markets in Africa* (1962) Polanyi's followers Dalton and Bohannon were forced to reduce the 'market princi-ple' to the operation of a 'law of supply and demand' and then using this as a criteria tried to make an entirely extraneous and arbitrary distinction between the economic and non-economic aspects of the markets they confronted. [2] In this chapter I try to provide an integrated discussion of horse-trade without analytically privileging one moment of these exchanges.

5. I NEO-CLASSICISM AND ACTUALLY EXISTING MARKETS

Economic and other anthropologists have for long attacked the use of neo-classical models which predicate the 'individual maximiser of utility' as an ahistorical universal category. Even Stuart Plattner, a relatively formalist economic anthropologist – he is pleased by explanations which avoid reference to 'differences of cultural or economic values and goals' (1989:221) – points out some 'unrealistic assumptions' (1989:8) in the utility maximisation theory. This does not impinge however on Plattner (*inter alia*) remaining attached to much else in the neo-classical paradigm. [3]

My chapter however takes a different critical perspective and questions the use of another basic concept in economics, the notion of rational calculation as an analytical tool in understanding the activity of market agents. My aim is not so much to prove the irrelevance of neo-classical economics to Gypsy behaviour in horse-fairs: that bourgeois economic thought is profoundly inadequate to the social processes ob-served here, even if we restrict ourselves to the so-called 'purely economic aspect' of horse-traders, ought to be apparent from the presentation of the ethnography. My aim is rather to throw into relief some of the unstated assumptions of our economic models as the first step towards understanding Gypsy trading in its own terms.

Neo-classical economics is a powerful statement of the idea that the economy can be conceived of as a market, that all the processes of making a livelihood can be seen as market-type exchanges. The suggestion that by metaphorical extension production can be seen as a special instance of buying and selling has of course been widely criticised by economists of the left. My critique instead concerns the relevance of neo-classicism to the object from which it claims to be directly drawn.

The neo-classical paradigm can be laid out adequately if crudely: the starting block is an ideal type market of a single, standardised product. The theory attempts to describe the conditions (prices, quantities and qualities) under which this market will reach what is known technically as 'equilibrium', that is the state in which as a result of perfect competition a market will clear (and by implication all buyers and sellers will be maximally satisfied). Note that the theory does not primarily concern itself with the process by which equilibrium comes about, rather with the nature of market clearance as a state and its necessary conditions. If there is a social force at work leading to equilibrium it is the law of supply and demand: as explained on the blackboards of Economics lecture halls the intersection of the market supply curve with the market demand curve gives on the one hand the price and on the other hand the output towards which the market tends and at which it clears.

For anthropologists interested in the nature of cosmological systems there are a number of striking features about this one. First, contrary to appearances it is not only a formal model of economic linkages, but it is also a model of social co-ordination or social integration since it is asserted that through the price mechanism the decentralised activities of numerous agents are co-ordinated so that in equilibrium all plans of the agents at any one time are fulfilled. At a global or societal level it is thus that (Pareto) optimal allocation of all resources is achieved. Note that equilibrium is not some weak form of co-ordination, but a perfectly harmonious state in which by definition there can be no room for change because perfect functional integration has been achieved.

This can be put slightly differently. In the neo-classical model people are assumed to have perfect knowledge of the world and of the intentions of others: consumers are aware of all purchase opportunities, resource owners are aware of all selling opportunities and firms are aware of all cost and revenue conditions. As Israel Kirzner, a critic, puts it, the state of equilibrium is:

> one in which *no* market ignorance is present. We […] then have a pattern of perfectly dovetailing decisions. No decision made will fail to be carried out, and no opportunity will fail to be exploited. Each market participant will have correctly forecast all the relevant decisions of others … . Clearly, with such a state of affairs the market *process* must immediately cease. (1973: 11).

Or, as an anthropologist might see it, in equilibrium we are in nirvana, a religious state of utopia where not just the market process but all social process has come to an end.

The neo-classical approach with its emphasis on the economic conditions necessary for equilibrium obviously does not lend itself to empirical analysis of real-life markets where it is the *market process* above all which catches the attention of an observer and which one wants to explain. The market process rests, among other things, on the existence of actors' ignorance: it is precisely the uneven distribution of knowledge (and as we shall see of trading skills) between traders and peasants which allows profits to be made: if peasants 'knew' how to buy horses as cheaply as the Gypsies fewer would come to market.

There is a further implication, though, of neo-classical price theory which has equally restrictive implications. This is a point which Kirzner brings out: 'the price system in equilibrium presents each decision-maker with a fully coordinated set of signals, which, if followed, will permit all plans to dovetail' (1973: 219). That is to say that rational economic action in this system implies accepting that at any time there is a single optimal course of action which can be determined by calculation using one's present state of knowledge. Action in a market is then encompassed by Lionel

Robbins's model of allocation of known scarce resources to given ends. The point I wish to stress is the implicit opposition here between the ideas of rational calculation and intentionality. For economic man to react rationally to the world is to accept the given conditions in which we live, to fit like a cog into a machine of moving parts the motor of which is quite invisible to us and far beyond our manipulation. Anything else, any attempt to take fate into our own hands appears in this model as irrational. But since almost all market behaviour can be analysed precisely as attempts to alter the terms of trade, to back one's hunches, to grasp imaginatively possibilities unforeseen by others and then persuade one's exchange partners to see the world as one sees it oneself, the main object of market studies appears to be irrational behaviour. The expanding literature on the irrationality of bazaars where peasants 'interfere' with rational methods of price determination (for example Geertz 1979) is evidence of the influence of this view within anthropology.

Now Gypsies, despite being at the very bottom of the Hungarian social pile (indeed, perhaps precisely because they have no claim on the system whatsoever) do not conceive of their relationship to horse-markets in the passive, accepting way called for by rational calculation. Gypsy models of trade and price setting have inscribed in them notions of actors' agency over the terms of trade and potency over their exchange partners. Robbinsian economising is not, I suggest, going to be of much help in understanding this behaviour, however appropriate it may be for describing the allocative actions of managers within firms.

So there are three crucial assumptions or implications of the neo-classical model which make it a priori difficult to use for understanding real-life market behaviour: its focus on assumed principles of action rather than actors' behaviour; its assumption that we can talk as if equilibrium pertained; and its implication that rational economic behaviour is effectively responsive, that actors in markets are passive price-takers, not imaginative brokers.

5. 2 AN ENTREPRENEURIAL MODEL OF MARKET BEHAVIOUR

Frustrated by the inapplicability of Robbinsian models of economic action I, among others, have hunted for alternative accounts of market behaviour. P. Alexander (this volume) provides a critique of one such alternative model of price formation: that developed by managerial studies and the economics of information. Using my research among Gypsies, I will consider an alternative attempt to get beyond the theoretical cul-de-sac of neo-classicism. My source is the work of one of Hayek's pupils, a member of the Austrian school whose writings have a surprisingly direct bearing on the analytical problems I face.

Israel Kirzner's starting-point is that of his teacher Hayek: he rejects the idea that the market is an effortlessly functioning computer because this assumes away all the crucial problems of economic co-ordination. These arise from the fact that in human society the information necessary to make decisions is dispersed as 'bits of incomplete and frequently contradictory knowledge which all the separate individuals possess' (Hayek 1945:520). Hayek's major argument is of course that the competitive market process is the best means known for co-ordinating this knowledge. In this chapter I take over instead Kirzner's stress on the disequilibrium pertaining in markets at any time and his development of the concept of entrepreneurship. Disequilibrium is patently the order of the day in horse-fairs (there are information asymmetries; there is a range of prices for goods of one quality and the market does not clear) and so Kirzner is already better equipped to act as guide than the neo-classicists. More importantly in Kirzner's hands the concept of entrepreneurship, which he explicitly seeks to make psychologically plausible, appears to come close to capturing some crucial features of Gypsy market behaviour. [4]

The first notable feature of Kirzner's work is that he is concerned with market process, that is the process by which, amongst other things, prices change over time due to the action of human agents, or put more generally how people change their plans as a result of market participation. In other words, there is a concern with time, with perception of possibilities and with active intervention by actors. In attempting to characterise the behaviour of entrepreneurs Kirzner is led to look at the creative process of adaptation (learning) involving fertility of the imagination, flashes of insight and the readiness to take on uncertainty and risk. Whereas neo-classicism offered no model of behaviour, Kirzner has at least provided a theory which can be challenged.

Second, Kirzner views entrepreneurial action as arbitrage: entrepreneurs notice price discrepancies and act on them (1973: 16). There are other market roles in Kirzner's model (for example, for asset owners) but that of the entrepreneur is specific in that all that is involved is perception of the possibility of pure gain. [5] All an entrepreneur has to do is to become aware of arbitrage possibilities and so 'the opportunities [the entrepreneur] thus offers to the market can in principle be made available by anyone' (1973:16).

Though Kirzner's economics is open to several lines of attack, this account of market behaviour will be seen to have an uncanny resemblance to the activity of Gypsies. It is precisely because of this unexpectedly neat fit between theory and data that the ultimate failure of Kirzner's model is significant and tells us something about the nature of capitalist folk-models of the economy.

At this point before launching into the ethnography, I must enter a caveat. In this chapter I will at times construct an oversimplified contrast between Gypsy notions of trade and prevalent capitalist ones. It is agreed by most anthropologists now that in any society there are a diversity of models and metaphors of livelihood which are to some extent in conflict and competition with one another. In making my model of Gypsy models and contrasting it with a dominant one of our own I do not wish to deny this important fact.

5. 3 SOCIALIST HORSE FAIRS

Before describing Gypsy trading behaviour I should say a few words about the place of horse-markets in the Hungarian socialist economy. At the outset of the socialist period it was thought that the role of such 'primitive' economic instruments as fairs would gradually diminish. But Kadar's 'Goulash' socialism being what it was, by the time of fieldwork in 1985 there was a fairly healthy trade in horses and the livestock fairs I attended were impressive affairs easily filling the whole market-field. [6] At a large market in the centre of the country in May one might find 400 or more horses for sale.

At this time Gypsy involvement in horse dealing was intense: some 70 per cent of the horses driven up to market were in Gypsy hands. [7] It is crucial, however, to realise that Gypsy wealth in horses resulted less from a sudden wave of success as traders in a market over which they had never had control than from better wage-labour opportunities Gypsies have enjoyed since the mid-1960s. In a word, most Gypsies I knew in 1985 were only able to acquire horses by using money originally earned in wage-labour in factories. The most common route to the acquisition of a horse was for a man to invest the better part of a month's wages in a set of piglets. Six piglets bought for 3,000 forints could be sold as pigs for 23–30,000 forints six to nine months later at minimal financial outlay thanks to the efforts of Gypsy wives and daughters who scavenged the rubbish bins of the Hungarian housing estates for fodder. When the pigs were then sold to the state slaughterhouse by the male household head the proceeds and the better part of another month's wages provided the means to acquire a horse of average quality (about. 25–30,000 forints).

Note also that although there are a few Gypsies whose horse-trade has 'taken off' and who successfully 'turn horses round', for the majority of men buying a horse is a gamble that only rarely pays off. It is hard to calculate profit in dealing - Gypsies invariably exaggerate their takings and for many men a profitable deal is one which allows them to buy another horse and try their luck again rather than one which produces an absolute profit. But at least half the deals I observed failed to produce a financial return once one had taken into account fodder and travel expenses. In many more than a few deals I recorded an outright loss.

Despite this, I argue that through trading Gypsies assert a degree of control over the outside world, or at least a rejection of the control which outside forces try to exert over the Gypsies. The money which Gypsies appear to win in trading, provides a basis, ideologically at least, for a cycle of feasting and celebration in which Gypsy brotherhood, the key idiom of community, is established (see Stewart, 1989). Earnings from wage-work, though more important economically are by contrast ideologically devalued. In horse fairs-macro-economic forces and micro-level powers which shape Gypsy lives are thus effectively denied.

5. 4 A DAY AT THE MARKET

In presenting the activity of Gypsies at markets I wish to invert the actual temporal order of exchanges. Horse-markets are divided into two partially distinct phases as far as the Gypsies are concerned: firstly, Gypsies buy from and sell to (*kinel / bikinel*) the peasants, then later in the day as the peasants leave and before the police move in to clear the Gypsies from the square, they 'swap' (*paruvel*) their remainng horses with one another. I will begin with this moment of the market because it is then that the Gypsies set the terms of exchange, then that they can be said to be in control of the market-event.

During the main part of the day dealings with peasants are tortuous and complicated affairs but the shouting matches that Gypsies lock themselves into to achieve

Figure 5.1: A Gypsy Horse Dealer (Photograph by I. Németh).

their 'swaps' provide even more intense excitement. There are a number of distinctive features of Gypsy-on-Gypsy deals but most important is that they are represented as 'swaps' (*parumos*). That inter-Gypsy deals ought to be governed by the logic of a swap does not have to be literally interpreted. Money can be given in whole or part exchange and in most cases this is inevitable as it is rare to find two horses of precisely equal value, but neither Gypsy should be seen to profit over the other from the deal. It is in part this ideal which makes deals among the Gypsies such tiring and tortuous affairs.

This idea of the 'swap' derives from the pervasive Gypsy ideology (see for example Stewart 1988 and 1991) that all Gypsy men are brothers to one another and are obliged to help one another.[8] Swapping implies an exchange of like for like, an equalisation of the diverse entities that are horses. This is a task in which much honour (*patjiv*) is at stake. A man's status is linked with the kind of horses he buys and sells and so Gypsy men stand by an animal and do not willingly admit its faults. Yet half the nature of dealing as Simmel appreciated (1978: 79–81) is giving in and accepting, compromising.

This equalisation is all the more problematic given the symbolic representation of horses at this stage of the market. When dealing with the *gazo*s, horses are primarily commodities, that is abstracted tokens of value which can be shuffled as rapidly as possible between buyer and seller. Later in the day it becomes clear that horses are also rather more than commodities, they are in effect representatives of the non-Gypsies and of Gypsy women.[9] One is not faced here with some casual joking but a fairly elaborate set of images and practices based on a metaphoric association of horses with femaleness.[10] Now, throughout the day Gypsy women are kept away from the horse-trades in person. It is when the peasant-producers of the horses retire from the stage that the Gypsy men start up their second order game.

The significance of the exchange of horses as metaphorical women will perhaps be a little clearer if I say that in all other contexts the very suggestion that Gypsy women are swapped by Gypsies is subject to taboo, and any hint of marital exchange (such as sister exchange) is supressed. More generally, the idiom of affinity is remarkably played down in Hungarian Gypsy life as befits a community whose idiom of unity is one of brotherhood.

So it is that the horses become a means to represent a form of (male) Gypsy potency to create a fantasy social order at once appealing and terrifying, involving objects gendered as female and therefore symbolic of the one part of the world that Gypsy men have some control over. In their 'swaps', then, Gypsies are playing on the deeper meanings and possibilities of exchange through a truly remarkable appropriation. Through the horses produced by non-Gypsies and represented as non-Gypsy/female by the Gypsies a kind of utopian fantasy of exchanging and swapping women around can be enacted. In doing this the Gypsies are playing with fire: evoking both the dangerous potential of exchange for their brotherhood and of dealings with non-Gypsy women.

5. 5 THE SALE

Whatever the nature of the 'swap', for the first few hours of trade Gypsies try to deal with peasants and during this phase horses are clearly commoditised, conceived of in terms which allow them to be measured in that abstract symbol of human relations, the price.

Horse-markets begin slowly, almost imperceptibly. Some traders may spend the night on the market square to let their horses rest but most arrive by lorry as the dawn mist lifts. Still it takes a few hours before the cries and shouts of the dealers ring through the air. So at the outset Gypsies wander slowly round the market to see what is being 'done' that day.[11] Information gathering continues at the bar where Gypsy men gather toasting each other. Several shorts may be put away but men restrain themselves at this stage of the day knowing full well that more than one deal made while drunk has been regretted later.

Once a suitable horse has been found it has to be carefully inspected, a task which demands considerable knowledge, a good eye and patience. At this stage of the dealing an important issue, the horse's temperament, is normally touched on: a frisky or nervous horse will prove difficult to shoe and may prove tricky to handle in other tasks as well. The gestures of both buyer and seller are designed to reveal the horse's true nature in a dramatic fashion. The seller, knowing his own horse, may crawl under its genitals or even rub against them. Any but the most calm horses will react violently to such provocation, in the latter case spraying urine all over the owner before trying vigorously to kick him.

If both parties are serious about trying to deal with the other they may well agree to 'drive' (*tradel*) the horse, or 'do the test' (Romany *zumavel la*, Hungarian *csinálja a próbát*), both dramatic displays of the horse which are designed to establish its strength and stamina.

There are no conventions as to when bargaining begins and offers may be made or demanded at any time. Before the tests when the buyer was glancing over a range of horses there may have been talk of a price though no one likes to make the first move and both parties demand that the other 'Names a price' Hungarian (*mondjon egy árat!*) Making an offer or request demands a dramatic gesture with each partner slapping his hand into the other's saying for example 'Give me 45' (that is 45,000 forints). As one man put it 'we like to strike our hands. For us this makes trade … it warms our ears'. As each slap rings out the onlookers know that here money may be made to move. This theatrical gesture may be repeated by each side throughout the bargaining: it shows a willingness to bargain further and in a sense creates the bargaining situation, for if one party is trying to get the other going they will pull out the other man's hand and slap their own into it.

Come the second round of bargaining, after the 'trial', several more drinks may have been had and the atmosphere will have heated up. Crowds of onlookers gather now to watch and close in without embarrassment on the two contestants. In market dealing, both parties know there is a premium on wit, on keeping up good relations with the other, of always appearing the more generous party though typically extravagant claims are made both for and against the animal. Throughout, the claims of the Gypsy dealer are backed up, guaranteed as it were, by blood-curdling curses.

Gypsy men are quite surprisingly persistent in their argument and will not take a refusal from a peasant as final. During one inspection of a horse a peasant dealer was told with monotonous regularity by four different Gypsies to tie the horse up to the cart and try it out if he doubted its strength. He was asked why he did not want to tie it up, told to do so again and generally treated in a brusque, familiar though not offensive fashion. Gypsies dealing with *gazo*s always use the formal Hungarian '*maga*' forms that establish respect and distance, yet at the same time leave the peasant in no peace to 'make up his own mind', and instead appear as if trying to impose their view of things, bossing around the *gazo* buyer or seller.

It is an odd thing about horse markets that everyone likes a deal. That is what the crowd are standing around waiting for and so in all these ways dealers put the pressure on the buyer to make a move, not to let the deal fall through, not to seem to be the one who failed to bring it off.

5. 6 THE ROLE OF THE MIDDLEMAN

One way to begin to make sense of the Gypsies' horse-dealing is to look at a role which both Hungarians and Gypsies believe the Gypsies are cut out for. This is the role of the *cincár*, or middleman [Kiss, 1939:279]. The logical extension of the idea that Gypsies go to market as dealers, as circulators (H. *forgatók*) of animals, is for Gypsies to take on the role of the pure intermediary ('*közvetito*') or *cincár*.

On the market the *cincár* has to make a drama of his role. A very smooth and professional-looking middle aged Gypsy at one sluggish market set up the first action of the day in a duel of a deal with another Gypsy on behalf of a peasant buyer. The market had been lifeless till then and it took ten minutes of terrible cursing, shouting and a tough 'trial' on the horse for the *cincár* to get an agreement. As he did and the money passed hands, the *cincár* called for the 'drink to bless the deal' (*aldomás*) to be drunk and strode out through the crowd drawing it along behind himself knowing that he was the centre of attention, and even admiration; knowing that all wanted to know for whom he had bought and how much he had earned for his speech in this deal.

Gypsy men tend to be rather proud of their ability as *cincár* and of the 'fees' (*mita*) they collect. After a particularly successful intervention one man told me 'I'm a King!' (*Kraj sim!*) as he reminded me for the fifth time how he had successfully completed the deal. He added that anyone can 'do' the *cincár* role 'if they have the words' (*te si les i vorba*).

5. 7 DEALERS, ENTREPRENEURS AND BOSSES

In the role of *cincár* Gypsies appear to be a real world instance of Kirzner's pure entrepreneurs. Like these, the Gypsy middleman simply sees an opportunity for trade which no one else perceives. Gypsies spend much of their time when they are not at work for wages dealing with peasants and trying to gain an advantage over them. In this perspective the horse market is just one moment in a continual effort to profit from the 'foolishness' of the non-Gypsies. When I was doing research I was often struck by the willingness of Gypsy men to convert their resources into almost any number of different assets (cows, pigs, second-hand cars) which would allow them to realise arbitrage opportunities. Although men may like to have a horse in the stable their eyes are always out for the greater opportunity. The analogy established, I now want to suggest that Kirzner's entrepreneurial account of market behaviour leaves out crucial aspects of what the Gypsies are doing.

My critique runs on three lines. Kirznerian entrepreneurship ought to be open to anyone but empirically in Hungary horse-merchants tend to be Gypsy. Secondly, the Gypsy focus on the horse-trade (in contrast to trade in other livestock) was probably not arrived at as a result of the greater profits to be made there, that is, as a result of entrepreneurial perception of oppportunity. Third, in Kirzner's model the role of the entrepreneur is to lead the market away from disequilibrium, but I will show why Gypsy behaviour is unlikely to do so.

It is an important part of Kirzner's theory that because an entrepreneur simply exploits arbitrage possibilities the 'opportunities he thus offers to the market can in principle be made available by anyone' (1973:16). Entrepreneurship entails no 'entry costs' and is therefore perfectly competitive.[12] In practice, however, it is the Gypsies who tend (and are said) to dominate the horse-markets of rural Hungary as traders. Why should this be?

The reason, I suggest, for this Gypsy specialisation lies not in some innate trait of entrepreneurship but in the historically constructed ethnic division of labour between them and their sedentary peasant hosts. I have shown elsewhere (Stewart n. d.) that Gypsy horse-trading has to be understood in contrast to the work-ethic of the surrounding non-Gypsy, especially peasant population. The peasant, and more recently the socialist, work ethic urges self-sufficiency and nobility through work. The peasant's identity is tied up with his land which offers him the possibility of autonomy. Through punishing toil the peasant makes a 'proper' person of himself and provides the means for an independent life for his household (see Fel and Hofer 1961 and 1969 for the ethnography on which I base these claims).

Since the Gypsies have no land and no means of production they have to achieve autonomy in exchange. In dealing the Gypsy tries to achieve independence, only in his case by making money grow without effort and labour. If they 'work on' anything it is the human parties to the deal, not the horse. They do so through their ability to talk. As one horse dealer explained:

> I need to have speech. If I don't have that then I can't do anything. You see, most people don't have this … You have to talk someone into buying a horse. You have to talk the horse up [literally, 'beside it'], so someone will buy it. You have to take a person's hand to make them do business – otherwise they won't come together.

For the peasants and for the Gypsies the market is an arena of game. For the peasants this game is associated with risk and immoral earnings. For the Gypsies it is in this uncertain game that the normal rules of life, which they well know are no game, are suspended. It is in the context of the game of dealing that the Gypsies are willing to display a passion and absorption which is alien to most of the peasants on the market who adopt a bored phlegmatic air in trading.

In this game it is words which are the source of the dealer's power. To profit publicly from one's use of words is a pleasure very dear to the Gypsies (both as actors and observers) and it seems to me that it is in order to enjoy the pleasure of creating a deal, as much as for any remuneration, that Gypsies play the role of *cincár*. Through their speech Gypsies 'make money turn around, turn around and come to us', and they stress the ease with which this may be done as a dealer 'rotates' goods between customers. A familiar model for what the Gypsies do in horse-dealing could be Ricardo's formula of commodity exchange: Money-Commodity-Money (1). Certainly Gypsies fondly express an analogous fetishisation of money: on receiving money in a deal a Gypsy man may spit on it and say, in Hungarian, 'Your Father! Your Mother! Come here!' (*Apád, Anyád, Ide jöjjön!*).

Though Ricardo's formula well captures the fetishisation of exchange which Gypsies revel in, the suggestion implicit in the model that any C will do so long as it leads to M (I) is strictly speaking inaccurate. This relates to my second criticism of Kirzner. Kirzner's model entrepreneur ought to be totally uninterested in the nature of C but this is not always the case for the Gypsies. In material terms Gypsies have left the other livestock markets (cattle and pigs) almost untouched. In ideological terms, among all their pecuniary activities it is horse-trades which Gypsies stress rhetorically in their conversation and in their songs which celebrate their way of life.

The reason for this cannot be said to be narrowly economic/entrepreneurial, but surely rests in the symbolism of horses in European rural life. By dominating the trade in horses the Gypsies achieve a victory over their peasant adversaries that surpasses all their other efforts. According to Fel and Hofer it was a peasant's demeanour with horses which marked him out amongst his contemporaries (1969:380). Indeed the desirable category of 'proper peasant' was only used for people who knew how to use horses and did not apply to men who only used cattle in agricultural work. A Gypsy, whose social status is still lower than any cattle-using landless labourer, achieves a vicarious domination of the *gazo*s in the market by demonstrating his 'superior' knowledge and mastery of these favoured animals.

This aspect of Gypsy market behaviour also allows us to see why their arbitrage activity is unlikely to lead the market towards equilibrium. According to Kitzner the result of entrepreneurial activity is a spread of knowledge among market participants: 'exposure to the decisions of others communicates some of the information these decision-makers originally lacked' (1973:10). As a result 'the overambitious plans of one period will be replaced by more realistic ones; market opportunities overlooked in one period will be exploited in the next' (1973:10). That is to say market actors make 'systematic plan changes' which result from the 'flow of informaton released by market participation' (1973:10). I have already indicated that there are cultural and historical reasons why peasants are unlikely to do so. Gypsies ought to, but do they?

At the micro-level Gypsy horse-merchants are continually testing the market; major traders will for instance make trips to distant markets to test the water in the overall system. But at the macro-level alertness to profit opportunities (or at least to loss dangers) is restricted for Gypsy men who are thus unlikely to follow Kizner's model and abandon their 'overambitious plans'. This is due to factors which Kirzner's market-oriented model overlooks, that is the means by which horses are 'produced' for the Gypsies. As I have said, for most men horses are subsidised by the joint input of wages and unpaid female labour in raising pigs. Gypsy entrepreneurs are thus less than acutely sensitive to their pecuniary profit since it is not primarily their labour and effort that is being risked. (Unsurprisingly the attitudes of Gypsy women are more complex. Women are more aware of the discrepancy between model and actuality, and one woman's words convey a common feeling: 'horses don't interest me; it's my husband who wants to keep them'. They rarely however impede their husbands' desires.) For a Gypsy man if horses are hard to sell, or go for a loss this is not a reason to give them up. Gypsy men are in Kirzner's terms protected from 'competitive pressures' and the market process is 'impeded'.[13]

The reason for this can only seem obscure from within the framework of bourgeois economic thought which attributes an implausible paucity of motives to its actors. For Gypsy men the horse-market retains its attraction since it is in their trade that Gypsy men achieve their most satisfying victories over the 'arrogant' (*barimasko*) peasants. Even more importantly, because the money from trade is 'won' and not earned it is ideal for creating brotherhood with other Gypsies. Wage-labour money, Hungarian forints, carries with it the alien intentionality of the non-Gypsy work-provider, the state, according to whose ethic money is to be saved, accumulated and wisely spent on civilising one's living conditions (see Stewart forthcoming). But the 'silver' (*rup*) which Gypsies acquire from horses is free of the taint of the *gazo* giver and can thus be painlessly shared with one's brothers.

5. 8 LUCK AND THE DETERMINATION OF PRICES

It ought to be clear by now that for Gypsies the generation of a flow of goods and the determination of their prices does not rest on an impersonal price mechanism, a balance of supply and demand into which Gypsies rationally slot themselves. For Gypsy horse-dealers everything happens as if prices are the result of the game of bargaining.

To some extent establishing a deal is a matter of coercing unwilling peasant partners to part with their money. But Gypsy notions of the moving forces in trade are not exhausted by images of coercion and domination. Equally as important is the concept of *baxt* (luck, efficacy, prosperity, happiness). *Baxt* is a complex concept to the elucidation of which I have already devoted a separate paper (Stewart, n. d.). One obvious parallel is with our notion of windfall gain but *baxt* for the Gypsies only bears an overlapping relationship with our own idea of 'chance'.

This is in part because, as Geertz has pointed out in his discussion of the Indonesian concept of *Tjotjog* (Geertz, 1960:31) we think of co-incidence as uncertain and therefore self-evidently trivial. In contrast for Gypsies 'luck' is the rightful consequence of righteous behaviour, it is the natural state of being a Gypsy. This is so because *baxt* is established in the preparations any serious Gypsy horse-trader makes before going to market. Since all success in dealing relies on powerful and persuasive speech it is appropriate that the seat of luck is a man's head. In order to preserve his luck a man must avoid too close contact with polluting objects and persons (women's lower bodies, their skirts, priests and so on). Above all it is avoidance of the pollution associated with Gypsy women's fertility which preserves a man's luck.

So while it might at first sight seem that a concept of 'luck' determining trade would be a variation of capitalist images of impersonal, non-intentional models of exchange, for these Gypsies 'luck' as efficacy, as the successful manipulation of the *gazo* trader implies a background level of intentionality. When a man receives the price he is looking for for his animals, he is lucky (*baxtalo*) and he is that because he is a true Gypsy.

5. 9 CONCLUSIONS

This ethnography of actual market behaviour offers the chance to transcend the now rather sterile conflict between supporters of a so-called 'market principle' and its critics. The barrenness of this debate derives from the fact that both of these camps cleave to the belief that there is such a thing as a 'market principle', as 'market forces' or the 'logic of the market'. In this way, as Chris Hann points out in this volume, Polanyi and the leading modern Hungarian economist Kornai agree that a price mechanism operates in markets which mediates the distribution of goods on a mechanical basis according to available supply and demand. Both concur that in a market or capitalist economy the economy is 'self-regulating', free from social or political determination.

It is hard to recognise the Gypsies' market behaviour in these models. The nature of the horse-market, the division of labour between traders and peasants and the nature of the bargaining process itself are all shaped by social and political features which are an inherent, constitutive part of the market process. This should be clear from my description of actor's behaviour during sales but is particularly apparent if one considers the 'swap' that Gypsies also go in for during the market. Here it is clear that through trade (making commensurable objects that appear initially non-commensurable) the Gypsies are doing far more than is encompassed in bourgeois market models of whatever sophistication.

The sceptical reader may object that this 'swapping' goes on at the end of the day and is truly peripheral to the main activity of the market. But, as a thought exercise, imagine the market the other way round: the first part of the day composed of swaps between Gypsy men followed by the arrival of the peasants when the Gypsies tired of their own game. The only reason the market is not organised this way is of course the power (political and economic) of the non-Gypsies who set the terms of trade, and whose policemen move in at the end of the day to shut down the market and clear the remaining Gypsies from the field. Were the Gypsies able to determine the order of play who would then presume to apportion analytical priority to one or other moment of the market and claim that this is the *real* market process?

An important contribution of anthropological economics has been to view economics and economic institutions as cultural phenomena. Because neo-classical economics was predicated on a separation of market (utility maximisation) from culture (unquantifiable and therefore non-commensurable values/morality) it has often seemed to anthropologists to be rooted in a mistaken view of the social process. In the compartment of life devoted to utility maximisation humans were supposed to behave with machine-like regularity, or at least analysts said one could talk as if they did. S. Gudeman (1986) has pointed out the uniqueness of these mechanical models of livelihood. [14]

Hayek and the neo-liberals, to their credit, tried to set the ball rolling in the opposite direction with their concern for knowledge and beliefs. Indeed they put market theory back at the centre of social theory by claiming that markets offer the most perfect form for realising human freedom and social integration. Though they did not use the terms of our debates, Hayek and his followers effectively put economics and culture back together.[15]

Unfortunately they did so while attempting to retain the notion of 'the economic' as a distinct sphere of activity. As I hope to have shown this attachment to the 'economic' and consequent blindness to the forms in which social power is enshrined, and to the range of motives at play in real-life markets, scupper the best efforts of bourgeois economics to account for real-life market behaviour. Perhaps this should hardly surprise us. Western folk models of the economy were, as Agnew argues, devised either as an 'ideological solution to the cultural confusions produced by the spread of market exchange' or as an attempt at the level of ideas to conceive the sort of market predictability that institutions such as the Royal Exchange were meant to establish in practice (1986: 2–6). There is thus little reason to try to apply these schema outside their original contexts. Our tasks should rather be to understand those schema, in their own context and to make the leap of imagination necessary to grasp other people's trading activity in its own terms.

Gudeman recommended that anthropological economics ought to study divergent models of production and distribution (1986). When we do so, he argues, there will be no simple relation between material practice and ideal model. I hope to have illustrated his argument in relation to an area of livelihood, haggled exchanges, which he passes over in that work. I do not, however, want to suggest that model and practice are only arbitrarily linked. So, by way of closing, I would ask whether the kind of active, entrepreneurial model of trade and exchange which the Gypsies adhere to might be related to their position on the underbelly of Hungarian society. Field reports of entrepreneurial activity seem to derive from lumpen groups in the slums and ghettos of semi-industrial societies (Hart 1975: Pardo n. d.). These people lack the organisational power to establish associations and firms with which they could, like the rest of us, restrict 'market processes'. Could it be that the true bearers of the capitalist spirit, ever willing to act on an entrepreneurial hunch, are those excluded from the capitalist system in almost every other respect?

NOTES

1. I was, for instance, told that under normal conditions the price of a top-quality horse was the same as that of two hectolitres of home-made wine sold at the house. This equivalence had been maintained over the lifespan of my peasant informants (some sixty years) with divergences especially during the 1950s when livestock fairs were suppressed by the communist authorities.

   The horse-markets were also integrated to some extent with the world economy, at least at their extremes, because of the sale of horses via the state export agency to western European countries for horse-meat. Gypsies were the prime movers in this trade as well and I often saw horses removed from the Hungarian fair circuit in order to be more profitably sold on the meat market.

2. Just as J. and P. Alexander report (1991) the glossing of indigenous terms as 'wholesaler' and 'retailer' marginalises the emically central fact that one tends to be male and the other female.

3. Plattner (1989) puts especial emphasis on risk aversion in poor and informationally faulty economic environments. P. Alexander (this volume) indicates some of the theoretical and empirical limitations of this approach.

4. The concept of entrepreneur has a long intellectual history carrying the meaning of risk-taker since at least seventeenth century French (Cantillon) (Kirzner, 1979:39). Kirzner's usage is distinct from Schumpeter's in a number of respects (see for example Schumpeter, 1965). Whatever its intellectual credentials, one is bound to note that we English still use the French term having been unable to come up with an alternative to undertaker!

5. As Kirzner puts it:
   > whereas the market participation of asset owners is always to some extent protected (by the peculiar qualities of the assets possessed [no two assets being exactly the same no opportunity offered can ever be exactly and therefore competitively duplicated by another agent]), the market activity of the entrepreneur is never protected in any way ... (1973:16).

6. For a few years at the height of the Stalinist terror in Hungary in the early 1950s horse-fairs and all markets in livestock were suppressed. But with the liberalisation of economic policy from the mid-1950s the fairs emerged again. Despite a legal ban on holding horses for personal agricultural use which remained in force until 1977 (see Swain, 1985:73) in the more liberal economic atmosphere of Kadarite Hungary many peasants seem to have found ways to keep some horses. The continued importance of household plots alongside other under-capitalised forms of private agricultural production (see Hann 1980; Swain 1985) and increased private carting in rural areas (see, for example, Doman 1984:124) meant that the number of (officially registered) single and dual horse-owners rose from nearly 18,000 in 1964 to a peak of 56,000 in 1969. In 1980 it stood at some 40,000, declining but still significant.

7. Gypsy involvement in this trade was a source of irritation to the authorities who saw this as a failure of the official policy to assimilate Gypsies into the proletariat.

8. For instance while a Gypsy may trick a *gazo* whenever he likes, to set up a deal with a Gypsy based on a lie, or not to give full information about a horse is reason for having to accept a horse back.

9. As commodities they appear to be things with a social life. But as swappable women/non-Gypsies they appear as the material, tangible form of social relations. Because they are objects horses provide a means to act on these social relations (compare Tambiah, 1969).

10. Men tell stories in which horses stand in for women; boys dress horses with their mother's scarves and men on the way to market talk jokingly of going to swap wives (see Stewart 1988 for more details).

11. Gypsies are restricted by their range of contacts and their knowledge of the different markets. In the hilly areas of the north of Hungary, for instance, heavy and powerful horses are needed by the *gazo*s. Other constraints on the Gypsies are the sex of the horse since mares tend to be preferred by *gazo*s. The wealth of the Gypsy also plays its part as horse prices range from around 12,000 forints (three times a monthly basic wage) to 50,000 forints, an equivalent in real terms to £3,000.

12. Note the circularity of the model, the way it creates its own reality conditions. By treating entrepreneurial activity as the only true 'market' activity, Kirzner can maintain that markets are perfectly competitive, since entrepreneurship *ex definitio* is competitive! The horse-markets which offer such perfect opportunities for entre-

preneurial competition rather undermine the empirical basis of Kirzner's model.

13. Kirzner might argue that in acting thus the Gypsies are in effect establishing firms which protect them from the effects of competition and thus cease to be entrepreneurs. The question would then be whether there are any 'pure entrepreneurs' in the real world who trade on markets without the aid of associations which impinge on their competitiveness.

14. A favoured illustration of the bizarre symbolic practices to which our notion of a disembedded, asocial market economy leads lies in the basement of the London School of Economics where a large piece of hydraulic machinery was built to model a phantasmagoric image of a sealed British economy. In the early heady days of British monetarism as a salutary example of corporate sponsorship a Japanese foundation paid for the model to be restored into full working life. Unsurprisingly, sceptics might say, the model shortly sprang a leak, leaving disconcerting puddles under sections marked credit and money supply. Debate then raged in the Senior Common Room as to the state in which the machine provided a more accurate representation of the British economy: rusting, effortlessly functioning or plain bust.

15. It is thus not surprising that Kirzner for example is interested in 'perception' and thereby imagination and creativity (see Kirzner 1979), nor that his work has provoked discussion about the contexts in which entrepreneurial activity is encouraged (Kirzner 1980).

REFERENCES

Agnew, J. C. 1986. *Worlds Apart: The Market and the Theater in Anglo-American Thought. 1550-1750*. Cambridge: Cambridge University Press.

Alexander, J. and P. Alexander. 1991. 'What's a Fair Price? Price-Setting and Trading Partnerships in Javanese Markets', *Man*, 26(3):493-512.

Dalton, G. and P. Bohannon, 1962. *Markets in Africa*. Evanstone: Northwestern University Press.

Doman, I. 1984. *A Szarvasi Cigányok [The Gypsies of Nagykörös]*. Kecskemét, Petofi.

Fel, E. and T. Hofer, 1961. 'Az átányai gazdálkodás ágai' *Néprajzi Közlemények*, 6 (2): 1–220.

Fel, E. and T. Hofer, 1969. *Proper Peasants. Traditional Life in a Hungarian Village.* Viking Fund Publications in Anthropology, No. 46. Chicago: Aldine.

Geertz, C. 1960. *The Religion of Java.* Chicago: University of Chicago Press.

Geertz, C. 1979. 'Suq: the bazaar economy in Sefrou', in C. Geertz *et al.* (eds.), *Meaning and Order in Moroccan Society.* Cambridge: Cambridge University Press.

Gudeman, S. 1986. *Economics as Culture: models and metaphor of livelihood.* London: Routledge and Kegan Paul.

Gregory, C. 1980. 'Gifts to Men and Gifts to God: Gift Exchange and Capital Accumulation in Contemporary Papua'. *Man*, 15 (4): 626–52.

Hann, C. 1980. *Tázlár: A Village in Hungary.* Cambridge: Cambridge University Press.

Hart, K. 1975. 'Swindler or Public Benefactor? – The Entrepreneur in his Community', in J. Goody, (ed.), *Changing Social Structure in Ghana,* London: International African Institute.

Hayek, F. A. 1945. 'The Uses of Knowledge in Society', *American Economic Review*, 35 (September): 519–30.

Hollos, M. and B. Maday (eds.), 1983. *New Hungarian Peasants: An East Central European Experience with Collectivisation.* East European Monographs Series, no. 134. New York: Brooklyn College Press.

Kirzner, I. 1973. *Competition and Entrepreneurship.* Chicago: University of Chicago Press.

Kirzner, I. 1979. *Perception, Opportunity and Profit: Studies in the Theory of Entrepreneurship*. Chicago: University of Chicago Press.

Kirzner, I. 1980. *Prime Mover of Progress: The Entrepreneur in Capitalism and Socialism*. London: Institutue of Economic Affairs; No. 23.

Kiss, l. 1939. *A Szegény emberek élete, elsö kötet* [*The Life of the Poor, First Volume*]. Reprinted in 1981, Budapest, Gondolat.

Pardo, I. n. d. 'Socialist Visions, Naples and the Neopolitans'. Paper presented to A. S. A.. conference on Socialism, April 1991.

Plattner, S. 1989. *Economic Anthropology*. Stanford: Stanford University Press.

Schumpeter, J. A. 1965. 'Economic Theory and Entrepreneurial History', in H. G. Aitken (ed.), *Explorations in Enterprise*. Cambridge, Mass: Harvard University Press.

Simmel, G. 1978 [1900]. *The Philosophy of Money*. London: Routledge.

Stewart, M. 1988. *Brothers in Song: The maintenance of Gypsy Identity and Community in Socialist Hungary*. Ph. D Thesis, University of London.

Stewart, M. 1989. 'True Speech: Song and the Moral Order of a Hungarian Vlach Gypsy Community', *Man* (N. S.), 24 (1): 79–102.

Stewart, M. forthcoming. 'Gypsies and the Socialist Work Ethic', in C. Hann (ed.), *The Anthropology of Socialism*, London: Routledge.

Stewart, M. n. d. 'Gypsy Horse Dealers, Peasant Producers and the Idea of Luck'. Unpublished paper.

Swain, N. 1985. *Collective farms which work?* Cambridge: Cambridge University Press.

Tambiah, S. 1969. 'Animals are Good to Think and to Prohibit', *Ethnology*, 8: 424–59.

6

Trade in Kufra
(Libya)

JOHN DAVIS

If you travel along the coast eastwards from Tripoli in Libya, after about 800 kilometres you come to Ajdabiya, a small town near the coast which was the headquarters of the Sanusi administration for a few years of uneasy accommodation with the Italians and was a centre of battles in the second world war. It also has what must be one of the more romantic signposts of the world: there is a T-junction, to the east you can arrive in Benghazi, Alexandria and Cairo (1,000 kilometres); to the south you can travel 800 kilometres and reach to Kufra and then a further 1,200 to Khartoum or 1,500 to Ndjamena in Chad.

In the years 1975–9 I was fortunate enough to spend rather more than two years in Libya, doing fieldwork among a group of people who called themselves by the collective name Zuwaya and who occupied a territory which stretched from the Mediterranean coast to the borders with Egypt, Sudan and Chad. Although, at least in the 1970s, rather few of them were engaged in trade, they regarded themselves as traders, and they were in fact the principal traders on the route which leads from the coast into black Africa. In the past they bought slaves and animals from Sudan to the coast for export to Alexandria, and also engaged in smaller trade – one very old man, for instance, remembered bringing ostrich feathers northwards, for export to Paris, at the turn of the century. The trade even then was not a principal occupation of Zuwaya, but was integrated with a cycle of nomadic movement from the oases in the south and the catch-crop grain-farming areas in the north, in the sub-desert land around Ajdabiya: most people farmed and herded, a few (energetic young men) went off from Kufra for a few years to trade in the markets of Sudan, Chad and, from the 1870s, into Niger, Nigeria, Cameroon, before rejoining the annual south–north movement.

Zuwaya were not the only people who traded along this route: other Libyan groups, some Egyptians and even Turks are thought to have travelled through Kufra. Other groups had settlements in the oases of Jalu and Aujla and were engaged in what seems to have been a classic struggle with Zuwaya for control of those important staging posts. But Zuwaya did control Kufra and the other smaller oases within 200 kilometres or so (Tazerbu, Buzaima, Rabbiana), a control which gave them a decided advantage over other travellers: these were the only major watering places on the

2,000 kilometres journey to Melitt and then to Omdurman. Of course water itself was a free good: you did not refuse water. But the control of Kufra permitted Zuwaya to offer protection from thieves, brigands and murderers whom travellers might encounter. Zuwaya had a monopoly of protection, since there were no other stable bases of settlement which could support a powerful force of men. If you consider that Zuwaya were also the people best placed to thieve, murder and maraud, it is clear that they were very well placed indeed to threaten and then to protect, at a price, from the threat which they themselves constituted. It was a significant part of Zuwaya livelihood.

Kufra seems very distant from the signpost in Ajdabiya; and indeed Evans-Pritchard refers to it as one of the most remote places in the world (Evans-Pritchard 1945). But it had been the headquarters of the Sanusi movement in the late nineteenth century, a centre from which they expanded into the Sahel and attempted to lead a resistance to French imperial expansion through Niger and Chad. With the closing of the Nile route into black Africa in the 1880s, Kufra's importance as a trading centre was enhanced; people began to settle there because it was so central: only three months' journey from Khartoum, two months' from Kharga and the Nile, two or three months' from Tripoli. But from 1911 Kufra again became valuable for its remoteness, attracting refugees from the Italians who invaded the northern plains but did not gain control of the Kufra depression until the battle of Hawaria in 1932.

The Italians compelled Libyan nomads to settle by setting up a pale between the desert and the catch-cropping areas of the north: these were designated as future agricultural zones and were banned to herders and grazers. Many of the refugees in the south had, in any case, their own good reasons for not going north; thus the pattern of movement and of livelihood changed significantly in the 1930s. During the second world war the Italian and other armies fighting in the territory were responsible for a new development: using old army trucks it became possible for the nomads to make the journey between Kufra and the coast in a week or so. After the discovery of oil and the creation of new wealth, with more modern vehicles Zuwaya could make the round trip to Khartoum in a couple of weeks, to Ajdabiya or Benghazi in a week or ten days. Wheels, especially Mercedes Benz trucks, made it possible for Zuwaya to settle and to travel without taking their families with them.

In 1975 the population of the thirteen Kufra oases was about 9,000. Of these, 5,000-6,000 were Zuwaya, claiming ownership of the archipelago of oases in the depression, organised in lineages each with a shaikh and a territory, a system of mutual support and in emergencies operating a series of claims of mutual responsibility. Another 500-600 were Tibbu: black men who were generally accepted as the aboriginal inhabitants of the Kufra area. They spoke Tibbu as well as Arabic, had an organisation of lineages with shaikhs and had connections with other Tibbu elsewhere – in Chad and in the Tibesti mountains. They were the only inhabitants of the district who had an effective organisation which was independent of Zuwaya; Zuwaya resented this indipendence and treated Tibbu with suspicion as a result. A third group of inhabitants were Ikhwan, the term used for officials of the Sanusi order and (in 1975 after the abolition of the order by the revolutionary government) still applied to those men and their families and descendants. In Kufra they were mostly clerks and shopkeepers, were often respected people, but were usually not significant in politics. They numbered about 1,000 in all. A fourth category (which had no pretensions or attributes of groupishness) were the foreign workers, of whom there were about 2,000.

Most of the Libyan inhabitants of Kufra were children: about 60 per cent were less than sixteen years old; and rather more than half of the population were women. The effective political population was therefore rather less than 1,500; about the same number of Libyans in Kufra were officially defined as economically active. Most of them worked for the government as clerks and committee members, teachers, police-men and soldiers. About 15 per cent had no employment and lived by trade, gardening, herding and shopkeeping. It was, however, also very common for a government employee to run a subsidiary occupation – a shop, a garden, which brought in extra income and which allowed him to claim that he too was *Zuwai hurr*, a 'free Zuwayi' beholden to no other.

So, about two hundred men got their living principally from trade and many more got a subsidiary income from shopkeeping. In addition, quite a large number of people – at a rough estimate another three or four hundred – bought goods in Libya and sent them abroad as they could, in expectation of socialist restrictions on private wealth. If you had a brother or a cousin who trucked goods to Sudan, Niger, or Chad it made sense, in the political climate of the 1970s, to get him to trade goods on your behalf and to place the proceeds in a foreign bank account. And in fact, at the end of the decade, the government did change the currency, compelling Libyans to change old money for new, but restricting the amount of new money they could hold (the balance held in frozen bank accounts).

Kufra was none the less a substantial entrepôt in the desert trade. You could acquire Deutschmarks, US dollars, Central African francs and South African rands on the local unofficial currency market, as well as most of the sub-Saharan monies (although I think some people collected them more as curiosities than as an investment). I do not think anyone from Kufra traded directly into South Africa, but the currency filtered indirectly into the Sahara, in no doubt small quantities, though, in the nature of the case, it was difficult to make an accurate assessment of the size of the market.

The volume of trade was also quite substantial: near Ajdabiya the authorities ran a truck park, a sort of marshalling yard for drivers bound southwards. There were rarely less than thirty trucks there at any time I observed it; four or five would leave in a caravan each morning, four or five again in the evening. About half the drivers went to places in Libya: to the oases, to Kufra, to the oil and agricultural camps in the desert. About half continued southwards from Kufra, but that was variable with the seasons and with the state of the frontiers. Some of these trucks were small Fiat ten-tonners; some were huge machines: I once saw a forty-ton flatbed truck owned by a Sudanese but with Irish number-plates, and one or two people had Deutz trucks. The workhorse of the desert, by the mid-1970s, was the twenty-ton Mercedes Benz, with three driving axles, sixteen gears and specially fitted 1,000-litre fuel tanks. Some trucks did not pass through the Ajdabiya truck park; many of the small shopkeepers of the oases had their own transport. Toyota pick-ups were the favoured vehicle, carrying a hundredweight or two of shoes or fresh vegetables or soap. Not all loads are equally heavy: cigarettes, for instance, are light, but relatively bulky. You could make a very rough guess, of perhaps 100 tons of goods arriving each week in Kufra and rather less than half that amount continuing southwards (allowing for political restrictions on trade).

The goods carried included all that was needed for a wealthy population living in a non-productive area: most fruit and vegetables, quite a lot of meat were produced in the oases. But all other food (pasta, rice, tea, sugar, flour, cheese, tinned milk, fish, tomatoes, beans and so on); all clothing, shoes, household equipment, insecticides, furniture were imported and carried south to Kufra. With the provision of twenty-four hour electricity in the oases, people had begun to acquire refrigerators, air-conditioning and freezers; with the expansion of popular democracy and control of government there had been a huge demand for office equipment: desks, chairs, filing cabinets and typewriters. With the expansion of salary-based incomes, people began to build themselves houses of a substantial sort, requiring bricks, cement, timber, paint. With the expansion of trade, it was important to have local supplies of fuel and spare parts for motors. All that arrived in Kufra.

Zuwaya traders who continued southwards usually carried cloth, subsidised food-stuffs and some household goods such as radios and electric fans, as well as occasional bargain goods and special deals for which they hoped to find a market. Sudanese and other traders carried cloth, consumer goods and people. It was very common to see a truck loaded with the driver's goods, with a number of passengers sitting on top, each with a charged quota of luggage slung on the sides of the driver's cargo. The Sudanese traders were on a return journey: the typical pattern was that they sent meat northwards on the hoof in the spring, used the proceeds to buy cloth and other goods in Benghazi or Tripoli and then negotiated the return journey to Melitt or Omdurman with whichever truckers would provide a reasonable truck at a reasonable price. These were sometimes Zuwaya, more often those relatively inexperienced in the trans-Saharan journeys.

That is the traffic from north to south. Of course, about as many trucks travelled south-north (though not the Irish giant); most of them, however, were empty and the costs of the return journey were included in the charges for the southbound trade. The most profitable goods were empty cola bottles, for which one man had a contract – a guaranteed return cargo. Zuwaya also carried some agricultural produce: early onions, some millet, some dates usually for sale in Zuwaya-owned shops in Ajdabiya or Benghazi. From further south they brought small quantities of scented wood, spices, sheep and people – labourers on their way to the north. Finally, and again this was seasonal, camels. The Sudanese traders usually walked their beasts as far as Kufra and then negotiated a trucking fee for the journey to the slaughterhouses of the northern cities. A Mercedes carried about twenty-four camels and made the journey in two or three days against the six weeks or two months required to walk from Kufra to Ajdabiya.

Zuwaya charged about 1,200 Libyan dinars to carry a twenty-ton truck-load from Ajdabiya to Kufra, and about the same again to go on to Melitt. This was intended to

cover the costs of the return journey and was equivalent to £2,000 ($3,000) at the
official rate of exchange in 1979, about £1,300 ($1,700) on the black market. Any
return freight was a bonus, and the man with the cola-bottle contract (for which he
was paid 400LD) was sitting pretty. Zuwaya varied their charges for a load of camels,
Kufra to Benghazi, according to the number of people waiting in the Kufra quaran-
tine station to ship their camels northwards: in the low season they could not get
much more than 400LD (£600 to 700), but in March and April the charge rose to 600
to 650LD. On most journeys the passengers – herders rather than the controlling
traders who travelled independently, a few weeks or months after the camels – sat in
the back of the truck and provided their own food. When prices rose, they would try
to negotiate a ride in the cab and to share the driver's food. Zuwaya tended to resist
this: they said the herders were smelly, they did not have much conversation and in
any case were black. At the higher price, and without the comfortable ride and
without the free food, some herders preferred to walk; the charges then began to fall
again. I have notes of conversations in which Zuwaya truckers discussed the pretensions of the herders, noted who among the truckers was wavering and might be
prepared to lower his price, and tried to hold the common line on charges.

In Ottoman times (until the 1870s) Zuwaya ran an effective protection racket for
travellers in the desert, offering guides and security in exchange for a fee. Some
Zuwaya said that their control of the desert was recognised by the Turkish governors
of Benghazi, who had granted them an exclusive licence to conduct traders through to
Kufra. It is clear, however, that such monopoly as Zuwaya may have achieved from
time to time was contested by other groups in Cyrenaica: by Mjabr in Jalu, for
instance, and perhaps by Magharba (Mason 1977). From the 1870s the control of
trade passed from Zuwaya to the Sanusi family, whose order established a series of
lodges along the trade routes into the Sahel. Zuwaya still traded, and were no doubt
the main guides across the desert. But safe conduct was in the control of the Sanusi
family who, for instance, ordered Zuwaya to guide Rosita Forbes and Hassanain Bey
from Ajdabiya to Kufra in the 1920s (Bey 1925). In the period of Italian control trade
was more or less disrupted, and after the second world war there was no question of
Zuwaya re-establishing what they had lost. Nevertheless, they had decided advantages
over other traders: quite apart from the local knowledge and support networks, which
were important assets in a territory which is still incompletely mapped, compared
with other persons who live (say) in Bengazi, they were in a much better position
having fixed bases in the desert, to supply food and other goods to the oil exploration
teams and the surveyors, labourers and administrators engaged in agricultural
projects. In the 1970s it was still the case that Zuwaya had a decided advantage over
other people using the route through Kufra: they had no difficulty for instance in
borrowing water or fuel while *en route* across the desert. When Zuwaya crossed paths
with other Zuwaya in the desert they often stopped to eat together and to exchange
information: the northbound driver told of the prices and movements in Kufra; the
southbound reported on cargoes available in Benghazi, people who needed transport
from Ajdabiya, and so on. Non-Zuwaya whose trucks broke down found that spare
parts were very expensive in Kufra, while a Zuwayi could usually find a friend or

kinsman who had a spare fuel pump or radiator hose at the same price it would fetch in Benghazi. The most devastating costs for strangers were for transporting vehicles which could not be repaired on the spot: a Fiat had to be loaded onto a Mercedes; a Mercedes onto a Deutz, and the pick-back operation back to Benghazi could cost three or four thousand dinars. Zuwaya were much more accommodating to other Zuwaya.

The trucker's costs were fairly low: a normal journey, fully laden, used rather less than 500 litres of fuel, at a cost of about 100LD; then oil, wear and tear, spare parts, food and cooking fuel – it cost less than 200LD to run a Mercedes truck from Benghazi to Kufra. The major cost was the trucks themselves: a Mercedes was priced in Benghazi at about £70,000 with the extras needed for desert travel. Some men had worked their way up a ladder of ownership: they had started with old army trucks, Austins and Bedfords abandoned by the British army. A few of these were still running in the 1970s, though they were only used for local traffic within the oases. A year or so of a Bedford and, at any rate in the heady days of oil exploration, a driver might expect to graduate to a Fiat, comfortable and reliable, but very slow because it had only one driving axle and the gears were not good for soft going, and relatively expensive to run because the trucks could not carry more than about ten tons. After a year or two of driving these vehicles, a successful man might graduate to the Mercedes, a vehicle so powerful it could dig itself out of a sand dune.

By the 1970s however, the commonest way for a Zuwayi to acquire a Mercedes was by a form of partnership known as *al thalth*, 'by thirds'. Two Zuwaya were by then millionaires, and a handful of other men were really quite wealthy. In technical legal terms they owned fleets of Mercedes trucks: one man was said to possess fifteen of them, another between ten and fifteen, several had three or four. In fact, however, most of these were subject to the informal and unregistered contract of partnership which gradually transferred ownership of the vehicle from the purchaser to the partner. The terms of the contract were that a wealthy man would purchase a truck, and his poorer partner would agree to drive it, for a wage. They kept a note of the cost of the truck, and of the running costs, including the driver's wage, and they recorded the income got from freight charges. When the net income equalled the cost of the truck, the junior partner became owner of one third of the truck. They could sell the truck and divide the proceeds or they could then continue with a second stage: the driver no longer got a wage but one third of the net earnings from the journeys. And when the net earnings again reached the original cost of the vehicle, he became owner of half the vehicle: the second stage of the relationship was called *al-nus* 'by halves'. And so on: the contract (which was never a written document so far as I know) was advantageous to both parties. From the wealthy man's point of view, his money was 'working' for him, producing an income, in a way which was conformable with Islamic law since it involved no interest; it was also a way to benefit a friend or kinsman, at least a fellow Zuwayi, and added to his standing. From the junior partner's point of view, it provided a fairly certain step up the ladder to independence and wealth without the stigma of employment, and associated him as a partner with a man of standing and prestige. And the stages of the contract could be passed fairly rapidly: I knew one man who had just begun his contract in 1975 when I first arrived in Libya, and who had just bought his own new Mercedes in 1979 when I finally left. Four or five years was the normal expected period, though there were some contracts which lasted longer and some which went sour and were never completed.

From the point of view of an economic anthropologist, the contract is important in various ways. First because it shows wealth to be in motion: it suggests an economy in which the crucial and unequally distributed elements of wealth are not fixed and static methods of accumulation, but are mobile and in continual transfer. When Qaddafi's regime attacked private commerce in terms which suggested that traders and shopkeepers were capitalist exploiters, adding nothing to the value of the goods which they traded, Zuwaya defended themselves in his terms. They argued that socialist distribution was synonymous with shortages and absence of goods in the shops and was thus the same as no distribution. They argued that capitalism was more effective than socialism as a way of getting goods where they were needed. In fact it was not an appropriate argument, however, or not entirely, because the wealthy Zuwaya were not inveterate accumulators of exchange value. It was also the case that in the 1970s wealthy Zuwaya did not constitute a class in any reasonable sense of the term: none had inherited his wealth; choice of partners in marriage was not significantly determined by wealth. Nor was wealth a correlate of any of the secondary characteristics of class: better education, health, segregated housing or enhanced political power. So when Zuwaya defended themselves by saying that they were efficient capitalists, it seems to me that it is better to take that as a response to Qaddafi's power to set the terms of argument, than as a correct identification of their economic role.

It is not, in fact, really very important whether Zuwaya were capitalists or not, except that an academic point hangs on the issue: we think of markets as producing capitalists – that is what markets do, what they are for. But in this case, the intensely market-oriented activities of wealthy Zuwaya, and the market aspirations of moderately wealthy and even poor ones, did not produce capitalists. The point is that we can remind ourselves that markets are not in fact univocal, producing only one sort of social consequence.

Zuwaya distinguished three sorts of exchange: 'we have', I was told, '*zakat, tijara,* and *sdiqqa*'. *Zakat* is alms, the exchange which is enjoined as one of the holy duties of Muslims. *Sdiqqa* is the exchanges which mark relationships between kin: at funerals and circumcisions, for instance, the gifts which a person brings as a contribution to the feast and as a part of his own entertainment are *sdiqqa*; they are a substantial part of a household's expenses. The colloquial word for bridewealth (indirect dowry, *mahr*) is *sdaq* and both words are related to *sadiq*, friend.

Tijara is trade; I remember being excited (in 1975) at discovering yet another case in which a North African model seemed to correspond with the flowers of anthropological classification: for were these not really very similar to the substantivists' reciprocity, redistribution and market? However, the thought that I might be able to trace an intellectual genealogy by which (like segment) these terms had infiltrated social science via French colonial scholarship, soon vanished as I began to understand more about trade. I have already mentioned the way in which capital moves from person to person and does not result in a labour market stratified into buyers and sellers of labour. Similar features are apparent as soon as you look at the organisation of trade, the techniques of trade and the aspirations of the traders.

In the early years of this century the basis of the Zuwaya trading network was the series of Sanusi lodges in the Sahel. And, although I was never able to accompany Zuwaya traders across frontiers into Sudan or Chad, it is clear that in the 1960s and 1970s the basis was the diaspora of the 1930s: the Italian conquest of the oases of the central Sahara resulted in the exile of many Zuwaya who then established themselves in Chad and Sudan. These men maintained relations with their kin in Libya and constituted a network of trading relationships: Libyan Zuwaya traded to them, carrying goods for their market activities in sub-Saharan Africa. The sub-Saharan Zuwaya in fact came home to marry and to die, in the 1970s, in some cases taking up land which they had abandoned forty years before. A further source of links was created by the introduction of conscription after the revolution: the doctrine that defence was a popular duty and that it was an offence punishable under military discipline to ask how long an individual's military service might last, caused some young men to decamp to the south. They too became contacts for their fathers, brothers, uncles and cousins who were engaged in the trans-Saharan trade. Even when there were no such permanent settlers, people were able to construct similar sorts of organisation. A shaikh in Ajdabiya, for instance, had a business in Niger: he and his eldest son bought cloth in Tripoli, exported it to Niger, had the cloth made up into clothing by cheap labour in the south, and then reimported some part of it to Ajdabiya, where they sold it at the going Libyan rate. In order to put the business on a sound and safe footing, they maintained two households, one in Ajdabiya, one in Niger, and they each had a wife in each place, taking it in turns to live in one or the other: the father travelled to Niger with a truckload of cloth, and relieved his son who returned with the truck loaded with clothing and other goods. He stayed in Ajdabiya for a few months, before returning to Niger to spell his father.

The point I wish to make is that Zuwaya success and confidence was built on trust in friends, kin and spouses rather than on trust in the working of a market. Zuwaya were more confident in kin, you might say, than they were in the impartiality of economic forces; that is how they made their money.

The evidence about Zuwaya accounting procedures tends to the same conclusion. Very few Zuwaya kept account books: in response to direct questions on the subject, the two richest men claimed to do so, and said that they kept track of their ramified enterprises with the aid of specialist accountants (of whom Libya possessed very few at that time). I have no reason to doubt them, but I was never privileged to see their books. Two other people, both small shopkeepers, showed me account books in which they kept notes of loans they had made to their friends, or credit they had granted to their customers – the distinction was vague, and the books were multi-purpose *aides-memoire* rather than representations of the costs and returns of a business. 'Do you make a profit?' I would ask; and then, 'But how do you know you make one?'. In every case (except for the two millionaires) people replied that they sold their goods for a bit more than they paid for them: you buy Korean tinned pilchards at 40LD a gross and you sell at (say) 0. 35LD a tin; you get 50LD in return for an outlay of 40LD and that is a profit of 10LD. Well it may be or it may not: most British shopkeepers, for instance, include more in their accounts than the cost of stock; the notion of a rate of return over a period of time seems to be an important ingredient of capitalist calculation. Zuwaya accounting procedures were skimpy, and they did not seem to use the notion that shelf-space is a valuable commodity or that turnover is a measure of efficiency. They certainly used money to purchase commodities to sell for money but it is not at all clear to me that they calculated their enterprise. They varied their prices, ate their stock, loaned their spare cash to friends for no return.

It may be that the notebooks in which partners *al-thalth* kept a record of outlay and income represented a more accurate accounting, of a sort which would make a rational appraisal of the success of effort easier and more precise, and would moreover do so in a form which made it possible to compare one enterprise or partnership with another. But in fact I think it is not stretching the case to argue that this is not what they were used for: the notebooks (which, again, I never saw; I think because they contained details of the terms of trade and of the charges made to different individu-als) were for recording the achievement of successive targets, rather than for calculat-ing the profitability of enterprise. They recorded the dispersal of capital, rather than its accumulation. The point I wish to make is that no one really knew if he was making a profit, unless he had money to spend on more stock, on *sdiqqa*, on *zakat*. What relation that money in the pocket might have to outlay, to the time taken to achieve the return, was not available knowledge: in my understanding of capitalist markets, however, those are essential components of successful entrepreneurship.

Another aspect of Zuwaya trade concerns risk. I think it fair to say that every trader and trucker I met was against risk, and would have been happiest to know that he had succeeded in eliminating it altogether from his enterprise. The men who considered themselves most successful, and who were generally agreed to be so, had gone some way to ensure that they did not lose money in any intrepid commercial adventure. I once sat with a trader in his shop and we watched a man selling Polish shoes from a Toyota truck: he disposed of his stock in an hour or so and I commented on his success. My companion was full of contempt: the adventitious trader had made some money, but he had done so on speculation, had taken too much risk; his business could have gone the other way: that was the behaviour of a small man, without standing and without substance. The real trader never speculates. He himself, for instance, only brought goods down to Kufra against a firm order for them. He envied the man who had a contract to supply the army barracks with food and cigarettes: although he never made more than 500LD on a trip from Benghazi, he made it every ten days and he knew in advance that he would make it: anything else he carried was a pure bonus. This was real commerce. To have that contract and the cola-bottle one would be more than a man could desire. The trader's attitude was widespread: the best way to trade was to work without risk of loss, for a small profit if necessary, but in any case for a sure one. 'Poor man; he isn't sure'. Risk is associated with struggle, with uncertainty; a strong man and one who can be trusted is a man who is sure, reliable and (for instance) not likely to betray you because he is forced by circumstances to retrench or to weigh his priorities against you. Risk-taking brings the trader into a cloud of uncertainty which may affect his associates as well, if things turn out badly.

These elements suggest that the Zuwaya distinction between *tijara* on the one hand, *zakat* and *sdiqqa* on the other, were perhaps not so clear as they first appeared. It is true that, with strangers, Zuwaya thought and acted as if 'business is business'; but they behaved differently towards other Zuwaya, making special prices, for instance and the internal organisation of their enterprises was remarkably personal. Zuwaya relied on kinship and marriage to establish their trading networks, on the obligations of shared membership of a collectivity to secure market information and to regulate prices. Emrys Peters remarks of bridewealth (in the 1950s) that because of the rapid succession of exchanges, relatively few camels could create a rather large number of relationships; bridewealth is one of the ways (as Goody teaches) in which wealth is diffused in a population. But this is also the characteristic of partnerships *al-thalth*, for instance: business, at any rate among Zuwaya, had some of the qualities of social exchange. Although Zuwaya distinguished them sharply it is clear that they overlapped. Their capitalism diffused wealth internally and did not result in concentration. Similarly, avoidance of risk, the lack of a clear calculus of capital, suggest that Zuwaya engagement with an international market was very much on their terms: so far as they were able, they tamed it and domesticated it, made it safe; when they could not do so, they tried to avoid it.

What I have done so far is to contrast Zuwaya entrepreneurs with an image of capitalists which is derived from nineteenth-century economists' analysis of market activity, mainly in Europe. In those terms, Zuwaya appear exotic and their market decidedly imperfect. But it is clear that when you contrast them with the actions and institutions of actual entrepreneurs (as opposed to theoretical ones), they do not appear so aberrant. Stock markets, commodity markets in London or New York or Chicago; local labour markets in Britian, are also associations of people, more or less formally organised and bounded and (often) with an equal amount of face-to-face interaction and acquaintance. It is by no means clear that a Morgan a Carnegie or a Nuffield would give up the opportunity to maintain a commercial advantage, even a monopoly, on the theoretical ground that the greater perfection of the market required him to do so: competition is as unwelcome to a classical entrepreneur as it was to a Zuwayi trader. It is even more difficult to see modern corporations embracing risk for its own thrill: ICI and Siemens do not produce adrenalin. Modern companies, at any rate in Europe and OECD countries, do produce accounts and have got more detailed ways of forecasting profits. But it is not altogether clear that these are an objective technology of capitalist accumulation. On the one hand, some corporations go bust through their own ignorance of their internal affairs. On the other, many of the detailed items of accounting are related more to the requirements of taxing authorities than they are to the scientific conduct of a business.

Business is business wherever it is, and businessmen are not distinguished by the fact that some operate according to the laws of economics, while others are constrained by social institutions to work in an imperfect market. The differences lie chiefly in the external controls on business activity.

The Libyan government, in the 1970s, introduced a series of measures to eliminate private trade and transport, which were defined as anti-socialist (probably true) and capitalist (probably mistaken). But it is important to remember that Libya was – and still is – a relatively unusual kind of revolutionary state chiefly because more than 95 per cent of revenues came from petroleum companies in the form of royalties. What is peculiar about all hydrocarbon societies is that the state flourishes without the need to tax its citizens, and that it creates the characteristics of modern welfare without the concomitant revenue-collecting service. In revolutionary hands, the inspector of taxes, when he exists, is a useful instrument of social policy: it is easier to tax class-enemies than to hang them. Without that apparatus of state's men, however, a revolutionary government has to find other ways of eliminating private enterprise. In Libya, the planned vehicle was the creation of co-operatives and the one-off imposition of quantitative limits on cash through currency change. I have said that Zuwaya and others found ways to circumvent the limits on cash holdings. They also managed to limit the damage co-operatives might do to business by participating in them whole-heartedly. The government offered subsidies for buildings and for stock to properly registered and constituted co-operatives, on condition that the goods were sold at prices fixed by government. Profits would go to shareholders in the co-operative, by a formula established in conformity with social and economic justice. When I left Libya in 1979 there were some thirty-five co-ops in Ajdabiya, Ajkharra and Kufra which had members and officers who were Zuwaya: most of them were shaikhs and traders, although some had recruited Zuwaya schoolteachers and professionals to the committee. The names of the co-ops were redolent of Zuwaya history and independence of the state: Bu Zadma, Ghazala, for instance were the names of Zuwaya lineages which had fought against the Italian colonial state with particular distinction and Hawaria co-op was named after the battleplace where Zuwaya made their last stand against Field Marshal Graziani.

And so on. It is tempting to see this enthusiastic adoption of co-operativism as a potentially successful Zuwaya subversion of state socialism. But it is difficult to assert that without understanding fully what was in the minds of the revolutionary authorities, who surely expected different things from co-ops in the large cities with relatively uprooted populations from those in the smaller settlements with lineage territories and shaikhs. In any case, it is worth noticing that the state's regulation produced an economic regime which conceptually overlapped with the aspirations of local Zuwaya traders: absence of competition, cheap stock, low risk and good fellowship among market operators.

In a state, like most OECD ones, where the government has to tax its own citizens the priorities are rather different. It is essential, for instance, that the citizens are productive – that they make wealth that can then be taxed, for only then can the state afford to provide them with protection and to reward the state's men for their dedication to public service. In this case it makes sense among other things to generate an expectation of rising living standards and to establish a regulated market which approximates in some respect to the conditions of perfect competition: monopolist or corporatist citizens become too powerful *vis-à-vis* the government and it is more fruitful from the revenue-collector's point of view to have a large number of producers, in conditions of uncertainty, striving to produce taxable wealth. Only if the market is structured to preserve risk can government be sure that no one will succeed in eliminating competition to achieve the kind of certainty that Zuwaya traders quite reasonably regarded as the most desirable conditions of business. Only if government intervenes to prohibit insider manipulation can the state's men be sure that sufficient citizens will trust the market to be impartial between them to enter the game of wealth creation and generate revenues. Accounting standards (to return to an earlier point) are one means of ensuring competition, as well as a conventional measure of the taxable profitability of market-players.

Of course, there are other differences between markets than the extent and intent of government regulation: the scale of operations varies, the kinds of goods which are traded are also important, as are the kinds of social relations among traders (the difference between agnatic segmentary organisation and the bureaucracy of OECD corporations, for instance, although exaggerated, is none the less significant). But it is the case that conditions approaching perfect competition have only been achieved – as many economists point out – where governments intervene to maintain them; this is a contradiction in terms of the nineteenth-century theories of economic competition. When that government action fails or is missing, the conditions of trade approximate to those desired by Zuwaya.

The Bohannans argued (as Pirenne had done before them) that markets are the objects of political struggle: even the smallest Tiv market place was an important political resource to the local authorities. What I want to add is that the form a market takes is also politically determined: a free market, in classical terms, is always the product of political control rather than the automatic outcome of unrestricted exchange. The techniques of the calculus are also related to the forms of political and social control. The markets in Kufra are different from OECD ones in large measure because the polities which control them (very schematically, 'segmentary anarchy', religious order, revolutionary Islamic committees) are different and have different priorities. I would certainly want to mention Islam in any general account of Libyan market organisation and to contrast it with the ideas and notions associated with the Protestant and Roman Catholic ethics. But I also suggest that it is unnecessary to leap immediately to the divine economies in order to explain some of the differences among mundane ones. One of the important differences is the kind of political organisation which establishes and maintains the peace of a market. The social consequences of the market also depend in my opinion on the kind of political controls to which it is subject. The tendency of OECD markets is to reproduce stratified and centralised economies, of a kind which the political authorities can control; Zuwaya markets – permeated with kinship and marriage, with an internal organisation which was related in important respects to the institutions of social exchange – again seem to have reproduced the political order of a collectivity whose members thought of themselves as egalitarian and free from government control.

REFERENCES

Bohannan, P. and L. Bohannan, 1968. *Tiv Economy*. London: Longmans Green and Co.

Evans-Pritchard, E. E. 1945. 'The Sanusi of Cyrenaica', *Africa*, 15:61–78.

Goody, J. R. 1973. 'Bridewealth and Dowry in Africa and Eurasia', in J. R. Goody and S. J. Tambiah (eds.), *Bridewealth and Dowry*.

Hassanain Bey, A. M. 1925. *The Lost Oases*. London: Thornton Butterworth.

Mason, John P. 1977. *Island of the Blest: Islam in a Libyan Oases Comunity*. Athens, Ohio: Ohio University Press.

Peters, E. L. 1980. 'Aspects of Bedouin Bridewealth among Camel Herders in Cyrenaica,' in J. L. Comaroff (ed.), *The meaning of marriage payments*. London: Academic Press, pp. 125–60.

Pierenne, H. 1925. *Medieval Cities*. Princeton: Princeton University Press.

Part III

The Articulation of Modes of Discourse

7

Divine Protection and Liberal Damnation

Exchanging Metaphors in Nineteenth-century Potosí (Bolivia)[1]

TRISTAN PLATT

A Manichaean would say: that the genius of evil in battle has triumphed over the genius of good, and that the evil devils captained by the infernal Ahriman have defeated in Bolivia the good angels of the celestial Ormuz; but that evil genius, that Ahriman of the Manichaeans, is none other than our own mercantile madness ...
(*Anónimo*, Cochabamba 1854)

INTRODUCTION

Concepts of the market must be understood in relation to the historical and representational settings in which they are reproduced and transformed. But this is not a straightforward task and my approach to South Andean markets in the nineteenth century may be introduced with a question. If it is true that every ethnographic perspective is as valid and as contemporary as any other, then this assumption should naturally be extended to different historical epochs, where the other projects itself in time with no knowledge of those who may later choose to assign it a place in a temporal genealogy. Efforts at this tele-empathetic process are the historiographical equivalent of fieldwork. But what happens when, as with the case of liberalism, one is seeking otherness in a period or space still so close as to be part of one's own life? And anyway, is not one reason for seeking otherness in the first place the obscure intimation that in so doing one may better recognise oneself?

Sources for markets in nineteenth-century South America are redolent of contemporary liberal spirits which still condition our possibilities under many different guises. The otherness of these spirits is therefore shot through with a sense of intimate recognition; it is this uncomfortable tackiness that makes the sources so difficult to handle. Free trade is, after all, part and parcel of the New Right's thinking, and the argument over the virtues of public intervention versus those of private initiative is likely to get more intense in the coming years. The triumphalist accents of some neo-liberal formulations are accompanied by an almost apocalyptic fear of the spectre of protectionism: the imminent fragmentation of the 'world-market' into trading blocs is always somewhere on the liberal agenda.[2]

The tone of this liberalism, which mingles aggression with self-righteous desperation, is given in a recent number of *The Economist* (8. 12. 1990), whose main editorial discussed the possible failure of the Uruguay round of GATT talks. On the cover,

Figure 7.1: A Lifeboat for Trade (reproduced by kind permission of *The Economist*).

Figure 7. 1, a romantic picture of a lifeboat in stormy seas showed the crew of a sinking schooner being rescued. Beside the picture was the legend: 'A lifeboat for trade'.[3] Inside the editorial affirmed that, of all the tasks facing western leaders at the present time, the most vital was 'to maintain and extend the post-1945 order of liberal trade'. The other side of the coin was invoked discreetly, without mentioning the obscene word 'protection' (Borges once quipped: 'In a riddle whose answer is "chess", what is the one word that is forbidden?' …); but the emergence of trading blocs was subliminally associated with the anarchy and violence of the natural elements, which threatened to overwhelm the valiant crew of the liberal lifeboat and their precious human cargo. The article ended by pleading that 1990 'must not end by *ditch*-ing trade-enlightenment' (my italics: note the supercilious urban assimilation of protection to farm drainage).

As so often in post-independence Latin America, the early years of the Bolivian republic witnessed the advantages of protection pitted against the encroaching forces of free trade. The issues were summed up in a remark attributed to George Canning: 'South America is free, and, unless we sadly mismanage our affairs, it is British'. In the historical and political literature on nineteenth-century Bolivia, the protectionist current has generally been characterised as a survival from the colonial period: it was free trade which, with all its attendant risks and dislocations, held out the promise of modern progress (Benavides 1972, Mitre 1981, Klein 1982). This has culminated in the fatalism with which the (mainly liberal) historiography tends to construct its image of this century. The power of nineteenth-century liberal discourse, which engineered the Bolivian national economy's change of direction, still dominates most historical interpretations of the period.

The main ideologue of Bolivian liberals was Adam Smith. Whether cited explicitly[4] or adopted wholesale without acknowledgement, Smith was a key point of reference for Bolivian free-traders in the nineteenth century. However, even then there were economists in Europe who tried to refute the free-trade assumption from various standpoints. In 1834 another Scottish economist, John Rae (Scotland, Canada, US, Sandwich Islands) published his *New Principles of Political Economy* which criticised Adam Smith for assuming that the resources permitting accumulation are distributed equally in different regions, parts and nations of the world. The notion of a self-adjusting mechanism based on the division of labour, the action of supply and demand and the unleashing of individual self-interest does not necessarily produce beneficial results for the whole society.[5]

The debate between liberalism and protection is complex but central, both to the history of Bolivia and to the theme of this volume. It raises issues in South American political economy which are with us today: freedom, justice, colonialism and the sources of the poverty as well as the wealth of nations. At the same time, the debate was not confined to those nineteenth-century creoles who may have been fluent in classical economics or European political theory: Andean indians, the majority of the new republic's population, participated in ways barely recognised by the governing élites. I shall emphasise here this variety of discourses that jostled together, merging and diverging in accordance with shifting political realities at the local, regional, national and international levels. Rather than prejudging some discourses or suppressing others, I shall suggest that Andean metaphors, rationalities and ritual forms of expression offer an equally valid perspective on the secular process by which the ideologues of free trade strove to impose their will on a society out of step with North Atlantic economic interests.

7. I ADAM SMITH, BULLION AND THE HOME MARKET

Smith discusses the problem of the home market in Book IV of *The Wealth of Nations*. Indeed, the famous metaphor of the 'invisible hand'[6] lies embedded in an extensive polemic with mercantilism, where Smith argues that freedom will automatically ensure a sufficient degree of protection for the home market. Interestingly, he accepts protection in matters of military defence (compare with the Westland affair) or as retaliation against those unwilling to give freedom of access to their own national markets (US threats against Europe or Japan); he also accepts that governments may decide to raise revenue by taxing imports. But these are all riders to his central assumption that unregulated freedom to exchange will ensure that the local market is glutted before overseas expansion can begin.[7]

Though seldom concerned with countries whose main produce is gold and silver (which he considers mainly as sources of bullion and coin for the manufacturing countries of the north), Smith does observe (IV. v. a. 19) on the futility of Spain and Portugal trying to stop the outflow of precious metals, since inevitably only that much will stay inside these countries as they can afford to employ in coin, plate, gilding and other ornaments. The rest must necessarily be smuggled out. Smith argues that protection establishes an abundance of relatively cheap metal which raises the price of manufactures, thereby discouraging home industry and encouraging imports. He recommends the abolition of the tax and prohibition: this would provoke a fall in the nominal value of goods and a rise in the real value of gold and silver, a smaller quantity of which would cover the needs of coinage and circulation. Exported metal would then bring back 'materials, tools, and provisions, for the employment and maintenance of industrious people'.

This critique of Spanish attempts to restrain the export of precious metals seems to have provided a textbook model for Bolivian free-traders. In Book I we read that coinage should ideally show its true metallic content, that is weight, on its face, and that it should circulate at its market price. This idea partially underlies the outrage of Bolivian free-traders who insisted that all coinage, even debased small change, should be valued according to its price on the world market. In fact, as other Bolivian economists were aware, during the nineteenth century this practice was not followed by such highly capitalised nations as Switzerland, Britain, the US or Chile, whose debased coinage of small denominations was exchanged internally at its nominal value for the larger denominations where intrinsic and nominal values were supposed to coincide (Santibañez 1862).

Finally, the argument is inapplicable to the Bolivian case, where there was no such mechanical relationship between monetary debasement and price inflation as many free-traders predicted. For, as the Potosí economist Tomás Frías pointed out in 1871, sufficient demand for means of exchange rendered unnecessary any reduction in the price of money (calculated in kind) that might end by precipitating price rises among other commodities (Platt 1986). We must retain this lucid creole rejection of any naïve extrapolation of liberal ideas to an alien reality.

Nevertheless, echoes of the Scottish Enlightenment resound between the lines of Bolivian liberal pronouncements. For example, Smith derives the division of labour from what he calls the human 'propensity to exchange': the extent of the division of labour depends on the extent of exchange, that is, on 'the market'. He thereby implies that where there is no exchange, there can be no true humanity. So when the Bolivian land commissioner Narciso de la Riva (1885) argues, 110 years after the publication of *The Wealth of Nations*, that the propensity to exchange is reduced to its minimal expression in the case of Bolivia's indians, he is immediately enabled to draw the conclusion that indians are therefore irrational and savage. Again, when Adam Smith argues that a 'greater market will give rise to a greater division of labour and hence industrialisation', the conclusion drawn in Bolivia is that, in so far as indians appear to be resistant to the demands of the mining market, they can also be thought to block an increase in the extent of the division of labour and with it the industrialisation of the country. From this stems directly the notion of indians as a millstone round the neck of the nation, preventing it from moving to the tune of progress. These positions may seem naïvely racist but behind them lies a canonic text.

The silence surrounding the concept of 'protection' in recent political and economic discourse is therefore suspicious. During most of nineteenth-century Bolivia, it was in fact liberalism rather than protectionism which was often associated with the destructive fury of nature.[8] For protection was favoured by all who stood to gain from the consolidation and expansion of the internal market – cloth-manufacturers, food and fuel producers, small retailers of home produce, manufacturers of wines and spirits (*singani*), maize-beer and coca dealers, and small mining companies in 'mineral sharecropping' arrangements with their workforce (*caccheo*), as well as the tributary indian majority. For these, the liberal assault was perceived as the threat of chaos against order. Hence the predominance of fiscal policies derived from those of the colonial tributary state, which had sought to secure an internal market with a potential for capital accumulation in periods of flourishing peasant production and mining growth (Assadourian 1982; Platt 1982, 1986, 1987c; Annino et al. 1987; Langer 1988, 1990).

During the republic, the state legal monopoly on the purchase of uncoined silver remained until 1872, when the contraband export trade in silver bullion was finally legalised.[9] To what extent was the liberal overdetermination of South America during the nineteenth century – 'ideological' in the terminology originally coined in an *educational* context by the official ideologue of the Bolivian republic, Destutt de Tracy (Mesa and Gisbert 1976, Tomo II: 15 ff. ; see Kennedy 1978) – in fact contested from a similarly *trans–Atlantic* protectionist position? Early republican Bolivian writers cite Smith, Say, Flores Estrada, Yumandreau, as well as Sismondi and Colbert (Dalence 1848) and the example of Hamilton is visible in the texts of the period.[10] But historical research has still to establish whether the ideas of List and the German school of National Political Economy may not have reached the Altiplano before the liberal triumph of 1872.

7. 2 SILVER IN CIRCULATION: NOURISHMENT FOR THE SOCIAL ORGANISM

The most significant commodity in nineteenth-century Bolivia was therefore silver, whether 'raw' or 'minted' (as Olivia Harris suggestively expresses the Andean way of contrasting bullion and coin). Harris (1989) begins her analysis of Andean ideas about money with the opposition between 'romantic' views of money's dissolvent influence on the collectivity, and 'liberal' views which see money and the spread of exchange as part of the process of civilisation. She then seeks traces of both in the discourse of Laymi peasants,[11] before arguing that, for them, money in circulation is predominantly associated with cosmic fertility and increase.

The notion of cosmic fertility suggests a possible convergence between Andean ideas and those associated with pre-Enlightenment European physiocrats (Gudeman 1986). Such convergences are clear in other contexts. A romantic attitude, for example, was also present among creoles, and was dismissed scoffingly by Santa Cruz's Finance Minister, Dr José María de Lara, in 1831:

> Those who feed off fantasy say that all a Nation needs is two or five hundred Citizens with 20, 50 or 1000 head of cattle, with lands in equal proportion; and that prosperity lies in each farmer having his own lands, a couple of oxen to plough them, 20 or 100 sheep ... and no need to buy his food; ... but let us not waste time inventing paradises.[12]

At the other extreme, the liberal utopia remained a beacon for many passionate spirits among the new nation's white leaders (Latin American liberalism was in many ways very romantic). For the real politico–economic antagonist to free trade was not romanticism but protectionism.

It could of course be argued that protection is premised on a romantic (and deeply conservative) nostalgia for the *Ancien régime*. It was to avoid self-delusion on this point that Bolivian Trotskyists later refused to condemn the opening up of Bolivia to the world market, since this allowed the mining proletariat to emerge as the force for the future (Lora 1967–80). Such an argument, however, misunderstands the nature of the protectionist project, which did not involve simply harking back to the late colonial order, but included efforts derived from Hamiltonianism and practical experience to build on the internal market inherited from the empire in order to develop an internal process of capital accumulation.

Liberal and protectionist positions differed crucially over monetary policy. Till January 1873, the legal procedure by which miners could dispose of their product was by selling it at a fixed price to the National Mining Bank in Potosí.[13] The bank would then resell it, after reducing the silver to bars, to the National Mint. The mint would pay for the silver bars from the bank with coins made from previous silver purchases and the bank would then put the money into circulation via a number of different routes. It might return it to the miners in payment for their product; they would then use it to pay their labourers and purchase food and industrial inputs. Alternatively, payments would be made direct to import houses for supplying the silver industry with overseas consignments of mercury and iron, or providing foreign arms for the army.

One way or another, the coins would divide up into two distinct flows. The first, consisting of the higher denominations with a higher silver content, would be exported at its 'intrinsic' (that is, world market) value to pay for imports; the other, made up of the smaller denominations and with a higher admixture of copper, would enter the internal market-places and circulate at its nominal value, facilitating the process of exchange over an area far wider than the national territory of Bolivia, from Ecuador to Buenos Aires and from the nitrate fields of the Pacific coast to the gold mines of Cuiabá, Brazil (Mitre 1986).

My concern here is mainly with this second flow, and, specifically, with the spatial, social and temporal paths traced by an important part of it. In nineteenth-century Bolivia 'tributary indians'[14] formed the bulk of the population. Most of these culti-vated land held collectively from the state on the basis of the early colonial land-grants (*repartimientos*), which were themselves derived from the ethnic and territorial divi-sions of the Inka and pre-Inka periods (Platt 1982, 1987c). In exchange, the collective possessors of the land paid *tasa* (indian tribute) to the state. Since the sixteenth century this had been delivered twice a year through a hierarchy of ethnic, regional and state collectors amidst elaborate ceremony at the solstitial feasts of Saint John and Christmas. But tribute money could only be acquired through the sale of labour or goods. In this sense, the tributary demands of the state functioned like a pump, forcing the circulation of coin through successive social exchanges until it reached Potosí once more to be deposited in the public treasury. Here it was ready for re-emission in the form of fiscal payments to the army or to public functionaries and administrators who, along with the miners, would be the main purchasers of indian produce.

Free-traders denounced the unfairness of this system: silver-producers had to sell their raw metal for a price fixed by the bank several points below the price it would fetch on the open (i. e. international) market. They argued that, whatever its denomination, silver coinage was simply bullion so far as the foreign purchaser was concerned, and would always fetch a sum calculated in relation to the quotation in the London metal markets. As the only legal purchaser of silver at a price fixed by law below 'free market' levels, the National Bank was exercising a monopoly which stifled the development of the mining industry.

Capitalised through commerce (Mitre 1981), the new liberal mine-owners also argued (the intertextual echoes with Adam Smith resound) that to debase coinage was tantamount to ruining the national credit abroad, since a debased coinage had a higher denomination than its 'inherent value'. In this situation, vast quantities of uncoined silver were smuggled out of the country prior to 1873, in exchange for imports which could then be retailed by the silver-miners. Free-traders argued (and liberal historians repeat) that such contraband was inevitable, the logical result of the iron laws of supply and demand and that the law of 1872 was simply the historic result of economic necessity, the political expression of a lack of any possible Bolivian autonomy.[15] An alternative interpretation (which I shall not pursue here, although it is essential to a critique of the Whig view of Bolivian history) could argue that the silver-barons and their politicians managed to get the law through parliament just in time for them not to be controlled effectively by the Bolivian army stationed in the mining camps.

In Bolivia as elsewhere, then, discussion of the market goes hand in hand with discussion of forms of political authority (Hart 1986). It was clearly impossible to separate the market issue from that of the state, as free-traders were demanding. On the other side, the Bolivian tributary state system was felt by its supporters to allow a process of capital accumulation through the internal market, in a context of sufficient means of circulation, 'forced commercialisation'[16] and tariff protection. Our next aim, therefore, must be to examine the nature of exchange and tribute in an Andean society out to constrain free trade.

7. 3 ETHNO-HISTORICAL APPROACHES IN NINETEENTH-CENTURY POTOSÍ

As anthropological analyses of money and markets move beyond the old formalist–substantivist dichotomy and the role of the political becomes recognised in the formation of any possible referent of the word 'market', the search for new concepts has been accompanied by renewed attention to other ways of representing the nature of exchange. Evolutionary ideas, linking the growth of money and markets to the triumph of calculating individualism over the moral economy of the past, have been replaced by a more open approach, with greater attention to consumer preferences as vectors of economic change, and a search for new clusters of comparative ideas as the old ones dissolve. Greater concern has also been shown for alternative cultural metaphors employed to represent different perspectives on the nature of exchange.

Some have tried to overcome the Maussian opposition between western concepts, which contrast gift-giving and cash transactions, and those of 'primitive economies', where the difference between the two does not exist: in these views, capitalist commodities are 're-fetishised' as possessed by *spirit* and gift-exchange becomes prey to rational calculation (Appadurai 1986). We shall find some use for this view, which also qualifies the traditional Marxist distinction between capitalist and pre-capitalist forms of exchange. [17] Besides the 're-animation' of commodities, Appadurai argues further that things may move through several phases in their exchangeable 'life' as they enter and leave the status of commodity. Studies of monetary circulation in Potosí give some support to this too, as we shall see. He also maintains that commodities may leave their previous channels of circulation in a spirit of entrepreneurial initiative (thus opening new ones that are then 'customised' for the purposes of future reproduction) – a suggestive metaphor for the ever-extending network of monetary transactions that spread over the Andes from the Potosí money-manufacturing industry. It can also characterise moments of expansion of the network of Andean vertical exchange partners, whose maize and salt, wheat and potatoes have each their female spirits which are said to make the exchanges in the valley. These transactions, however, must also be affected by the choice of the valley farmer, who feels attracted by the design in one storage sack rather than another: for the sacks bear magical designs which bespeak a person's social, ethnic and ecological origin, guarantee the duration of the product, encode references to the spiritual exchange which is hoped for in the valley, and measure the sacks' contents (Torrico 1990).

Others have meanwhile insisted on the need to situate all forms of exchange within the cycles of production and reproduction that form their strategic context. Here, long-term cycles of social reproduction are schematically contrasted with short-term cycles where individual interest predominates (Parry and Bloch 1989). One nineteenth-century Bolivian case might appear to fit the dichotomy quite well

(Platt 1987c). Llama-herders from the Potosí Province of Lipez operated a rigorous economic calendar. In it mining demand for llama-transport to bring ore down from the mine to the refinery was only attended to during a couple of months each year. During this period, the llama-herders showed a preference for higher rates of pay, switching their services from one mine to another according to the rates offered. But from May till October each year they abandoned the mining sector and dedicated themselves to exchanging salt for maize, at carefully calculated rates of exchange, with exchange partners resident in the distant, warm valleys. During these months nothing the mine-owners could do – 'not even offering them the same goods their journey would provide, plus a profit four times greater than the product of their own labour ...'[18] – would deflect them back to the transport of minerals. The first rationality might appear, then, to be based on short-term *private* calculation; the second on a longer-term cycle of *social* reproduction involving both partners to the exchange.

But this dichotomy does not really do justice to the situation. It omits the role of mensual time and the Andean-Catholic calendar in the distribution of different social activities, *including* monetary exchange, throughout the year in relation to the two semestral periods when tribute payment to the state was expected. Lipez indians would dedicate October to December to hunting vicuña, vizcacha, chinchilla and Andean rhea, to be sold on the Pacific coast; at the same time their llamas would rest while waiting for the rains to renew the pastures. In December, with the arrival of the rains, the llama-herders would take their animals to transport ore until February. Then they would return and immediately celebrate their first annual tribute-payment ceremonies for the Christmas solstice. Following these, they would collect llullucha (freshwater kelp) before travelling to the great Altiplano salt-pans to collect salt. They then returned to their homes for Holy Week before migrating to the valleys. Now they disappeared for three or four months, reaching as far as the Chaco, exchanging salt and llullucha directly for maize, or providing labour in exchange for grain. After this diaspora they would return to the highlands just in time to celebrate their St John tribute-payment ceremony in September, and attend the great commercial fair at Colcha the same month. Here any surplus cash could be spent on products brought up from both sides of the Cordillera as well as on overseas imports. Finally they left their llamas to rest and returned to hunting (Platt 1987c).

Note that, in this calendar, different economic rationalities are themselves distributed on a monthly basis among the same population, rather than serving to contrast different populations. One of these is based on a shorter-term individual relationship with the miner who pays most, while the other is predicated on an extended social relationship through time. But the reproductive process benefits the corporative landholding group as a whole: tribute-payment is a social affair and the calendar is devised to allow all domestic units to monetise themselves, pay the collective tribute and acquire the subsistence necessary for their survival. The rhythm of herding activities is part of two longer *tributary cycles*. Both forms of rationality therefore have their place within the collective strategies of social reproduction of the ethnic groups concerned.

Here, another of Appadurai's proposals benefits from close comparison with the Potosí situation. Small *diversions* of these seasonal llama-trains are sometimes engineered by the mine-owners, in ways which suggest the 'impediments' to the 'flow of the commodity' (in this case, animal traction) analysed by this author. Again, let us see what happens. The seasonal migration of the llama-herders occupies three or four months (May to September) of their yearly calendar. This movement was regarded by the great silver patriarch Felix Avelino Aramayo as an 'instinctual' phenomenon (Aramayo 1862) of the natural world; indeed, it was almost as hydraulic engineers dealing with the gravitational flows of a 'natural economy' that the mining companies, desperate for animals to transport the raw ore from the mine-mouth to the refinery, organised a diversion of the descending llama trains into a siding. The llama-herders were first presented with tempting advances and credits, and then prevented from departing until they had worked off their debts. Finally, the mining company issued certificates stating that each herder was free to travel to the valley with a specified number of llamas. The herders then reverted to their journey down to the distant maize-producing valleys.

It would be idealistic to suggest here (with Appadurai) that the commodity is itself seeking new channels of exchange. But the 'animate' metaphor for the nature of the commodity need not therefore be abandoned. The diversion through an institutional block, arranged by the mining capitalist, can also be thought of as a 'trap' into which indian labour is lured to make it available to the mining sector, before 'releasing' it to revert to the maintenance of long-term familial and *casero* [19] relations with valley exchange-partners. The conceptualisation of exchange as a 'trap' is, of course, well-known from Taussig's (1987) study of discourses and debts on the banks of the Putumayo during Colombia's nineteenth-century rubber boom.

What were the consequences for the rural tributary economy? It is sometimes assumed that the expansion of the commodity sector implies automatically an increase in monetary exchange (Parry and Bloch 1989). But in Bolivia (as is to be expected from the application of liberal economics in a bullion-producing country), foreign trade, expanding to the inner margins of the country, sucked all the silver out, including minted coin, in exchange for a deluge of imported goods, thereby forcing most of the population – including the tributary indians – on to the *inner side* of these margins. [20] In many rural areas, traditional exchange on the basis of non-monetary equivalences increased, as the process of demonetisation and the reorientation of mining demand overseas[21] gathered pace. The growth of liberalism therefore produced the opposite to what was intended: the internal market sector shrank, industrial activities were sacrificed to extractive ones and by the end of the century a relatively trivial sum of tribute had become an almost insuperable problem for most Bolivian peasant households.

7.4 THE MEANINGS OF TRIBUTE (*TASA*)

The role of money as commodity and/or means of exchange is accompanied by other functions. Money has two sides to its coin (Hart 1986): one is the side which shows the nominal value, thus referring to the coin's function as means of circulation; the other, showing the head of the sovereign, president or head of state, refers to the hierarchical relationships between the people who use it and the state which emits it (Knapp 1924, cited in Bradby 1982). This second side [22] brings us to the tributary relationship between the indians and the Bolivian state (Platt 1982), a relationship which involves both a sacrificial dimension and a tinge of contractual obligation, while throwing out an influence that affects strict commodity exchange inasmuch as labour or produce is sold with the aim of acquiring tributary coin (Platt 1982 and 1983). Thus, where Gose (1986) contrasts *sacrificial objects* (tribute) with *individually owned commodities* (exchange), I shall again reject simplistic dichotomies, preferring to show how both aspects are co-present in the tribute-paying ceremonies.

Tribute payment ceremonies were celebrated (as we have seen) twice a year at the solstitial feasts of St John and Christmas. At each ceremony [23] tributary coin was delivered into the hands of the representative of the state, in amounts reflecting the extent of each land holding and the degree of security of tenure (Platt 1982). At the same time, the indian authorities would call out the names of the fields for which the tribute was being paid. These ceremonies, celebrated with chicha and coca-leaf, were the most important in a series of obligations levied on Andean communities,[24] and the close link between tribute and land is emphasised by the use of the same word, *tasa*, to refer to both. In this way, coins abstracted from market circulation by indian tributaries were formally returned to the state by dispatching them, on muleback, for the final step of their journey, back to the Departmental Treasury in Potosí.

A first image now emerges to characterise money in its tributary role. The silver peso coin is today given the same indigenous name by which it was known in the sixteenth century: *uj sara*, 'a maize (cob)'. The reference is apparently to the extensive maize plantations tended for the Inka in Cochabamba by rotative labourers (*mitayos*) from the highlands (Wachtel 1980). The implications of this are far-reaching: the production of maize for the Inka state, which then redistributed it as corn-beer (*chicha*) to the army and to those involved in public works (including the state maize fields in Cochabamba) (Murra 1975), has served as a model for interpreting and legitimising the production and redistribution of silver and coin among participants in the home market by the colonial and republication states.

The date of the tribute-collecting ceremony varied according to each ethnic calendar, which organised the year's activities in relation to the sequence of Catholic religious fiestas. Ceremonies could be postponed up to three months if the activity required to obtain tributary coin overlapped with the solstitial date. If the Lipez tributaries did not pay their June tribute till the early days of September, in Chayanta Province one ethnic group did not celebrate the Christmas tribute-paying ceremony until Quasimodo after Carnaval (February to March).[25] But the Departmental Treasury applied double-entry book keeping methods based on a comparison between tribute collected (in advance or on time) and tribute owing: indian tribute was also the shaky mainstay of fiscal revenue (Sanchez Albornoz 1978). Failure to deliver invited sanctions for what could easily lose its semi-gratuitous appearance and reveal itself as an order backed up by political and military force.

For the tribute-paying ceremonies also encode a more complex statement concerning the nature of the tributary state. Tributary coin could be seen as an indicator of the extent of each indian's participation in the urban and mining markets: it registered the success of the state's attempts to oblige indians to provide a minimum of labour and produce to the mines and cities. In the early republican period, we even find *receipts* issued by mining companies or the military in exchange for goods or services received or expropriated, which are then presented direct to the state as tribute instead of coin. The conceptualisation of money *as receipt* for forced market participation is an important aspect of Andean tribute.

Two sacrificial aspects of the tributary relationship must also be distinguished. The sacrifice of offerings to the divine patrons of production (such as the so-called 'devil' of the mines) in return for precious metal should be contrasted with the final sacrifice of coins as offerings to the state. Both situations are fraught with ritual danger: the first from the underground 'devil', who may reject the offerings or compensate for their insufficiency by devouring the indian sacrificer himself;[26] and the second from the state which may transform exchange of the *means of fertility* (coins and land) into a demand backed up by military violence. However, while the first expression of violence cannot be contested provided it keeps within its own 'interior' jurisdiction (*ukhupacha*, the 'Inner World'), the second can be rejected in the name of an alternative, more legitimate form of state, if governmental threats of force seem to deny the established bases of the moral order, thereby signifying a diabolic intrusion into the 'Upper World' (*janajpacha*) of the solilunar state.

At tribute payments the state's own coinage returns to the hands of the power which minted it, and the ceremony thus marks the completion of a tributary cycle of circulation. Libations poured for the sacrificed coins refer both to their tributary characteristics (the maize-cob) and to their fertility. Today, banknotes are often referred to as 'flowers', *t'ika*, symbolic of life and increase. An ethnographic detail from 1986 is suggestive: among the Macha ethnic group (Northern Potosí), the modern banknotes with which tribute was paid during the St John ceremony were held from flying away 'like butterflies (*pillpintu*)' by stone weights libated to as *inka mayku*. This is the 'Inka-with-authority', who makes present and personifies the highest level of the state. The aptness of Andean metaphors for expressing economic processes is again manifest: the Inka pins down the helpless 'butterflies' which might otherwise fly off to metamorphose themselves into flower after flower in a natural return to circulation. Thus the state intervenes to restrict the propensity to exchange of these living forms of money-commodity.

At the same time, however, the state confirms their nominal value by recognising it in tributary accounting: the liberal-provoked crisis at the end of the century was marked by tributaries clamouring to be allowed to use the old rates, rather than accepting the devaluation that followed the slow transformation after 1862 of the old *pieces of eight* into the Bolivian *peso* of 100 *centavos* (Platt 1986, 1987b). Moreover, the state's demand for tributary coin was itself a factor which helped debased coins of the smaller denominations to circulate at their nominal value, forcing them through the tributary system with a velocity which maintained the rhythm of transactions necessary for inflation to be avoided. In this sense, the tribute-payment ceremony validates both aspects of money and represents the culmination and final destiny of money as means of exchange.

The money-sacrifice also reflects the authority of the paternal state as *source of justice.* Tribute-payments are an important mechanism by which the enlightened solilunar state's authority was legitimated. The devotional aspect of this republicanised piece of colonial tradition must be contrasted with the pressure towards abuse and illegal practice inherent in a system based on the public auctioning of administrative posts.

It is as part of the devotional perspective that we can understand a reform of the tribute-collecting system proposed in 1855 by the most extreme of the nineteenth-century protectionist regimes, that of Manuel Isidoro Belzú (1848–55). Here, the Bolivian tributary state reveals its interest in the *theatrical* form of self-presentation common to many states (Geertz 1980, Hobsbawm and Ranger 1983). A new post, that of the state collector, was to be created in order to eliminate abuses and illegal practices by the provincial governor. Each new collector was to wear a silver medal on a chain round his neck, and to bear a silver-banded staff of office. He was also empowered to name his indian agents within each canton.[27] We do not know what design was stamped on the medal, but we can expect it to have been some symbol of state authority (Burnett 1986). The staff of office is clearly a republican transformation of the colonial staffs of different sizes still to be found in the hands of indian authorities today. In this sense, the collector's medal and staff legitimised the link between minted coin and state authority (see Platt 1991).[28]

Such attempts to legitimate the authority of the state must be contrasted with the opportunities for corruption offered by the tributary system. For tributary coin could still re-enter circulation by a number of loopholes *after* the tribute-paying ceremony was completed but *before* reaching the Departmental Treasury in Potosí. It could even function as productive capital in the collectors' private mines during the interval between its delivery by the indians and its final surrender to the Treasury. For the collectorships were public posts auctioned off to the highest bidder, who was then entitled to try and recover the value of his bid and make a small profit into the bargain. Tribute money was therefore a 'sacrifice' of potential means of exchange from the perspective of the indian tributaries, but also industrial credit and potential source of profit for the local authorities.

In this context, the notion of 'desire' introduced by Appadurai (1986) expresses the insertion of personal advantage and interest into the structure of public administration, with an inevitable increase in the opportunities for corruption. The purpose of this arrangement, from the state's point of view, was to use personal interest as a motor for ensuring the collection of public revenues. It represents a compromise position between the pure tributary model and the liberal utopia; indeed, it confirms what was argued above, namely that the liberal spirit was present *within* the protectionist project, which simply insisted on making conscious and deliberate use of the controls to hand in order to ensure the strengthening of national production for the home market.

The Potosí case therefore requires us to recognise the different understandings which may be brought by each party to the tributary relationship: what can be seen by one party to the transaction as a tributary sacrifice appears to the fiscal intermediary as a source of credit and personal enrichment. It becomes pointless to try and impose over-simplified dichotomies on situations which in their very nature are shifty and ambiguous: the reality of the situation lies in the *political* institutions and discourses in which are carried out these constant negotiations between tributaries, fiscal authority and private entrepreneurs over the nature and meanings of the money yielded up at tribute-paying ceremonies.

7. 5 THE MEANINGS OF PROFIT (*WAKI*)

The previous section offered various perspectives on the tributary relationship as a diagnostic feature of the Bolivian protectionist state. We now return to the economic debate of the nineteenth century, and with it to the circulatory perspective on coin. A debate parallel to the argument over tariff barriers and the free export of silver bullion also developed at the local level. Here, however, it concerned the way in which trade between rural areas and the towns should be organised, and popular fury could express itself openly at the impoverishing impact of the liberal 'principles of economic science'. [29] In this debate, the notion of the 'free market principle' is subjected to a vigorous popular critique in the light of the political and institutional reality of the local Andean market-place.

Unlike the Amazonian societies discussed by Joanna Overing (this volume), Andean peasants have intervened in the market for centuries,[30] and consider it perfectly reasonable for a middleman or woman to take a profit (Platt 1987a, Harris 1989). The idea of the *redistribution* of goods and services has enjoyed legitimacy in the Andes since pre-Hispanic times (Murra [1955] 1980). In the nineteenth-century sources, the term *guaque* (Aymara, *waki* meaning 'fair share, portion, part') occurs with the meaning of 'commercial profit': deriving from the vocabulary of non-monetary redistribution, its semantic transformation suggests that the redistribution of goods was still regarded in Andean thinking as a legitimate activity, in the mercantile idiom as well as in non-market terms. [31]

In the nineteenth century, the *waki* was seen as a share of the final price charged by market-women (*gateras*), as well as by the administrators of the municipal *cancha* or *casa de abastos* (provisions house). The term should be contrasted with another native term that appears in the nineteenth-century sources. This is the *alakipa*, or 'wandering vendor', who buys and sells small quantities of many different effects, without a fixed place of sale, and thus with no obligation to pay the tax on a fixed selling place.[32] The debate over the best form of supply to the mining towns and cities was further affected by the attempts of the authorities to curb both street vendors and *gateras* in order to secure this tax for fiscal purposes.

7. 5. 1 A Market-place in the Making

The argument can be observed clearly at mid-century, when a sudden spurt of speculation injected renewed capitalist rationality into several mining camps within the overall protectionist framework established by Belzú. Till then Carguaycollo, site of the richest of these mid-century speculations, had remained abandoned to the mineral share-croppers (*cacchas*). But in 1852 the Corregidor, José Bacarrega, painted an intense picture.

> Since the regeneration of this mining camp, both producers and consumers have been the victims of uncontrolled violence, of monopoly transformed into an industry, of deceits and theft. The purveyors who manage to escape the clutches of the 'food-lifters' [*forsadores de viveres*] on the roads, who pay the price they please and on terms of their own choosing, must then face the insolent rabble who attack them in scattered bands as they enter the town; their goods, or at least their sacks [*costales*] are mislaid; or else they fall into the tyrannical care of astute inn-keepers … who after receiving a gift [*regalo*] at the first greeting demand a weighing tax [*romaneaje*] of 2 *reales* per *peara* [10 animal loads], and use an infinity of tricks in order to buy their wares at the lowest price, and then resell them dearer; and as to the flour-sellers, they sleep in the streets or on the outskirts, at the mercy of thieves and those who take flour on trust and then never pay them … [33]

The situation described by Bacarrega shows a pre-market-place situation, where unregulated freedom reigns: the main organising principle is violence by middlemen and consumers against the indian producers obliged to visit the town in search of tributary coin. I have previously suggested that market-place negotiations over the 'just price' may have been interpreted in terms derived from Andean ritual warfare (Platt 1987a). Yet there are signs that even in this situation some buyers were singled out preferentially by the producers through the offer of a 'gift', as though in search of the preconditions for the renewal of a peaceful organisation of exchange. These were the *posaderos* (innkeepers) who could offer in exchange a protected roof for the night. [34]

How did the *gateras* (mainly though not always women) manage to impose themselves on the indian producers (mainly though not always men)? Many tricks are effective when the producer is away from home. He does not want to delay his return; has no time to go from door to door; is unwilling to have to face the administrators in the provisions house. Food-purveyors are often content to be able to sell their whole load for cash, even if more cheaply, to an intermediary who will take on the onerous task of selling the produce to the ultimate consumer. The direct producers can thus remain wandering vendors (*alakipa*): they then make their own purchases, and begin the journey home. Only when at home again can the peasant feel safe: he can then complain at ease to his family and comrades about the *gateras'* behaviour and the low prices they have 'forced' him to accept.

Travel time, including all perambulations before the full load is sold, is therefore calculated carefully, and the savings on this 'cost of realisation' provided by the *gatera* is one reason for accepting the low prices she tries to impose. Later in the century, the *gateras* chose to pursue the producer to his own home; here prices were even lower to cover travel time and expenses incurred directly by the *gatera* herself. The logic of the situation thus allowed the intermediary to press down purchase prices, while forcing up prices of resale, at the same time as she intercepts the producer ever farther from the city gates, finally appearing in the community itself to buy next year's harvest before the seed is in the ground. In this contentious space opened up by their efforts, a modest accumulative potential is in the hands of intermediaries prepared and able to invest time and capital in the process.

For Bacarrega, the only way of dealing with such mafias was through the centralisation of transactions in a municipal provisions house (*casa de abasto*):

> The debate is ancient as to which system is of more benefit to the Public: the isolation of foodstuffs in the *Casa de Abasto*, or their free introduction and sale. The departmental and provincial capitals have resolved the problem in favour of the former.

So the town council of Carguaycollo ordered that food-supplies be brought to the town square where transactions were made under the eye of the police. 'Gifts' (reconceptualised as 'extorsion', compare Platt 1987b) were forbidden and the weighing tax reduced to 1 *real* per *peara* (a troop of 10 mules). But the problem continued: the purveyors had no other place to sleep, and continued to go to the innkeepers. For as long as some intermediaries could offer the indians the counter-favour of a roof, therefore, the functions of the absent market-place would inevitably gravitate towards the inn.

Bacarrega, therefore,

> rented the *tambo* (inn) called Belarde, and ordered the purveyors to sleep there, in order to distribute their wares fairly, giving preference to the mine-owners. The tax they pay is only 1 *real* for a day and a night, even if they have more than 20 loads … they pay according to the nights they spend in the tambo's lodging-rooms, and those with a few loads are dispatched the same day without being charged a cent …

Thus the traditional 'gift' to the innkeeper was captured by the municipality as 'tax'. The purveyors were apparently convinced and the situation relieved:

> food is now so abundant that we even have loaves weighing two and a half ounces [35] … there has been no more talk of purveyors being assaulted on the roads; the monopolies are disappearing; more and more purveyors keep arriving … the consumers buy direct from the producer, contracts are free and not forced.

However, the response of the intermediaries, fighting to keep hold of their indian clientele, was to denounce the provisions house as an interference with commercial freedom:

> Persistent rumours circulate [wrote Bacarrega] about the Provisions house preventing the arrival of supplies; that it keeps the purveyor away because (it is said) taxes or alcabalas are charged. This is a specious name given, in the chaos of obscurantism, to the tambo charges (*tambeaje*) … It is the monopolist rabble which has spread these falsehoods.

Note that the language usually deployed by liberals against the 'feudal yoke' of the *ancien régime* is here directed against the free-traders themselves. 'Free' commercial interests are denounced as 'obscurantist'; they are 'monopolists', because they corner the supply before it reaches the town and fix prices among themselves; freedom of contract itself is represented as something that can only occur under protection. On the other hand, the confusion between *alcabalas* and *tambeaje* shows the free-traders retaliating for their loss of *waki* by accusing the Corregidor of reintroducing colonial taxes, while the Corregidor insists that a fair rate is being charged for accommodation. Such inversions are evidence of a confused semantic field of battle over *waki* between municipality and private enterprise: protectionist republican authorities seek to replace traditional 'gift-exchanges' with municipal taxation by denouncing *waki* as a sign of 'corruption', while themselves being accused by their free-trading rivals of interfering with 'freedom' and the right to profit by reintroducing a colonial 'extortion'. Meanwhile, the indian purveyors themselves, immersed in the 'moral economy', of the *ancien régime*, seem to have been happy to pay *waki* to anyone, provided they offered the reciprocal favour of protected conditions in which to acquire tributary coin at 'just prices'.[36]

The political correlates of the dispute are further clarified by Bacarrega's observation that

> the monopolists have been supported by those trouble-makers [*descontentos*] who are never lacking in the towns, who try to destroy without rebuilding, without producing one idea, one useful project in favour of the future and to the benefit of this mining camp.

The 'trouble-makers' (compare with the 'demolitionists' of note 8) are obviously supporters of Belzú's liberal rival, José María Linares (President, 1857–61). The battle between free trade and protection on the national and international level is here articulated at the grass roots with a local contest concerning the organisation of supplies to the mining-camps.

This sequence of events illustrates the ideological fissures which underlay the argument over provisions. Disagreements over the desirability of 'free market' principles here found their pragmatic expression in the difficulties of forming a local market-place where the producers would truly negotiate with the consumers. The scale and intensity of the political polarisation (as well as the prophetic nature of the debate with regard to the present-day ideological shindy[37]) was confirmed in 1865, when the Belzú regime was denounced as 'communist' by liberal authorities![38]

7. 5. 2 A Provisions-house in Action

It is in the city of Potosí itself that our sources allow us to observe more clearly a provisions-house system in action. Like the local authorities discussed in the previous section, the post of administrator was rented out to the highest bidder, who could then pocket all funds collected as taxes from the purveyors in the hope of covering the rent and make a profit as well. The administrator, or *Canchero*, was thus another speculator, well placed to foster precisely the abuses which it was his function to prevent.

In Potosí, too, the purpose of the provisions house was to centralise all produce where its sale could be supervised by municipal officials. According to a *Reglamento* of 1845, all goods entering the city by any of its four entry roads were to be intercepted by the guards (*celadores*) and the quantities registered in notebooks. After sale under supervision in the provisions house, the administrator was to give a certificate (*valé*) to each purveyor, which could be checked by the guards on departure by confronting it with their own register. This would ensure that sales had not taken place outside the provisions house. According to the regulations for 1846, consumers could make their purchases at cost prices direct from the purveyors between seven or eight and eleven o'clock in the morning; thereafter, until three in the afternoon the storekeepers and other intermediaries could buy at the same prices for resale in town stores (*pulperias*). Consumers who had bought goods in the early hours were forbidden from reselling them. All sales in the centre were to be 'free' agreements between buyers and sellers, and the administrator was not to touch or put aside wares for himself to resell to private customers for profit (*waki*). [39]

All these prohibitions obviously reflect practice to some extent. One case[40] which was brought in 1830 shows the intermediary María Moscoso placing an injunction on municipal officials and their dependents. In her *Questionnaire* to witnesses she tells us that

> when the purveyors arrive and unload in the centre, the officials hide most of their goods in rooms apart until the sales to consumers have ceased, and then they distribute them to the intermediaries [*gateras*] with an increase of 2 *reales* over their just price, and this is paid as *guaque*, to the profit of the official ...

Here we see the official assuming the role of an additional middleman between the purveyor and the *gatera*.

In this case, the complaint comes from the *gatera*. In another we find an urban indian, Mariano Apasa, a candlemaker from San Sebastián parish, complaining about the municipal authority's interest in securing *waki* on the sale of grease, a necessary input for Apasa's business. The official had refused to allow direct sale from producer to consumer, forcing sale on credit terms to himself and then reselling it for cash to another customer willing to pay a higher price. But this price simply served to provide *waki* for the authority, rather than being passed on to the producer. As Mariano Apasa explained:

> three months ago he went to the centre at Munaypata, and saw the son of Reynaga [an official] take 1 *quintal* and 5 pounds of grease from an indian purveyor, depriving the witness of the chance of buying 2 *arrobas*; he then resold it to Dr Garrón [miner and bank official] for 16 *pesos*. He showed the money to the witness and then paid the indian purveyor 15 *pesos* 2 *reales*, with a clear profit of 6 *reales*, without having previously given the owner a cent ...

Apasa's complaint, it seems, is not simply that he is thereby deprived of cheaper grease. He also thinks the transaction was carried out on false pretences: if he was acting as a middleman, Reynaga's son should first have purchased the grease himself before reselling at a profit. Behind the dispute probably lies the scarcity of small change and the ambiguity of credit. Reynaga had *imposed* credit terms on the producer; he also seems to have had a prior arrangement with one of the most powerful creoles in the city. Hence he was able to acquire six *reales* in cash on the deal (as a virtual 'tip' from Garrón?), while the candlemaker who had saved the necessary cash to make the purchase found himself denied the transaction altogether. This was precisely the sort of situation forbidden in the 1845 *reglamento*.

If officials were going to behave like this, however, *waki* or no *waki* the purveyors had to find an alternative way of getting rid of their wares. So it is that the administrator of the provisions house in Puna (capital of Porco Province) lamented in 1858, shortly after Linares' coup:

> no one wants to sleep there now; the purveyors go to private houses in the outer suburbs, and so do not pay their dues [*canchaje*]; the bakers bring wheat-flour into their houses illegally, and don't pay their dues; the slaughterers bring in cattle to be eaten in the town without paying either; the result being that I am the victim ... of the excesses of a few speculating citizens; it is now six months since the auction of the post, and I've barely made 20 *pesos* ...⁴¹

Here, then, the wheel had turned full circle: the purveyors had fled back to the 'monopolists', selling goods and 'giving *waki*' in exchange for lodgings in order to escape the greater monopoly threatened by the municipal officials.

7. 5. 3 *The Devil and the 'Principles of Economic Science'*

What produced ambiguity in the indians inspired debate in the creole press. As silver coin and bars poured out of the country in exchange for imports from 1873 on, a rearguard action against free trade was mounted at the local level. In 1872 itself, with free trade in silver bullion the issue of the day, we find the opposition pointing to the effects of free trade in the local markets:

> *Free Trade* ... has begun to produce its effects, for potatoes have risen 3 *pesos* without any reason, meat is scarcely to be had ... for since trade is free, the traders are free to ask the prices they wish and to traffic us all at their pleasure. If the authority does not act to relieve the people, the people will suffer the plagues of Egypt, with the madnesses of modern science.
>
> The poor indians, who live from the bread they make in Yotala, pay the Provision-house keepers so high a contribution on introducing their produce into the city that their industry is killed. The onion-ladies pay the same again which makes the price of their product rise to the level of the shop, et sic de ceteris. How excellent is Free Trade! How the consumers have benefited! What a brilliant application of the *principle* of the economic fathers!⁴²

The creole as consumer feels the conflict with free trade and is able to ironise liberal economic discourse itself. Here, then, the debate is resolved *against* free trade at the level of local market-place organisation. Where the municipality is corrupt, or does not intervene with sufficient force, we are told, the result shows that 'Free Trade is most advantageous for a few and has been the tyranny of the stomach of the poor ...'⁴³ However, the indians' reasons for favouring sale to the intermediaries remained, and in the twentieth century we can observe both systems of supply functioning simultaneously in Bolivian mining towns. At least the provisions house is useful as a refuge and offers a protecting roof for the night, in moments of scarcity and heavy speculation with food.

Let us now return to my Manichaean epigraph. A clear association is suggested between 'market madness' and the principle of evil. The text indicates both the existential effects of rampant liberalism on the crucified nation, and a further convergence with the Andean religious world.[44] For the 'Devil' is the producer of raw metal which is changed into means of circulation in the mint. And protectionism continued strong among a majority of the population well after the silver-barons' political victory in 1872. In 1875 we can even hear the dance-groups (*comparsas*) chanting during the bull-running at the Sucre Carnival:

> Comes the bull with the black horns,
> Death to the free extraction of silver![45]

In this heated moment, it almost appears as though 'Ahriman' himself, in the form of the black-horned bull, is about to burst into the streets and market-places.

The devil's presence is also signalled by the rampant trade in silver bullion in the last decades of the century – overflowing from the mines in greater quantities than ever before, only to by-pass the Potosí mint and flow in torrents along the new roads and railways towards the ports of exportation. In 1890, sacrificial battles in the silver-mining city of Colquechaca, staged traditionally by the indian communities, were enlarged by the mining work-force who, furious at the disappearance of their salaries overseas, organised riots against the foreign export houses. Amidst this cosmological crisis, the indians clung to the idealised memory of the old tributary state, with its imagined orderly circulation of state-minted coins: under siege from the devils of liberalism, it was this memory which, at the end of the century, provided a psychological trampoline for the great uprising of Aymara and Quechua communities during the Bolivian Civil War (cf. Platt 1987b, 1991).

CONCLUSIONS

The referential and poetic aspects of metaphor run through this account of the liberal–protectionist debate and its consequences for Andean forms of exchange. The frustrations of late twentieth-century capitalism have shifted interest from politico-economic structures to the analysis of the discursive strategies by which these structures are empowered. The frontiers between 'economic science' and 'native models' can thus be interrogated and subverted – a belated academic response, no doubt, to the needs of the people on the receiving end who have long queried the authority of 'the economists'. It becomes possible to recognise the way in which economic policies are themselves embedded in and controlled through discourse: the rampant triumphalism of the New Right, like the liberalism of nineteenth-century Bolivia and its associated historiography, is only one example of this. More generally, neo-liberal economics can be confronted with many other discourses which do not pretend that economic and social policy can be deduced simply from the 'natural human propensity to exchange'.

In nineteenth-century Bolivia, the protectionist camp converged with an Andean counter-discourse of tributary justice and the socio-political correlates of exchange under divine protection. If the discourse of free trade overwhelmed the protectionist alternative, this was not because it was more efficient or beneficial, but because it managed to leave its rival behind in the invocation of scriptural authority and in the manipulation of parliamentary politics in order to attract foreign capital and reinvest in an internationalised mining industry. Protectionist monetary policy did not produce price inflation, as was denounced by free traders, because the demand for means of exchange throughout the Andes – intensified by state tributary demands – ensured a sufficient speed and volume of circulation for it not to do so (Tomás Frías). For the protectionist opposition, *Freedom needed Protection*. It is at this point that the modern history of Bolivian democracy begins.

Indian demand for coin was conditioned, in the first instance, by tributary pressures: different rationalities were integrated into tributary cycles organised by ethnic calendars. Tribute-payments defy any simple analysis because they were perceived differently from such varied political perspectives. From the indian point of view, money functioned as a *receipt* for labour and produce supplied to the mines (receipts and land-titles, as well as bank notes, may sometimes be represented as 'flowers', symbols of reproduction, by Andean peasants). It was also sacrificed to the state in celebration of another completed cycle as means of exchange. Both aspects (tributary/circulatory) influenced each other: to separate them distorts the way in which they were represented. In Andean tributary metaphors, the 'butterfly' was pinned down by the weight of the stone Inka, while maize-cobs were presented to the state as source of means of circulation.

Andean tributary indians conceptualised 'just' commercial profit as a 'fair share' for the intermediary or the administrator of the provisions house. Complaints against the 'free' market-place seem to have come particularly from consumers tired of cartel agreements among the intermediaries, although indian producers and *alakipa* also objected to the 'jungle' conditions prevalent in many towns. Even where such conditions dominated (as at Carguaycollo in 1852), the Andean purveyors attempted to manage them in moral terms through 'gifts' to the innkeepers. Such 'gifts' were increasingly reconceptualised by the authorities as 'extortions': to the emerging liberal structure of authority, they were a euphemism for the corruption of the *ancien régime*. But, at the same time, the perception of tribute as 'gift-sacrifice' was itself transformed into 'extortion' through the use of public means of violence by the state (compare Condarco 1965, Platt 1987b). In these conditions, appeals to republican law and citizens' rights begin to alternate with and complement the moral and common law perspective of the tributary state, in which 'gifts' to market intermediaries, the state or the church may be legitimised in terms of reciprocal favours received.

Politico-economic models can be recognised through the Andean metaphors in which these models are expressed. The sacralisation of Andean coin as product of the earth was complemented by the theocratic nature of the solilunar state (symbolised by the silver medals of Belzu's collectors). I have suggested that the unleashing of 'raw' silver exports at the end of the century will have appeared to many as a cosmic catastrophe, in which warring forces from inside the earth were let loose upon its surface. A Potosí variant of the Andean–Christian understanding of historical transitions (Bouysse and Harris 1987; Harris 1982, 1987; Platt 1987a, 1987d, 1991) may underlie the carnival song of 1875, where the 'black bull' suggests the imminent appearance of the underground 'devil' of the mines. For it was through such metaphors and representations that Bolivians of all cultures could understand and interpret accurately the *effects* of 'trade-enlightenment'.

Liberal discourse, in a creole reading of Adam Smith, was therefore, against all its own expectations, responsible for the destruction of the internal market, the demonetisation of the country, the internationalisation of mining capital and the creation of an export/import-dominated form of economic dependency which has continued to crucify the country for most of the twentieth century. Such issues in Bolivian historiography acquire added significance today, when the dominant capitalist interests in the western world – regrouping, diversifying and shedding labour in the face of the declining rate of profit, as well as cynically triumphalist in the face of the collapse of East European 'socialism' – increasingly fail to legitimate themselves through the historicist slogan of nineteenth-century liberalism that 'there is no other way'.

NOTES

1. This text is based on materials collected during a research project (Assadourian et al. 1980) on 'Mining and Economic Space in the Andes' (1980–3), sponsored by the Institute of Peruvian Studies (Lima) and the National Archive of Bolivia (Sucre) with funding from the Inter-American Foundation. It has been further developed by work with the Anglo–French Project on 'State control and social response in the Andes, XVI–XX centuries' (1985–7), funded by the ESRC and the CNRS (with Thérèse Bouysse, Olivia Harris and Thierry Saignes). Useful suggestions were forthcoming at the St Andrews conference on 'Concepts of the Market' (1991), and I am particularly grateful to Roy Dilley for his comments. During the final revision I derived additional benefit from discussions in St Andrews with Luis Javier Ortiz, of the Universidad de Medellín.

2. At this moment (January 1991), the EC contemplates yielding to US demands that price subsidies to small European farmers be sacrificed to liberal 'economic principles' which coincide neatly with US and big capitalist farming's material interests while leaving the smaller farmers at the mercy of this *field of power* we imagine as 'the market'.

3. The classical metaphor of the 'ship of state' was already identified with commercial trade in seventeenth-century England (L. Platt, personal communication).

4. For example by Dalio Fernandez, Subprefect of Chayanta province, see *Informe del Subprefecto de Chayanta al Prefecto de Potosí*, Potosí 1889 (p. 18).

5. A similar preception underlay the neo-protectionist current of 'national-economic' thought, exemplified by Hamiltonianism and given theoretical expression by Friedrich List, whose *National System of Political Economy* (1841–4) defended the necessity of a German customs union to achieve the national objective (see Hobsbawm 1990).

6. See Heinz Lubasz's chapter in this volume for the Providentialist overtones of this over-invoked phrase.

7. Smith attributes this to such factors as the uncontrollable risks abroad, transport costs and the lack of trusted agents. Though possibly true of the behaviour of many eighteenth- and nineteenth-century British capitalists, the argument was of little consolation (as Rae pointed out) to those societies whose home industry was being destroyed by foreign capital.

8. An exchange of insults at the end of the century between the country's Constitutional and Liberal parties illustrates the point. In 1890, the Constitutionalists maintained that the insult 'conservative' (*conservadores*) had been hurled at them by the Liberal party out of resentment at being called themselves 'demolitionists' (*demoledores*) by the government (*La Industria*, Año IX, no 1058, 4. 1. 1890) – not to mention 'social Darwinists', which was certainly true (see Demelas 1980; Langer

1988). In a *world-jungle* still dominated by the liberalism of Victorian Britain, many Bolivians felt that 'human nature', or what Adam Smith had called the 'propensity to exchange', needed restraint and regulation if Bolivia was not to be 'demolished' entirely.

9. The 1872 law was heralded by the decimalisation of the currency (1862) and by Melgarejo's overtures to Chile's highly capitalised wheat and cereal farmers (Grieshaber 1977, Platt 1982, 1986) in the name of American unity. It has been argued that the Chilean product was able to penetrate the Andean market because its costs of production had been reduced through economies of scale. The notion of price advantage is, however, insufficient to explain the imported product's success where the local competitors are tributary indians prepared to sell at any price in order to amass their tribute-money. In fact, the *whiteness* of Chilean flour seems to have attracted the preferences of a certain type of consumer: the racial symbolism is confirmed by the existence in Sucre, within living memory, of a loaf made from native wholemeal mixed with Chilean white, and called *pan mestizo*. We should therefore leave open the possibility of consumer preferences both encouraging *and limiting* the 'penetration' of the Bolivian market by imported flours.

10. See Anónimo 1854.

11. The example of Laymi 'romanticism' given by Harris is ambiguous: miners without money with which to buy peasant produce may appear less abusive, not because money is thought to dissolve solidarity, but because they lack the basis for initiating a transaction.

12. Ministerio de Finanzas, *Memorias e Informes*, 1831 (p. 9).

13. For a fuller description of the system see Assadourian 1982; Mitre 1981, 1986; Platt 1986 (also published in Annino et al. 1987).

14. 'Indian' is mainly used in this paper as a *fiscal* category (*indio tributario*); though this does not deny that tributary communities (or ethnic groups) had each a specific social and cultural identity whose similarities underpinned the nineteenth-century creole notion of an 'Indian Caste' (or 'Class') at the labouring base of nineteenth-century Bolivian society.

15. Not only Liberals but also, later, Trotskyists. See Lora 1967–80, Dunkerley 1980.

16. This concept (Kula 1974; compare Platt 1978, 1987c) roughly covers the minimum indian participation in the markets required by the Andean tributary state.

17. Significantly, however, Appadurai refuses to pursue the consequences of treating the commodity *labour* as though it had been reinvested with 'spirit'. If he did so, he might simply find himself confronted with the free individual who, in classical political economy, presents his labour in exchange for a wage from the owner of the means of production – a result which might appear positively pre-Marxist.

18. Compañia Esmoraca, *Segunda Memoria*, Sucre 1886 (p. 10).

19. Meaning 'regular exchange-partner'.

20. I have suggested elsewhere (1986) that this situation can be conceptualised as an *inversion* of the proposition (associated with Elizabeth of England's financial advisor Thomas Gresham) that 'weak money drives out good' where both share a sphere of circulation and exceed the public need for means of exchange (compare Fetter 1932). In nineteenth-century Potosí, we find the country increasingly incorporated into the sphere of circulation of silver as bullion, while the 'weak' denominations are expelled towards the internal margins of the country where they continue to circulate at their nominal value. The situation reflects the continued need for means of exchange at the local level, but also the growing *political* control of free trading miners and commercial interests over most of the country.

21. A key expression of this was the collapse of the national refining industry as the railways made it more profitable to export unrefined ore (Mitre 1981).

22. There is also a third side, generally neglected: patriotic slogans are sometimes inscribed on the *milled edge* of the high quality silver peso coin, which is in fact a shallow cylinder rather than a disc (compare Burnett 1986). The whole adds up to the slogan: State, patria and circulation.

23. Quechua *kawiltu*, from Spanish *cabildo* meaning 'council'.

24. Others included service in the post-houses, labour on the roads and in the mines, refineries and the mint, and acceptance by turn of other political and fiscal duties to church, state and *ayllu*.

25. For other Chayanta tribute-paying dates, see Platt 1984.

26. For example, through a mining 'accident', see Nash 1979, Taussig 1979, Platt 1983, Salazar 1987, Sallnow 1989.

27. *La Nueva Era*, Sucre, Tomo I, no 13, 8. x. 1855.

28. Such medals may represent the state's equivalent of the old coins, no longer legal tender, which are today associated with earlier mythic ages, and which Harris has argued (1989) are similar to *illa*, the lightning-struck stone or metallic sources of fertility which ensure the multiplication of flocks and humans. Coins, it is thought, reproduce themselves like organic matter (very like Marx's pear-fetishes) and multiply through circulation; the medal on the new collector's breast would complement the message of hoarded silver coins by reaffirming the solilunar state's willingness to protect the reproduction of minted money.

29. Although this fury reached a head after 1872, the terms of the debate were constant throughout the earlier part of the nineteenth century, and reached back well into the imperial period (see Tandeter 1975).

30. In the sixteenth and seventeenth centuries Potosí and other ethnic groups worked in the mines and refineries, producing the avalanche of silver-bullion which provoked the European price revolution and with it the emergence of modern capitalism (Hamilton 1936, Assadourian 1982, Bakewell 1984, Arduz 1985, Cole 1985).

31. An earlier version of these ideas was put forward in Platt 1987a.

32. For alakipa see Archivo Histórico de Potosí, Prefectura Departamental (Correspondencia) 574 no. 15, Mariano Terán to the Prefect, Potosí 13. 6. 1847. *Plazaje* was charged for the *gateras, canchaje* for direct producers in the provisions house.

33. Archivo Histórico de Potosí, Prefectura Departamental (Correspondencia) 701 nos 16, 17, 21 et al.

34. The weighing tax was in any case already in place in many towns (in Sacaca, Chayanta's 'dry port' for grains and flours sold to La Paz and Southern Peru, it funded the local school).

35. As in Potosí, the price of bread was constant, and the weight governed by a sliding scale in relation to the price of flour.

36. Compare E. P. Thompson on late eighteenth-century bread riots in England. Platt (1982, 1987c) and Rivera (1984) deploy the concept of 'moral economy' in the Andean context (compare with Scott 1976 for a south-east Asian version). Tandeter and Wachtel (1983) have shown how, for the indian tributary, 'just prices' tended to be seller's rather than buyer's prices: thus, it was low prices which helped precipitate the Andean insurrection of the 1780s, rather than the high prices of flour identified by Thompson (1971) for England and Labrousse (1973) for France as contributing respectively to riot and revolution.

37. Maastricht is a topical example of the confused battle between intervention and liberalism.

38. Archivo Histórico de Potosí, Prefectura Departamental (Correspondencia) 1140 no 20, José M. Esteves, Subprefecto de la Provincia de Porco, al Prefecto, Puna 1. 4. 1865.

39. Archivo Histórico de Potosí, Prefectura Departamental (Correspondencia) 544 no.

7, *Reglamento para las Canchas de Abasto*, Mariano Terán, Junta de Propietarios, Potosí 29. 7. 1845.

40. Archivo Histórico de Potosí, Prefectura Departamental (Expedientes) 209 f. 4r–v (1830).

41. Manuela Mayora de Jimenez, to the Lieutenant-Colonel Governor of Porco Province (Puna 5. 2. 1858), concerning her rental of the administration of the provisions house. Interestingly, the rentee is here a woman, and no doubt herself a practised 'middle-woman' on the model already described. In this document, the word '*contrabandistas*', commonly used for those illegally exporting uncoined silver, is used by Sra Mayora for all purveyors who evade paying taxes by seeking private outlets in the town for their product. Archivo Histórico de Potosí, Prefectura Departamental (Expedientes) 4663.

42. *El Lábaro Constitucional*, II. 39, 10. 10. 1872.

43. *El Obrero*, Año 1 no 13. 12. 1. 1876.

44. The passage probably ironises the masonic metaphors of influential contemporary creoles, which had entered the country from Argentina and Chile. Indian religious thought, however, does not share this Manichaean approach to good and evil (see Izko 1981, Harris 1982, Platt 1983, 1987c).

45. '*Viene el toro de las negras astas,/Muera la libre estracción de pastas!*. This *estribillo* is quoted in the Potosí newspaper *La Discusión* (No 46, 30. 4. 1875), edited by Modesto Omiste. The Sucre correspondent ('Julius') told how he had refused to give charity to a Sucre chola, who had answered, 'ashamed, that they were in difficulties due to the free extraction of uncoined silver'. 'Julius' then remembered the Carnival chant … He himself rejected the explanation offered, as the 'artesans of Sucre are in enviable conditions. Their women attend the distribution [in the provisions house] to re-sell articles of first necessity, and thus maintain their husband and children: the husband only attends his workshop two or three days a week to get a few pesos for his vices'. La Plata, the capital of the colonial Audiencia of Charcas, now converted into Sucre, the capital of the republic, was of course well-supplied with the product of the Potosí mint.

REFERENCES

Annino, A. , M. Carmagnani, G. Chiaramonti, A. Filippi, F. Fiorani, A. Gallo and G. Marchetti, 1987. *America Latina dallo Stato Coloniale allo Stato Nazione (1750–1940)*. Milan: Franco Angeli.

Anónimo, 1854. *Tratado sobre los medios de proteger la industria en Bolivia*. Cochabamba.

Appadurai, A. (ed.), 1986. *The Social Life of Things: Commodities in Cultural Perspective*. Cambridge: Cambridge University Press.

Aramayo, F. A. 1862. *Proyecto de una nueva vía de comunicación entre Bolivia i el Océano Pacífico*. Sucre: Tipografía del Progreso.

Arduz Eguía, G. 1985. *Ensayos sobre la historia de la Minería Altoperuana*. Madrid: Editorial Paraninfo.

Assadourian, C. S. 1982. *El Sistema de la Economía Colonial*. Lima: Instituto de Estudios Peruanos.

Assadourian, C. S., H. Bonilla, A. Mitre and T. Platt, 1980. *Minería y Espacio Económico en los Andes, siglos 16–20*. Lima: Instituto de Estudios Peruanos.

Bakewell, P. 1984. *Miners of the Red Mountain: Indian Labour in Potosí, 1545–1650*. Albuquerque: University of New Mexico Press.

Benavides, J. 1972. *Historia de la Moneda en Bolivia*. La Paz: Ed. Puerta del Sol.

Bloch, M. and J. Parry (eds.), 1982. *Death and the Regeneration of Life*. Cambridge: Cambridge University Press.

Bouysse-Cassayne, T. and O. Harris, 1987. 'Pacha: en torno al pensamiento Aymara', in

Bouysse-Cassayne *et al.*, *Tres reflexiones sobre el pensamiento andino*. La Paz: Historia Social Boliviana (HISBOL).

Bouysse-Cassayne T., O. Harris, T. Platt and V. Cereceda, 1987. *Tres reflexiones sobre el pensamiento andino*. La Paz: Historia Social Boliviana (HISBOL).

Bradby, B. 1982. '"Resistance to capitalism" in the Peruvian Andes', in D. Lehmann (ed.) *Ecology and Exchange in the Andes*. Cambridge: Cambridge University Press.

Burnett, D. 1986. *Bolivian Proclamation Coinage*. Virginia: Latin American Press.

Cole, J. A. 1985. *The Potosí Mita. 1573–1700: Compulsory Indian Labor in the Andes*. Stanford: Stanford University Press.

Condarco, R. 1965. *Zárate, el temible Willka: historia de la rebelión indígena de 1899*. La Paz: Talleres Gráficos Bolivianos.

Dalence, J. M. 1975 [1848]. *Bosquejo Estadístico de Bolivia*. La Paz: Editorial Universitaria, Universidad Mayor de San Andrés.

Demelas, M. D. 1980. 'Darwinismo á la criolla: el darwinismo social en Bolivia, 1890–1910', *Historia Boliviana* 1(2). Conchabamba: Amauta Books. pp. 55–82.

Dunkerley, J. 1980. 'Reevaluación del caudillismo en Bolivia', *Historia Boliviana* 1 (1).Cochabamba: Amauta Books. pp. 59–77.

Fetter, F. W. 1932. 'Some neglected aspects of Gresham's Law', *The Quarterly Journal of Economics*, 46 (3): 480–95.

Geertz, C. 1980. *Negara: The Theatre State in 19th Century Bali*. Princeton: Princeton University Press.

Gose, P. 1986. 'Sacrifice and the commodity form in the Andes', *Man* (N. S.), 21 (2): 296–310.

Grieshaber, E. 1977. *Survival of Indian Communities in Nineteenth Century Bolivia*. Ph. D thesis, University of North Carolina.

Gudeman, S. 1986. *Economics as Culture: Models and Metaphors of Livelihood*. London: Routledge and Kegan Paul.

Hamilton, E. J. 1936. *American Treasure and the Price Revolution in Spain, 1501–1650*. New York: Octagon Books.

Harris. O. 1982. 'The dead and the devils among the Bolivian Laymi', in M. Bloch and J. Parry (eds.), *Death and the regeneration of life*. Cambridge: Cambridge University Press.

Harris, O. 1987. 'De la fin du monde: notes depuis le Nord-Potosí', *Cahiers des Amériques Latines 6 Nouvelle Série*. Paris: Institut des Hautes Études d'Amérique Latine. pp. 93–118.

Harris, O. 1989. 'The earth and the state: the sources and meanings of money in Northern Potosí, Bolivia', in J. Parry and M. Bloch (eds.), *Money and the Morality of Exchange*. Cambridge: Cambridge University Press.

Hart, K. 1986. 'Heads or tails? Two sides of a coin', *Man* (N. S.), 21 (4): 637–56.

Hobsbawm, E. J. 1990. *Nations and Nationalism since 1780*. Cambridge: Cambridge University Press.

Hobsbawm, E. J. and T. Ranger, 1983. *The Invention of Tradition*. Cambridge: Cambridge University Press.

Izko, J. 1981. 'Magia espacial y religión telúrica en el Norte de Potosí, *Yachay, Revista de Cultura, Filosofía y Teología*. Cochabamba: Universidad Católica Boliviana. pp. 67–107.

Kennedy, E. 1978. *A Philosophe in the Age of Revolution: Destutt de Tracy and the Origins of "Ideology"*. Philadelphia: Memoirs of the American Philosophical Society, Vol. 129.

Klein, H. 1982. *Bolivia, Origins of a Multi-Ethnic Society*. Oxford: Oxford University Press.

Knapp, G. F. 1924. *The State Theory of Money*. London: Macmillan and The Royal Economic Society.

Kula, W. 1974. *Teoría Económica del Sistema Feudal.* Mexico: Siglo XXI.

Labrousse, E. 1973 [1962]. *Fluctuaciones económicas e Historia social.* Madrid: Editorial Tecnos.

Langer, E. 1988. 'El liberalismo y la abolición de la Comunidad Indígena en el Siglo XIX', *Historia y Cultura (La Paz)* 14: 59–95.

Langer, E. 1990. 'Espacios coloniales y economías nacionales: Bolivia y el Norte Argentino (1810–1930)', *Historia y Cultura (La Paz)* 17: 69–94.

Lora, G. 1967–80. *Historia del Movimiento Obrero Boliviano* (4 vols.) La Paz-Cochabamba: Editorial 'Los Amigos del Libro'.

Mesa, J. de and T. Gisbert, 1976. *La Vida y Obra del Mariscal Andrés Santa Cruz. Tomo II.* La Paz: Casa Municipal de la Cultura 'Franz Tamayo'.

Mitre, A. 1981. *Los Patriarcas de la Plata.* Lima: Instituto de Estudios Peruanos.

Mitre, A. 1986. *El Monedero de los Andes.* La Paz: Historia Social Boliviana (HISBOL).

Murra, J. 1975. *Formaciones económicas y políticas del mundo andino.* Lima: Instituto de Estudios Peruanos.

Murra, J. 1980 [1955]. *The Economic Organization of the Inca State.* Greenwich, Conn: JAI Press Inc.

Nash, J. 1979. *We Eat the Mines and the Mines Eat Us.* New York: Columbia University Press.

Parry, J. and M. Bloch (eds.), 1989. *Money and the Morality of Exchange.* Cambridge: Cambridge University Press.

Platt, T. 1978. 'Acerca del sistema tributario pre-toledano en el Alto Perú', *Avances: Revista Boliviana de Estudios Históricos y Sociales* 1: 33–46.

Platt, T. 1982. *Estado Boliviano y Ayllu Andino: tierra y tributo en el Norte de Potosí.* Lima: Instituto de Estudios Peruanos.

Platt, T. 1983. 'Conciencia proletaria y religión andina: *qhuya runa* y *ayllu* en el Norte de Potosí', *Historia Social Latinoamericana* (HISLA), 2: 47–73.

Platt, T. 1984. 'Liberalism and ethnocide in the Southern Andes', *History Workshop Journal*, 17: 3–18.

Platt, T. 1986. *Estado tributario y librecambismo en Potosí (siglo XIX): mercado interno, participación indígena y lucha de ideologías monetarias.* La Paz: Historia Social Boliviana (HISBOL).

Platt, T. 1987a. 'Entre *ch'axwa* y *moxsa*: para una historia del pensamiento político Aymara', in T. Bouysse-Cassayne et al. , *Tres reflexiones sobre el pensamiento andino.* La Paz: Historia Social Boliviana (HISBOL).

Platt, T. 1987b. 'The Andean experience of Bolivian Liberalism: roots of rebellion in 19th century Chayanta (Potosí)', in S. Stern (ed), *Resistance, Rebellion and Consciousness in Andean Rural Society (18th–20th centuries).* Madison: University of Wisconsin Press.

Platt, T. 1987c. 'Le calendrier économique des *ayllus* de Lipez en Bolivie au 19éme siècle', *Annales ESC*, 42(3): 549–76.

Platt, T. 1987d. 'The Andean Soldiers of Christ: confraternity organization, the Mass of the Sun and regenerative warfare in Northern Potosí (18th and 20th centuries)', *Journal de la Société des Américanistes*, 73: 139–91.

Platt, T. 1991. 'Simon Bolivar, the Sun of Justice and the Amerindian Virgin: Andean conceptions of the *Patria* in 19th century Bolivia', in M. Ziolkowski (ed.), *El Culto Estatal del Imperio Inca.* Warsaw: Centre of Latin American Studies.

Riva, N. de la. 1885. *Informe del Revisitador de tierras de origen de la provincia de Chayanta.* Sucre.

Rivera, S. 1984. *Oprimidos pero no vencidos: luchas del campesinado aymara y quechua 1900–1980.* La Paz: Historia Social Boliviana (HISBOL).

Salazar-Soler, C. 1987. 'El *Tayta Muki* y la *Ukupacha*. Prácticas y creencias religiosas de los mineros de Julcani, Huancavelica, Perú', *Journal de la Société des Américanistes.* 73: 193–217.

Sallnow. M. 1989. 'Precious metals in the Andean moral economy', in J. Parry and M. Bloch (eds.), *Money and the Morality of Exchange.* Cambridge: Cambridge University Press.

Sanchez Albornoz, N. 1978. *Indios y tributos en el Alto Perú.* Lima: Instituto de Estudios Peruanos.

Santibañez, J. M. 1962. *Estudios sobre la Moneda Feble Boliviana, seguidos de un Proyecto para la Reforma del Sistema Monetario Actual.* Sucre: Tipografía de Gutierrez.

Scott, J. 1976. *The Moral Economy of the Peasant: Rebellion and Subsistence in Southeast Asia.* Newhaven and London: Yale University Press.

Smith, A. 1976 [1776]. *The Wealth of Nations* (eds. Campbell, Skinner and Todd), Vol. 1. Oxford: Clarendon Press.

Tandeter, E. 1975. 'El Papel de la Moneda Macuquina en la Circulación Monetaria Rioplatense', *Cuadernos de Numismática, 4 (14): 1–11.* [Buenos Aires: Centro Numismático.]

Tandeter, E and N. Wachtel. 1983. 'Conjonctures inverses: le mouvement des prix à Potosí pendant le XVIIIe siècle', *Annales ESC*, 38 (3): 549–613.

Taussig, M. 1979. *The Devil and Commodity Fetishism in South America.* Chapel Hill: University of West Carolina Press.

Taussig, M. 1987. *Shamanism, Colonialism and the Wild Man: Terror and Healing on the Putumayo.* Chicago: University of Chicago Press.

Thompson, E. P. 1971. 'The moral economy of the 18th–century English crowd', *Past and Present,* 50: 76–136.

Torrico, C. 1990. 'The weaving designs on the *kustalas* of Macha'. Unpublished MS.

Wachtel, N. 1980. 'Los *mitimaes* del valle de Cochabamba: la política de colonización de Wayna Capac', *Historia Boliviana*, 1 (1): 21–48. [Cochabamba: Amauta Books.]

8

Kinship, Witchcraft and 'the Market'

Hybrid Patterns in Cameroonian Societies [1]

PETER GESCHIERE

The aim of this chapter is to study various reflections on the market in south and west Cameroon. The focus will be on kinship and witchcraft/sorcery [2] – spheres of life that in the west are not primarily associated with the market. In the societies discussed here, however, it is difficult to separate these spheres from 'the market'. To understand how these groups are coping with the impact of the world market – to recognise their own reflections on what western people call 'the forces of the market' and the peculiar expressions of these forces at the local level – it is especially the more intimate spheres of life, like kinship and sorcery, that we have to study.

The penetration of the market into these personal spheres – which still constitute the core of the local patterns of organisation – is all the more surprising since several of these groups did not know the institution of a market-place until the colonial conquest (around 1900). This applies especially to the societies of the southern forests where exchanges between the groups were couched in terms of kinship and an ideology of reciprocity. Yet, it is precisely in these societies 'without markets' that nowadays idioms of the market have emerged with surprising force on nodal points of the kinship organisation: in funeral rites and marriage ceremonies, in sexual relations and the domestic division of labour. Apparently an ideology of reciprocity and market-like behaviour can go very well together.

The Duala on the coast and the Bamiléké and the 'Grassfielders' in the western mountains had a much longer experience with the market-place as an institution. Especially in the mountains, social formations had developed which were based on a regional network of trade, linked to long-distance exchanges (Warnier 1985). During colonial and post-colonial times, these groups adapted relatively well to the new market conditions. The more successful entrepreneurs in present-day Cameroon come from these areas. However, even though the market penetrated fairly easily in these areas, developments hardly corresponded to classical economic theory. Here, specific metaphors of the market emerged, especially couched in a discourse of witchcraft, which were of direct – albeit variable – consequence to economic behaviour.

A comparison of these different examples can help in deconstructing western notions of the market – a task which seemed overdue to many participants of the St Andrews conference.[3] During my first fieldwork one of the most shocking experiences

– an unexpected kind of 'culture shock' – was the confrontation with market-like behaviour in what to me were intimate spheres of life. Precisely because I was shocked, I came to realise to what extent my own western notions of the market were culturally circumscribed.[4] Such an experience makes one conscious of the fact that the western image of the market does not reflect a self-evident reality but rather a specific folk model which has become enormously influential by its scientific elaboration in economics (and in economic anthropology).

In a more specific sense these examples can serve to indicate the untenability of a standard feature of western stereotypes of the market: the notion that 'traditional' forms of organisation will by definition resist the impact of 'modern' market forces. This vague but general notion has particularly impeded better insight into the various ways in which African societies tried to cope with the further penetration of the world market in colonial and post-colonial times. The ongoing significance of old organisation patterns, although in constant transformation, has certainly influenced the impact of the market. But often these modern transformations of 'traditional' idioms prove to express not a refusal of the market as such but rather a determined struggle to gain access to it on the people's own terms.

The main merit of a collection of articles edited by Parry and Bloch (1989) on a parallel topic – the penetration of money in non-western societies – is in my opinion that it effectively defuses this stereotype of a self-evident resistance of 'traditional' societies to money and the market. Like the penetration of the market, monetisation is not an automatic process: its variations and diverging trajectories are determined by different cultural constructs of money, which certainly do not always imply a refusal of money as something evil or threatening.[5] The classical image from Marx – and many other authors – of money 'as an acid attacking the very fabric of society' (Bloch 1989:169) is often not very helpful. In the literature of Africa, examples abound of how precisely the upholders of the old order – the elders – welcomed money and used it to reinforce their position.[6]

Yet I wonder whether Bloch is not overplaying his hand when he concludes from this that the specific role of money is to be drastically relativised: in his analysis monetisation seems to play only a minor role in processes of change.[7] For the societies discussed here, the penetration of money as a (more) general means of payment did constitute an important turning point and the circulation of money did start processes with dynamics of their own. The unintended consequences – unintended to all parties involved and often highly variable – of the monetisation of bridewealth in many parts of Africa are good examples that money can play a specific and independent role.

Similar caveats against an all too drastic deconstruction apply in my view to debates on the notion of 'the market'. It is doubtless highly worthwhile to bring out the folk model behind western scientific constructions of the market. Yet, such attempts at deconstruction should not hide that these western constructions have acquired considerable force on a global scale. The Cameroonian societies where I worked have had dramatic experiences of the capriciousness of market forces and the image of 'the market' as an impersonal agent is to them therefore all too real. The

Various groups in South and West Cameroon

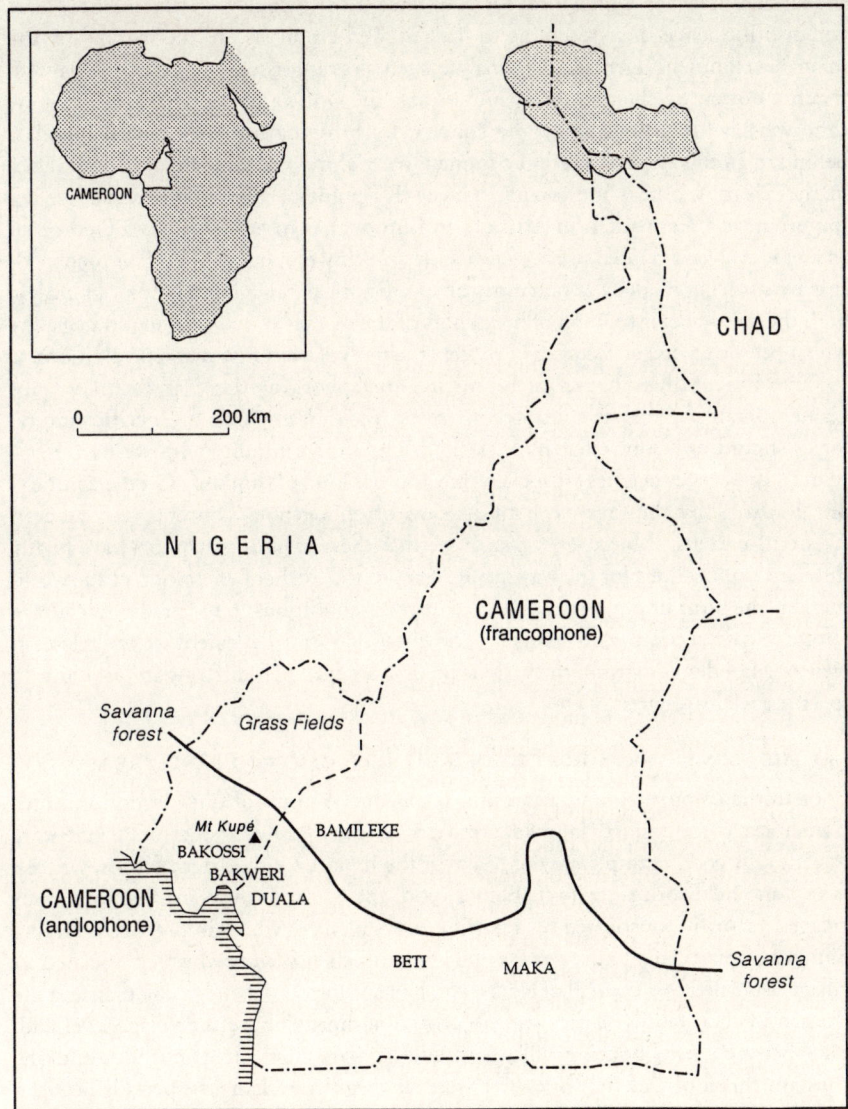

Figure 8.1: Various Groups in South and West Cameroon.

devastating effects of the recent crisis – many peasants suddenly have no cash because they simply cannot sell their cash-crops any more – are only one example of this. All markets introduce an open-endedness in social networks which may be experienced as a threat, and the deepening penetration of the world market reinforces this vulnerability.

Especially in view of the recent crisis in Africa, it is urgent to gain more insight into the different ways in which local societies have tried to cope with 'the market'. This will also influence their reactions to the renewed emphasis on 'the market' by the main development agencies. To analyse such pressing issues, it seems we have to retain a notion of 'the market' (which equals the world market ?). Yet, at the same time we have to problematise the concept by bringing out the cultural premises behind it. In this respect, a recent comment by Mahmood Mamdani on IMF policies in the Third World is important. 'The IMF's point of view is ahistorical, having forgotten that the market, in Africa as in Europe, has never existed as a God-given entity; it is always created, *through social struggle*'(my emphasis, Mamdani 1990:457). It is by studying markets as outcomes of specific social struggles that one can analyse both the cultural construction of metaphors of the market and the varying strategies by which people try to get access to or protect themselves from new market conditions.

The aim of this chapter is to discuss metaphors of the markets in various Cameroonian societies as cultural constructs. Yet this emphasis on specific cultural logics should not imply that there is an absolute discontinuity with western metaphors – that these societies are locked into another kind of thinking. On the contrary, one is struck by the creative hybridisation of endogenous concepts and modern (western) patterns. Moreover, we shall see that these various metaphors have highly different implications for the way people react to the further penetration of the world market: they can imply a refusal of new market conditions, but can also encourage efforts to gain access to new markets. The question is to what extent we can relate, in view of Mamdani's dictum, the various metaphors and their differing implications to specific social struggles?

8.1 THE SEGMENTARY SOCIETIES OF SOUTHERN CAMEROON AND THE MARKET

Prior to the colonial conquest (around 1900), social forms of organisation in south Cameroon corresponded in many respects to the classical model of 'segmentary societies'. A good example are the Maka in the remote south eastern forests, where I have done fieldwork since 1971. Before 1900, the Maka lived in small autonomous villages, formally constituted by a patrilineal segment to which in practice a varying number of matrilateral kin (*mita*, 'nephews') and clients (*miloua*) were associated. A village was ruled by a council of elders who had authority over the young men and the women of their family. There was no central authority above the village level and, even between neighbouring villages, relations were marked by hostility and the constant threat of violence. But there were also regular exchanges especially between related villages. These exchanges primarily concerned women and prestige goods which were controlled by the elders: bundles of small iron bars (*mimbesj*), other iron objects, bags of locally produced salt. In their stories about the past, my Maka informants always discussed these exchanges in terms of reciprocity. Two groups could thus meet to put an end to a blood feud. On such an occasion, the receiving group had to offer a girl for each man killed, in order to 'restore a life' to the other group. A few weeks later, this group had in its turn to act as a host and offer a girl for each man they had killed. Similarly, regarding marriage, the elder of the groom had to offer over a period of time a series of bridal gifts to the bride's elder. But on receiving the gifts, the elder was under a strict obligation to use these goods in order to 'buy' a woman on behalf of his own group (Geschiere 1982).

A network of exchanges, especially between affines, bridged the gap between patrilineal villages. When in the course of the nineteenth century the traders from the European factories on the coast penetrated ever deeper into the forests of the interior, they were channelled into this network of affinity and kinship.[8]

After 1905 the Maka were subdued by the Germans. In 1914 this part of Cameroon was conquered by the French. Both Germans and French considered the Maka region to be particularly backward. The Germans, who had to make a considerable effort to subdue the Maka, called them *'die Primitivisten aller Primitiven'*. One of the reasons for this contempt was that the Maka seemed to be impervious to the forces of 'the market'. As one of the first French administrators expressed it: these *'primitifs imprévoyants'* did not react to *'la loi de l'offre et de la demande qui est un puisssant levier pour l'action productive chez les peuples civilisés'*. And he tersely formulated what was both to the French and the Germans the obvious remedy to this insensitivity: *'l'unique remède est l'obligation au travail'.*[9] Up to 1940, the rather desperate efforts of the successive colonial administrators to stimulate the *'mise en valeur'* of the area were all based on coercion: forced levying of labour, *'cultures forcées'* of cash-crops and many other attempts to enforce strict administrative control in order to stimulate the productive activities of the villagers.

However, after 1945, the Maka suddenly proved to be less 'resistant to the market'. After forced labour and other coercive government schemes had been abolished, and when higher prices made the advantages of cash-cropping clear, the villagers rapidly began to expand their cocoa and coffee plantations on their own initiative. Since then, the penetration of the market and a money economy has proceeded in a less spasmodic manner. Since the 1950s, nearly every family head in the village has had an annual cash income from the sale of his cocoa and coffee harvests. The women's food plots still assure the basic subsistence of the villagers. But many women earn a little money on the side by the sale of some of their products. Moreover, many young men and women have succeeded in getting salaried jobs in town, for shorter or longer periods. Money has become an integral part of the domestic economy in nearly all households.[10]

8.2 MARKET AND KINSHIP

When I started my fieldwork in this area, I was already familiar with the colonial history of the Maka and the many problems the French had had in mobilising the Maka for the *'mise en valeur'* of the area. I had read some of the colonial administrators' long complaints of the insensitivity of these people to 'the law of supply and demand'. Therefore, I was all the more surprised, not to say shocked, by the mercenary behaviour of the villagers, especially at occasions where it was, in my view, highly inappropriate. My first experience of this came as soon as on the second day after I had settled in the village, when I was invited to a wake for someone who had died a year ago. The women's dancing group was supposed to honour the occasion by dancing, in principle from sunset to dawn. Their dance, very 'traditional' and very impressive, was however interrupted rudely, only an hour after they had started. One of the women had discovered a coin of 10 francs CFA in the bowl where all the bystanders were supposed to put their offerings, and she accused me of having made this ridiculously small offering. All the women joined in her protests. Their leader added that in any case the people were not offering enough for their dancing and five minutes later the group marched off. Nobody could make them return. I was very indignant, not only because I felt unjustly accused, I had certainly not put this coin there, but also since I felt that a dead man's wake was not the appropriate occasion for such mercenary behaviour.

I was to encounter many more examples of similar behaviour, but of a more structural kind. The second week after my arrival I assisted for the first time at a Maka funeral. To the Maka, funeral rites are one of the climaxes in the 'acting out' of the kinship organisation. Especially when the deceased is a prominent man or woman, people gather from all the neighbouring villages to participate in the rites. The Maka say that a deceased person is an important link in the network between the patrilineal groups. Therefore, all the groups involved have to participate in order to reaffirm these links. This leads to theatrical 'performances' in which the complex balance of solidarity and hostility between the groups involved is 'acted out', especially between the patrilineal kin of the dead and the other parties involved: 'mothers'-brothers', 'daughters-in-law', 'sons-in-law' and 'sisters'-sons', all of whom are supported by their own patrilineal kin.[11]

Daughters-in-law especially play a spectacular part. Their relation to their husband's family is highly ambivalent: they have to be ostentatiously obedient, particularly to their father-in-law, but they can also indulge in small 'rituals of rebellion', mocking the old man and singing lewd songs to his face. The funeral of their father-in-law, or of one of his 'brothers', is a special occasion for such 'ritual rebellion'. As soon as the *tam-tam* of mourning has sounded, the daughters-in-law start to 'enliven' the scene: they dance and sing all night, mock the patrilineal kin of the deceased, and engage them in 'dancing duels' to humiliate them. They are obliged to behave in this way, and the more aggressive their performance, the more satisfied the deceased's spirit is supposed to be, for their display shows that he has acquired numerous, 'dynamic' women for his group.

The climax of their performance is the *kombok*. The women suddenly appear dressed up in the deceased's clothes. Aided by the sons-in-law, who are dressed as warriors, they attack the deceased's house which is shaken dangerously. The patrilineal kin offer symbolic resistance. But after a few skirmishes, the daughters-in-law suddenly rush off with the bier on their shoulders, the body bouncing up and down. They 'hide' in the bushes just outside the village, singing merrily and dancing. The first time I witnessed this, I could not help feeling that all this was not the appropriate way to 'honour' the deceased. But I was really shocked by what followed. The elder of the deceased's group has 'to buy back' the body from the daughters-in-law, and this requires hard bargaining. The elder then claims for instance that there is no money since the cocoa harvest has not yet been sold. He counts out a few banknotes, but the women push him away, saying that they should be better remunerated for all the care they have lavished upon the deceased. The elder adds a few banknotes, but the women continue to refuse using different arguments and so on. Usually, they accept once the elder has raised his prices again. Especially in the beginning, such scenes strongly reminded me of the flea market near my house in Holland, and I realised that I found such behaviour utterly inappropriate at a funeral.

Moreover, this is certainly not the only moment for bargaining at a funeral. Just before the actual burial, the elders of the deceased's group have to 'buy the body' once more, this time from the mother's-brothers. Unlike the daughters-in-law, this last group has a very strong sanction at their disposal. They have to bury the body and they may leave without doing so, if they are not satisfied with the price offered to them. On this occasion therefore, the bargaining has more serious undertones. The elders of both groups confront each other – next to the open grave – with much rhetorical prowess. The slamming of banknotes and fists, again accompanies fairly banal arguments: there is no money, because the tax has just been paid, the other party still has not paid an outstanding debt and so on. The amounts paid on these occasions are also substantially higher (in the 1970s they were usually several ten thousands of francs CFA, in other words amounts up to £100) but they can vary considerably.

These negotiations with the daughters-in-law and the mother's-brothers are the most spectacular moments of bargaining, but in the coulisses many more exchanges take place with other groups of kin. Moreover, the rites seem to be constantly enriched by new 'inventions'. In 1973, when I attended the funeral of a young woman I noticed that the road through the village had been blocked by a rope and some branches. Apparently, the rope had been attached by the women of the same generation as the deceased. All the men who wanted to pass had to pay a few coins to the women. This led to unexpected complications when a French priest, who regularly visited the villages and who was known for his fierce temper, approached at great speed in his car. It seemed at first that he wanted to drive right through the barrier but at the last moment desisted. One of the women explained that he had to pay some money whereupon the priest replied that he had never heard of this. When the women insisted, he became red in the face and started to shout that this was a heathen custom, that they were turning their funerals into a market with all this money business and so on, and so forth. He restarted the engine and the women just had the time to lower the rope, else he would have broken it. I was especially surprised by the comment of my assistant, himself a staunch Catholic: 'Le Père is right, this is a new thing and the women are exaggerating. They borrowed this from Yaoundé (the capital). These women, they are making a market of everything'.

The kinship organisation of the Maka offers many more occasions for hard bargaining. Another key-moment in this respect is the conclusion of a marriage when the groom's group comes to the bride's village to offer bride-price. Again the elders of both groups have to confront each other with much rhetorical display and again the arguments used are often highly prosaic. The groom's elder has to offer a protracted series of presents: bottles of whiskey, crates of beer, demijohns of red wine, blankets, wrappers and so on, but the climax is the counting of the money and the bargaining over the bride-price. The groom's elder solemnly counts out the notes, one after another, while everybody looks on in dead silence. When he stops, the bride's family – the women foremost – utter their indignation with shrill cries of protest. The bride's elder declares in stately manner that this offer is an insult to the family and that he is not prepared to give his daughter away so cheaply. His opponents reply with the usual arguments – everybody knows that there is no money now, it is the slack season and so on. And again, a final agreement is only reached after hard bargaining.

In this context as well, it is not self-evident that an agreement will be reached. I know of cases where the bride's elder has rejected the offer and the groom has had to return without his bride. Moreover, the amounts on which both parties agreed varied considerably. There is a certain standard: in the 1970s for instance prices fluctuated between 80,000 and 100,000 francs CFA (about £160 – 200) but there were also cases in the village where I lived when considerably more (up to 120,000 francs CFA) or less (60,000 francs CFA) had been paid.[12] Sometimes only part of the agreed sum is paid, with the promise to settle the rest later. This invariably leads to serious complications, especially when the couple's first children are born. Then the bride's family insist on all sorts of extra payments.

All this bargaining has, of course, a ritual aspect. The negotiations between the groom's elder and the bride's representative follow fixed patterns, but despite this ritual canalisation, the bargaining can lead to conflicts which are all too real. Especially in cases when part of the sum has to be paid later or when there are conflicts about subsidiary payments for the children, it is not uncommon that one of the parties takes the matter to court – to the village chief or, which is more serious, to the official courts in town. People can be heavily fined or even imprisoned, particularly in the latter cases.

The Maka are certainly not exceptional in their strong emphasis on monetary affairs during kinship rituals. Their western neighbours for instance, the Beti, have acquired a certain reputation for the hard bargaining that takes place during their marriage ceremonies. The Beti, a prominent group in present-day Cameroon, have similar patterns of organisation to the Maka. But due to their central position in Cameroon – Yaoundé, the capital, is in their territory – they became much earlier and much deeper involved in modern politico-economic developments. With them the penetration of a money economy into kinship rituals seems to have taken on even more spectacular forms. One of the newest fashions during their marriage ceremonies is, for instance, that the groom's party has to pay additional money in order to buy the 'plane ticket' for the bride. Only after enough money has been put on the table is the bride, who was hiding in one of the neighbouring houses, 'flown in'. Of special interest is that people from other parts of Cameroon – from the west or the north – profess to be shocked by such extremely mercenary behaviour. 'With these people a marriage becomes an auction' said one of my informants.

Moreover, this monetarisation of kinship, affinity and other personal relations is certainly not confined to formal occasions, like funerals or weddings. One could quote also the numerous complaints – often by men – about the monetarisation of sexual relations. '*Aujourd'hui les femmes se mettent elles-mêmes sur le marché*, as one of my neighbours bitterly remarked. The young men especially complain that it becomes impossible for them to conclude a decent marriage. Again, such complaints refer particularly to women from the southern forests groups.

One can of course quote many parallel examples from other parts of Africa of how money and hard bargaining quite easily penetrate intimate spheres of life. It seems, moreover, that this trend is especially strong in societies which until fairly recently could be characterised as 'societies without markets' – that is societies which prior to colonial rule had little or no direct experience of the market as a 'place'. Apparently, this did not impede the rapid spread of principles of the market right into the core institutions of these societies.

8.3 DISCUSSION: 'RECIPROCITY' VERSUS 'THE MARKET'?

An obvious question is whether these practices of hard bargaining at funerals, weddings and other personal occasions are something new: are they to be seen as consequences of the penetration of the money economy in colonial times – a perversion of local rituals by the impact of 'the market'? Or are they rather continuations of older patterns of behaviour?

Some authors emphasise the dramatic effects of the penetration of money and the market in these societies. As early as 1948, Furnivall insisted that the most uninhibited forms of capitalism emerged, not in the countries of its origin, but on the periphery where the market had penetrated from outside and where it was therefore much less impeded by social restraints.[13] Following this perspective, one could suppose that precisely in societies like those of the Beti and the Maka, where the market was something new, money and hard bargaining could penetrate all the more easily into personal spheres of life.

On the other hand, our examples of hard bargaining have many precedents in more 'traditional' contexts. There are similar examples in classical anthropological monographs – even in their archetype, Malinowski's *Argonauts*. In this perspective, the bargaining of the Maka over bridewealth and funeral exchanges might rather be a continuation of older patterns of behaviour. Moreover, according to some, such haggling would not be related to real markets but rather to gift exchange, social prestige and reciprocity.[14]

A rapid summary of a few historical data can help to answer these questions. It is clear that in these societies money penetrated into personal spheres of life almost immediately after the colonial conquest. In the Maka area, money had already emerged around 1930 in the bride-prices. At first it still constituted a complement to the *mimbesj*, the bundles of small iron bars which were traditionally the main prestige goods. But around 1935 the *mimbesj* seem to have disappeared altogether from the marriage payments. This is fairly early, because in those years money must have hardly circulated within the villages.[15]

A more spectacular example of how quickly money could spread comes from the Beti area. In 1913, Paul Rohrbach a German journalist from the *Frankfurter Zeitung,* travelled along the road from Kribi on the coast to Yaoundé in the interior. This road had only recently been constructed (after 1900) to facilitate the rapidly growing rubber trade. Already in 1903, according to some estimates, 1,000 carriers passed daily on this road (Wirz 1972:137). Rohrbach was surprised to see groups of women standing along the road and singing a cheerful song. On his request his boy, who spoke '*Neger-Englisch*' translated their song: 'We are happy to sleep with the strangers who pass. But they have to pay us well. Else we run away when they want to have us.' Whereupon the boy added: 'Oh, these Yaoundé people, they like money too much'.[16]

The boy's comment in particular is quite striking. There is a remarkable contrast here with the later complaints of the French administrators who considered these people to be insensitive to '*la loi d'offre et de demande*'. Instead, it seems that the villagers were so keen on earning money that they did it by means which were fairly shocking, both to the European and his boy from the coast. This rather suggests that these societies knew remarkably few barriers to the spread of money.[17]

The introduction of money must none the less have constituted an important turning point. It must have greatly facilitated the development of hard bargaining during kinship rituals described above. Prior to this such ritual 'payments' had to be made in prestige goods which lend themselves less easily to haggling. Moreover, it was more difficult to use these goods for individualistic pursuits. The prestige goods received as bridewealth, for instance, could in principle only be used to acquire a new woman for the group. But as soon as money penetrated bridewealth, things became different. In contrast to the old prestige goods, money could be used for any purpose. In the French archives, complaints about '*l'escroquerie de la dot*' – bridewealth swindling – had already emerged by the 1920s. Complaints by women that their elders had 'eaten' their bridewealth – that is, had used it for personal consumption, often for buying western luxury goods, instead of keeping it to acquire a wife for a son – are nearly as old. The fact that money offered new possibilities for enrichment must have greatly reinforced the stimulus to bargain in the exchanges between kin groups.

But this does not mean that the developments in these forest societies did correspond to Furnivall's image of 'capitalism' and the market spreading without any restriction or social channelling in peripheral areas. On the contrary, among the Cameroonian forest groups, the spread of money and the market clearly followed the circuits in the local patterns of organisation. The more spectacular manifestations of bargaining emerged in the relations between the kin groups – that is, in the local arenas regulating the exchanges of prestige goods and women. From folk tales, it is clear that these encounters between such groups had always been marked by an atmosphere of confrontation and intimidation. The Maka have a saying: 'Marriage is war' which means that one can only marry one's potential enemies. Marriage is only possible outside the bounds of kinship – that is outside the sphere of peace. The fact that marriage is possible implies automatically that there is the danger of 'war'. No wonder that in these relations of affinity, one has to prove one's worth with much ostentation in the face of a partner who could always turn into an enemy.

In some respects, therefore, the hard bargaining at weddings and funerals does continue the old rivalry between lineages linked by ties of affinity: it fits in with the precarious balance between aggression and solidarity which some anthropologists call 'a joking relationship'. In this sense, one could say that the new contacts with the market economy have been integrated into a traditional idiom of exchange. But one should add that the exchanges are now carried out with a completely new means of payment: money. This innovation is of great consequence for the practical effects of the bargaining. Money has given a new dimension to the relations between elders and young men, which is of crucial importance in these societies. The young began to complain, for instance, about the elders 'eating' the bridewealth. From their side the elders apparently viewed the monetisation of the bridewealth as an opportunity to gain access to the money economy on their own terms: they felt free continually to raise the bride price – the amounts demanded increased steadily – and to use at least part of the money for their own consumption.

The monetisation of marriage and funeral exchanges also had direct consequences for the way in which these societies became integrated into the colonial economy – or, in broader perspective, into the world market. Rey (1971) tried to show for an area in north-west Congo that the monetisation of the bridewealth played an important role in solving the labour problem of the *colons* and the colonial authorities. This interpretation applies to the Maka area as well. In my interviews with the first migrants from the village where I lived (they had left the village as young men in the 1930s) one of the standard answers to the question, why they had left, was that their parents wanted them to earn money for the bridewealth. Thus, in a very direct sense, the development of the 'market of kinship' was related to more orthodox markets of labour and commodities.

Against this background it seems clear that the practices of hard bargaining discussed above cannot be explained as simply a continuation of old forms of rivalry – after all, money adds a new aspect to this rivalry which is of crucial importance to the encapsulation of these societies in the colonial economy. But neither can this hard bargaining be viewed, à la Furnivall, as simply a result of the perverting influence of money – the monetisation process was channelled into the local circuits of exchange between the groups. Instead the 'market of kinship' seems to be a hybridisation of old forms of rivalry and new idioms of the market.

In this light it may be clear why the old conceptual opposition anthropologists tended to make between 'reciprocity' and 'the market' is not very useful: it is of little help in understanding the importance of such forms of hybridisation for the present-day predicament of these societies. Of course elements of reciprocity in the exchange of gifts and 'ostentatious consumption' to enhance one's status are to be recognised in the examples discussed above. At funerals and weddings in Maka villages, for instance, bargaining always takes place in public and is marked by much pathos and theatre. The examples above indicate, however, that such 'traditional' forms of rivalry and exchange are easily linked to new market conditions. Apparently, the opposition between idioms of 'reciprocity' and 'the market' is not that absolute. The above also provides a clue of how to analyse such processes of hybridisation.

It seems characteristic that the articulation of local patterns and new market conditions took form around a crucial contradiction in these societies – around bridewealth, that is in direct relation to the struggle between young men and elders over the redistribution of women and prestige-goods. It was because they were grafted upon this old contradiction that the new market conditions could so rapidly transform these societies from the inside.

8.4 SORCERY AND OTHER METAPHORS OF THE MARKET

In many respects, societies in the western parts of Cameroon nowadays offer a marked contrast to the southern forest societies. The most successful entrepreneurs in present-day Cameroon come from western groups like the Bamiléké or the Grassfielders and from Duala on the coast. In these societies other metaphors of the market dominate.

Historically it is of importance that these societies knew the institution of the market-place much earlier than the southern forest groups. The Duala on the coast had intensive contacts with European traders, probably from the 1600s onwards. These trade contacts stimulated the rise of 'kingues' and new forms of authority which surpassed the old kinship networks of Duala society. In the western Grassfields and the Bamiléké area, a complex regional network of market-trade had already developed centuries before, and this constituted the base for the emergence of even stronger chieftaincies in this area (Warnier 1985). The Bamiléké area was probably already in contact with the coastal trade by the seventeenth century. Consequently, these groups had experience of different types of money over a long period; local iron hoes as means of payment had been superseded by 'brass manillas' and beads (and occasionally cowries from trade to the north and the north-east with the Hausa). These moneys were used not only for bridewealth or long-distance trade but also for local exchanges (Warnier 1985:90, 149).

To these societies, the further penetration of the European market and the introduction of European money after the colonial conquest was therefore less of a rupture than in the forest areas. These groups also adapted themselves relatively well to the new market conditions. This does not mean, however, that developments in these areas followed the classical economic paradigm. Of interest is that especially in these more 'entrepreneurial' societies a very powerful metaphor of 'the market' emerged in terms of sorcery and occult power. According to some, this metaphor has deep historical roots: it might even refer to earlier experiences of the slave trade. But it has remained up to the present day of great importance to people's perceptions of 'the market' – albeit that there are important regional variations in the ways these beliefs affect people's reactions to new economic opportunities.

The archetype of this belief is the *ekong* of the Duala, the first group to come into contact with the European trade. To the Duala, *ekong* is a special form of witchcraft which is closely related to wealth, especially to new forms of wealth. *Ekong* people do not eat their victims as witches are commonly supposed to do, but they transform them into something like 'zombies' and put them to work. There is a special connection with Mount Kupé, about sixty miles to the north of Duala, in the land of the Bakossi. *Ekong* people are supposed to send their victims there and make them work on 'invisible plantations'. Their new wealth is explained as the fruit of their victims' labour.

Bureau illustrates how this *ekong* belief functions in modern Duala, nowadays the economic capital of Cameroon:

> A person who is interested in *ekong* goes to visit an 'ekoneur' [French for '*ekong* owner' – a neologism which is commonly used], who puts him to sleep by hypnosis. In his dreams, this person will see a land where money flows and many labourers work for him. An estate owner will offer him his plantations on condition that he offers the life of, for instance, his mother in return. His first reaction will be to refuse. When he wakes up, the 'ekoneur' will say to him 'Now you have seen, now you know what you have to do'. His client will ask for some time to think about it. Some day he will make up his mind. (Bureau 1962:141; compare also Mallart Guimera 1981:115)

De Rosny, a Catholic priest, who studied these beliefs in Duala in the 1970s, gives a vivid picture of the other side – the anxiety of the potential victims:

> when someone dreams that he is taken away as a slave, his hands tied, towards the river or the Ocean and that he cannot see the faces of his capturers, he knows that he has to see a *nganga* (witch-doctor) as soon as possible. (de Rosny 1981:93)

'Ekoneurs' are supposed to steal their victims' bodies from the grave and then 'sell' them to one of their customers.

This idea of 'selling someone' and de Rosny's dream picture seem indeed to refer to the old practices of the slave trade. So does the fact that the Duala and other groups in the area tend to make a close connection between *ekong* and the Europeans. This is what de Rosny found out to his distress. He had visited an old *nganga* (witch-doctor) and a chief in a village near Duala and he had offered them both a bottle of whiskey. When he wanted to leave again, he found that the road was blocked by youths from the village who behaved very aggressively and refused to let him pass. Apparently, both the chief and the *nganga* were suspected of having *ekong*. The rumour that a white stranger had come to offer them a present, was apparently enough to resurrect old fears of people being 'sold' to the whites.[18]

De Rosny rightly points out, however, that contemporary *ekong* beliefs also reflect more modern forms of the market. He emphasises that *ekong* as such existed among the Duala long before the colonial conquest. In these earlier days, *ekong* was a well-respected association of chiefs, notables and traders – that is, of those groups who controlled access to the market and the trade with the Europeans. Nowadays the *ekong* has been 'democratised': it seems to be in the reach of anybody who wants to have a try at it. According to de Rosny, there is a direct link here with economic changes which have occurred since the colonial conquest – such as the development of new forms of wage labour and the spread of money – by which access to the market became no longer the prerogative of family-heads or rich traders. All this has certainly not made the economy more transparent. Rising and falling prices of cash-crops and the uncertainty of the labour market have become crucial for the survival of most city people. But these 'forces of the market' are absolutely unpredictable, certainly for the ordinary people, and they seem to be outside everybody's control. One of the attractions of *ekong* beliefs is – according to de Rosny – that they can 'integrate' the mysteries of the market. They have persisted among the popular strata because they can still offer at least some form of explanation for the glaring differences in wealth under the new market conditions. Just as the market has been 'democratised', so *ekong* now seems to have become much more widespread.

At first sight, this metaphor seems to characterise the market as something unequivocally weird. In this respect, *ekong* seems to correspond to the stereotype, which is still so common among western observers and development experts, of sorcery/witchcraft as a 'traditional barrier' to modern changes and 'development'. However, on further consideration, things turn out to be more complicated. The *ekong* belief has not remained restricted to the Duala, but has also emerged throughout the western and south-western regions of present-day Cameroon. In these areas it has been closely related to the progressive penetration of the market economy and to new opportunities for enrichment. But among the various groups this metaphor of the market has different implications. In some areas, *ekong* beliefs seem to express less a refusal than an eagerness to participate in the market. Clearly, the same metaphor allows for different reactions to the new market conditions.

Among the Bakweri, the western neighbours of the Duala, these beliefs have strong negative connotations. They use the term *nyongo* for representations that are nearly identical to the Duala *ekong*. Older Bakweri even claim that *nyongo* was introduced to their area by the Duala. This is supposed to have happened quite recently, probably at the beginning of the colonial era (Fisiy and Geschiere 1991). Prior to that time, the Bakweri, living on the steep slopes of Mount Cameroon, were largely bypassed by the trade routes from the coast into the interior. Only towards the end of the nineteenth-century were they affected by the efforts of Duala traders to create cocoa plantations and recruit labour for these plantations in the interior (Wirz 1972). The Bakweri elders, who now tell stories of how the Duala brought the *nyongo* to their land, often add fairly negative comments about the avariciousness and the venality of the Duala traders.

To the Bakweri, this *nyongo* is still unequivocally evil. In a seminal study, Ardener (1970) showed how, for a long time, this belief constituted a formidable barrier against any attempt to profit from the new opportunities for enrichment. People did not even dare to build the new type of house with a tinned roof – in this region the new status symbol – because then they would certainly be accused of *nyongo* witchcraft. In 1955, at the time when Ardener worked in this area, there was a sudden breakthrough, when people from Lysoka (a Bakweri village) brought in Obasinjom from the Banyangi (more than 160 miles to the north). This powerful *juju* was supposed to be able to flush out *nyongo* witches and take their powers from them. There followed an intensive anti-*nyongo* campaign during which village after village was cleansed. Significantly, all this coincided with the 'banana-boom' in this area. Due to better transport facilities and a new co-operative organisation, the Bakweri peasants had for the first time a chance to profit greatly from the colonial market economy by cultivating bananas. But they could only do so after Obasinjom had liberated them from *nyongo*. People felt free to profit from the 'banana-boom' only because this *juju* 'had put an end to *nyongo*'. Now they could even build modern houses without being suspected of this dreadful form of witchcraft.

Of course, *nyongo* was not completely eradicated. There have been rumours about *nyongo* up to the present day. Recently, Obasinjom even experienced a spectacular revival in the mountain villages – apparently because there was growing unrest about *nyongo* activities. Again, there seems to be a direct link with a sudden economic change – this time the serious crisis and the austerity measures drawn up by the state since 1987. Up till today, *nyongo* remains something evil to the Bakweri which has to be combated and eradicated at all costs.

De Rosny (1981) described similar attitudes in present-day Duala. To the city people, *ekong* is an omnipresent evil lurking everywhere in their modern, urban surroundings. The *nganga* (witch-doctors) who figure in his book see themselves as protagonists in a continuous war against *ekong*. But, as remarked earlier, the image of *ekong* was not always so negative among the Duala. According to de Rosny it was formerly (probably prior to the colonial conquest when Duala society was still a slave society)[19] a respected association of notables and rich traders. De Rosny (1981:92) underlines that, in those days, the *ekong* 'did not yet have the odious character it has acquired today'.

In this respect, there is a striking contrast with more recent developments among the Bamiléké and the Grassfielders, in the western mountains, who now have the reputation of being the most entrepreneurial groups in Cameroon. Here similar conceptions prevail but they are called *kupe* (after the mountain) or *famla* (after a quarter of Bafoussam, the new centre of Bamilékéland). Again these beliefs refer to the 'selling' of one's own relatives, to the stealing of the bodies of the victims who are transported to Mount Kupé and to new riches created by the labour of these 'spirits'. But in these societies the condemnation of these practices seems to be less unequivocal than among the Bakweri or the Duala. Apparently there are here special possibilities to 'whitewash' the wealth thus acquired.

These areas are of special interest, since, as remarked above, entrepreneurs from this area are supposed to dominate now important sectors of the national economy. Indeed rumours of *famla* abound especially about the Bamiléké entrepreneurs, who now control important assets in Yaoundé and Duala. But in practice, this hardly seems to affect their position. Apparently, their *famla* associations are supposed to be so well organised that it would be futile to try and combat them. The only way to escape them is by moving away. This seems to be the other side of the famous '*dynamisme bamiléké*'[20] – their propensity to migrate and their economic success throughout Cameroon. *Famla* and *kupe* are popularly considered to be the obvious explanation of the success of these entrepreneurs. This endogenous metaphor of the market has thus acquired considerable importance for the national economy.

The question is of course why precisely in these areas such beliefs were accepted as a more or less normal element of entrepreneurship. In another article (Fisiy and Geschiere 1991) – to which I can only briefly refer here for reasons of space – we tried to explain this by the special position of the chiefs (*fons*) in these societies and their role in processes of accumulation. It seems that *kupe* is fairly new to the Grassfields and the same might be true for *famla* among the Bamiléké.[21] But it is clear that these beliefs fitted in very well with special patterns of accumulation that had developed in these areas over the last centuries. Warnier's challenging interpretations of the relation between chieftaincy and trade in the Grassfields indicate how important the *fon*'s role was to the expansion of networks of accumulation (Warnier 1985). For each chieftaincy, the *fon*'s prestige determined the scope of its trade relations and inversely the success of its traders reinforced the prestige of its *fon*. The main export products were palm-oil, iron objects and slaves. According to Warnier (1990) one of the peculiarities of this area was that the export of slaves was based mainly on the sale of people by their own kin. He tries to show how enterprising individuals in this area could realise their ambitions by delivering people from their own group – often less protected youths from the larger compounds – into the hands of slave dealers. A key element of the *famla* conception, the 'selling' of one's own relatives, would therefore be derived from a historical reality.

Another characteristic of the relations in these chieftaincies is that, in the last resort, it is the *fon* who legitimises the wealth of his subjects. The relation to his court determines whether wealth is considered to be social or asocial (Fisiy and Geschiere 1991). This principle is of direct relevance to the integration of new forms of wealth. By dedicating one's wealth to the *fon*, modern entrepreneurs can 'whitewash' their riches, despite all rumours of *famla*. Conversely, any form of accumulation which is not related to the court is bound to be considered as asocial. This may explain why modern entrepreneurs from these areas are so keen to reinforce their links with the court, for instance by buying 'traditional' titles in the associations around the throne. The *fons* for their part seem to be eager to participate in the new forms of accumulation by creating all sorts of pseudo-traditional titles and selling them to the new rich (Goheen in press). Again, this is not really an innovation. After all, the position of the *fon* has always been based on their control of the networks of accumulation.

To summarise: in the societies of the west, the strong position of the *fon* – his ideologically heavily buttressed control over accumulation – offers an institutional arrangement to legitimise wealth begotten by *famla*, which is lacking in the south-western societies.[22] In the west therefore, this type of belief functions less as a barrier to new forms of accumulation and more as a powerful incentive to try and profit from the new opportunities in the market economy.[23]

8.5 CONCLUSION

The comparison above, brief and limited by a lack of space, raises a whole array of questions which should be further elaborated. Here, I can only mention a few.

First of all, these various metaphors of the market do indeed raise questions concerning the cultural construction of our own (that is western) market notions. The very fact that westerners tend to be shocked by the uninhibited display of market-like behaviour – such as haggling over money – in kinship rituals and other intimate spheres, begs the question of how exactly we construct a conceptual distinction between kinship and economy or 'the market'. In an interesting argument, Bloch

(1989:172) tries to show how vital such distinctions are to the reproduction of capitalist relations: in his view they serve to maintain the separation, which is basic to capitalism, between the individual as private citizen and as worker (compare also Strathern 1985). Yet, how exactly these distinctions are reproduced in western thinking is not yet very clear.

More specifically, our examples can serve to defuse the current western stereotype of 'traditional' societies almost by definition resisting the market. All the examples above indicate that things are much more ambiguous than this. The various metaphors embody elements of fear and can be seen as attempts to control the market, for instance by personalising it. But they can at the same time encourage determined efforts to gain access to the market and the unknown opportunities offered by new market conditions. It is rather striking, for instance, that even the elders, whose position of authority was supposedly threatened by the penetration of money into these societies, seemed to have put up little resistance. Apparently they allowed money to penetrate rapidly into the central kinship rituals. This suggests that, instead of resisting the impact of money and the market, they welcomed these specific opportunities for gaining access to new riches.

In this sense, Appadurai (1986:57) seems right to conclude that such cultural constructions – around exchange, commodities, money or the market – are 'political' and should be studied as such. They cannot simply be analysed in relation to specific cultural or symbolical logics – by which one risks overrating their stability and coherence – but they have to be related to changing political relations. Without further specification, however, the term 'political' risks becoming an inane label. Some indication is required of how the different political conditions and implications of these metaphors are to be analysed – how we are to relate them to 'specific social struggles'[24]. Or, to be more concrete, how are we to explain that the metaphors discussed above could have such different implications for the way these societies reacted to the penetration of the world market?

At least for the societies discussed here, a valuable lead might be found in Rey's insistence on the key role of local contradictions in the articulation of these societies with new market conditions (Rey 1971 and 1973). To Rey, these local contradictions and the alliances of local power-holders with capitalist interest groups were crucial in the subjection of African societies to capitalism.[25] However, these contradictions differed according to region, as did the ways in which they were transformed and articulated with new politico-economic inequalities. The modern transformations of these local contradictions offer, therefore, a good starting-point for analysing different trajectories – scenarios – in the articulation of local forms of organisation with new relations of control and opportunity (compare Rey 1973, Geschiere in press).

This focus on local relations of power and their different articulations with new inequalities seems helpful to clarify the different tenor of the examples discussed above. It can serve to specify how we have to study the 'politics' of these metaphors. For instance, to understand the different ways in which 'the market of kinship' affected the reactions of these societies to the penetration of the world market, variations in the position of the elders and their position vis-à-vis the new power relations seem to be crucial. In the same way, the different implications of sorcery metaphors of the market proved to be related to specific power relations – in this case to the strong position of the chiefs among the Bamiléké and the Grassfielders, a position which was reinforced during the colonial period. Because these chiefs still had the power to 'whitewash' the new wealth, even when there were rumours of sorcery, these metaphors could have a special impact here – less levelling and more congenial to accumulation than in other societies.

These are, of course, only sketchy comments. A real comparison would require more space. Yet, the above discussion may indicate how local metaphors of the market express creative processes of hybridisation. Such processes are better understood in terms of analysing variations in time and space à la Rey, than by the kind of binary oppositions – such as 'reciprocity' versus 'the market' – which still tend to inform much anthropological discourse. The emphasis on hybridisation and variations may serve to gain deeper insight into the recent predicament of these societies: at a time when conditions on the world market are dramatically deteriorating for them, they are confronted by a renewed emphasis on 'the market' by development agencies. Such paradoxes indicate the wider context in which these local metaphors of the market have to be analysed.

NOTES

1. My thanks to Roy Dilley who was untiring in giving me his stimulating comments.
2. I use both 'witchcraft' and 'sorcery' for lack of better terms. In several respects, these terms distort the meaning of the African terms of which they are supposed to be the translation. The problem is especially that both 'sorcery' and 'witchcraft' have strong pejorative overtones, while the African terms often have a much broader meaning, covering also more positive aspects of the occult forces. A more general translation like 'occult forces' would therefore be preferable. However, terms like 'sorcery', 'witchcraft' or 'sorcellerie' have been appropriated by Africans. Nowadays, they return time and again in the newspapers and there are current debates about, for instance, 'Développement et Sorcellerie'. To relate to these current debates, I use, albeit with misgivings, these same terms. I shall use both terms interchangeably since in the Cameroonian societies discussed here, it is difficult to distinguish sharply between 'witchcraft' and 'sorcery'.
3. Compare also Gudeman 1986.
4. Compare similar experiences described by Bloch 1989 and Harris 1989.
5. The problem here seems to be anthropology's predilection for clear-cut binary oppositions (societies with and without markets, pre-money societies and monetarised ones and so on) all of which amount to the basic opposition 'them and us'. It has been clear for some time already that in practice such oppositions are untenable. Yet Harris (1989:236) warns that such oppositions are still 'built into the very structure of anthropology as a discipline' as does Appadurai (1986:12): 'anthropology is [still] excessively dualistic' (compare also Geschiere in press).
6. Compare for instance, Parkin (1972) on the 'cultural paradox' of Giriama elders promoting the impact of the money economy which came to undermine their own position; or Dupré (1982); compare also Appadurai (1986:26) on money as a 'Trojan horse of change'.
7. Compare Bloch (1989:169–70) and Parry and Bloch (1989:16,19).
8. Wirz (1972:100) describes this process in detail. When a trader wanted to establish contacts in a region unknown to him, the obvious way to do so was by marrying one

of his daughters to someone from this area. Then he could profit from the kinship and affinity networks of his son-in-law to expand his trade network. Thus, new trade goods mainly entered the existing circuits by means of the exchange of women and prestige goods. Near the coast, bride-prices already consisted of European goods towards the end of the nineteenth century.

9. Chef de la région Briaud', Abong-Mbang, to Commissaire de la République, Douala, 14.12.1920; Archives Nationales, Yaoundé, APA 111643.

10. Since 1988, however, the market for cash-crops has collapsed. In 1988, the co-operative which had a monopoly over the sale of cocoa and coffee in the area, ceased paying farmers. In subsequent years, farmers were paid after much delay and at much lower prices. This has had dramatic consequences for most households.

11. All these terms are used in a highly 'classificatory' sense. 'Daughters-in-law' include all the women that have married into the patrilineage of the deceased, the 'sisters'-sons' are all the sons of women born to the patrilineage of the deceased but who married elsewhere, and so on.

12. In the 1980s the price rose to 150,000 francs CFA (nearly £300), but then also considerable variations were possible. It is not yet clear how the recent collapse of the cash-crop market and the concomitant problems of raising money will affect the level of the bride-price in the villages.

13. Furnivall (1948) developed this view in discussing colonial developments in Burma and the all-pervasive influence of market forces in this colony.

14. Compare Polanyi (1957:263) who speaks of 'haggling with fixed prices' – apparently to make a contrast with true market situations. Compare also the critique on Malinowski for rigidly opposing gift exchange (equalled with prestige) and trade (equalled with profit) in his analysis of the *kula* (see Hart 1986 and Bloch 1989:169).

15. Until the end of the 1930s, French administrators really had to squeeze tax money from the villages. Nearly all of the little money the villagers earned – mostly by working on European plantations in the area – was drained from the villages by the tax collections. Only after 1945, did money begin to circulate more regularly (see Geschiere 1983).

16. *Frankfurter Zeitung*, 25.5.1913; see also Staatsarchiv Potsdam, Reichskolonialamt, Bnd 4, file 4226, p. 57.

17. Nowadays, money has penetrated into all sorts of relations. As an exception one could mention that there is now a strong ban on any attempt to use money in order to acquire land. At least in the Maka area, any rumour that someone is trying to sell or rent his land for money, evokes fierce reactions from his own kin who reproach him for tampering with their communal domain. However, it seems that these fierce reactions are fairly new; probably they are related to the feeling that there is a growing pressure on land. At least in the beginning of the colonial period, 'chiefs' – in reality often colonial strawmen – did 'sell' land to Europeans and their auxiliaries for money – mostly for derisory low sums.

18. Other aspects of *ekong* rumours are more reminiscent of the forced colonial labour recruitments. The Bakweri (the western neighbours of the Duala), for instance, believe that the victims are transported *in lorries* to Mount Kupé. The Bakossi, to the north of the Duala, talk about huge working camps on Mount Kupé (Ardener 1970; Balz 1984).

19. Compare Wirz 1972 and Austen 1977; in this respect as well there seems to be a direct link between *ekong* and slavery.

20. The title of a book by Jean-Louis Dongmo (1981) about the rise of the Bamiléké entrepreneurs.

21. The term *famla* might not be older than the colonial period. See Miaffo and Warnier (in press), Pool 1989, Pradelles de Latour 1991, Rowlands (in press) and Warnier 1985 and 1990.

22. Among the strongly segmentary Bakweri, chieftaincy was only weakly developed (according to some there were no real chiefs prior to the colonial conquest). The Duala had their 'kingues' whose position was highly dependent on their contacts with European traders and who lacked the elaborate ideological reinforcement of the *fons* in the west; after the colonial conquest, the Duala 'kingues' lost much of their influence.

23. The Bakossi, half-way between Duala and the Bamiléké in the interior, exhibit yet another pattern. Mount Kupé, the magic mountain, is in their territory and *ekong*-like ideas – here called *ekom* – are strongly developed among them. In their conception, *ekom* is not necessarily evil. It seems rather to be considered as a piece of good luck if someone succeeds in enriching himself with the help of *ekom*. This seems related to the idea that the zombies who are slaving away on the invisible plantations on Mount Kupé are mainly people from other groups (Bakweri, Duala). Among the Bakossi, these beliefs seem to reflect a sort of ideal of absentee landlordism which corresponds to the way Bakossi tried (and try) to profit from strangers – formerly slaves, now immigrants – by making them work on their ancestral lands (compare Balz 1984 and Ejedepang-Koge 1971).

24. Compare the quotation from Mamdani in the introduction above.

25. I realise, of course, that it takes some courage nowadays to resurrect these discussions of the 1970s on modes of production and their articulation. It seems no accident that these debates ended in a cul-de-sac due to the heavy jargon and the obsession with definition and classification of modes of production. Probably these debates focused too much on the notion of 'mode of production' (which proved to be fairly cumbersome) and thereby neglected the more open and creative notion of 'articulation'. It seems therefore still worthwhile to pursue Rey's explorations around this latter notion (compare also Laclau and Mouffe 1985 and in general van Binsbergen and Geschiere 1985).

BIBLIOGRAPHY

Appadurai, A. 1986. 'Introduction: Commodities and the Politics of Value', in A. Appadurai (ed.), *The Social Life of Things*. Cambridge: Cambridge University Press.

Ardener, E. 1970. 'Witchcraft, Economics and the Continuity of Belief', in M. Douglas (ed.), *Witchcraft Confessions and Accusations*. London: Tavistock. pp. 141-60.

Austen, R. A. 1977. 'Slavery among Coastal Middlemen: the Duala of Cameroon', in S. Miers and I. Kopytoff (eds.), *Slavery in Africa*. Madison: Wisconsin University Press. pp.305–33.

Balz, H. 1984. *Where the Faith has to Live. Studies in Bakossi Society and Religion*. Basel: Basel Mission.

Binsbergen, W. M. J. van, and P. Geschiere (eds.), 1985. *Old Modes of Production and Capitalist Encroachment: Anthropological Explorations in Africa*. London: Kegan Paul; Leiden: Afrika Studiecentrum.

Bloch, M. 1989. 'The Symbolism of Money in Imerina', in J. Parry & M. Bloch (eds.), *op. cit.*, pp.165–191.

Bureau, R. 1962. *Ethno-sociologie religieuse des Douala et apparentés*. Yaoundé: Recherches et Etudes Camerounaises 7/8.

Dupré, G. 1982. *Un ordre et sa destruction*, Paris: ORSTOM.

Dongmo, J.-L. 1981. *Le dynamisme bamiléké*. Yaoundé.

Ejedepang-Koge, S. N. 1971. *The Tradition of a People: Bakossi*. Yaoundé.

Ejedepang-Koge, S. N. 1975. *Tradition and Change in Peasant Activities: A Study of the Indigenous People's Search for Cash in the South West Province of Cameroun*. Yaoundé.

Fisiy, C. and P. Geschiere, 1991. 'Sorcellerie et accumulation: Variations régionales', *Critique of Anthropology*, 11 (3): pp. 251–77.

Furnivall, J. S. 1948. *Colonial Policy and Practice.* Cambridge: Cambridge University Press.

Geschiere, P. 1982. *Village Communities and the State: Changing Relations in Maka Villages (S.E.Cameroon).* London: Kegan Paul International; Leiden African Studies Centre.

Geschiere, P. 1983. 'European Planters, African Peasants and the Colonial State: Alternatives in the "mise en valeur" of Makaland, Southeast Cameroun, during the Interbellum', *African Economic History,* 12: 83–108.

Geschiere, P. 1988, 'Scorcery and the State', *Critique of Anthropology,* 8: 35–63.

Geschiere, P. in press, 'Anthropologists and the Crisis in Africa: Beyond Conceptual Dichotomies?'. The Hague: IMWOO.

Geschiere, P. & P. Konings (eds.), in press. *Les Itinéraires d'Accumulation au Cameroun.* Leiden: African Studies Centre; Paris: Karthala.

Goheen, M. in press, 'Men own the fields, Women own the Crops: Gender and Accumulation in Nso', in P. Geschiere & P. Konings (eds.), *op. cit.*

Gudeman, S. 1986. *Economics as Culture: models and metaphors of livelihood.* London: Routledge & Kegan Paul.

Harris, O. 1989. 'The Earth and the State: The Sources and Meanings of Money in Northern Potosí, Bolivia', in J. Parry & M. Bloch (eds.), *op. cit.* pp.232–69.

Hart, K. 1986. 'Heads or Tails? Two Sides of the Coin', *Man,* 21 (4):637–56.

Laclau, E. and C. Mouffe, 1985. *Hegemony and Socialist Strategy, Towards a Radical-Democratic Politics,* London: Verso.

Mallart Guimera, L. 1981. *Ni dos, ni ventre,* Paris: Société d'ethnographie.

Mamdani, M. 1990. 'Uganda: Contradictions of the IMF programme and perspective', *Development and Change,* 21: 427–67.

Miaffo, D. and J.-P.Warnier, in press. 'Accumulation et ethos de la notabilité chez les Bamiléké', in P. Geschiere and P. Konings, (eds.), *op. cit.*

Parkin, D. 1972. *Palms, Wine and Witnesses.* London: Intertext Books.

Parry J. and M. Bloch, 1989. 'Introduction: Money and the Morality of Exchange', in J. Parry & M. Bloch (eds.), *op. cit.* pp.1–33.

Parry J. and M. Bloch (eds.), 1989. *Money and the Morality of Exchange,* Cambridge: Cambridge University Press.

Polanyi, K. 1957. 'The Economy as Instituted Process', in K. Polanyi, C. M. Arensberg and H. W. Pearson, *Trade and Market in the Early Empires.* New York: Free Press.

Pool, R. 1989. *There Must Have Been Something – Interpretation of Illness and Misfortune in a Cameroon Village.* Amsterdam: University of Amsterdam.

Pradelles de Latour, C.-H. 1991. *Ethnopsychanalyse en pays bamiléké.* Paris: EPEL.

Rey, P.-P. 1971. *Colonialisme, néo-colonialism et transition au capitalisme.* Paris: Maspero.

Rey, P.-P. 1973. *Les Alliances de classes.* Paris: Maspero.

Rosny, E. de, 1981. *Les yeux de ma chèvre – Sur les pas des maîtres de la nuit en pays douala.* Paris: Plon.

Rowlands, in press. 'Economic Dynamism and Cultural Stereotyping in the Bamenda Grassfields', in P. Geschiere and P. Konings, (eds.), *op. cit.*

Rowlands, M. & J.-P.Warnier, 1988. 'Sorcery, Power and the Modern State in Cameroon, *Man* (N.S.), 23: 118–132.

Strathern, M. 1985. 'Kinship and Economy: Constitutive Orders of a Provisional Kind', *American Ethnologist,* 12: 191–209.

Warnier, J.-P. 1985. *Echanges, développement et hiérarchies dans le Bamenda précolonial (Cameroun).* Stuttgart: Steiner.

Warnier, J.-P. 1990. 'Traite sans raids au Cameroun', *Cahiers d'Etudes Africaines,* 113: 5–32.

Wirz, A. 1972. *Vom Sklavenhandel zum kolonialen Handel – Wirtschaftsraume and Wirtschaftsformen in Kamerun vor 1914.* Zurich: Atlantis.

9

Wandering in the Market and the Forest

An Amazonian Theory of Production and Exchange [1]

JOANNA OVERING

The Piaroa, a people of the Amazon Territory of Venezuela, subsumed 'shopping in the market-place' within the domain of production, and not, as one expect, within their own indigenous category of exchange. The salient distinction in the Piaroa understanding of sociality was that of production and exchange. As types of activity, production was about the acquisition or transformation of resources for use through the work of self or that of close kinsmen, while exchange was about the acquisition of goods created by a person from a foreign domain. Most importantly, the contrast centred upon the different types of *social* relationship that were involved in the flow of food and materials between people. On the one side, there were the internal relations of community life built through productive work, co-operation, sharing and the creation of intimacy and high spirits,[2] while on the other there were the external relations of exchange which, through the competition of individuals, created a world ever hovering on the edge of violence, coercion, predation and even war. Thus, the tranquil and *safe* community of insiders structured by the principles of sharing and production was in sharp contrast to the competitive and individualistic relations of foreign politics structured by the principle of exchange. It was a distinction of identity and difference that was complete, one that opposed the inside and the outside, safety and danger, friend and foe. The image of alterity always carried with it at the very least the potentiality of 'the cannibal other'. As will be discussed in the next section, it was the view of the Piaroa that going 'shopping' in a Venezuelan market town – as light-hearted productive activity and not dangerous exchange – involved the *social* relationship of insiders and not the competitive, foreign ones of exchange.

In order to unfold the logic of the Piaroa in their linkage of types of social relationship with the flow of things between people, it is necessary to follow Piaroa classification, and not received anthropological wisdom. The tendency in anthropological theory has been to over-value the place of exchange to the neglect of production and consumption in the social structure of so-called 'primitives'. Lévi-Strauss (1969:61), following the reasoning of Mauss, stresses the social value of 'primitive exchange' as a 'total phenomena'. The view of both is that it is through exchange and the reciprocal transfer of things and people that both peace and social relationships are created among 'primitive' peoples. Clastres (1977), writing on the tropical forest peoples of South America, went so far as to reduce their sociality to exchange, whereas it is in fact the dialectics of production and exchange that needs to be examined to reach the indigenous theories of sociality – and indeed its reality. The start must be indigenous and not structural theory, else a focused picture of indigenous reality never comes into view.

Throughout this chapter I am reserving the term 'exchange' to refer to those situations in which the Piaroa applied their term *palou*, which referred to the competitive process of trading, bartering and negotiating for goods carried out between men of different communities and territories. Because of its specific dangers, *palou* belonged to the political domain of foreign relations and was therefore carried out in the main by powerful leaders. With the exception of the relatively informal trading carried out between men of the communities of the same territory, *palou* relationships were formalised as long-term and individualised trading partnerships within one of the vast indigenous networks of trade. The term *palou* was not used to describe the process of buying axes, machetes and so on from shopkeepers within a Venezuelan market town, nor did *palou* occur within the internal boundaries of community relations. Unlike Lévi-Strauss, the Piaroa saw production and not exchange as conducive of peace; even marriage, which ideally was endogamous to community, was put at a remove from both the domain of exchange and reciprocal gift-giving.

Within a community 'gifts' were given: the Piaroa distinguished between those gifts for which reciprocation was expected (*mifona*) and the 'free gift' (*mifona chiya'a*) which carried in the giving no expectation for reciprocation. In terms of daily production and consumption, however, most flows of items followed the principle of *sharing* (see Overing 1989), a process to be distinguished from both exchange and the giving of gifts. For example, all products of the jungle were shared among the members of the community, as too were many of the items acquired through trade shared by sets of them. Sharing was a process critical to the achievement of safety in daily social living, for it ensured that those who lived together became over time 'of a kind' with one another – it led to equality and created homogeneity. This was in contrast to the process of exchange which in the Piaroa view is the marker of social differentiation and the potential creator of relations of hierarchy. The oppositions unfolded through 'elementary structures of reciprocity' were for the Piaroa more conducive of war than peace [3] and thus more appropriate to the external world of foreign relations than to the internal realm of kinship relations.

In the section below I shall address more fully the 'puzzle' of the Piaroa separation of 'shopping' and exchange. Here, as throughout the remainder of the discussion, the emphasis will be upon the contrast between the social relationships of production and exchange. The section that follows will then deal with the history of the Piaroa's relation with both the Venezuelan market economy and the indigenous networks of trade of the Orinoco basin. The final sections concentrate on the community – the realm of productivity activity – and the dialectics of production and exchange in its creation.

9.1 THE SHOPPER AND THE HUNTER

The Piaroa linked the shopper in the market-place with the hunter in the forest. The relation was first of all a linguistic one. Both 'shopper' and 'hunter' were designated by the noun, *emaekwa*, a term literally translated as 'taker' which was a cognate of the verb *emehisae*, 'to take'. In the Piaroa view, when a hunter went to the forest he took from it, just as a shopper did from the market-place. Further parallels appear between activities in the market and the forest. They would tend to use the same term for expressing an intention to go shopping as for going on a foray in the forest to seek any type of food, be it fruit, nuts, insects, fish from the streams of the forest or its birds and animals. A person would announce when planning to go shopping, collecting, fishing, or hunting that 'I am going wandering',[4] a phrase that might be followed by specific desires, such as 'I am going wandering' to eat a particular fruit, or to fish with traps – or to find a machete, a piece of cloth or some fish-hooks. Often enough, however, a person used the phrase 'I am going wandering' to signify that he or she was going off 'to see what could be found'.

The question that I shall address is the obvious one of why did the Piaroa extend the forest into the town? What were the similarities between using the forest and going shopping in the market-place? It is tempting to see the critical relationship between the two, especially the homology of hunter and buyer, as being that of predation. Certainly in western understanding, the metaphor of predation for market behaviour does not sound particularly strange; the Piaroa were certainly aware of the humour of subsuming the behaviour of the (predatory) shopper with the predatory stalking of the hunter. However, such a solution can only be partial since in Piaroa understanding *all* activity allowing for human existence in this world was founded upon predatory, and indeed cannibalistic capabilities. Thus while it was true that both shopping and hunting were considered predatory performances, so too were collecting, fishing, gardening, making artefacts, having children, chanting, curing, talking, trading, going to war and so on. In gardening, for instance, trees were cut down and killed in order that plants, which (who) were once human beings, could be grown, processed and eaten. The Piaroa definition of human life as a predatory process will be further discussed below, but it is relevant to note that such a view of existence is not unusual to indigenous peoples of tropical-forest South America where the themes of predation and cannibalism have been highly pertinent to most of their ontologies of being.[5] The point is that predation was not for the Piaroa a feature peculiar to hunting and shopping, since all human agency – in their view – had its predatory (and indeed cannibalistic) aspect.

The better answer to the similarity between shopping and hunting is that first of all neither fell within the category of exchange, but of production; second, within this classification they were distinguished as a particular type of productive activity. Food collection in the forest was different in certain ways from other productive activity, such as gardening and the making of artefacts. The work of these other productive pursuits was more focused than hunting, shopping and collecting. In the terrains of forest and market- place a person could wander, perhaps without specific aim, to pick up whatever caught his/her eye. For the Piaroa such adventure in wandering was especially pleasurable, an attitude they often expressed.

Also, the taking of resources of the forest, as when one shot an animal or gathered nuts, demanded a smaller degree of productive knowledge than did gardening or the making of artefacts. In the latter tasks, a person used transformational skills that went far beyond those needed for the act of killing an animal or of foraging for food and shopping for manufactured goods. When making curare or a blowgun a man created from raw materials the means enabling him or other men to shoot and kill an animal; in making a garden the land was transformed – a man cut down its trees and burned them, and his wife furthered its transformation by planting, growing and nurturing new plants upon it. To make a garden a person had to plan well ahead, while wandering in the market-place and the forest usually required little forethought for its success.[6] Bringing in game and fruit from forays into the forest required lesser creative capabilities than gardening, those somewhat akin to the skills a person would use for the harvest alone – but even so it would have been a harvest from the garden cultivated by someone else and not created through his/her own productive skills. It can be seen, then, why 'taker' as the description for the hunter and the shopper was particularly apt: in shopping and hunting one 'took' animals, plants and manu-factured goods that one had not created through one's own skills.[7]

In exchange a person also acquired goods that he/she had not created or made, but what is above all clear is that the Piaroa separated the activities of the market-place from those they would classify as 'exchange' (*palou*). As already stated, the skills of 'taking' from both forest and market-place were firmly placed by the Piaroa within the domain of production. Although the results of any productive activity may have been used for the purpose of exchange – whether of hunting, shopping, gardening or the creation of artefacts – these activities were sharply contrasted by the Piaroa with the process of trading.

We are still faced with the question of why the Piaroa classify shopping as a type of productive activity and not as exchange? The answer to this classification takes us into the arena, not of capitalism and the 'market economy', but that of social relation-ships. The random and impersonal relationships of both forest and market-place were totally different in concept from the highly personalised and enduring relationships of exchange and trade. A shopper did not normally form personal relationships with the shopkeepers of the market-place, nor did the hunter and forager establish them with the animals and plants of the forest: these were fleeting and impersonal relation-ships, made randomly in accordance with chance and circumstance.[8] In any event it was the Piaroa view that neither the animals of the forest nor the fish of the rivers could engage in social action: because their capabilities for intentionality and reason had been taken from them at the end of mythic time, they thereafter lacked for eternity the capacity for forming personal relationships (see Overing 1985a). In the market-place the impersonal relation between shopper and shopkeeper carried over to the goods themselves, in the sense that the products bought there were disembodied ones: with market-place goods the power of their creator was not a factor with which to be reckoned, which on the contrary was the case for most goods acquired in exchange (see below). Who, from the shopper's point of view, was the maker of western manufactured goods?

Unlike the encounters of forest and market-place where dealings were usually with unspecified others, exchange relationships were personalised and therefore highly significant in their specificity. Neither random nor accidental, the exchange relationship was established to endure through time, a feature that especially held for long-distance trading. Men chose their trading partners in foreign lands with great care. Although personal and enduring, these dyadic relations of exchange (*palou*), through which men bartered and negotiated for the goods of their partners, were understood by the Piaroa as falling within the domain of foreign politics: exchange was an inherently dangerous process which as part and parcel of the world of external politics entailed the competition of *individuals*.

There are three points here to be stressed. First, exchange was always between men who were more or less foreigners, for the process of exchange was out of place within the domestic relations of community life and did not occur there. Second, exchange was between individuals, and not groups. The Piaroa tended to individualise their relations with all who lived outside their own domestic relations of community life. Within the boundaries of community life, where people engaged in the safe, co-operative, and productive relations of group existence, the prevailing flow of goods and food was through sharing and then through the continual giving of gifts. But immediately beyond the safety of community began the individualistic and competitive relations of exchange which, as the social distance between actors increased, became ever more likely to be acted out with force and coercion.

Third, exchange itself was the primordial mode, a violent one, for external political relations in general. During creation-time history when all the resources of the world were being created, as well as the capabilities for using them, it was the desire on the part of creator gods for the powers and resources of other domains that led them to initiate relationships with one another. From the start, the political relation was envisioned as a matter of taking from strangers of other realms. The archetypical exchange–political relationship of mythic time was that of affines (as brothers-in-law or father-in-law/son-in-law) foreign to one another who exchanged, and then captured, thieved, demanded, murdered for and cannibalised the forces and resources (including people) that belonged to each other's respective domain. This mythic backdrop of affinal violence and greed gave form to the Piaroa treatment and understanding of all their own relations with outsiders in their own 'present-day' time.

The dangers of exchange entailed more than the mere physical relationship between traders, for the goods themselves carried power. Each indigenously made item that was acquired in trade contained its own force for action that had been given it by its creator as part of the production process. As I shall explain more fully below, all products of work were in the Piaroa view of things a manifestation of the producer's 'thoughts' (*ta'kwaru*). Verbal expression was given to such an understanding of materiality when they referred to a product of work (a blowgun, a garden, a child) as one's *a'kwa* (thoughts). By accepting an article in exchange, a trader was in danger of being poisoned by the powerful alien capacities (thoughts) incorporated into the object by the one who produced it. Thus all such items could be said to be embodied ones, each with an agency distinct to itself. Exchange was always a matter of taking the power of another, and therefore a danger to the self. Because of the particular dangers of foreign objects, land and people, successful trade told of the power of the warrior. Thus, in Piaroaland, only the most powerful of men, their leaders (*ruwatu*), could engage in exchange, especially foreign exchange involving expeditions into territories belonging to distant Piaroa and other indigenous peoples.

The presence of danger, however, was not in itself the distinguishing mark of exchange, for as already stated productive activities (as predatory processes) also carried their danger. Animals had danger for hunters and others who wandered in the forest; they could inadvertently pass disease to the Piaroa – as too could the large fish of the rivers. The contrast was not between safety and danger *per se*, but between types of social relationship, those created through production as opposed to exchange: the first was with safe insiders, while the second was established with dangerous outsiders.

A person's success in gardening depended upon his or her intimate relationships with others of the community: gardening was both with and for other kinsmen of the community. The same can be said for the *social* relations of hunting, collecting, fishing – and shopping; production accomplished through both gardening and 'wandering' in forest and market-place was with safe insiders of a person's own community.[9] The *social* relations of danger affecting activities in the forest were between the communities' powerful leaders (plural *ruwatu*, singular *ruwang)* and the beings of other worlds, such as the Masters of forest and rivers who might order the animals and fish to send their diseases to the Piaroa. The relationship a *ruwang* established with such beings formed part of his duties in external politics – of defending his community against enemy forces and in general dealing with the dangers and powers of foreigners. As held for his trading partnerships, a *ruwang* formed relationships for his negotiations with the spirit world that were highly specific, individualised and therefore personal to him. These relationships, as foreign ones, pertained to the world of exchange, and not of production. In contrast, the productive activities within the forest (and market-place), centred as they were upon the safe and interior relations of the community, could be carried out by everyone; any person – whether man, woman or child – could join in forays into the forest, just as anyone could shop in the market-place and also share the adventure of going shopping with almost anyone else from the community.

There is a history, of course, to the relation the Piaroa had with the market-place which allowed them to introduce the market into their indigenous theory of social relationships of production and exchange in the way they did. Some of this history needs telling before the discussion above on the inclusion by the Piaroa of the market-place into the safe and internal domain of production, and not the foreign, external realm of exchange, can be further unfolded. The salient contrast in the next section is between the historical relation the Piaroa had, on the one hand, to indigenous networks of trade, and, on the other, to the Venezuelan market economy.

9.2 WHITE MAN'S GOODS, THE MARKET-PLACE AND INDIGENOUS NETWORKS OF TRADE

Although to a certain extent the Piaroa have always been affected by the development of the Venezuelan market economy, the majority of them did not become incorporated into it until the 1970s. Since then, due to the policy and intervention of a new government which had intense interest in the development of the resources of the Amazon, social and economic change has come to the Piaroa with great speed and with a vengeance (see Mansutti Rodriguez 1986:64–72).[10] Today most of the 7,000 Piaroa who dwell in Venezuela have moved down river into concentrated settlements that are close to market-towns and often controlled by New Tribes Missions. However, in 1968 at the time of my first fieldwork with them, the majority of Piaroa dwelt in their traditional communal houses scattered along tributaries of the Middle Orinoco, and though highly aware (and wary) of the Venezuelan society neighbouring them to the north, they continued to follow their own existence separate from it. Their polity, their social organisation, their language, their knowledge and their learning were indigenous to them, and most of the methods through which they transformed the resources of the forest and the rivers were their own. Their food came from their gardens and from the forest, and for the most part the means they used to acquire their food or to cultivate it and process it into edible form were indigenous to the area, either produced by themselves or by neighbouring indigenous groups. To use the forest they produced their own blowguns, curare, quivers, darts, traps and hunting dogs. For fishing in the streams they made their own traps. They grew up to forty varieties of vegetables (basically a root culture, supplemented with maize and squash) and fruit in their gardens, most of which were indigenous to the area.[11] The digging stick was the primary garden implement used for cultivation. Their hearth was made of stones of the area, and they still used their own fragile, black, pottery baking trays. They made the graters and the basketry that enabled them to transform cassava into edible form. They made their own torches, wove their own cotton for their loincloths, grew the hallucinogens upon which their ritual was dependent for its efficacy, and wore powerful amulets made either by themselves or by their indigenous neighbours. In short, as held for other areas of life, their material existence (their production and their consumption) was still largely indigenously based.

The important exception was their use of axes, machetes, knives and fish-hooks – items upon which they have been dependent for several centuries. Their dependency on such tools had not led to an increase in the production of food; normally each garden remained at less than a hectare in size. Rather, it was the leisure that these efficient steel tools provided that was so highly valued. The leisure gained, especially by the men in their garden work where it was their task to cut down the trees of the forest, could then be used for the production of items for exchange within the vast indigenous trade networks of the Orinoco basin. It was somewhat ironic that it was partly to acquire the items of the industrial west that the Piaroa engaged in this trade. At the same time it was the existence of these active networks of trade that spoke of the health of indigenous social organisations. I tend to agree with Henley's conclusions (1982:214), in writing about the Panare who are the neighbours of the Piaroa, about the effect that the introduction of manufactured tools might have upon an indigenous group. Henley observes that he sees no reason to argue that this process brought about any major changes in Panare social relations of production. As was also true for the Piaroa, no social prestige was attached to the ownership of such goods, which were for the most part shared as property within a community and even territory. Thus, among these highly egalitarian peoples (certainly from a material point of view) they served no basis for any form of internal social differentiation.

It is only in the recent past that the Piaroa acquired their industrial goods from the market-place. Puerto Ayacucho, the capital of the Amazon Territory, was not established until 1924, and it is this town, situated on the Middle Orinoco, that was the closest to many traditionally located Piaroa territories. During the seventeenth and eighteenth centuries, western goods could at times be acquired from mission stations. However, reflecting the state of turmoil general to the region of the Orinoco during that period, the missions along the Middle Orinoco were not very successful, and were both intermittent and short lived.[12] There is also no evidence that the Piaroa ever settled in them. Practically never mentioned in the early missionary chronicles, by 1800 the Piaroa were, however, well known by the Franciscan missionaries on the Orinoco (Humboldt and Bonpland 1821,V:15–16).[13] Piaroa settlements were only two to three days' journey from one of their missions, and Piaroa from them frequented it for trading purposes.[14] According to subsequent reports,[15] the Piaroa never became incorporated into the missions, until some groups of them, from the late 1950s to the present, became increasingly affected by the tenacious New Tribes Protestants.

Until two decades ago, it was through the indigenous trading network that most Piaroa acquired their western goods. Industrial items were introduced into the system by indigenous peoples, both by Piaroa and by those from other groups, who lived close to markets or who dwelt on the edges of indigenous territories in the neighbourhood of creole settlements. According to Mansutti Rodriguez (1986:50), there were three principal ways that these more peripheral Piaroa obtained commercial articles from the creoles. A few of their communities were in the unfortunate position of being attached to a company store. The members of such communities sold their labour to a creole 'patron' in return for western goods. Though most did not, some communities tolerated the visits of a creole 'travelling salesman'. It was in part to hide from the world of the whites, their aggression and their diseases, that the majority of Piaroa lived high in the headwater regions, many along unnavigable tributaries – the same strategy that had served to protect them during the conquest from the ravages of the Conquistador and then later from the raids of the Carib and Arawak slave raiders into the Middle Orinoco. Especially fearful of the wandering, lone male who fits their image of both Conquistador and their own powerful and wild 'Master of the Jungle', the Piaroa did not welcome the travelling creole salesman to their communities.

The third method of obtaining industrial goods was by trading their own products (basketry, parrots) to either missionaries or to market shopkeepers. Because the town of Puerto Ayacucho was only recently established, the Piaroa were late in entering the money economy, and their main use of Venezuelan money was for decoration – their ear and lip ornaments were pounded metal, made of Venezuelan coinage. By the time I visited them in 1968, the Piaroa in communities near to Puerto Ayacucho had to a certain extent incorporated money into their economy for both internal and external use. When they occasionally went to the market-place they sold their products and shopped for their axes and machetes with money. They sometimes gave money instead of products in exchange for services among themselves. The latter use of money was adopted in the case of help in highly specialised tasks, such as house building. The practice of paying for specialist services was at any rate indigenous to Piaroa culture, where one had always been expected to pay for the receiving of specialist knowledge, the learning of it and benefiting by it. In the past the payment was usually in specialist goods, the topic of the next section. In 1968 it was still often the case for the members of communities who dwelt high in headwaters regions to receive their industrial goods through the indigenous trading network.

9.3 SPECIALISATION AND THE NETWORKS OF INDIGENOUS TRADE

The work of ethno-history attests to the antiquity of the vast indigenous trade networks of the area. They linked the two great basins of the Amazon and the Orinoco, and the islands of the Caribbean with mainland South America (see Dreyfus 1983/4). Piaroa territory was criss-crossed with paths specifically created for trading purposes (see Mansutti Rodriguez, 1986:44–50). In the excellent account that Mansutti Rodriguez gives (1986) of the intra- and inter-ethnic networks in which the Piaroa until the last decade participated, he makes several important generalisations. First of all such trade was premised upon economic specialisation, and allowed for the distribution of highly valued, scarce resources throughout the indigenous territories of the Middle Orinoco. The presence or absence of good raw materials for reproducing the technical aspects of the indigenous material economy, which included items of ritual, was one main incentive for trade. These networks of trade also ensured that everyone had access to the needed western goods – the axe, the machete, the knife, fish-hooks and matches.

To guarantee access to all such resources communities specialised in the making of particular items, either of productive or ritual utility, that would give them a secure place within trading networks. For instance, one community in the territory in which I dwelt specialised in the making of cassava graters. From the start this speciality entailed long-distance trading, for the stone fragments set in the resin on these boards were acquired from the Mako whose home was along tributaries of the Ventuari, a good distance from the producers of the graters who dwelt on a tributary of the lower Cuao. The Mako, in turn, acquired the stone fragments from another ethnic group (the Ye'cuana) who neighboured on Mako territory. All of the indigenous peoples of the region depended on trade, either directly or through networks of trade, with these same Ye'cuana for the production of blowguns, for it was only in their territory that the sacred reed grew from which the inner tube of this hunting weapon was made, which gave it the force for the hunt. The Ye'cuana, renowned as great river traders, were the centre of several inter-ethnic trade networks. The Piaroa were also closely involved in trade with their neighbours, the Panare, the Pemon and the Guahibo.[16]

Mansutti Rodriguez (1986:17–19) gives us a list of fifty products that were exchanged within this complicated system, among which edibles were not prominent. While some Piaroa might exchange processed foods (cassava bread, manioc flour) with creoles in order to obtain western goods, such food was not used within the sphere of indigenous exchange. The items valued in indigenous trade were either powerful means of production – canoes, blowguns, hunting dogs, curare, resin (used in the making of many implements), poisons, cassava graters, pottery cooking pots and trays, axes, machetes, knives – or potent ritual objects – maracas, hallucinogens, tobacco, crowns, hunting charms, amulets, quartz stones, beads, body paints. For the Piaroa these were not separate spheres of exchange, for any of these items could be exchanged for any other (Mansutti Rodrigues 1986:38) – one blowgun for one cassava grater, or one container of curare, or two toucan feather crowns. Canoes were costly, and could require one machete, one axe and two blowguns in exchange. Hunting dogs could also be expensive, and a good one could fetch a canoe. The variety of equivalences were fairly standard to both intra- and inter-ethnic trade; gain was not a factor. Profit, as will be seen below, would have been too dangerous a principle to follow. According to Mansutti Rodriguez (1986:38), the value of a product responded more to tradition, utility and the amount of time necessary to produce it, than to anything we could label 'laws of supply and demand'.

9.4 THE PREDATION OF POTS AND BLOWGUNS

Most of the indigenous items – and to a certain extent those of western origin – had crucial elements in common that united them intellectually into one sphere of exchange. First, from the Piaroa point of view, they were all critical to the production process; each played its own role in the culinary arts, and thus was important to the process of transforming resources of jungle and rivers into edible form. This process entailed many other-worldly duties, and required therefore the agency of hallucinogens, quartz stones and maracas; and because production was a dangerous, if not deadly, business, it required as well the protection of amulets, charms and body paint. Crowns and beads told of the productive powers of their wearer, and in metonymic fashion were related to these forces (see Overing 1985a, 1989).

The second factor that linked all the indigenous products is further indication of the degree to which the trade networks were integrated not only into the indigenous religion and metaphysics, but also with indigenous polity. To give them their efficacy in the productive process all of the indigenous items had been sacralised by religious specialists. A blowgun would not work unless a Ye'cuana specialist had given its inner reed the agency to kill. Similarly, the cassava grater would be useless for the grating of manioc without the aid in its making of the specialist who knew the chant that gave it its efficacy. Nor would pots cook and dogs hunt, and so on down the list.

Thus, in Piaroaland, most utensils used in the culinary arts – the means from start to finish through which resources were transformed into edible form – required for their creation the assistance of a powerful *ruwang* (the Piaroa leader and religious specialist). His powers for production and protection were incorporated into them. This meant that the production of some objects, the very dangerous ones, were in the hands of the specialists alone. Only powerful *ruwatu* made curare and hallucinogens, which they always shared with other men of their communities, while the cassava graters which were made in the territory where I lived were produced as a joint effort by the women of a particular community and its *ruwang*.

The efficacy of all objects produced indigenously and exchanged within the networks of exchange depended, then, upon the potency given them by the specialist *ruwatu*. As I have already explained, this also made the objects a potential danger, for they carried in their use the force of the manufacturers' 'thoughts'; each object was a manifestation of the 'thoughts' of all the people who participated in their production. In Piaroa metaphysics, it was *ta'kwanya*, an aspect of thoughts (*ta'kwaru*), that provided the personal power for fulfilling material needs, and this included the capacity for creating tools of production. The Piaroa said that *ta'kwanya* were the particular capabilities a specific type of people could acquire that enabled it to live as it did: it referred to a people's way of doing things in the material sense. The Piaroa had the *ta'kwanya* for making blowguns, curare and producing manioc, while white people had the *ta'kwanya* for making machines, tall buildings and tinned foods. Our term 'knowledge' is too weak a label for capturing the meaning of *ta'kwanya*, although it was a concept that included the notion of knowledge. For instance, through *ta'kwanya* a Piaroa knew the forest, the habits and the history of all its inhabitants, both plants and animals. However, *ta'kwanya* most importantly referred to those active, powerful forces of the mind that allowed a people to act upon the world, transforming it for use in their own particular way.

For the Piaroa, *ta'kwanya* were transcendental capacities which they received from the crystal boxes of their Tianawa gods. These powerful celestial gods were the owners of guardians of all *ta'kwanya* to which the Piaroa had access, and it was only upon request that the gods gave these powers to the *ruwatu*, who then brought them back to earth to incorporate as beads of knowledge within the individual members of his community. I never heard a *ruwang* (as one who was knowledgeable about such matters) elaborate on how non-Piaroa, either the whites or other indigenous peoples, acquired their powers of *ta'kwanya*. It is none the less pertinent to note that while the objects created by other indigenous groups were treated by the Piaroa in the same manner as those of a Piaroa source, the 'inner power' or danger of the white man's objects never seemed to be a concern for them, and this was perhaps because they did not have a specific maker.

The Tianawa gods kept the forces of *ta'kwanya* tightly contained within their crystal boxes because they were too dangerous to be let loose in their fullness in the world. According to Piaroa cosmogony, *ta'kwanya* were a source for violence in this world, and in their origin these forces were the capabilities through which the predator captures and processes his prey.[17] Because tools for the productive process – pots and blowguns, curare and cassava graters – were physical manifestations of their creator's *ta'kwanya*, each contained within it the force of their predator creator. Creator and pot were therefore 'of a kind' with one another.

The capabilities for production contained within a person were highly individualised, for no two people had the same amount and type of *ta'kwanya*. The forces of *ta'kwanya* were so poisonous that the Piaroa could take them from the Tianawa gods only in small doses at a time. In each community there were those who chose to have only a moderate amount of *ta'kwanya* and those who desired the more dangerous course: the great *ruwatu*, so long as they could manage it, continued to take from the Tianawa gods throughout their adult life. Through their powers of 'thought', they were the great protectors and warriors of their community who also endowed it with all possibilities for existence; as such they also had the potential for being very dangerous men. It was they who engaged in long-distance trading for their communities.

9.5 THE DANGERS OF LONG-DISTANCE TRADING

As already discussed, exchange in Piaroa theory pertained to the volatile world of foreign relations, and thus was a process that could easily shift from the peaceful trading of goods to warfare and the killing of people. The reason for the exchange relationship being so dangerous was that it was premised upon contact with the alien and therefore cannibal 'other', the one who was a predator of one's own domain.[18] A man did not engage in exchange with those of his own community – with those whose powers were similar to his own – but with the stranger who owned desirable resources to which he did not otherwise have access.

It was indeed normal to the history of the Orinoco basin for trade and warfare to be two sides of the same coin. According to the ethno-historical work of Dreyfus (1983/4:49), from pre-conquest times until well into the eighteenth century, the extensive expeditions of the Kalinago in their great war canoes took them from their islands in the Caribbean onto the continent well into the Guianas. The network of river routes they followed were chosen with care for the purpose of re-establishing their relations with both favourite enemies and favourite friends, the latter being their formal trading partners (Dreyfus 1983/4:46). They were involved in trade of a sort with friend and foe, for from them both they acquired precious items to take back to the islands. They raided their enemies for goods, women and slaves to use and/or exchange, and for prisoners to eat in anthropophagous ritual performances back home (Dreyfus 1983/4:43). From the very same ethnic group they would receive from formal trading partners desired products of the Amazon; green stones, feathers, jaguar pelts (Dreyfus 1983/4:45).

It is the argument of Dreyfus that the vast trading and raiding networks linked the Caribs and Arawaks from the islands and the continent into one large, but fluid, political unit of ethnic groups. The political institutions of the groups involved were dependent upon their continuous war and trading parties. In the Kalinago islands, the political structure 'was clearly based upon the complementary relationship that held between the war chief, the shaman and the ceremonial rituals of anthropophagy' (Dreyfus 1983/4:48). While the use of these vast networks of intertribal communication have long since lost their function as routes for raiding, their other function – that of exchange – remained strong well into the 1970s (also see Butt Colson 1973; Thomas 1972:20, 1982:124).

It was on the southern edge of this grand network into which the Piaroa were incorporated as traders. We do not know how they fit into its history, nor the extent to which they were subjected to Carib and Arawak raiding. Neither Arawak nor Carib, the Piaroa speak an independent language. They are also known for their extreme peacefulness. Indeed, one would think that armed conflict would have been unthinkable to the Piaroa, since their sanction against violent killing in the physical sense was generalised to all humanity, and not just to close kinsmen or members of one's territory. On the other hand, they were renowned in the Orinoco basin for their capabilities as sorcerers, and their warriors were probably always men 'of thoughts', not arms. But given the history in the area of the expeditions of great war chiefs who traded for goods and raided for prisoners – for women to be taken in foreign marriage, for men to be used either as slaves (and in the seventeenth and eighteenth centuries for European use) or for anthropophagous rituals – the intensity with which the Piaroa linked exchange and danger, cannibalism and the stranger, is understandable. Affinity was also incorporated into this paradigm of danger. As already noted, their root metaphor of exchange was that of two (male) affines preying upon each other's respective domains.

Because of the dangers of the peoples, the spirits, the objects and the terrain itself of alien lands, it was the duty of the Piaroa political leader, the *ruwang*, in his capacity as a great 'man of thoughts', to conduct all trading expeditions into foreign lands both within and without Piaroaland. Most dangerous were the sorcerers (*ruwatu*), for in Piaroa understanding all their deaths were caused by the sorcery attacks of malevolent men from foreign territories. Such sorcerers could indeed be the rival specialists with whom the *ruwang* traded. Therefore the trading relationships a *ruwang* developed with foreigners were highly formalised towards the aim of keeping them as safe as possible. Another means that *ruwatu* used to 'domesticate' their relationship with distant trading partners was to transform them through the relationship nomenclature into 'kin' relations by classifying them as 'father', 'brother' or 'son'. A *ruwang* never addressed such formal trading partners by affine terms, for the dangers of affinity were too great to be made overt when dealing with powerful *ruwatu* of foreign lands. Affinity stated a difference in powers and therefore a relation of competition, while consanguinity entailed an obligation of benevolent protection. The 'kin' classification carried with it the pretence that the men were of the same domain, of 'a kind' with one another, and not (the truth of the matter) competitors with powers dangerously different from each other. The practice of labelling was different for the safer, yet still competitive, relations of exchange within a man's own territory, where exchange followed its archetypical pattern in the matter of labelling. The relations between communities within the same territory were created through the continuous exchange of goods and services, and although marriage was ideally endogamous to community most alliances were initiated between the communities of a territory. In order to facilitate one's place within this system of multiple exchange, a man would relate to men of other communities as affines, classifying them (if not too closely related as kin) as 'father-in-law', 'brother-in-law' or 'son-in-law'. Social visiting between communities was often accompanied by the casual exchange of goods and services, particularly between the *ruwatu*, who in the main were responsible for the political, economic and ritual relations that held between communities. The ritual specialisations of the *ruwatu* could thereby be utilised by all: the 'master of chants' could exchange his skills with the man who had the powers for curing sorcery attacks.

Although powerful *ruwatu* conducted most inter-territorial and all long-distance trading, other members of the trader's community and even territory[19] were involved in it. The trade was not to the personal material gain of the *ruwang*. Members of his community contributed to the goods that he would take on his trip, and many of the items he brought back, especially tools for production of both western and indigenous origin that were scarce to the community (curare, blowguns, axes, knives, graters), were shared by its members. Such sharing of foreign goods was usually among those of the same gender, because it was they who closely co-operated in certain daily tasks of production (Mansutti Rodriguez 1986:11). For very scarce items, such as a canoe, the entire territory shared its use, in which case all of its members considered themselves as its owner. The *ruwang* would also exchange on the personal behalf of others, bringing them back powerful amulets or hunting charms.

With the topics of sharing and co-operation, however, the discussion has shifted away from the competitive and basically foreign relations of exchange, and turned instead to the internal domain of community life where it was the tranquility of relations that was above all valued as the type of sociality most conducive to its productive endeavours. Before continuing on the subject of production, several points should be made about Piaroa community life. The first has to do with the size of the community. In 1968 the membership of the communal house, the physical centre of village life, ranged from fifteen to sixty people. We have no data on the size of villages in earlier centuries, but even in Piaroa memory these dispersed and relatively autonomous social units were once much larger. This is important since in the view of the Piaroa the community set the boundary for safe, and therefore *social* relations, beyond which began in varying degrees the *asocial* relations of exchange and foreign relations. The second point to make is that the *ruwang's* relation to his community was very different from his relations to the outside. He had no right to use coercion within the community. In his relationship to his community he could with legitimacy only make manifest the productive side of his power, and never its violent coercive side that was so necessary to the success of his relationships with outsiders. Relations internal to the community were primarily about co-operation, production and consumption, and not exchange and competition. This was a principle of sociality that pertained as much to relations between in-laws as to those of leader and follower.

9.6 SAFETY, SOCIALITY AND THE PRODUCTIVE RELATIONS OF COMMUNITY LIFE

In the view of the Piaroa there was no practice of exchange between members of the same village. This is a remarkable fact, since the right to join a community was established through a person's marriage into it. Communities were created, and they expanded, through the establishment of marital and in-law ties within them; the affine relationship, both between males and between females, was critical to their structure. At the same time, the Piaroa considered their community to be comprised of close kinsmen, who through time and work could become 'of a kind' with one another, rather than dangerously different. In the Piaroa metaphysics of human existence the relation of alterity was necessary to the creation of relations of identity; the very fact of human fertility – the production of children – was dependent upon people interacting with others alien to themselves.

Specialisation within the networks of trade was as much based upon this metaphysics of difference as upon economic need, understood in its more obvious sense: the culinary arts were impossible without the acquisition of foreign implements to provide alien force to the production of food. In similar vein, sexual relations were barren unless between people essentially different from one another. Thus, affines were essential to life; it was through relations with them that one acquired the forces necessary for both the production of food and of children. It was only through the acquisition of powers both external and potentially dangerous to it that the internal life of the community could be created. Within the community the danger of necessary affines – the actual father-in-law, brother-in-law and son-in-law – was averted through a process of daily, productive living that had the effect over time of transforming the dangerous affinal relationship from one of exchange to one of sharing. In the Piaroa view, the principle of difference was too dangerous a matter to play out in any overt manner within the context of the highly *informal* and intimate relations of community life. The 'cannibal other' must become nurturant kin. Through the proximity of daily living within the same village, affines slowly became even physically 'of a kind'.

The process of 'becoming of a kind' included having children, working and eating together. It depended upon the mutual caring for one another through daily work and the sharing of the products of it; thus the village as a collectivity of kinsmen living and therefore working and eating together was ideally a community of nurture. Generosity in sharing was an important social principle, and in some areas an obligation. In hunting, fishing and collecting – and in the past, shopping – a person appropriated in large part on behalf of the collectivity. In short, personal work and social linkage were constitutive of one another. Without the tranquil and co-operative relations of good community life, one could not be productive; and without production, there was no community.

9.7 THE GIFT WAS NOT EXCHANGE

Affines who lived together within the same community, in contrast to classificatory affines who dwelt in different villages, emphasised the altruism of their relations. The stress of women with female in-laws was upon the comfort of co-operative relations in work; co-resident male affines, in the realm of politics, carefully refrained from competition. All actualised in-law relations, both those of males and those of females, were to be relations of sharing. It was the moral obligation of affines within a community to work at achieving friendship, a process which male in-laws enhanced through the continual giving of gifts and favours.

As discussed in my introductory remarks, the Piaroa made the absolute distinction between exchange (*palou*) and the giving of gifts (*mifona*). *Palou* entailed the trade in goods, the haggling over them and was conducted between two *ruwatu* of different communities. In contrast, gifts were given within the context of community relations, where the further distinction between the gift to be reciprocated (*mifona*) and the 'free gift' (*mifona chiya'a*) was made. When a person gave a gift to a close kinsmen (a mother, daughter, father, son or sibling), it was assumed that the gift would eventually be reciprocated. A person could even demand a specific gift from such a relative, but with the expectation of reciprocating with a return gift at a later date. However, with gifts between affines (and between follower and leader) there was no expectation of return – these gifts were 'free'. A primary means through which two male affines intensified the social side of their relationship towards the end of domesticating it was through the continuous giving of small 'free gifts' to one another – a comb, some curare or tobacco. The gift freely given to an affine was a sign of peaceful intentions. It also gave the message that the giver's relation with the receiver was one of altruistic sharing, and not of exchange and competition. The institution of the free gift released affines from the strain of worry that their gift given would not be a gift reciprocated – such lack of reciprocation being the most persistent reason for the disintegration of relations between the creator gods of the Piaroa mythic past.

Balanced reciprocity, where there is always the expectation of the return of the gift, perpetuates opposition; and it is highly significant that the Piaroa used this type of gift most liberally where it would do the least harm. Close kinsmen were already 'of a kind' with one another. With them, a person could joke, banter and make demands, all with the confidence that they would not retaliate in a dangerous way. A person demanded a gift or gave one with the expectation of return only to those with whom one's sociality was secure and without question. But to bind a male in-law with the *obligation* of reciprocity, to demand it of him, was an unwise and even dangerous procedure: the affine might not return the gift, a negligence that would state a refusal or a closing of the social aspect of the relationship. As the Piaroa explained it, in the arena of affine relations one had to be very careful not to ask for war and for the retaliation of 'the cannibal other'. As Mauss similarly understood (1990[1950]: for example, 39ff), the failure to give, to receive or to reciprocate is equivalent to a declaration of war; it is a refusal of alliance and communication. The Piaroa, who certainly stressed this aspect of the gift, paid an attention to its danger that Mauss did not foresee in his discussion of primitive analogues of the social contract. The Piaroa did not want to gamble with the safety achieved with the potentially competitive and dominating alien other. By denying the weight of the reciprocated gift and its necessity between affines (and between leaders and followers), they chased the notion of exchange outside the domain of community relations.

To a large extent the successful community was one that as a whole embodied the spirit of sharing, or the generalised reciprocity expected of affine relations internal to it. This is a complicated statement that requires much more explanation than can be unfolded here. It takes into account the Piaroa idea, and the very Amerindian one, that human fertility itself was dependent upon the dangerous interaction of forces from different domains. In the realm of marriage, it meant that safety was to be achieved in this dangerous coming together of (predatory) forces only if its establishment could be withdrawn from the area of foreign politics and exchange, and instead be squarely placed within the domain of the sharing and productive relations of community life.

9.8 CONCLUSION

In Piaroa thought, the gift was not as innocent as it presumes to be in anthropological theory. If the Piaroa had had more experience with the market economy, they would not, as Lévi-Strauss does, have made the absolute opposition between gift-giving, as it is experienced in 'primitive exchange', and exchange for profit as it is enacted in the market-place of the west (1969:61). I speak of a hypothetical understanding on the part of the Piaroa, because if their knowledge of the capitalist system had been complete, which it was not, they would never have categorised 'shopping in the market-place' with the productive activities of the forest, and even less with the co-operative and sharing relations of community life. They would have understood too well its place within their own aggressive domain of exchange and foreign relations. But since in their view the *social* relations involved in shopping, unlike those of exchange, were centred around the internal relations of community life, the activity of going to market pertained also to the interior and safe realm of production, and not to the external, competitive domain of foreign relations.

The point is that anthropological theory about the gift can miss the mark with regard to indigenous thought and practice, which is precisely what as its minimal requirement it should capture. The distinction made by Lévi-Strauss between the giving of a gift and the predatory, profit-making of market exchange would not have been valid for the Piaroa (given that their knowledge of the western system was more complete), since in their view the one could easily slide into the next. The value in either process could be centred on the goods exchanged, and not upon the social bonds that the gift in theory should cement. In their view, there always remained a competitive edge to their own exchange relations, despite the social obligation that they, again in theory, should have fulfilled (for example the attainment of a state of friendship between foreign territories). They would also judge as exceedingly naïve the assumption of Mauss about what he refers to as 'all the societies that have immediately preceded our own', when he comments on them that 'there is no middle way: one trusts completely, or one mistrusts completely; one lays down one's arms and gives up magic, or one gives everything, from fleeting acts of hospitality to one's daughter and one's goods' (Mauss 1990[1950]:81).

In anthropology, the 'problem of the gift' incorporates, of course, the 'problem of exchange'. The western idea of reducing civil society to the competitive area of exchange would have been a strange and contradictory equation for the Piaroa, one with abhorrent implications, since exchange for them was on the continuum that more likely ends with war, not peace. Yet Lévi-Strauss stresses the social value of '*primitive*' exchange. As he sees it, 'primitives' are social in so far as they engage in exchange: their sociality is constituted as 'a total exchange, comprising food, manu-factured objects, and that most precious category of goods, women' (1969:61). For him, reciprocity, reason and the social state are all conjoined, and the gift becomes the means through which the unreasoned disorder of the primordial world (of animality) is overcome.[20] In both the Maussian theory of the gift and in Lévi-Strauss's theory of alliance – but in contrast to indigenous understanding – it is through exchange that wars are prevented and peace achieved.

Very little attention is paid by either to what in indigenous theory is often understood to be the salient force conducive of peace – the social relations of production and its morality. In the view of Mauss and Lévi-Strauss, it is exchange and *its* rationality that among 'primitives' serve as the moral and good cementing force of social relationships. In part this is their argument because the transfer 'of things and people' that they are envisioning for the 'archaic' or 'primitive' world is one free of the harshness of the profit-making and competitiveness of the 'real' market-place. For them it is 'primitive' exchange that – in its innocence and as its strength – embodies a morality that obliges a person to give, and not just to take. Perhaps such anthropological theories can be understood as attempts to cleanse the market mentality; they re-fashion and give it to the alien 'other', telling of ideals unreachable in our own world of the social, identified as it is with the adult world of independent men competing in an economic arena free from the moral allegiance of tribe and family.[21]

Such an understanding of the gift, exchange and alliance also projects an innocence that the Piaroa would reject as highly unlikely. It is, however, a cleansed theory of exchange that transforms our own aberrant notion of civil society into a more realistic, and certainly more satisfactory theory of sociality. As such it has great appeal and is therefore one widely held in anthropology as belonging to and descriptive of (our own) more youthful, primitive space. This is despite the fact that many of the indigenous peoples of tropical South America might well be highly sceptical of the idealism and moral simplicity of any theory that stresses the moral rationality of exchange as constitutive of the social.[22] For the Piaroa, exchange was understood as necessary to production and therefore to the achievement of the social precisely because of its danger, and not its safety. It was a more cerebral and perhaps more realistic theory of exchange upon which they acted than that envisioned for them by Mauss and Lévi-Strauss.

NOTES

1. I give my warm thanks to the Leverhulme Foundation who in awarding me a Research Grant for the academic year of 1989/90 gave me the time to work on many of the issues of this article. I would also like to thank Roy Dilley, Peter Rivière and Fernando Santos for their constructive comments on an earlier draft of the paper.
2. See Overing 1989 where I describe the importance of the creation of tranquility and high spirits to production.
3. See Overing 1981, where I draw attention to the Piaroa discomfort over the placing of marriage within the framework of exchange – which for them would have been to treat the marital relation itself as an aspect of trade.
4. *tu tsutsae* (m.) or *tu tsaehutsae* (f.)
5. For example, see Lizot (1985); Crocker (1985); Viveiros de Castro (1986).
6. Of course both hunting and shopping were dependent upon certain previous activities. The inner tubes for blowguns had to be acquired in exchange, and the

materials for traps collected from the forest; while the acquisition of money was a pre-condition for shopping.

7. This statement would hold only for the ordinary hunter who was not also a powerful shaman. It is one of the tasks of the shaman/leader to make plentiful the forests around his community. He filled the forest with game through the danger-ous ritual of transforming humans who dwelt beneath the earth into animals to dwell upon it; thus in a sense he was a 'creator' of animals. See Overing Kaplan 1975, Overing 1988.

8. To acquire the money which could then be used for shopping, the Piaroa did tend to use in a more steady fashion particular shops or middlemen. The most common source for money were those mission stations whose missionaries had a certain commercial bent; they would buy artefacts from the Piaroa for resale in Caracas. Also, certain shops bought indigenous artefacts and manioc flour from the Piaroa.

9. Part of the treat of 'wandering' was being able to *choose* one's company. While in gardening both men and women had specific obligations to particular kinsmen (to a wife, father-in-law, a mother or daughter), this did not hold for forest and market activities. A boy could hunt with a favourite uncle rather than with a father; collecting, fishing and shopping activities tended to be *ad hoc* in composition – anyone who wished from within the community could participate once a plan was suggested.

10. The policy towards its Amazon Territory has once again changed, for the Venezue-lan government has announced its intention to close it to development for the next ten years. This is in conjunction with the establishment of the Humboldt Research Centre which will begin an intense environmental study of the region.

11. For the list of the plants cultivated by the Piaroa, see Overing and Kaplan 1988.

12. See Overing Kaplan 1975 for a brief history of missionary activity along the Middle Orinoco.

13. Also see Bueno 1933 [1801–4].

14. In the words of Humboldt and Bonpland (1821, V:16), 'having obtained what they [the Piaroa] sought, knives, fishhooks, beads, they returned to the woods, weary of the regulations of the mission'.

15. For example, see the writings of the Salesian, Defarrari (1945:14).

16. Both Jean-Paul Dumont and Paul Henley, ethnographers of the Panare, northern neighbours of the Piaroa, tell of Piaroa traders visiting Panare settlements in recent years. Dumont (1978:149–50) tells of twelve Piaroa men arriving at the Panare settlement where he lived to barter resin for tobacco and curare, and Henley (1982:25) mentions Piaroa traders coming to Panare communities, again with resin, in order to obtain curare.

17. See Overing 1985a, 1986, 1989 on Piaroa cosmogony and the creation of the culinary arts.

18. I have written elsewhere that humans and animals of the forest were prey of each other (Overing 1986). We are speaking here of relative danger. A trading partner was much more dangerous for a man than was the animal for the hunter. As already stated, the animal in the forest had lost all capabilities for intentionality; thus its danger to humans was *un*intentional.

19. There might be as many as six communities dispersed throughout a political territory (see Overing Kaplan 1975).

20. Which is not so far from the reasoning of the Piaroa – except for their different understanding of 'reciprocity' and their variation on his meaning of 'social state'.

21. See Hegel (1821:Sec.152).

22. Also see Clastres (1977), who although convincingly argued against evolutionary theory in his work on the relation between political power and egalitarianism

among tropical forest peoples of South America, still manages to trivialise the indigenous understanding of power by reducing the topic to a theory of exchange.

REFERENCES

Bueno, R. 1933. *Apuntes sobre la provincia misionera del Orinoco e indígenas de su territorio, con algunas otras particularidades* [written in 1801-4]. Caracas.

Butt Colson, A. 1973. 'Inter-tribal trade in the Guiana Highlands', *Antropológica*, 28: 25–58.

Clastres, P. 1977. *Society against the State: the leader as servant and the humane uses of power among the Indians of the Americas.* Oxford: Basil Blackwell.

Crocker, J. C. 1985. *Vital Souls: Bororo Cosmology, Natural Symbolism, and Shamanism.* Tuscon: The University of Arisona Press.

Defarrari, E. 1945. 'Tribus Indígenas de la Prefectura Apostólica del Alto Orinoco', *Tercera Conferencia Interamericana de Agricultura*, Caracas. XL:6-30.

Dreyfus, S. 1983/4. 'Historical and political anthropological inter-connections: the multilinguistic indigenous polity of the "Carib" Islands and Mainland Coast from the 16th to the 18th century', in *Themes in Political Organisation: the Caribs and their Neighbours* A. B. Colson and H. D. Heinen, (eds.). *Antropológica* 59-62: 39-55.

Dumont, J-P. 1978. *The Headman and I.* Austin and London: University of Texas Press.

Hegal, G. W. F. 1821. *Grundlinien der Philosophie des Rechts*, Sec. 152 Berlin. [English Translation by T. M. Knox. *Hegel's Philosophy of Right*, Oxford: The Clarendon Press 1942.]

Henley, P. 1982. *The Panare.* New Haven and London: Yale University Press.

Humboldt, A. de and A. Bonpland, 1821. *Personal Narrative of Travels to the Equinoctial Regions of the New Continent during the Years 1799–1804.* (Translated from French by H. M. Williams). Vol.V. London.

Lévi-Strauss, C. 1969. *The Elementary Structures of Kinship.* (Revised Edition, translated from the French by J. H. Bell, J. R. von Sturmer and R. Needham.) Boston: Beacon Press.

Lizot, J. 1985. *Tales of the Yanomami.* Cambridge: Cambridge University Press.

Mansutti Rodriguez, A. 1986. 'Hierro, barro cocido, curare y cerbatanas: el comercio intra e interétnico entre los Uwotjuja', *Antropológica*, 63: 3–75.

Mauss, M. 1990 [1950]. *The Gift: The Form and Reason for Exchange in Archaic Societies.* (Translated by W.D. Halls.) London: Routledge.

Overing Kaplan, J. 1975. *The Piaroa, a People of the Orinoco Basin.* Oxford: Clarendon Press.

Overing Kaplan, J. 1981. 'Review article: Amazonian anthropology', *Journal of Latin American Studies*, 13 (1): 151–164.

Overing, J. 1985a. 'There is no end to evil: the guilty innocents and their fallible god', in D. Parkin (ed.), *The Anthropology of Evil.* Oxford: Basil Blackwell. pp.244–78.

Overing, J. 1985b. 'Today I shall call him "Mummy": multiple worlds and classificatory confusion', in J. Overing (ed.), *Reason and Morality.* London: Tavistock. pp. 152-279.

Overing, J. 1986. 'Images of cannibalism, death and domination in a "non-violent" society', *Journal de la Société des Américanistes*, LXXII:133–156.

Overing, J. 1988. 'Personal autonomy and the domestication of the self in Piaroa society', in G. Jahoda and I. Lewis (eds.), *Acquiring Culture: Cross-Cultural Studies in Child Development.* London: Croom Helm. pp. 169-192.

Overing, J. 1989. 'The Aesthetics of production: the sense of community among the Cubeo and Piaroa', *Dialectical Anthropology*, 14: 159–175.

Overing, J. and M. Kaplan, 1988. 'Los Wothuha', in J. Lizot (ed.), *Los Aborígenes de Venezuela*, Vol. 3. Caracas: Fundación La Salle de Ciencias Naturales, Monte Avila Editores.

Thomas, D. 1972. 'The indigenous trade system of Southeast Estado Bolivar, Venezuela', *Antropológica*, 33: 3–37.

Thomas, D. 1982. *Order without Government: the society of the Pemon Indians of Venezuela*. Urbana: University of Illinois Press.

Viveiros de Castro, E. 1986. *Arawete: os deuses canibais*. Rio de Janeiro: Jorge Zahar Editor LTDA.

Part IV
Development Discourse and the Informal Economy

10

'Good Government' and 'the Market'[1]

R. L. STIRRAT

On 6 June 1990 the United Kingdom Secretary of State for Foreign Affairs, Douglas Hurd, gave a speech at the Overseas Development Institute. Its theme was 'good government' and the necessity for aid donors in general and the ODA (the Overseas Development Administration – the aid wing of the British Foreign Office) in particular to support 'good government' in the developing world, and it has begun to be seen as marking a major shift in British government aid policy. Yet the nature of 'good government' was never made precisely clear, and the linkage between good government and a set of other concepts which appear to be central to the proposed future direction of British aid policy remained obscure. What I want to do in this chapter is discuss in a preliminary fashion some aspects of the content of Hurd's speech. In particular, I am interested in the relationship between 'the market' and 'good government' in official thought about development policy, for much of what Hurd had to say was concerned with the relationship between 'government' and 'the market'. In part this is an academic matter, but there is much more to it than that. In the design of development projects, one of the main forms that development interventions take, there is frequent recourse to terms such as 'market forces', 'transparency of the market', 'accountability', 'empowerment' and so on, concepts derived from policy statements such as Hurd's speech. Yet what precisely these terms mean, what implications they have and their relation to wider political positions is often unclear. Indeed the very ambiguity of these concepts is a central theme which for all it may encourage and allow a certain amount of subversive activity, prevents rather than encourages debate about development strategy and the nature of development interventions.

10.1 HURD'S SPEECH

The conference at which Hurd delivered his speech was concerned with the prospects for Africa in the 1990s, and thus most of what Hurd had to say focused on Africa. Whilst acknowledging that there has been some 'progress' in the last thirty years, he contrasted Africa with the success of countries in South-east Asia and the Pacific rim. Hurd claimed that the reason for this difference in performance was in large part a result of the differences in the nature of governments and policies followed by governments in Africa and Asia. In the former, as in Eastern Europe, governments have been 'inefficient and authoritarian', and this is the major cause of economic failure.

> Centralised political, economic and social structures have failed to deliver the goods in eastern Europe, and in those African countries where similar models have been attempted.

On the other hand,

> Economic success depends to a large degree on effective and honest government, political pluralism and observance of the rule of law, as well as freer more open economies.

Furthermore, the role of aid agencies is, according to Hurd, to assist in the formation of 'healthy societies'.

> Countries tending towards pluralism, public accountability, respect for the rule of law, human rights and market principles should be encouraged. Governments who [sic] persist with repressive policies, with corrupt management or with wasteful and discredited economic systems should not expect us to support their folly with scarce aid resources which could be used better elsewhere.

And just in case it might be thought that Africa was being singled out for criticism, the Secretary of State went on to say that the same criteria are being applied in Eastern Europe. Furthermore, such values are not being supported because they are 'uniquely Western but because where they are accepted they are effective and beneficial. No-one has found a better set of values by which to live'.

The speech then went on to discuss the problems Africa faces. Having lauded the beginnings of economic reform – in effect the policies of structural adjustment – Hurd outlined what he saw as the major issues which have to be faced in Africa. Whilst admitting in passing that they may not all have been caused by 'bad government', he claimd that they certainly require 'good government' if they are to be solved. Such problems include population growth, environmental degradation, migration, health and education, poor physical infrastructure and the burden of overseas debt. And then in conclusion he returned to the contrast between Africa and Asia.

> The main lesson from the success of South East Asia's economies is that, where individual skills and enterprise are released and where creativity is rewarded, economic development will follow. Eastern Europe provides ample evidence that economic and political liberalisation are inseparable. The more open a society is and the more transparent the decision of government, the more difficult it is to hide corruption and the abuse of human rights. Political accountability is increasingly seen as a pre-condition for economic reform. The release of the human spirit has a vital part to play in setting the right environment for development.

The themes in Hurd's speech have been taken up on a number of occasions by Lynda Chalker, the Minister with responsibility for Overseas Development. In December 1990 in a speech to the Africa Private Enterprise Group entitled *Africa: the Way Ahead*, Chalker recognised that '[good government]...is a concept which could suffer the fate of meaning all things to all men'. In an attempt to make its meaning clearer, Chalker went on to list a number of characteristics of 'good government'. First, she said, 'Good government is about sound economic management'. Second, it is about 'effectiveness'. Third, 'It must provide a sense of personal responsibility' as well as 'provide a strong rule of law and the independence of the judiciary, which are as much pillars of democracy as its parliamentary institutions'. And finally, 'It must ensure that decisions are made based on market principles and the right to private property'.

Similar themes are spelt out at greater length in her speech on 'Good Government and the Aid Programme' made to the Royal Institute of International Affairs in June 1991. Here, however, greater stress is placed on what she described as 'Respect for human rights', for, 'It is self-evident that individuals will not be able to play a full role in development unless their rights are fully respected'.

10.2 HURD AND THE WORLD BANK

Hurd and Chalker are not alone in their views about the role of government in Africa and the relationship between 'good governance' and the market economy. In the 1980s the World Bank became increasingly concerned with the nature of government in Africa, a shift culminating in the publication of *Sub-Saharan Africa: From Crisis to Sustainable Growth* in 1989. Indeed, there is more than a passing similarity between the phrases used by Hurd and those which crop up in the Bank's document, and one can only assume that Hurd's speech-writer was working under some pressure.[2]

In its 1989 publication, the long-term policy of the Bank is summarised thus:

> It aims to release the energies of ordinary people by enabling them to take charge of their lives. Profits would be seen as the mark of an efficient business. Agricultural extension schemes would be seen as responding to farmers, not commanding them. Foreign investors would be welcomed as partners, not discouraged. The state would no longer be an entrepreneur, but a promoter of private producers. And the informal sector would be valued as a seedbed for entrepreneurs, not a hotbed of racketeers. (World Bank 1989: 4–5)

As far as the Bank is concerned, the way in which this will be brought about is through both a reduction in the size of government and a shift in the role of government. 'Underlying the litany of Africa's development failures', writes the Bank, 'is a crisis of government' (ibid.:60). What is required is that government should retreat from the economy and instead concentrate on creating an 'enabling environment' in which the energies of ordinary people can be mobilised through the workings of the free market. Even where state enterprises are efficient, 'in time and with imagination privatisation can work' (ibid.:55). And of course, people should pay for services such as education, water supply and primary health care for this makes people act responsibly and empowers them as consumers (ibid.:86). As in Hurd's speech, a close association is asserted between the free market and liberal democracies.

Unlike Hurd, the Bank makes few direct statements about the need for government in Africa to take the form of western liberal democracies. Yet implicitly the same connection between a free market economy and a particular form of government is asserted. The vision of government in the World Bank document is one based on a distinction between a representative legislature and the executive, with an autonomous judiciary, and a 'scrupulous respect for the law and human rights at every level of government' (ibid.:192).

10.3 THEORIES OF HISTORY

Both the ministerial speeches quoted above and the World Bank's policy statement are primarily concerned with what they see as the practical problems of aid and development in Africa. Indeed, the World Bank document repeatedly stresses the need for a 'pragmatic' approach, and the same pragmatic interest is also present in Hurd's speech. In her speech at the Royal Institute of International Affairs Chalker refers to the 'sensible and pragmatic approach' which she sees as characterising British aid policy, and claims that 'Both developed and developing countries...recognise that we have no ideological axe to grind'. Yet underlying their approaches to development is a common view of history and a certain philosophy which underpins not only much of ODA's development work but that of most, if not all, the major western bilateral donors, and probably the multilateral donors as well. Furthermore, this theory of history is subscribed to by at least some of my undergraduates.

The last sentence of a quotation I gave earlier from Hurd's speech sums it up: 'The release of the human spirit has a vital part to play in setting the right environment for development'. Put more generally, and in a way my undergraduates appear to agree with, Douglas Hurd's theory of human history works something like this:

In all human beings there is a certain spark of humanity. In primitive societies, this is constrained by the forces of tradition, custom and hierarchical control. Human history is the process by which this spark is released from its chains until true freedom and the potential for individual fulfilment is released. Clearly, in such a picture, the regimes of Eastern Europe were a temporary blip on the upward path of human liberation. So too were the African states of the 1970s. Furthermore, the nearest approximation we have to this state of liberation is Western Europe and that is why the model for political, social and economic development is the west. The end product of history is the individual untrammelled by society.

A very similar theory of history underlines the World Bank's approach to development in Africa with its talk of the 'rapidly expanding urban centres [which] are crucibles of acculturation to modernity and to the market economy' (World Bank 1989:49). But whilst Hurd sees culture as at best irrelevant and at worst a barrier to the release of the human spirit, the Bank does at least recognise the relevance of culture. 'Far from impeding development, many indigenous African values and institutions can support it' (ibid.: 60), although in practice when the report is read as a whole only those values and institutions which the Bank sees as supporting a market economy receive its blessing. Yet perhaps the clearest and most cogent version of this theory of history is that outlined by Francis Fukuyama, the Deputy Director of the Policy Planning Unit in the US State Department. In 1989 he published a paper entitled, 'The End of History' in a somewhat obscure conservative American periodical, *The National Interest*, which provoked widespread discussion in the press on both sides of the Atlantic.

Like Hurd, Fukuyama is fascinated by the recent changes in Eastern Europe, and whilst Hurd argues implicitly that history – in a Hegelian sense – is coming to an end, Fukuyama is quite explicit about what he sees as the end of history. Fukuyama writes of the,

> Unabashed victory of economic and political liberalism. The triumph of the West, of the Western *idea*, is evident… in the total exhaustion of viable systematic alternatives to Western liberalism…What we may be witnessing is not just the end of the cold war, or the passing of a particular period of postwar history, but the end of history as such: that is, the end point of mankind's ideological evolution and the universalisation of Western liberal democracies.

Fukuyama is an unabashed Hegelian as far as history is concerned. He claims that:

> Consciousness is cause and not effect and can develop autonomously from the material world; hence the real subtext underlying the apparent jumble of current events is the history of ideology.

Going on to attack the materialism of the left, he also takes a sideswipe at what he calls the '*Wall Street Journal* school of deterministic materialism that discounts the importance of ideology and culture and sees man as essentially a rational, profit-maximising individual'. Yet he does allow a role for the material:

> In particular, the spectacular abundance of advanced liberal economies and the infinitely diverse consumer culture made possible by them, seem to both foster and preserve liberalism in the political sphere…We might summarise the content of the universal homogeneous state as liberal democracy in the political sphere combined with easy access to VCRs and stereos in the economic.

Fukuyama goes on to discuss such matters as the fall of fascism and Marxism, in passing making the extraordinary claim that the 'egalitarianism of modern America represents the essential achievement of the classless society envisioned by Marx'. Fukuyama lauds the achievements of Japan which has followed 'in the footsteps of United States to create a truly universal consumer culture, both the symbol and the underpinning of the universal homogeneous state'. And like Hurd he praises the success of the other NICs (Newly Industrialised Countries) in Asia where 'political liberalism developed in parallel with economic liberalisation'.

Yet while these states are seeing the end of history, the same is not yet true of the Third World which 'remains very much mired in history' and thus will continue to be a 'terrain of conflict' which Fukuyama associates with religion and nationalism. In the end, however, such states will reach the end of history, a prospect which fills Fukuyama with a sense of nostalgia for the past and a fear of the eternal boredom – the result no doubt of endless video watching – which the end of history will bring.

Now, it may well be unfair to compare Hurd's speech with Fukuyama's article. Furthermore, it has to be recognised that there are differences between the two approaches. Whilst Hurd stresses the release of the human spirit, presumably an internal essence, unchanging and unmodifiable, Fukuyama talks in terms of a changing consciousness which becomes manifest in the material world. Whilst Hurd appears to see the social and the cultural as barriers to this liberation of the human spirit and thus to economic and social progress, Fukuyama accepts that cultural forms are at least as important as free markets and stable political institutions in under-pinning capitalist economic development. Indeed, he goes so far as to claim that there is, 'Not a single respectable contemporary theory of economic development [which] addresses consciousness and culture seriously within which economic behaviour is formed.'

But at the same time, both Hurd and Fukuyama share certain themes in common, themes which underlie much of the development debate since the 1950s, if not earlier. First, there is the idea that history is coming to an end in the sense that liberal polities and the market economy are the end point of human history and that all societies will converge on this ideal. Second, there is an assumption of some ideal relationship between the state and the economy. Third there is a claim that the development of material forces is in some way dependent on non-material forces. Finally, there is an assertion that the market is in some sense superior to non-market relations. Similar themes, although not always as explicitly set out, underline the thinking of the World Bank.

10.4 THE MARKET AND GOOD GOVERNANCE

Both Fukuyama and the British ministers are in a way looking backwards and representing a particular historical strand in American and British thought, whilst at the same time looking forwards and proposing what should be done. In Hurd's and Chalker's cases, the prescriptive elements are clear: we should support certain forms of intervention but not others. In Fukuyama's, the prescriptive element is less clear: after all, there is a certain logic in history which will take its course willy-nilly. Both assert a conjunction between one form of political organisation – political pluralism or liberal democracies on the western model – and a particular form of economic organisation – the workings of the market. This conjunction is seen in various ways: as inevitable (the end of history); as morally valuable and desirable (no one has found a better set of principles by which to live) and as efficient (the infinitely diverse consumer culture made possible by them).

Yet one of the problems with this vision of the world and its future is precisely how the various elements in this model fit together. The states of South-east Asia which Hurd (and Fukuyama) held up as examples to be emulated by those in Africa are by no means models of pluralistic democracies with a strong commitment to human rights. Looked at in a somewhat cynical fashion, one could argue that Hurd and Chalker are really stressing not the wider interpretation which could be put on the term, 'good government' but a rather narrower interpretation in which 'good govern-ment' becomes synonymous with the market economy. Thus when Hurd talks of 'authoritarian models of the past' these are defined in terms of *economic* authoritarian-ism, not the forms of political authoritarianism found, for instance, in South Korea, Singapore or Taiwan. When he talks of human rights and the 'human spirit', it is difficult not to interpret such remarks in terms of a narrowly defined *homo economicus* rather than in a wider context which might stress rights of expression or belief. Perhaps this linkage is most clearly seen in an article written by Lynda Chalker which appeared in *The Sunday Times* during August 1991. Here she draws an explicit linkage between 'human rights' and development. A 'key aspect of good government', she writes 'must be respect for human rights and the rule of law. Entrepreneurs will not start businesses, nor outsiders invest, if there is no redress against arbitrary confiscation or corruption.'

The same sort of tendencies can be seen in the World Bank document. Whilst acknowledging that 'People are both the ends and the means of development' (World Bank 1989:63), the emphasis is upon the means. Thus people are seen as 'human capital' which, unlike 'physical capital', 'grows through use' (ibid.:44). The rule of law, a free press, a representative judiciary, even health and social welfare are all viewed as means of attaining economic growth. In both the Bank study and Hurd's speech there is a strange confusion. On the one hand, it would appear that good governance is simply a means to development – and in that context development is defined in narrow economic terms. On the other hand, economic development is seen as a means to human development: to what might broadly be called 'social development' in which good governance becomes a goal rather than the means. The speech as a whole is based on a confusion of freedoms in which certain forms of economic rights based on market forces emerge as dominant. Underlying the whole tenor of his speech is the evocation of a particular type of economy organised in a particular way around the twin principles of the market and private property.

Yet what does not seem to be recognised in either of these formulations or indeed in Fukuyama's apocalyptic vision is that there is no necessary coincidence either in theory or in practice between the freedoms of the market and the freedoms of liberal democracies. Indeed, it can be argued, as for instance by Lane (1986), Dymski and Elliott (1989) and Rawls (1971), that the two are based on contradictory principles. 'Both markets and polities are want-satisfying mechanisms, the distinction being that markets satisfy wants individually, while polities satisfy collective wants'. (Lane 1986:388). And again, 'The market leads people to think about processes of allocation and deserts, whereas politics leads people to think about outcomes of allocation' (Lane 1986:390).

What Mr Hurd and the World Bank ignore is that there is no necessary congruence between the two systems of choice based as they are on different principles. The outcome of a liberal democratic system of governance may well result in a series of decisions which directly conflict with policies for encouraging the growth of the market which Hurd and the Bank see as necessary for economic development. The only way around this problem is to give primacy to one or other set of principles. In the models proposed by Hurd and the Bank, the market ultimately rules supreme: private property, the rights of the individual entrepreneur, the rights to make profit, all become ultimate values and defined as human rights of a greater importance than, say, rights to education or health care.

In sum, then, by focusing on the elements of choice in both the model of the market and the model of western liberal democracies, the potential contradictions between the two can be ignored, and the conflicting principles which underlie the two systems systematically masked.

10.5 MARKETS, EMPOWERMENT AND ACCOUNTABILITY

One of the ways in which a linkage is claimed between the market and 'good government' throughout is the concept of 'accountability', and this recurs through Hurd's and Chalker's speeches. Here the argument is that 'good government' – in other words European models of liberal democracies – involve governments being answerable to the people. By implication, corruption is associated with other forms of government, and the rather naïve suggestion is that corruption will somehow disappear if free elections are held every five years. Accountability is associated with the idea of 'transparency'. Markets are 'transparent' in that they allow people to see what is going on in the 'real' world and thus be able to make economically rational decisions over the allocation of resources. In contrast, subsidies, state-controlled prices and so on, make such processes opaque: the true relations between the various elements in the system are hidden. This usage of 'transparency' is linked to the idea that 'good governments' are also 'transparent'. Transparency of the workings of government, a system which allows the people to see why decisions are being taken in certain ways and not others, coupled with liberal democracy, makes the servants of government accountable to the people.

Yet at the same time, the market also introduces accountability: accountability to the consumer. The problem, as far as the Bank and Hurd are concerned, is that no matter how 'democratic' the government might be, state-run ventures are not accountable to their customers but answerable only to the state. Because individual choice is the motive force in the economic system, the source of all energy and dynamism, then the market acts as a means by which economic actions are made accountable to the consumer. The key to this notion of accountability is the idea of consumer choice: accountability takes the form of either being able to sell or not to sell one's product. Given the existence of the market, accountability is necessarily present and there need be no extraneous mechanisms to ensure accountability. This appears to be the logic for the Bank's support for the privatisation of efficient state-run ventures: given that by definition they are outside the realm of the market, they cannot be properly accountable. Thus whilst on the one hand accountability is used as a means of linking liberal democracies with the free market, on the other hand the division between the polity and the economy is maintained by in effect arguing that market accountability is a superior form of accountability to accountability through the polity.

Yet there is more to the Hurd/World Bank position than simply accountability: liberal democracies and market economies *empower* the citizen/consumer. Through the market, the consumer is able to exercise control over the producers. Through the market, power is reclaimed from the over-powerful state in a manner reminiscent of that described by Hirschman for eighteenth-century writers such as Montesquieu and James Steuart (Hirschman 1977). But whilst the writers described by Hirschman saw the empowerment of the consumer through the market as the basis of political freedoms, the position of the Bank is to see the political freedoms of restored liberal democracies as the basis of economic freedoms. In the end, the rationale for liberal democracies is that the market can prosper, not that a prosperous economy will generate political freedoms.

The notion of empowerment underlying the approach taken by the Bank is based on the ideal of a level playing-field on to which all actors enter, over and over again, as complete equals. It is ultimately a legalistic notion of empowerment which assumes the individual, in Dumontian terms, as the basic 'value' of society with semi-sacred status. Thus empowerment in this model of society assumes the primacy of certain basic rights – in the economic sphere rights to own property, rights to buy and sell at will; in the political arena rights to vote for X or Y or not vote at all. At the same time it ignores other rights such as the rights to education or health unless the individual is willing to pay for it. It is also a view of empowerment which ignores the social impact of the market on the distribution and allocation of resources which thus give rise to differentials in empowerment. Such matters are ruled out of court because it is a model which exists out of time (the end of history) and thus ignores the dynamic processes which give rise to distributional inequalities.

To be fair to the World Bank, however, (and even though not mentioned in Hurd's speech, to British aid policy too), there is a recognition that empowerment through the market and through the encouragement of liberal democracies is only partly the answer. Some groups or categories of people (one is tempted to describe them as the 'deserving poor') have to be helped onto the level playing-field. Such categories include women in particular and other less easily defined people. Whilst Hurd's vision of the world is of the individual breaking free from the shackles of tradition, culture and community which disempower such groups, the Bank's vision is slightly more complicated in that it sees a role for 'community'. According to the Bank, not only is there a long history of entrepreneurial talent in Africa simply waiting to be liberated from state repression (World Bank 1989:136); there is also a tradition of 'communal organisations' to be exploited. And thus whilst one road to empowerment is through the advance of the market, the other route is through the encouragement of community-based groups, local-level NGOs (Non-Government Organisations) and so on, which can take command of local-level affairs. On the one hand, through empowerment comes participation; on the other, through participation comes empowerment.

Local-level participation is a continual theme throughout *From Crisis to Sustainable Growth*. Thus,

> Every opportunity should be taken to support local, communal, and nongovernmental organizations of all types…These initiatives are most likely to succeed if the institutions have local roots…The challenge is to build on this solid indigenous base, with a bottom-up approach that places a premium on listening to people and on genuinely empowering the intended beneficiaries of any development program. (World Bank 1980:191)

Such an approach clearly links the Bank's policies on development and development planning to much more populist approaches such as that of Robert Chambers (a leading writer on development). Yet at the same time, the full implications of what is being suggested do not appear to have been realised. On the one hand, institutions such as the Bank are encouraging the growth of the 'entrepreneurial spirit' and a situation in which market forces (or an imitation of them) are allowed to rule supreme. On the other hand, at least on paper, they are attempting to encourage the formation of economically active groups which are organised on very different principles – that of group identity, group solidarity and a shared ideology of community endeavour.

Yet precisely how such groups can coexist with the world of independent individualistic entrepreneurs competing in the totally free market envisaged by the Bank and Mr Hurd is not made clear. Whilst it would be wrong to argue in the spirit of a latter-day Tocqueville that the forces of political and economic individualism will necessarily 'dispose each member of the community to sever himself from the mass of his fellow creatures', what is surely clear is that the vision of 'local, communal and non-governmental organizations' sits uneasily with a rampant free-market economy. Following Hirsch (1976) it could be argued that the market undermines the moral principles that underpin the communal solidarities on which such organisations are based. Furthermore, the suspicion remains that when push comes to shove, the Bank and Mr Hurd would rather favour the brave entrepreneurs of a new Africa rather than those who espouse an older 'community-based' programme of empowerment.

If, then, one elision in the contemporary rhetoric of development involves equating the market with liberal democracies, a second is through equating the empowerment which is said to be an aspect of consumer choice in the market with empowerment which comes through collective local-level action. These form two different modes of empowerment and are based on different principles. Indeed, frequently the strength of local-level organisations and NGOs is precisely their anti-market (and anti-state) orientation rather than their support for the market economy. Thus where they are most successful is dealing with the distributional failings of the market system rather than with aiding the establishment of that system. From a political point of view, the rhetoricians of the Bank have usurped the concept of 'empowerment' from a populist anti-capitalist critique and now use it as an element in the justification of a system which is as likely to disempower people as it is to empower them.

10.6 CONCLUSION

As I made clear in the introduction, this is only a preliminary effort to look at some aspects of the rhetoric of development. As such it has focused rather narrowly on a few documents, in particular Hurd's speech and the World Bank's 1989 report on Africa. Any satisfactory discussion of the rhetoric of the market, empowerment, development and so on clearly requires a much wider view of the official literature as well as of the views of development personnel – the aid community. Yet even so, there are some themes worth stressing out of even this limited examination of the subject.

First, it is clear that the discussions of the market and good governance provided by Hurd and the Bank are riven through with contradictions. The relation between the market and good governance is never made clear and the possibilities of contradictions between the two generally ignored. Where such possibilities are implicitly recognised, the market is given prominence over ideas of good government.

Second, the approaches adopted by Hurd and the Bank are based on rather peculiar and limited theories of history which argue for convergence and which are based on a particular view of human nature embedded in western culture.

Third and finally, in practice the statements from the Bank, from Mr Hurd and from Mrs Chalker, can only have limited impact on the design and formation of aid projects. In part this is the result of the poverty of their models of development which makes them unworkable; in part it is the result of the ambiguous nature of concepts such as 'empowerment' which allow and encourage 'anti-market' forms of intervention to continue.

NOTES

1. This is a revised and shortened version of a paper given at the conference in St Andrews. I would like to thank the participants at that conference for their comments as well as those who heard another version at the Social Anthropology seminar at the University of Sussex. In particular I would like to thank Alison Evans for her critical and helpful remarks.
2. For critiques of the World Bank report, see Bernstein 1990, Stein and Nafziger 1991, and Collier 1991.

REFERENCES

Speeches and Newspaper Items

Lynda Chalker: Speech to the Africa Private Enterprise Group, 12 December 1990.
Lynda Chalker: 'Good Government and the Aid Programme'. Speech at the Royal Institute of International Affairs, 25 June 1991.
Lynda Chalker: 'Giving Aid to the Third World, with Strings Attached'. *The Sunday Times*. 18.8.1991.
Douglas Hurd: Speech to the Overseas Development Institute. 6 June 1990.

Articles and Books

Bernstein, H. 1990. 'Agricultural "Modernisation" and the Era of Structural Adjustment: Observations on sub-Saharan Africa', *Journal of Peasant Studies*, 18: 3–35.
Collier, P. 1991. 'From Critic to Secular God: the World Bank and Africa: a Commentary upon *Sub-Saharan Africa: From Crisis to Sustainable Growth*'. *African Affairs*, 90: 111-17.
Dymski, G. A. and J. E. Elliott, 1989. 'Capitalism and the Democratic Economy', in, E. F. Paul *et al.* (eds.), *Capitalism*. Oxford: Blackwell.
Fukuyama, F. 1989. 'The End of History?', *The National Interest*, 16 (Summer): 3–18.
Hirsch, F. 1976. *Social Limits to Growth*. Cambridge: Harvard University Press.
Hirschman, A. O. 1977. *The Passions and the Interests*. Princeton: Princeton University Press.
Hirschman, A. O. 1982. 'Rival Interpretations of Market Society: Civilising, Destructive or Feeble', *Journal of Economic Literature*, 20: 1463–84.
Lane, R. E. 1986. 'Market Justice and Political Justice', *American Political Science Review*, 80: 383–402.
Rawls, J. 1971. *A Theory of Justice*. Cambridge: Harvard University Press.
Stein, H. and E. W. Nafziger, 1991. 'Structural Adjustment, Human Needs, and the World Bank Agenda', *Journal of Modern African Studies*, 29: 173–89.
World Bank, 1989. *Sub-Saharan Africa: From Crisis to Sustainable Growth*. Washington: IBRD/World Bank.

Market and State after the Cold War

The Informal Economy Reconsidered

KEITH HART

Like Hegel's owl of Minerva, we live in the twilight of the short twentieth century. The abrupt collapse of Stalinism allows us the wisdom of hindsight, giving us a perspective on the seven decades since the first world war and the Russian revolution which eluded us during their hectic passage. Vulgar triumphalism views the result in terms of a football match – the west won the cold war. Market capitalism beat state socialism; Free Enterprise and liberal democracy defeated The Plan and the one-party state. A revived bourgeoisie claims that we have witnessed the victory of economics over politics.

The immediate antecedent of this sudden transformation was the period of the 1980s, when neo-liberal conservatives swept to power in the west with the aim of dismantling the welfare state consensus which lasted from the 1930s to the 1970s. Responding to a half-understood sense that national autonomy had been under-mined by developments in the world economy and the people scared by unprecedented levels of inflation, Reagan and Thatcher (backed by Kohl and Nakasone) pinned their hopes on sound money and the revival of 'the market'. What they overturned was the twentieth-century idea that only the nation-state could fix the problems of capitalism. The right was quicker than the left (which had so much at stake in the welfare state) to see the political opportunity offered by accepting the fact that the ability of the nation-state to represent society was inexorably on the wane.

Even so, this 1980s rhetoric of the market obscures the universal dominance of the state over national economy from the first world war onwards – whether welfare state democracy or totalitarian regimes of the right and left. It was Keynes's (1936) supreme achievement to reconcile this fact with the intellectual tradition of economic liberal-ism, to legitimise state management of the economy as 'macro-economics'. The welfare state system he envisaged may have recently suffered from privatisation and a growing polarisation of rich and poor; but national governments are still holding out as best they can against the inevitable erosion of their economic power.

Following C.L.R. James and his associates (1950), I look on the convergence of state bureaucracy and corporate industrial capitalism in the twentieth century as a world-wide system of 'state capitalism', where the state, not the market, was primarily responsible for reproducing capitalist relations of production. The collapse of Stalinism, which was crucial to that system's maintenance from the 1930s, is the most dramatic evidence so far of its decline. The fall is yet to come and it will necessarily involve the heartlands of western capitalism. This linkage between the fate of east and west has been obscured by the polarities of cold war rhetoric, even more so by the exaggerations of the 1980s which would have us believe that the United States is a 'free-market economy', as if the Pentagon were not a huge bureaucratic collective and the Federal Government did not administer almost half of the nation's wealth.

The term 'command economy' is more conventionally applied to countries ruled by The Plan or to democracies at war; but, when compared with any nineteenth-century state, all modern economics are controlled from above to a degree that was previously unthinkable. Yet we have retained the rhetoric of liberalism versus socialism which flourished in an earlier age when each doctrine was predicated on the withering away of the state. In the late nineteenth century, the polarisation of political creeds around the respective dominance of individual and collective principles of social organisation was premised on the inevitable triumph of egalitarian society over the hierarchical legacy of agrarian civilisation. Our century has confused matters by imposing control from above onto one or other variants of popular egalitarianism, by representing, in other words, state capitalism as either liberalism or socialism, thereby discrediting both.

Our task is to rethink the relationship between the state and the market at this moment of history, to disentangle the confusion arising from the cold war opposition between market individualism and the communist state. The rivalry between the United States and the Soviet Union for world dominance as successors to European imperialism led to the conflation of one pair of essentially egalitarian ideas (individual and community) with another stressing the difference between control from above and below (state and market). Now, having become identified for a while with the nation-state, the concept of society has begun to struggle free from its embrace, without yet having found a new universal referent. This allows many variants of collective principle to flourish above and below the level of the state. The relationship between individual and society is more moot than for a century. That is our problem and our opportunity.

The protagonists of the cold war designated the poor remainder of humanity 'the Third World' and gave the name 'development' to their economic predicament. Third World development was inevitably construed through cold war rhetoric, even though the precarious structures of state capitalism established there began to unravel as early as the 1960s and had (with the exception of parts of Asia) become completely unstuck by the 1980s. The focus of this chapter is on the political economy of post-colonial Africa, roughly from 1960 to the present, and particularly on the concept of 'the informal economy' which arose to denote an aspect of the relationship between the state and the market there during that period.

I coined the expression 'informal economy' (sometimes also known as 'the informal sector') at the beginning of the 1970s, following anthropological research a few years earlier into the proliferating street economy of Accra, Ghana's capital city. I shall argue here that this neologism reflected the cold war ideology of a frozen opposition between the state and the market; that its popularity was indicative of the blindness of academics and policy-makers to real conditions and historical trends in Africa; and that the ongoing political struggle between the people and bureaucracy was obscured by an assumption of the latter's natural dominance.

II.2

I went out to Ghana in 1965 to do fieldwork for an anthropology PhD on the politics of the new states. Following the academic fashion of the day, I wanted to study migrants to the cities, to see how their free political associations helped them to respond to the novel demands of citizenship and development. Instead I soon found myself in a slum concentrating on the economy of the streets. The migrants I knew had no connection to the state, except for occasional harrassment by the police. They were alienated from politics and their formal associations were a shadow of what the literature had led me to believe existed. In sharp contrast, everyone seemed to be engaged energetically in a prolific range of self-employed enterprises, both legitimate and illegal. The organisation of this world of petty commerce became the main focus of my research; and I eventually wrote it up as a case-study in 'modernisation' (Hart 1969).

I felt that I had absorbed the lessons of economic life as seen from the perspective of the people I had studied; but, like them, I was unable to understand the wider social forces which shaped so much of their lives – the economic shortages resulting from the collapse of the world cocoa price; the army *coup* which displaced the Nkrumah regime. Moreover, my experience of that slum posed questions of history and social connection which I could not answer without exploring the broader international context of decolonisation and development. With this in mind, I joined a group of development economists at the University of East Anglia and began a life of teaching, consultancy and economic journalism. Active participation in the world of 'development' enabled me to fit my research findings into the prevailing economic discourse of the day, the early 1970s.

This led to my taking part in a conference on 'Unemployment in Africa', held at the Institute of Development Studies at Sussex University in 1971. The papers mainly addressed what was taken to be the phenomenon of mass unemployment in Africa's cities. Estimates of the number of jobs available were subtracted from the burgeoning urban work-force and the residue, in Keynesian fashion, was termed 'unemployed'. A typical example of the genre was a paper by Hans Singer, a prominent development economist from the host institution, entitled 'Rural unemployment as a background to urban unemployment'. Having arrived by dubious means at a figure of 30 per cent for urban unemployment, Singer was forced to conclude that, since migrants were still flocking to the cities from the countryside, rural unemployment must be even higher, possibly 50 per cent!

In my paper, 'Informal income opportunities and urban employment in Ghana' (Hart 1973), I argued that the new urban poor were certainly employed, if not always for wages. Their incomes were qualitatively more irregular and uncertain; but in quantitative terms they covered a wide range above and below the unskilled wage rate at which the majority of uneducated migrants found jobs. The goal of most people was to combine wages and self-employed incomes. I talked about an 'informal economy' or sector of urban income opportunities, drawing on Max Weber's (1981) theory of rationalisation to contrast the stable wage employment offered by corporate organisations with the more unpredictable commercial activities I had studied in Accra. The exposition combined vivid fieldwork descriptions with speculation on the significance of this zone of economic activity for development prospects. I left it open whether the informal economy might be the basis for productive accumulation or was merely a redistributive mechanism.

Before long the idea took off as an organising theme in academic and policy-making circles (ILO 1972). A new branch of the development industry concerned with Third World urban poverty found a measure of coherence in debating the forms and functions of the 'informal sector'. It was criticised heavily by Marxists, who preferred the expression 'petty commodity production'. Since I was undergoing a Marxist conversion at the time, I did not feel like taking up the cudgels on behalf of a concept whose value I had never been entirely convinced of.

Nevertheless, the shelf-life of the 'informal economy' has turned out to be longer than that of many ideas produced in the 1970s. Having become an entrenched part of the International Labour Office (ILO) bureaucracy, it has recently been taken up by the World Bank as a major theme of their latest attempt to redress Third World urban squalor. The term crops up with increasing frequency in the sociology of countries like Britain and has been recognised as a part of economic doctrine (Hart 1988a). Hernando De Soto's book *The Other Path* (1986) used the idea to make quite an impact on public opinion in the New World. In my own field of economic anthropology, 'the informal economy' has come to indicate a division of the sub-discipline (Plattner 1989, Smith 1990).

The phenomenon of self-organised urban commerce, often on the wrong side of the law, was not unknown before my article; and there are many other labels for it – the 'second', 'black', 'hidden' and 'underground' economy, to name just a few. How then do we account for the prominence of the 'informal economy' as an organising concept in some sections of the intellectual division of labour, especially those concerned with Third World development? The short answer, in my view, lies in the language of paired negation. 'Informal' refers to the absence of form, to the lack of established regularity, in this case to economic evasion of the bureaucratic rules which underpin state management of the national economy. As such the informal economy is the conceptual negation of Keynesian macro-economics, of economic management from the state's commanding heights; and it expresses well within its own static parameters the cumulative failure of bureaucracy to contain the untamed market forces which have been undermining state capitalism on a world scale to increasing effect since the 1970s. By stressing what it is not (not 'good form', not amenable to the dominant form of rationality, beyond 'management'), the concept appealed to the sensibilities of an intellectual class who could not grasp what the economic activities in question positively represented.

Within development circles use of the idea of an informal economy has followed some huge swings in ideology. In the 1960s, when the world economy was booming under American hegemony, the emphasis of Third World governments and international agencies was on growth or bust, on capital accumulation at any cost, concentrating on cities, industry and mechanisation. This was reflected in my doctoral thesis's focus on 'modernisation'. By the 1970s, the costs and failure of this reckless programme were being recognised and the political threat of mass urban disaffection prompted a new concern for keeping the peasants happy on their farms. Under the prevailing Keynesian consensus of the time, this was called 'growth with equity' and its arrival as orthodoxy was signalled by World Bank President MacNamara's Nairobi speech in 1973. In the 1980s, following the electoral victories of neo-liberal conservatives in the west, the international agencies began a concerted attack on the post-colonial state in the name of the free market, a process highlighted by the publication of the 'Berg Report' on African development (World Bank 1981). Since the collapse of Stalinism, the International Monetary Fund and World Bank have been ever more explicit about linking economic support to 'good government', human rights and, above all, the free flow of capital.

In the early 1970s, when the concept of an 'informal economy' took off, it was a universally held assumption that only the state could organise a push for enhanced economic development. This led to the problematic of the day: how could the state (conceived of both as a planning agency and as welfare provider) meet the demands of a rapidly growing population for jobs, housing, education and healthcare? Above all, how could it cope with rising unemployment, the scourge of western politicians since the Great Depression and the *idée fixe* of Keynesian macro-economics? The informal economy offered itself as a form of self-organised unemployment relief and it was grasped eagerly by politicians and intellectual bureaucrats as a solution to their dilemma. A decade later, the attacks of the IMF and the World Bank on excessive public expenditure, state monopoly and restrictions on free trade and capital movement were reflected in promotion of the informal economy as an image of popular creative energies finding expression in an unregulated market. In this way the ideology of Third World development mirrored trends in the west and the concept in question swung with it.

11.3

The scale and character of the phenomena referred to by the term 'informal economy' are moot. In my original article I restricted its application to the economic activities of the Third World urban poor; and this has remained the principal referent since. But, as state capitalism continues to unravel at the seams, it becomes clearer that negation of the economic forms subject to bureaucratic regulation by the state goes far beyond rule infringement on the streets of cities like Accra. The rampant informalisation of economy is a global phenomenon embracing the international drugs traffic, bribery by multinational corporations, corrupt arms deals, tax evasion, smuggling, embezzlement by bureaucrats, peculation by politicians, offshore banking, 'grey' markets, insider trading, the black market of communist regimes and organised crime, as well as such legitimate activities as small businesses, own account dealing and do-it-yourself. In countries like Jamaica and Zaïre, the informal economy has taken over state bureaucracy. It is the origin of new mafias springing up in the aftermath of Stalinism in Eastern Europe and the Soviet Union. Thatcher's Britain became notorious for unconstrained greed. Everywhere, the commanding heights of the informal economy lie close to the centres of power and reach down to the petty enterprises which first caught my attention.

At first, the informal sector was seen by development economists as lying in the minor interstices of a bureaucratic economy controlled from above and afar, as the insignificant omissions of a largely effective system of statistical monitoring – match-stick sellers and the like, 'taking in each others' washing'. It certainly was true that economies like Ghana's were structured by the state to confine the commercial energies of the people into areas with restricted prospects for capital accumulation. But, in my original perspective, the informal sector was the bulk of the market economy in Accra and it supplied much of indigenous demand for food and drink, housing, clothing, transport, entertainment and so on. According to this view, the rapid growth of cities, in excess of the capacity of organised public and private sector production to supply the population's needs, was made viable only by spontaneous self-organised enterprise on a massive scale. Moreover, a dramatic development in the rural-urban division of labour was made possible in this way, laying the groundwork for substantial capital accumulation in the future (Hart 1988b).

National governments and, initially, the international agencies saw things other-wise. They preferred to believe their own statistics, which missed most of these activities, just as they virtually ignored the principal employment of Africa's food farmers and women. Policy initiatives aimed at improving the informal sector were cosmetic and piecemeal. They usually ended up negating it, making it official and rule bound – issuing licences, offering bank credit, organising market-places, setting up training schemes and, above all, taxing the operators made visible by formalisation. State intervention in the informal economy inevitably removed the cost advantages which made it commercially attractive in the first place.

In a book written at the watershed of the 1970s and 1980s (Hart 1982), I did point out that the post-colonial state in Africa rested on the pre-industrial contradiction between centralised power and the size of the agricultural surplus. Moreover, I suggested that the modern drive towards state expansion would collapse if African economies did not soon develop to a higher level of productivity; and this seems now to have happened in many cases. Survival, not development is the economic policy imperative of the day; and this is reflected in the dominance of the international undertaker, the IMF, in dealings between the west and the Third World. But it has taken the end of the cold war to reveal to me the full extent of the contradiction which I witnessed as a fieldworker twenty-five years ago.

I cannot help reflecting on the immense disservice done to ordinary Africans by all participants in the development industry over the last three decades. Most consult-ants, unlike their colonial predecessors, do not stay long enough to see what is happening on the ground, even if their economists' logic has not made them blind already. Dominance of the economy by state bureaucracy is a blatantly political process, whether it is abused or not; yet it was consistently laundered for public consumption as an essentially quantitative economic analysis. Economists have no room for political contradiction in their theories. In any case, they refused to comment on how post-colonial regimes stifled popular energies in the name of 'development'. The mystifications of the international state capitalist system, not to mention their own interest in retaining lucrative salaries, dictated otherwise.

It was obvious in the 1960s that the post-colonial state had become detached from its roots in the local society, a parasitic bureaucracy feeding in equal measure off its own downtrodden farmers and the international alliances which for a time were willing to sustain it (Hart 1986a). Africa was going to the dogs then; but nobody noticed or they pretended not to notice until it was too late. They just took the money and ran. I had no excuse. I had lived in a slum for two years; fieldwork had given me a chance to see what was going on, even to take the side of the people. It would be nice to say that anthropological method is inherently democratic and superior to the remote speculations of academic bureaucrats; and so it ought to be. I saw the alienation from politics, the economic energies. But I was so anxious to get the big picture, to go with the power and join the bureaucracy, that I transformed my fieldwork into a gimmicky idea that development economists were able to absorb into their Panglossian vision of the world.

It is worth stressing how little of what transpired in the Third World after decolonisation was picked up by intellectuals while it was happening. Parallel to Africa's deterioration was the rise of the South-east Asian NICs which were likewise diverging in the 1960s from the common pattern of economic backwardness. Neither phenomenon was recognised until years after it had become obvious to the inhabitants. This is a function of an intellectual division of labour in which the people with an overview never stir from their air-conditioned hotels and the people on the ground, such as anthropologists, lack any overview of the historical processes involved.

I did not refer explicitly to the cold war opposition of state and market in my original paper; but I reproduced it in the formal–informal dualism, two poles fixed for eternity in perpetual oscillation. The ahistorical rationalism of Keynesian economists in the 1970s assimilated the informal economy concept to the assumption of natural dominance of the state bureaucracy, making it a tool of employment creation. The neo-liberal rationalists of the 1980s claimed the informal economy for what it was, the untamed market; but they also chose wilfully to misrepresent the state capitalism that they served, disguising the ubiquity of bureaucracy behind a fetishised conception of 'the market'. Both were equally blind to the historical realities; and neither has contributed to the improved welfare of Africans.

11.4

The relationship between the state and the market came to be seen as antagonistic in the Anglo-American world of the 1980s. This conflict was already enshrined in the simplistic antinomies of the cold war; and before that it was expressed as the idea that individual and collective principles of social organisation (liberalism and socialism) are contradictory. The alternative position – that state and market may reinforce each other and that there are many ways of reconciling the individual and society – has underwritten, for example, the history of Germany and Japan for a century (Hart 1986b). It is embodied in the prominence now given in Europe to the concept of the 'Social Market', as well as in the search for new forms of political hierarchy based on the principle of subsidiarity – the assumption of limited powers by a higher level of organisation only when it has been shown that lower levels cannot cope with the social forces involved.

The context for our present theoretical dilemmas is a period in which the structures of state capitalism are being rapidly undermined. The decade beginning in 1989 is likely to see the emergence of a quite new political map of the world, with the formation of large trading blocs and increased concern for means of organising global society. In the process the nation-state will be forced to abandon its claim to represent the universal form of society, as it is squeezed by a combined movement towards internal devolution and incorporation into more inclusive political bodies. How the development of areas like Africa will fare in all this is anybody's guess; but the plight of Africa is likely to remain for a long time the sharpest reminder of humanity's need to find material and social expression for its collective conscience.

The failure of the post-colonial state in Africa was the first sign of the vulnerability of the international state capitalist system, its weakest point and most recent addition. But where did state capitalism come from? The political structures of the modern world were born in the turmoil of the 1860s. The decade began in 1861 with the American Civil War, Russia's abolition of serfdom and the Italian Risorgimento. It ended in 1870–1 with German unification, the Franco-Prussian war, the Paris Commune and the French Third Republic. In between Britain launched its class compromise with the second Reform Act of 1867, while Marx wrote *Capital* (1867) and the First International was formed. In 1868 Japan's Meiji Restoration began that country's meteoric entry onto the world stage. Thus in one turbulent decade all the major players on the stage of the twentieth century took their definitive political form as nation-states capable of containing and advancing the social forces of industrial capitalism.

The immediate context for this sequence was the transport revolution of the 1850s and 1860s (railways and steamships) which opened up the world market in staple commodities: food, industrial raw materials, textiles (Lewis 1978). The consequence of global economic integration was imperialist rivalry and the first world war. It was this last event which revealed the state's powers of economic mobilisation and precipitated the desperate competition between varieties of corporatism which has produced this century's economic boom, as well as its terrible toll of destruction. The period since the second world war has seen another revolution in communications – mass movements of people, goods, money and information on an unprecedented scale. Accelerated integration of the world market, especially in new areas of production such as industrialised agriculture, hi-tech manufacturing and long-distance services, has placed growing pressure on national autonomy. The war-making powers of the state capitalist system, having apparently pulled back from the brink of nuclear annihilation, now confront an uncertain period of international realignment.

It should not be surprising if, under these circumstances, a new critique of the state were to be launched, nourished by a desire to see its 'withering away' which goes far beyond the bogus rhetoric of Thatcher and Reagan (who assiduously built it up, while enhancing the private incomes of their friends in the name of the 'free market'). If the dominance of the state is to be reduced, scope arises for the development of new connections between individuals and communities at both higher and lower levels of social organisation. The dialectic of individual and society has been polarised in the twentieth century as an extreme contradiction between market individualism and state collectivism. This has had the effect of marginalising intermediate levels of association, many of which are compatible with the market. It has also diminished the power of more inclusive notions of civilisation, capable of unifying people across political boundaries through shared religious or humanist values.

The reproduction of social forms is intrinsic to human life. Formalism is crucial to the rational solution of problems of social organisation. It is worth remembering that western capitalism and science are the winning team so far; and modern economics is their intellectual synthesis. Even so, if the structures which sustained that synthesis are in decay, it may pay to develop an institutional approach capable of exploring the ground excluded by formal theory. Modern social science conceives of society as two levels: organisation from the top down (the state and bureaucracy) and organisation from the bottom up (the individualism of the market and democracy). These levels are more normally seen in isolation than in interaction. Other forms of association are left out; yet it is here that solutions to the problem of state and market are most likely to be found.

It is widely supposed that nation-states and their industrial capitalist economies broke down the ties linking individual citizens to the particularistic structures and religious identities of agrarian civilisation. At least that has been the prevailing intellectual orthodoxy. Ideological struggle focuses on the appropriate balance between co-ordinated public action (the state) and individual freedom (the market). I would suggest that intermediate forms of association, hitherto largely invisible to modern social theory, are essential to the functioning of institutions at all stages of economic development. Whereas states and markets may be plausibly described in terms of abstract social principles, membership in bodies between the two extremes is always specific and concrete. This is why social scientists have been reluctant to take associations seriously (it is too much empirical work to find out what they are), even though they have long been a preoccupation of anthropologists, historians and lawyers.

Participants in states as well as markets are represented as individuals whose aggregate patterns of behaviour are generated on the ground by a mass of independent decisions (Hacking 1991). A statistical logic postulates quantitative variation within a population made up of isomorphic units (voters, households, firms and so on). A highly centralised administration confronts a decentralised, anonymous mass. This is how the bureaucracy conceives of its antagonism to the people. But ordinary people seek some measure of protection from the power of the state and from their isolation as individuals. They find it in associations where they can identify with others like themselves, whether in corporations, political parties, churches, ethnic groups, classes or informal networks – a vast variety of social movements and semi-stable reference points in a chaotic, frightening world. Social life is impossible without such associations; one of their chief tasks is education.

British social anthropology announced its aim to concentrate on this intermediate level of social organisation in a collection of essays published fifty years ago (M. Fortes and E. Evans-Pritchard 1940). Here the customary political organisation of African societies was used to highlight the exclusion of this practical level of human life-forms from the abstract political philosophy then current in the west. To this critique we may now add the limitations of formal economics: we need to investigate both the place of associations in social life and the interaction of state and market mechanisms. The idea of an informal economy addressed the second of these issues, if not the first.

11.5

The informal economy is a market-based response of the people to the overweaning attempts of bureaucracy to control economic life from above. The social forms capable of succeeding state capitalism are likely to be grounded, at least embryonically, in that response. But where are we to look for evidence of how people construct the relationship between individual and community outside the dominating presence of the nation-state? Anthropologists have traditionally sought answers to this question in fieldwork-based ethnographies of so-called 'primitive' societies. Now that decolonisation and the ongoing process of global integration have undermined that strategy, it is likely that fieldwork will be used to show how people everywhere are making bridges between everyday life and world history (Marcus 1985, Grimshaw and Hart forthcoming). The social history of industrialising societies in the nineteenth century, before the dominance of economy by the nation-state, offers another fertile source for such an enquiry.

The post-Stalinist regimes of Eastern Europe, or at least their intellectuals, look to England's revolution in the seventeenth century, when the struggle between market and state took the form of a commercial landed gentry's attempts to emancipate itself from absolutist monarchy. The English concept of civil society, later adapted to the needs of a continental bourgeoisie (*Bürgerlich Gesellschaft*), now animates their desire to escape from the legacy of the totalitarian state. Their avid embrace of market principles will soon reveal the crippling lack of corporate structures which, although hidden by ideology, have organised western capitalism for at least the last century. Potentially more interesting, because less encumbered by historical precedent, will be the political experiments thrown up by the democratic revolution now sweeping through Africa.

For all its mystification by ideology, I am reluctant to abandon the concept of the market: buying and selling constitute a historically distinctive form of economic life. But the anomaly of using individual market competition as a model for the functioning of capitalist bureaucracy has to be laid to rest. Fortunately, this task is well under way, especially in the economic anthropology of Indonesia (Geertz 1963, J. and P. Alexander 1991), as well as elsewhere in this volume. In what sense then can the idea of market relations be retained?

Marcel Mauss (1925), while emphasising continuities in the forms of exchange, opposed the market to the gift in terms of the timing of a return for the thing given: in the latter case there was a delay, whereas in markets exchange is simultaneous. The instant equalisation of each party's interest made it unnecessary for the individuals involved to maintain a social relationship and this accounts for the impersonality characteristic of market dealings. This model for market relations is used by economists as an excuse for making society, time and space extrinsic to their basic approach. It is embodied in the financial institution of the spot contract. But market relations are rarely spot contracts involving two individuals in a narrowly bounded present time and place. Rather they extend backwards and forwards in time, normally requiring economic actors to engage with social organisation as a means of reducing the uncertainties involved.

Market relations consist of the buying and selling of commodities for money. The point of using money is that sellers do not have to find buyers who are selling whatever specific commodities they themselves want at that time (which is barter, Hart 1988c). Instead they take money for their sale and make their own purchases some other time. That is why we use different words for the two sides of market exchange. But it is also rare for buying and selling to take place in a temporal or social vacuum: selling entails past production schedules, buying entails future consumption or investment; and the money realised by sale can be held indefinitely for a variety of possible uses. Some of the key market contracts have time built into them: wages involve working before payment; rent involves payment before occupation. And credit, the basis of finance, is nothing if not a contract in time.

Moreover, the spatial dimension of market relations is always potentially infinite: attempts to insulate local transactions from the outside world are subverted by the market's proliferating connections with a social universe which can never be known or controlled. The decades since the second world war have seen a remarkable integration of market transactions on a global scale. The extension of market relations in time and space thus necessarily requires participants to face a source of profound uncertainty, which is compounded if their livelihood depends on successful negotiation of such uncertainty. Two principal methods arise for bridging the gap between the known and the unknown: social organisation and individual calculation. Market economy places a premium on finding ways of reconciling these needs. The resulting forms of individual and collective behaviour are highly varied. They are not given by the structure of markets as such; nor are markets practicable without them. Market relations depend heavily on ritual for their reproduction in that they attempt to bridge the gap between the known and the unknown (compare Durkheim 1976).

With the benefit of hindsight provided by such reflections in the context of the unravelling of the post war order, I can return to my own original fieldwork in Accra and ask what other lessons may be drawn from it than the existence of an informal economy. Now I find that the city's unregulated market economy was not just composed of an assortment of individuals, but rather had its own social forms, each reconciling the individual and the collective in a distinctive way. I have begun to explore these matters in a recent article (Hart 1988d). I would stress the following pertinent ethnographic observations. Because of a general scarcity of cash, market transactions were dominated by credit which entailed a wide range of strategies for projecting social relations forwards through time. The cultural material for market relations came from a variety of associations based on kinship and marriage, ethnicity, religion, political patronage, criminal fraternity, occupational status, personal friend-ship, legal contract and business partnership. At the same time, individuals had to base their calculations on idiosyncratic experience and could not afford to sacrifice their autonomy unduly to an over-restrictive system of rules. Out of this creative dialectic an innovative and highly variable pattern of economic life was spawned.

It remains to be seen what part will be played by relations established over the past few decades in what I once called 'the informal economy', now that democratisation and the market have begun to weaken Africa's rickety state structures. Having been adapted to the exigencies of a dominant bureaucracy, they may not be the ideal basis for a new political order. Even so, as in Eastern Europe, social forms which have learned to live with the market, often illegally, will be prominent in the uncertain times ahead.

The individual and society are thus not as contradictory as cold-war rhetoric would have us believe. Indeed both are indispensible to viable human life-forms. So the idea of an 'informal sector', resting as it did on the static negations of state capitalism, was always a vulgar and limited concept. But the social reality which gave rise to it – the initiatives of migrants living beyond the reach of the state in Accra's slums – yields alternative interpretations of the development process which are relevant to our own time. It is not the ideas of intellectuals but the people's struggles which offer hope for a better world; and a constructive anthropology of development would stress the tradition of fieldwork-based ethnography, not ways of conforming to the intellectual order of economists and bureaucrats.

We have to search for new social forms which are compatible with market economy. They are likely to be plural and opposed to an oppressive role for state bureaucracy. They should draw inspiration from the modern successors to world religion, ideologies such as free-trade liberalism, international Marxism, the Green movement, 'Greater Europe' and Pan-Africanism, which make sense of the need to transcend existing political boundaries. They will construct the relationship between the individual and the community in a harmonious, not an antagonistic way. Then perhaps public organisation and private interests will be combined flexibly for the general good. That at least is the meaning I have tried to rescue from my own participation in Africa's post-colonial débâcle.

One thing more remains to be said. The argument of this chapter owes more to Hegel than to Marx. Perhaps one can expect little else from the critique of ideas. But then Hegel was a better prophet of the twentieth century than Marx. State capitalism is the historical realisation of Hegel's prediction that capitalism would seek to resolve its contradictions through an absolute bureaucracy manned by a state-made intellectual class (Hegel 1819). The opposition of state and market represents the internal division within bureaucracy between those who organise public life and those who organise capitalist enterprises. Max Weber's (1978) gloomy prognosis that the future would be shared between state bureaucracy and market capitalism simply had the advantage of being historically closer to the thing itself. What neither took into account was the people's capacity to resist command from above; and for an understanding of that resistance and our own future we have to turn first to Marx.

Socialism is the extension of the political principle of democracy to economic life. Since work, the central fact of human experience, is still for most people organised in a disagreeably unequal and unfree way, it follows that the historical project of socialism is barely begun. Marx got his timing wrong; but he did discover that industrial capitalism would be a force conducive to the emergence of people power where it counts, in the organisation of production. That is why *Capital* (Marx 1867), written during the 1860s in the face of state capitalism's origins, must still be the intellectual starting point for our own moment of world history, its imminent demise in the aftermath of the Cold War (Grimshaw and Hart 1991).

REFERENCES

Alexander, J. and P. Alexander, 1991. 'What's a fair price? Price-setting and trading partnerships in Javanese markets'. *Man*, 26 (3): 493–512.

De Soto, H. 1986. *The Other Path*. New York: Harper and Row.

Durkheim, E. 1976 [1915]. *The Elementary Forms of Religious Life*. London: Allen and Unwin.

Fortes, M. and E. Evans Pritchard, 1940. 'Introduction', *African Political Systems*. London: Oxford University Press.

Geertz, C. 1963. *Peddlers and Princes*. Chicago: University of Chicago Press.

Grimshaw, A. and K. Hart, 1991. *C. L. R. James and The Struggle For Happiness*. New York: CLR James Institute.

Grimshaw, A. and K. Hart, forthcoming. 'Anthropology and the world we live in'. *Critique of Anthropology*.

Hacking, E. 1991. *The Taming of Chance*. Cambridge: Cambridge University Press.

Hart, K. 1969. *Entrepreneurs and Migrants: a Study of Modernization Among the Frafras of Ghana*. Ph.D Thesis, Cambridge University.

Hart, K. 1973. 'Informal income opportunities and urban employment in Ghana', *Journal of Modern African Studies*, 11 (1): 61–89.

Hart, K. 1982. *The Political Economy of West African Agriculture*. Cambridge: Cambridge University Press.

Hart, K. 1986a. 'Some contradictions in post-colonial state formation in West Africa', *Cambridge Anthropology*, Vol. 10.

Hart, K. 1986b. 'Heads or tails? Two sides of the coin', *Man* (N.S.), 21 (4): 637–56.

Hart, K. 1988a. 'The informal economy', in *The New Palgrave Dictionary of Economic Theory*. London: Macmillan.

Hart, K. 1988b. 'Rural-urban migration in West Africa', in J. Eades (ed.), *Migrants, Workers and the Social Order*. London: Tavistock.

Hart, K. 1988c. 'Barter', in *The New Palgrave Dictionary of Economic Theory*. London: Macmillan.

Hart, K. 1988d. 'Kinship, contract and trust: economic organisation among migrants in an African city slum', in D. Gambetta (ed.), *Trust: Making and Breaking Co-operative Relations*. Oxford: Blackwell.

Hegel, G. W. F. 1819 [1945]. *The Philosophy of Right.* [Translated by T. M. Knox]. Oxford: The Clarendon Press.

Internation Labour Office. 1972. *Incomes, Inequality and Employment in Kenya.* Geneva: ILO.

James, C. L. R. with R. Dunayevskaya and G. Lee, 1950. *State Capitalism and World Revolution.* Chicago: Charles H. Kerr.

Keynes, J. M. 1936. *The General Theory of Employment, Interest and Money.* London: Macmillan.

Lewis, W. A. 1978. *The Evolution of the International Economic Order.* Princeton: Princeton University Press.

Marcus, G. 1985. 'Contemporary problems of ethnography in the modern world system', in J. Clifford and G. Marcus (eds.), *Writing Culture.* Berkeley: University of California Press.

Marx, K. 1971 [1867]. *Capital.* London: Lawrence and Wishart.

Mauss, M. 1967 [1925]. *The Gift.* New York: Norton.

Plattner, S. (ed.) 1989. *Economic Anthropology.* Stanford: Stanford University Press.

Smith, M. E. 1990. *New Perspectives on the Informal Economy.* Lanham, MD: University of America Press.

Weber, M. 1978. *Economy and Society* (2 vols.), (eds. G. Roth and C. Wittich). Berkeley: University of California Press.

Weber, M. 1981. *The General Economic History.* New Jersey: Transaction Books.

World Bank, 1981. *Accelerated Development in Sub-Saharan Africa: an Agenda for Action.* World Bank, Washington DC.

Part v

Market and Plan in Europe and China

12

Culture, Market Ideology and Economic Reform in Czechoslovakia

LADISLAV HOLY

As elsewhere in Eastern Europe, the economic reform whose aim is the creation of market economy in Czechoslovakia is the result of the overthrow of the communist regime. Alongside the creation of a democratic political structure and a new system of central and local government, administration of justice, the reform of the system of education, health care, and so on, economic reform is part of the revolutionary process of the creation of a new post-communist social order. In many respects, it is the most important part of this process for the introduction of a free market will inevitably affect changes in all spheres of social and political life.

The need to introduce a market economy in Czechoslovakia is justified both in pragmatic and ideological terms. The view that the Czechoslovak economy has to be restructured to avoid its eventual total collapse predates the political change in Czechoslovakia. Considered in terms of the economists' standard criteria of economic performance, the Czechoslovak economy has been in poor shape for a considerable time and has increasingly acquired the character of an economy of a Third World country: productivity and the quality of manufactured goods are low, the rate of growth has been declining steadily, the internal and external debt of the country and inflation (so far mostly hidden through widespread subsidies) are rising, and international trade is heavily biased towards the export of raw materials and import of technology. All this was recognised a long time before the political change at the end of 1989, and an important part of the post-1968 old regime's political programme was the 'restructuring of the economic mechanism' – a phrase which replaced the previous slogan 'economic reform' which was ideologically tinted through its association with the reform attempts of Dubcek's regime of 1968. 'Restructuring of the economic mechanism' involved some kind of strengthening of market relations but did not aim at abolishing central planning and the public ownership of property. Its main aspects were better planning, tighter central control and more effective sanctions (mainly in the form of the distribution of state subsidies) and increase of productivity through the insistence on a better work discipline.

All this came to a halt in 1990 when the government programme of economic reform took the form of the complete abandoning of any central planning and its replacement by a liberal market economy in which the state would interfere only through its fiscal policies (taxation, control of the money supply, and so on). The possibility of a 'third road' which would combine some elements of a planned and a market economy was ruled out and the only issue discussed was the speed of the transition. Eventually the 'radical group' around the Finance Minister won the day over the 'gradualists' and a swift transition to a free-market economy became the government's policy. The three main elements of the economic reform are the liberalisation of prices which are to be determined solely by the market, the inner convertibility of the Czechoslovak currency and privatisation of all state enterprises. Property is being returned to its original owners or their direct heirs. Small state enterprises like retail outlets, workshops and restaurants which do not have original private owners or are not claimed by them, are being sold in public auctions. The large state enterprises are to be converted into limited companies. To make this conversion possible, the government will sell for a nominal price to all adults vouchers which can be used for the purchase of shares in any company of their choice.

12.1 THE 'VELVET' REVOLUTION

The economic reform was, and is still, however, motivated not only by the need to boost the ailing Czechoslovak economy. The notion of the 'market' has also strong ideological connotations and the transition to the free market is seen as the realisation of the goal of the 'velvet' revolution which ended communist rule in November 1989.

In spite of its technological backwardness, the Czechoslovak economy was, nevertheless, in better shape than anywhere else in Eastern Europe and the Czechs and Slovaks did not suffer any significant economic deprivation. The opposition to communist rule did not spring from any strongly felt economic hardship and the economic situation was not the motivating factor of the revolution at all. The revolution was started by students, actors and intellectuals. The most prominent of these belonged to a small circle of dissidents who, during the 1980s, had been increasingly protesting against the systematic persecution of scholars, journalists, writers, poets, musicians, pop singers and other artists who declared their open support for the reforms of 1968 and were unwilling to gain the regime's favour by publicly revoking their 'ideological mistakes'. Their opposition to the communist government was not an opposition to those who brought the country to the brink of an economic collapse but an opposition to those who systematically suppressed all basic human freedoms. The basic demand of the revolution was freedom. This demand became an effective rallying call for the masses because the government made its suppression of freedom publicly visible in its brutally violent suppression of the students' demonstration in Prague on 17 November 1989. This action precipitated daily mass protest rallies in Prague and other cities and towns, and culminated in a nation-wide general strike that eventually toppled the communist government.

What gave the 'velvet' revolution its impetus was the general feeling in the country that on 17 November state repression had reached an intolerable level. The self-image that the Czechs have of themselves played a significant role in fostering this general feeling. That image is of a highly cultured and well educated nation. The 'uncultured' use of brutal force by the state against the 'cultured' and peaceful demonstrators made it clear that the Czechs had a state which did not befit them as a cultured nation and that they deserved a better one. When the intellectuals started their revolt against the state power, the masses rallied behind them. This does not mean, of course, that the specific grievances of the intellectuals motivated the population at large. Most people even did not know who the leading intellectuals were. When Havel first addressed the mass rallies, most people perceived him as one of 'those mysterious dissidents' and when he later emerged as the only serious candidate for the presidency, Czechoslovak newspapers hurriedly printed articles explaining who he was. There were co-operative farmers and factory workers who genuinely believed that if he really was such a world-renowned playwright as he was suddenly made to be, his plays would surely have been staged in Czechoslovakia and they would have heard about him before.

But whatever may objectively be the cultural and educational level of those who expressed such views, they too were Czechs and saw themselves as part of a nation whose main characteristic is that it is cultured and well educated. What they resented as members of this nation was not the persecution of a few intellectuals but the affront which they felt when they had to obey the orders of those who not only knew less than they should have known in their leadership positions but who in fact often knew less than those whom they were supposed to lead. The image of those in authority as blithering idiots was all pervasive and an unceasing source of popular jokes.

The rallying of the masses behind the intellectuals who stood in the forefront of the revolution was of course considerably facilitated by the fact that the revolution took place in the television age. It was significant that the students were first joined in their strike by actors: these actors were seen as the main representatives of the intellectuals, for they had the visibility which writers, poets, playwrights and philosophers did not. Those who openly revolted against the state and with whom people could have identified were not unknown dissidents but men and women whose names and faces were known from television screens. This gave them an authority which the leading dissidents (including Havel), whose faces and often names were mostly unknown, could never have. All this contributed to the fact that the 'velvet' revolution could have been perceived as a revolution of the cultured, and of those who wanted to be seen as cultured, against the uncultured.

The image which the Czechs have of themselves as a highly cultured and well educated nation motivates what they presently describe as their 'return to Europe' and which they see as the ultimate goal of their 'velvet' or 'gentle' revolution. The Czechs have always detested being classified as East Europeans and are always ready to point out that Prague lies west of Vienna and west of the line between Vienna and Berlin. For the Czechs, Eastern Europe is Russia, Romania, Bulgaria and possibly Poland, but Czechoslovakia itself is part of Central Europe and it is common to describe it as lying in 'the heart of Europe' or even as being 'the heart of Europe'. The Czechs use the concept of *kulturnost* (a noun derived from the adjective 'cultured') to construct a boundary between themselves and the uncultured east into which they were lumped after the communist *coup d'état* in 1948, and they see their proper place alongside the civilised, cultured and educated nations of Western Europe. The idea of the 'return to Europe' dominated the election campaign in June 1990 when virtually every political party presented itself to the voters as the best party to lead Czechoslovakia back into Europe.

12.2 THE MARKET AS A CULTURAL SYMBOL

The transition to market economy is construed as a necessary part of achieving the re-entry of Czechoslovakia into Europe and of regaining the Czechs' place among the civilised nations of Europe to which they rightfully belong. This notion was clearly articulated by Vaclav Klaus, the Czechoslovak Minister of Finance and chief architect of the economic reform:

> As a slogan of our gentle revolution we chose the return to Europe, including the adoption of an economic system which is characteristic of the civilised world and which shows, in spite of all its shortcomings, that a better arrangement of economic relations does not exist. (*Lidove noviny* 10.3.1990)

The rhetoric in which the necessity of transition to market economy is couched, constructs the market as a symbol of civilisation which the Czechoslovak society now again aspires to achieve. As this symbol, the market is an integral part of the package of ideological notions, of which the other important elements are democracy and the pluralism of ideas. All these 'civilising mechanisms' were destroyed under socialism (Radim Valencik in *Tvorba* [42] 17.10.1990) when the society was pushed back from its development towards civilisation. As Radim Valencik expressed it in his analysis of the 'real existing socialism':

> the society which wanted 'to command the wind and rain' grossly distorted the forms of the organisation of production based on market relations which were gradually created in the process of historical genesis. The suppression of the market by the centralistic administrative-bureaucratic management resulted in the emergence and coming into prominence of pre-capitalist relations – feudal ones, those characteristic of the Asiatic mode of production and even those of lineage society. This social atavism led not only to stagnation (as it was euphemistically called) but also to an ever accelerating rot. (*Tvorba* [42] 17.10. 1990)

This market is, however, not only a symbol of civilisation and 'modern society'. It is also a symbol of the rational organisation of society or even of human rationality itself, and economic reform is often talked about as 'the return of rationality into our society' (*Forum* [10] 4.4. 1990) or as 'an experiment in the return to reason' (*Lidove noviny* 11.7.1990). The introduction of market economy is the return to 'the normal order' of things (Vaclav Klaus in *Literarni noviny* 2.8.1990).

The rationality of market economy derives from the fact that unlike a centrally planned economy it is not the result of an ideological construction imposed artificially on the society, but the result of the society's normal historical development or 'a great historical invention of humankind' (*Forum* [11] 11.4. 1990). In this respect, it is 'natural', whereas the planned economy is 'artificial':

> [In the centrally planned economy] the price of labour and goods was determined artificially and, moreover, even nonsensically according to ideological directives. However, modern society is organisationally directly dependent on

the free exchange of services and goods, i.e. on a monetary principle. (Vladimir Ulrich in *Tvorba* [42] 17.10 1990)

Planned economy is an ideological construct…, in essence it is violence which politics enforced on economics. Nobody constructed market economy – it developed naturally, what was useful survived, what was not useful, died out. (Otakar Turek in *Literarni noviny* 14.6.1990)

Market economy operates not only as a process of natural selection. It is itself the result of the process of natural selection and it is precisely this aspect of it which accounts for its effectiveness: 'Market mechanism is the most perfect means to the satisfaction of the needs of all people and was created in the process of the historical development of society' (*Lidove noviny* 26.5.1990).

Market economy achieves this perfection because it is a type of economy which is not guided by political or ideological considerations but an economy which was left to develop according to its own principles.

In this package of notions in terms of which the economic reform in Czechoslovakia is legitimised, the following characteristics of the planned and market economy are brought into opposition:

Planned economy	*Market economy*
atavistic survivals of pre-capitalist	civilisation
societal forms	modern society
stagnation	development
irrationality	rationality
artificial	normal
	natural
ideological construct	result of pragmatic considerations
subject to politics	independent of politics

All the terms in which the market economy is constructed in opposition to the centrally planned economy invoke a different kind of agency than the one invoked in socialist ideology. Part of the socialist ideology was the construction of man who, equipped with the scientific knowledge of the objective laws of historical development, is the creator of his own destiny. Equipped with the scientific knowledge of natural laws he becomes an unrestricted master of nature which he can shape to his own will. In terms of this ideological construction, man was the sole agent of social and economic processes. He was constructing socialism – the first just society – and he was constructing an economy in which people were rewarded according to their merit and not in virtue of inherited privileges, and in which they would be ultimately rewarded according to their needs. Human agency also positively affected natural processes for the new man, whom socialism brought into being, since he could 'command the wind and rain' as the slogan had it. Such slogans are now the object of ridicule and are routinely invoked as the ultimate proof of communist folly (see the quotation from Valencik above).

It is now part of the ideological packaging of democratic pluralism and market economy to point out that man's tampering with society led not to the freeing of human potential but to the suppression of all human rights; not to the creation of just society but to the creation of a totalitarian system; not to the gradual withering of the state but to its increased interference in all aspects of the citizens' lives, and not to the creation of a higher form of morality but to the destruction of all moral principles and to the disregard for even the most rudimentary principles of 'civilised' behaviour. Czech newspapers are full of critical comments about the rude behaviour of the officials, waiters, shop assistants or anybody else who is ostensibly employed to serve the public, and they incessantly compare the polite behaviour which permeates the public sphere of life in the west with the rudeness and haughtiness which is characteristic of the relations between people in the public sphere in Czechoslovakia. These negative aspects of behaviour are directly attributed to the absence of the market.

> Anybody who was in the west can testify that willingness, regard for others and respect for their needs are quite common there. This is not in spite of but because of the fact that the market has reigned there for more than two hundred years and its 'invisible hand' has educated citizens in this way. 'The baker bakes good and cheap rolls not because he is an altruist but because he is an egoist' says one of the basic maxims of classical economics. Readiness to serve, a friendly attitude to and interest in the needs of a customer are basic conditions of survival in the competition of the market and these qualities are then reflected in other inter-personal relations. (Anna Cervenkova in *Lidove noviny* 3.9.1990)
>
> Especially television commentators explain [market mechanism] as some kind of self-salvation which will automatically deliver smiling shop assistants, waiters ready to serve us, correct measures of beer and anything else we may only wish for. (Jan Hysek in *Forum* [44] 28.11.1990)

Man's belief that he can 'command the wind and rain' resulted in unprecedented levels of pollution and ecological devastation which only the market can again rectify. In the words of the Finance Minister:

> The only solution of our ecological problems lies in the introduction of normal market economy. We know well that the environment is most devastated in countries which lack a market economy. A normal functioning market economy is the crux of everything because it is an economy which lends to all goods, including water, air and everything else, their correct price (*Lidove noviny* 20.12.1990).

As far as economy itself is concerned, man's tinkering with it resulted in the transformation of Czechoslovakia from a country which before the Second World War enjoyed the tenth highest standard of living in the world, into a country which now occupies the forty-second rank, well below many Third World countries. The message is easy to grasp: the prosperous countries are prosperous because, unlike us, they never consciously tinkered with their economy; they left the market to do the job and they did not try to do it themselves. When talking about the aims of the economic reform, Vaclav Klaus clearly expressed where the agency should lie: 'The aim is to let the invisible hand of the market act and to replace the hand of the central planner' (*Forum* [18] 30.5.1990).

However, the necessity of introducing a market economy is justified not only in terms of the agency of the market which, as a self-regulating mechanism, is capable of avoiding all the errors and deficiencies of an economy, the agents of which were the planners, bureaucrats and ideologists. It is justified also in terms of the agency of those who participate in the market. The notion of the natural character of the market in particular is predicated on both types of agency. On the one hand, the market is 'natural' as a self-regulating mechanism which itself determines prices and values. Its 'natural' character derives its meaning in opposition to the centrally planned economy in which the prices and values were 'artificially' determined by human agents. The return to a market economy is thus a return to the 'natural' state of society. But the market is also 'natural' because it is an arrangement of economic relations that correspond to human nature. In consequence, when human nature is not interfered with, it always gives rise to the market. '[The market] is a great historical invention of humankind and it is never possible completely to destroy it. The striving of its participants for a bigger share has been so far the only basis of innovative movement and economic growth that corresponds to human nature' (*Forum* [11] [11.4.1990).

This 'human nature' is man's propensity towards private property, which in itself is the only effective motivational factor:

> In the case of small firms combined with the owner's direct work participation, private property is the most effective motivational factor. (Jaroslav Smrcka in *Forum* [10] 4.4.1990)
>
> It is a fact established through years of experience, that in most branches of human activity, private ownership is socially the most effective way of the management of material goods. (*Forum* [2] 7.2.1990)
>
> Repression of private property leads to diminished work motivation. (*Lidove noviny* 21.7.1990)

What was brought into opposition during the overthrow of communist rule in Czechoslovakia in November 1989 was not socialism and democracy but totalitarianism and freedom. In consequence, the debate surrounding the economic reform in Czechoslovakia does *not* suggest an ideological link of the free market to democracy through the notion of individual freedom, as most western analysts are inclined to argue. In western conceptualisation, the market is linked with democratic pluralism; in the same way in which only democratic pluralism guarantees an individual's freedom of political choice, only the market guarantees his or her freedom of economic choice. The notion of an individual's freedom, which ideologically motivates the introduction of market economy, is ultimately a freedom of choice among competing products, that is consumer choice. In this conceptualisation, the notion of a free market is part of an ideological package whose notions are pluralism, competition and freedom of choice. These stand opposed to the notions of centralism, co-operation in the realisation of a common social goal and the equity of needs. All these elements formed the package of notions characteristic of the socialist ideology. The market economy and the planned economy are the symbols of these contrasting packages of ideological notions.

By contrast in the Czechoslovak conceptualisation, the link between market and freedom is construed differently. It is not freedom in the sense of the exercise of choice so much as freedom in the sense of an unconstrained expression of human nature that is linked to the concept of the market. If private property is construed as part of human nature, only a free-market economy based on the private ownership of the means of production offers people real freedom for, unlike a planned economy, it does not constrain their natural propensity towards it.

The tangible symbol of freedom is not consumer choice but private ownership. This symbol is then actively invoked to justify the economic reform: to achieve freedom we must have a free market, the pre-condition of which is private ownership. Privatisation then logically becomes the key element in economic reform.

This construction of freedom, not as the freedom of consumers but as the freedom of producers (who are the owners), ties up with the emphasis on the productive side of the economy. In Czechoslovakia, consumer choice is at best only a distant ideal. At present, demand considerably outweighs supply and the emphasis on the production side of the economy reflects the reformers' goal to boost the effectiveness of production and to increase supply. They openly admit that achieving this goal would mean at least a temporary tightening of belts, for prices will rise as the result of removing subsidies. This emphasis on the effectivity of production is similar to the policy of the International Monetary Fund and the World Bank which insist on the introduction of various saving programmes as the condition for credit. That the terms 'market' and 'world market' are themselves terms which entail the emphasis on production rather than consumption is suggested by the rhetoric of 'penetrating the market' or 'gaining new markets'. The market is understood as a place where commodities can be disposed of; who and what is the source of the counter-value which is exchanged for the commodities in the market does not seem to be taken much into consideration. The Czechoslovak conception of the market corresponds to this conceptualisation.

12.3 MORAL RESPONSES TO THE MARKET ECONOMY

In line with this conceptualisation of the market is the fact that most people see themselves as the market's passive objects and not as its active agents who through the exercise of their choices affect the quantity, quality and price of commodities. They do not experience the working of the incipient market forces, but instead the practices of emerging entrepreneurs whom they evaluate by moral and not economic criteria. Private entrepreneurs, who, as a result of the government's policy of price liberalisation set their prices above the level previously determined by the state, are seen as profiteers whose objective is not customers' satisfaction but a quick profit without work. The state, which is pursuing the policy of minimum administrative interference in the running of the economy, tends to see the emerging profiteering as excesses that will automatically disappear once the free market gets fully established. The pressure on the government to bring under firm legal control any over-charging, which was a criminal offence when all prices were centrally determined, is countered by elementary lessons about people's envisaged role as active agents in the market and the power they exercise as customers. Women's magazines and daily newspapers now print articles whose message is: 'If you think it is expensive, do not buy it. If they cannot sell it for the asking price, they will have to lower it.'

The practical policy of economic reform has not been able to ignore all the objections to market economy, however, many of which stem from seeing entrepreneurs as the active agents of the market and the customers as its passive objects. When the legislation about the privatisation of retailing outlets, restaurants and workshops (the so called 'little privatisation') was being discussed, worries were often expressed that the new shop-owners would stop selling the goods which so far had been retailed in the shop and would start retailing merchandise which would guarantee them greater immediate profit. If the new private entrepreneurs were allowed unlimited freedom in choosing the goods they wanted to sell, the customers would suffer. The government eventually yielded to these arguments and legislation was passed which forces the new private owners of grocery shops to continue selling groceries for at least a year.

The main objects of moral scorn are the street money changers (*vekslaci*). As they operate without licences, their activities are as illegal as they were under the previous regime. Nowadays, however, they operate practically with impunity. The public at large see them as profiteers whose main objective is again a quick profit without work. Like private entrepreneurs who push up prices above what they should be, they likewise push up the exchange rate. Their activities are immoral because they destroy the 'just' price. However, the government has not so far yielded to the moral outrage of the public. Its tolerance springs from the view that the opening of the country's borders and the resulting influx of tourists has not yet been matched by the necessary expansion of banks and exchange offices. In this situation, the street money-changers provide a necessary service without which the tourist industry – an important source for the country of badly needed foreign currency – would break down. With the devaluation of Czechoslovak currency, the difference between the official and the black-market exchange rate has narrowed down considerably, and the government does not see the money-changers as a serious threat to the economy. In providing many companies with the hard currency they need, the services of the money changers are a welcome addition to the services otherwise provided by the underdeveloped banking system. Moreover, their activities are seen as those of market entrepreneurs who operate effectively according to the principle of supply and demand and thus contribute positively to setting the only 'realistic' exchange rate. The government is, on the whole, inclined to see them as people who will either gradually be absorbed into the emerging banking system or will eventually go out of business once the Czechoslovak currency becomes fully convertible and the necessary number of licensed exchange offices becomes established as the result of a fully operational market.

In the same way in which the shared cultural values are marshalled in support of the market by the architects of the economic reform, so they are also marshalled in support of the objections against specific aspects of the reform. One of these values is national pride which was distinctly heightened by the sweeping political change that took place in Czechoslovakia at the end of 1989 and, particularly, by the style of this change. The Czechs take a distinct pride in the 'gentle' character of their 'velvet' revolution which is for them a sign of their *kulturnost*. They compare themselves favourably with the Romanians whose revolution was distinctly bloody and messy, which showed that the Romanians lack the *kulturnost* that the Czechs possess. Similarly the Poles and East Germans, also lacking the Czech qualities, needed much longer than the Czechs to achieve the change. That the Poles and East Germans paved the way for the Czechs is conveniently disregarded when these, for the Czechs, favourable comparisons are made.

The self-image of the Czechs as a cultured and civilised nation is invoked in the moral condemnation of the money-changers and emerging private entrepreneurs. As they offer their services mostly to foreigners who do not know their way around, they destroy the reputation of the Czechs as a cultured nation and create the undesirable image of Czechs as cheats, swindlers and profiteers. In doing so, they hamper the Czechs' return to Europe: 'Would Europe really want us if we are not able to behave in a civilised manner?' is regularly the bottom line of moral reprehension about the activities of the private entrepreneurs.

12.4 NATIONALISM AND EGALITARIANISM

National pride and the notion that 'Czech is best' (expressed in the rhyme *co je ceske, to je hezke* – 'what is Czech is beautiful') leads also to the opposition to the participation of foreign capital in Czechoslovak enterprises. This is talked about as a sell-out of national wealth; opposition to it is based on three reasons. It is argued that the sale of shares in Czechoslovak enterprises to foreigners will lead to the exploitation of Czech labour by foreign capital, to the cheap export of labour and national wealth and to the subjugation of the Czechoslovak economy to foreign rather than to national interests. While, according to an opinion poll conducted in 1990, 46 per cent of people agreed with the sale of large loss-making companies, only 23 per cent agreed with a sale without restrictions, of which the most important one was that only Czechoslovak citizens and firms should be eligible as shareholders. Large firms especially are the object of national pride and the objection to foreigners participating in their ownership is particularly strong: while 44 per cent of people agreed with the sale of small enterprises to foreigners, only 18 per cent agreed with the sale of large companies.

Apart from nationalism, egalitarianism is another value which colours people's perception of the market and affects their attitude to specific practical aspects of economic reform. Social equality was of course an important aspect of socialist ideology and in Czechoslovakia it was realised in practice to a much more significant degree than anywhere else in Eastern Europe. Czechoslovakia had a very egalitarian income policy and the differences of income of the educated and highly qualified elite and unqualified labour were considerably smaller than in any other socialist country. This was seen by the economic reformers of the Prague Spring as dampening personal initiative and as a hindrance to economic development, but it was never an issue of popular concern. The levelling of income was reflected in the consumption of food and basic industrial goods as well as in housing. With regard to income level, patterns of consumption, legal conditions of employment and social security, Czechoslovak society developed a distinctly homogeneous character. A comprehensive school system contributed also to some extent to this development which the Czechs find distinctly comforting: as long as nobody has much more than I do, things are as they should be. Although it would be foolish to deny that forty years of socialism in Czechoslovakia has played its part in strengthening the egalitarian ethos, it seems to me that the ideal of egalitarianism was an aspect of the socialist idéology to which the Czechs objected least precisely because it built on Czech cultural values which pre-date the socialist period and which, like individualism in England, have deep historical roots. An important aspect of Czech history is the demise of the Czech nobility during the recatholisation of the country in the seventeenth century when the estates of the Czech Protestant aristocracy fell into the hands of German noble families. The major class and status divisions have since then paralleled this basic ethnic division. This situation did not change during the eighteenth and nineteenth centuries when the rising capitalist class in Bohemia was German or at least spoke German. National legends have always taken cognizance of this egalitarian ethos which preceded the building of socialism in Czechoslovakia, and in fact it might have been a factor which made possible to a greater extent than anywhere else in the socialist bloc, the elimination of the private economic sector. The Masaryk legend put great emphasis on his ordinariness. Every schoolchild knew that he slept on a simple military iron bed, enjoyed simple food, and nothing symbolised his hatred of ostentatiousness more than the only items that seemed to be in his wardrobe: his military style tunic and hat with ribbons in national colours. The stories about the headaches of his personal guards from whose watchful eyes he constantly tried to escape communicated his dislike of privilege. President Havel has steadily been acquiring a similar image. Recently the Czech newspapers and television reported that after his visit to the largest factory in Prague, he stopped in the local pub where he drank one beer.

The ultimate source of the egalitarian ethos is the belief in the equality of individuals in nature. It is acceptable to ascribe an individual's failure to the lack of effort or hard work but bad form to ascribe it to lack of intelligence, for that amounts to the admission of inherent inequality which is culturally denied. We may not all be good at everything but each of us is good at something, which proves our natural equality. I do not think that anybody was sorry when IQ tests disappeared, having been declared an invention of bourgeois pseudo-science; the illusion of equality in nature could be maintained without being openly challenged.

The market in which the entrepreneurs are perceived as active subjects and everybody else as passive objects offends the cultural ideal of equality, as well as the ideal that material disparities and the differences in life-styles within society should be limited. The market economy is perceived as a system which increases differences in wealth: only 40.3 per cent of those who voted for non-communist parties in the June 1990 elections, and only 18.5 per cent of those who voted for the communist party, find the increased differential acceptable. According to the opinion poll conducted in December 1990, only 43 per cent of people were afraid of the loss of employment but 61 per cent expressed their fear that the economic reform would make it possible for some people to become extremely rich (*Lidove noviny* 28.12.1990).

The deep-rooted feeling of social equality is seen by the architects of the economic reform as perhaps the most serious potential danger to its success. This leads to exhortations that 'to be responsible for oneself is the sign of human and civic maturity' (*Lidove noviny* 27.7.1990), that 'market economy gives a chance to those who are capable and hard working' and that 'each of us has to learn to look after oneself' as stated by Prime Minister Marian Calfa (*Lidove noviny* 11.7.1990). In its turn, this rhetoric led to the expression of feelings that 'the economic reform and all the changes which are connected with it address the citizens of the republic as if they all were only businessmen, managers and entrepreneurs' (Vaclav Slavik in *Rude Pravo* 15.11.1990).

The architects of the economic reform acknowledge the strength of egalitarian feelings but argue that this ideal has yet to be achieved and that the existence of inequality has to be acknowledged. Inequality existed even under communism but it was based on ideological and political privileges and not on the degree to which one contributes to the creation of wealth that guarantees a high standard of living to all. Given that inequality is a necessary condition of living in society, market economy is just, or at least less unjust than the centrally planned economy for 'only market relations will show who really deserves what' (V. Klaus in *Literarni noviny* 2.8.1990). The market economy is a just system because 'it builds on the ability, skill and wits of all, not only on the wits of the leading 'elite' as was the case in the system of centrally planned economy' (Otakar Gurek in *Literarni noviny* 14.6.1990).

However, the view that one's ability, skill and wits are the precondition of one's success in the market is far from widespread, and the view prevails that people's chances of success are greatly unequal. Those who 'worked honestly' under socialism see themselves as discriminated against, for they have never been able to accumulate capital which would enable them to start as entrepreneurs. Some commentators argue that the ideologically motivated preference for private property expressed through the policy of privatisation is 'the betrayal of the programme of the November revolution which expressed the equality of all forms of ownership and not only a preference for one of them' (Jiri Vrany in *Tvorba* [45] 7.1.1990). People express a similar view in that they see the market as again privileging those who ruled over the distribution of housing, higher education, cars and other scarce goods and who were in the position to command substantial bribes. Only those who prospered under totalitarianism will prosper again in the market economy. These people are nowadays referred to as the 'mafia' and the prevailing image of them is of an octopus which holds society firmly in its tentacles. With the approaching privatisation, the question of the laundering of dirty money has gained a prominent part in the debate about economic reform. The government's attitude that it is unfeasible to check on the source of the capital of the new private entrepreneurs and that any such legislation would only delay economic reform and thus worsen the already dismal economic situation, strengthened the fears that a new totalitarianism is creeping into Czechoslovak society. Many people now express their fears that the same people who controlled the country politically under socialism will now control it economically and the view that one form of totalitarianism was simply replaced by another is growing stronger.

NOTES

The Czech newspapers referred to in the text are: *Forum, Lidove noviny, Literarni noviny, Tvorba, Rude Pravo*. All translations from the Czech are by the author.

13

Market Principle, Market-place
and the Transition in Eastern Europe

C. M. HANN

I am concerned in this chapter less with the theoretical status of 'the market' in anthropology and in economics than with the images and understandings evoked by the term in Hungary in 1990. Long before the revolutions of 1989–90 Hungary was widely perceived to be on the front line of the insidious spread of a 'market principle' in Eastern Europe. I begin by asking how we can best understand the path followed by Hungary in the Kádár period (1956–88), with a particular focus on the concept of 'market socialism'. Next I offer a brief account of a certain climate of opinion in the country in 1990. I then turn in the main part of the chapter to materials concerning the area in which I first did fieldwork in the mid-1970s, and which I was able to revisit in the summer of 1990.

13.1 MARKET SOCIALISM AND ECONOMIC ANTHROPOLOGY

Market socialism is a concept which has generated a large literature in twentieth-century economic thought, with major contributions coming both internally, that is from theorists working within socialist countries, and from western authors. [1] In my view the concept can be plausibly applied to Hungary after the introduction of the so-called New Economic Mechanism in 1968. I have often used it myself as a shorthand for indicating Hungary's significant divergence from standard models of centrally planned economies (see Hann 1980:45, 1990:1). These reforms, which included a significant measure of devolution to enterprise managers, are conventionally summarised as an attempt to achieve an optimal combination of plan and market, leading to the establishment of what is variously termed a 'regulated', or 'guided' or 'simulated' market. [2]

The economic reforms in Hungary were periodically contested and renewed, and are now widely regarded as having led to an impasse by the late 1980s. Certainly the country's economic difficulties at this period were deep rooted, but it is perhaps too simple to blame the 'market socialism' strategy for this failure. Hungary would not necessarily have abandoned this course in favour of a headlong rush towards capitalism were it not for external political developments in 1989–90. Today the gradualist aspirations of socialist reformers have been jettisoned and the stage is dominated by neo-liberal politicians and economists who see 'the market' as utterly incompatible with any definition of socialism. The most distinguished economist, a scholar whose reputation is perhaps even higher in the west than in his native Hungary, is János Kornai. Kornai believes that piecemeal reforms of the post-1968 type were always insufficient to tackle the structural problems of a socialist economy. Enterprises were always subject to interference from the central authorities, budget constraints were never hard enough, capital markets hardly functioned at all, and so on. For Kornai, any talk of 'simulating' a market in order to improve economic co-ordination, whilst leaving ultimate power in the hands of the politicians and planners, is based on a contradiction. For him there is only one possible route, namely the creation of a 'genuine market economy', without simulation. For him, as for many intellectuals and perhaps most lay opinion in Hungary today, this true market can be conceived only in terms of capitalism as it has developed in the west. No alternative has any proven record, nothing else can offer Hungarians the living conditions they see close at hand in Austria and Germany. The socialist economies are presented as artificial and distorted, whilst capitalist market economies are seen as 'natural'. For example, when discussing the process of privatisation in contemporary Hungary Kornai argues that 'it is indispensable to thoroughly analyse the concentration structure of genuine market economies, where competition has resulted in a kind of natural selection (Hungarian: *természetes szelekció*)' (1990:83).

Locating himself explicitly in the tradition of von Mises and von Hayek, Kornai also gives considerable prominence to the dimension of property relations. For him the most fundamental problem is that in practice state ownership means that property belongs to no one. His own definition of a free economy runs as follows:

> A free economy is, of course, a market economy, but the concept is richer and refers not only to the fact that the main coordinator of economic activities is a specific mechanism, namely the market. A free economy is one that allows unhampered entry, exit, and fair competition in the market. The notion of a free economy also implies a certain configuration of property rights and a certain institutional and political structure. The system promotes the free establishment and preservation of private property and encourages the private sector to produce the great bulk of output. It is a system that encourages individual initiative and entrepreneurship, liberates this initiative from excessive state intervention, and protects it by the rule of law. A free economy is embedded in a democratic political order, characterised by the free competition of political forces and ideas. Given my own value system, the guarantee of these liberties has a high intrinsic value and should therefore enjoy top priority in economic policy-making. (Kornai 1990:22–3)

I shall return to some of these themes below in the context of fieldwork data. My purpose at this point is to note the triumphant emergence of late in Hungary of a current of opinion, promoted vigorously by the country's leading economist, which wishes to do away once and for all with half measures, tinkering and simulation, and introduce into Hungary the 'hard', authentic version of a 'market economy'. This version is perceived by many people as both natural and as scientifically verified: after all, Kornai has the enhanced legitimacy that is conferred by a university chair in

Boston, as readers of the semi-popular work from which I have quoted above are reminded in its blurb. His own proviso – 'given my own value system' – is over-looked, and the Kornai recipe is easily taken to be indispensable for the efficient organisation of all industrial societies. Any other recipe, such as talk about grounding a market economy on a hierarchical structure of property rights which would transcend the public–private dichotomy, is rejected by Kornai as naïve wishful thinking which is sure to disappoint the Hungarian people in practice.[3]

It is not my purpose to challenge Kornai's position in terms of how well it captures the economic realities of contemporary industrial societies. It seems to me that it clearly underestimates the role played by the state in the evolution of modern economies, and that his line of argument is deeply coloured by antipathy towards the values as well as the pragmatic achievements of his country in the socialist period. What I would like to suggest here is some affinity between this conceptual apparatus of Kornai and the arguments of a great compatriot of an earlier generation.

Karl Polanyi worked primarily as an economic historian, though his later writings had considerable impact upon the field of economic anthropology.[4] In *The Great Transformation* and *Trade and Market in the Early Empires* he argued that the industrial revolution had ushered in an era in which, for the first time, 'market exchange' provided the dominant mode of integration. Polanyi saw this development as dangerous and dehumanising. It allowed economic forces to escape from the social controls previously exercised through modes which he labelled 'reciprocity' (funda-mentally egalitarian) and 'redistribution' (fundamentally hierarchical). The idea of the all-corrupting 'market principle' was further developed by anthropologists work-ing in the substantivist school which Polanyi established. For example, Paul Bohannan and George Dalton in their introduction to the collection *Markets in Africa* elabo-rated the distinction between the market *principle* and market-*places* as anthropolo-gists had studied them in tribal and peasant societies. They pointed to the paradox whereby the extension of the market principle typically led to the extinction of earlier forms of market-place, with the loss of those integrating social aspects that were just as important as their economic functions. Our modern market systems are presented as lacking any comparable integration, as devoid of any social or cultural dimension.

This substantivist project has exercised some influence upon general theorising about socialist Eastern Europe. Ivan Szelenyi and George Konrád (1979) have sug-gested that the socialist states were governed by a principle of 'rational redistribution', in an argument that is constructed upon explicitly Polanyite foundations. Recent anthropological work on the region also continues to manifest elements of this approach. For example, Katherine Verdery has argued that socialist systems sup-pressed free markets 'precisely because they move goods laterally rather than vertically towards the center – as all redistributive systems require'. Like many others she seems to treat 'the market' as an unambiguous agent in the present wave of reforms.[5]

What I wish to point to is the congruence here between the substantivist tradition in anthropology with its suggestion of a (hidden) market principle and the contem-porary economist's reliance upon essentially the same concept in his critique of 'market socialist' experiments in the Kádár period. Of course the values at stake are directly opposed: Polanyi deplored the influence of the market principle, whilst Kornai sees it as the only road to salvation. It is worth pointing out that the latter has always disapproved of the term 'market socialism'. Unwilling to sully the concept of the market, he prefers to describe Hungarian policies after 1968 in terms of a consumerist orientation which in his view did nothing to alter the effective structures of control. The obvious fact that many market-places in Hungary have been well provisioned, efficient and competitive can thus be dismissed. These markets are 'peripheral' (to use the substantivist terminology) to the dominant principle of centralised redistribution, which is exemplified in other, less visible markets (for example industrial raw materials). But perhaps the concept of 'peripheral markets' will be dismissed as a typical anthropological fudge by the purists on either side. Both its neo-liberal proponents in Eastern Europe and its radical opponents in the west continue to need a strong concept of the 'market principle' for their differing ideological projects. Having recently edited a volume about economy and society in Hungary in which I placed myself more or less squarely in the substantivist tradition (Hann 1990) I am in no position to deny the convenience of such a concept.

13.2 MARKETS IN 1990: REPRESENTATIONS AND REALITIES

I arrived in Hungary in late July and stayed throughout August. This account is based upon observations and conversations in that month, and also upon media representations followed throughout the year.[6] In view of the work I had just edited (I was hawking copies of Hann 1990 around the deserted academies) I was pleased to find that the theme of 'market economy' (*piacgazdaság*) was still extremely prominent.[7] In particular the television news programmes highlighted a number of social problems that were projected as somehow associated with a wave of uncontrolled petty trading, prostitution and pornography, and new protection rackets. Thus there was footage at peak viewing times of chaotic market-place scenes, and interviews with concerned council officials, and long-suffering local residents who would bemoan the lack of any effective regulation by the council. Sometimes there were specific allegations to highlight moral issues. In one television news bulletin the scandal focused on traffic in young children, allegedly being routinely sold by their Gypsy parents. Another featured counterfeit currency disseminated on some of the larger market-places of southern Hungary by powerful gangs with origins in Yugoslavia and Bulgaria. Meanwhile newspapers carried analyses of violent disputes between Syrian and Algerian gangs for control of the money-changing business on the streets of central Budapest. Another news item alleged that Soviet soldiers were selling potentially lethal shells and rockets to local scrap metal dealers in a district I knew well from my earlier fieldwork. There was also a story which ran for weeks concerning the market sale of foodstuffs that were dangerous to health. It was associated with a serious outbreak of swine fever in countries bordering on Romania. This trade was associated particularly with 'tourists' from that country, and it was suggested that at least some of the tinned food unofficially imported from that country stemmed from supplies dispatched there as aid after the revolution which overthrew Ceausescu.

Without performing any sophisticated content analysis it was obvious to me that these stories had some common themes. Those guilty of treating family members as alienable property, those who accosted tourists on the streets for money-changing, and those who returned gifts of food as illicit commodities, could not possibly be ordinary respectable Hungarians. Ethnic and racial prejudice against outsiders was complex. The main culprits as far as the new unregulated market-places were concerned were the Polish dealers, conspicuous throughout the country in every large town by the end of the 1980s. Even when Poles were not in fact the most numerous group in the local market people tended to refer to it as the 'Polish market'. However, the media, in my view, showed somewhat less hostility towards these northerners than was blatantly displayed towards 'Balkan' neighbours and the principal internal enemy, the Gypsies. Hungarians who frequented such markets might argue that Poles deserved sympathy: they were to be found wheeling and dealing only because they had no other options open to them, given the chaos of the Polish economy. (A fuller explanation of the phenomenon which has seen Polish traders establish powerful networks from Stockholm to Istanbul, and from Berlin to Beijing, would take us too far away from the themes of this paper. It is certainly relevant to note that many Poles found themselves from the late 1970s in possession of passports that allowed them to travel much more freely than other East Europeans, but with no means of material support abroad...)

These market-places were also referred to as the 'Little Comecons', an ironic analogy with the international trading bloc that worked so imperfectly. The usual currency in these markets was the Hungarian forint, but barter was also common and by 1990 western currencies (above all the DM) were increasingly influential. Most of the items supplied were for domestic consumption: Hungarians could be fairly sure of getting towels from Poland at better prices than in the state shops, likewise shoes from Czechoslovakia, and various tools from Romania and the USSR. I also heard of teenagers who travelled to Hungary from East Germany and Czechoslovakia in order to buy denims originating in Istanbul from Polish middlemen. Others would go to these markets in search of some vital component for their car, a part perhaps not available in any country through the official channels. Major players, as in the 'second economy' generally, were those with good information networks (often through relatives in neighbouring countries) and the capital to enable them to exploit these characteristic shortages. Nevertheless I have the impression that these market-places have always been dominated by small dealers. There is a limit to the capacity of a Polski Fiat and trailer, even if by 1990 there was no limit to what amenable customs officials were prepared to wave through. At the extreme end of this petty trading were the efforts of ethnic Hungarians from the USSR to secure a few forints for local purchases when that frontier was opened to tourists and private visitors in 1990 (for the first time in forty years, and even then under very strict controls). All they could bring with them were one or two bottles of vodka or cheap wine, so they would set out their stall, complete with a single glass, to provide market-goers with a tipple. Unfortunately this is one sector of the economy in Eastern Europe where competitive principles are reasonably effective, so business was tough.[8]

These market-places were the scenes of occasional skirmishes with the police and local authorities in the 1980s. For this reason a research project would have been difficult to organise even in 1990. In general, tolerance increased over the decade, and (as in Poland in 1990) efforts were made to bring all forms of open-air trading under local council controls. At Lake Balaton (the country's main tourist centre) the council allocated a suitable field on the outskirts of a major resort, put up notices in Polish, and attempted to collect relatively small sums from traders as a daily levy. They did not go so far as to provide any sanitation, as the press was quick to point out, even though this site served many as a caravan park and holiday home for much of the summer. Hence as elsewhere dealers had little difficulty in resisting attempts to control their activities: markets could easily disperse and new ones emerge overnight.

Overall it seemed to me that the Hungarian media in the summer of 1990 were rather successfully fostering a sense of principled hostility towards everything that smacked of Polanyi's uncontrolled, 'disembedded' market. I think there was less concern in Hungary with 'negative egalitarianism' than in other socialist societies (compare S. and J. Potter 1990 and Holy, this volume). But the situation was one in which vital moral principles were at issue: Hungarians were being demeaned and exploited by every kind of mafia (this word was much used and discussed) and this was closely associated with the growing prominence of new market-places and the extension of market practices into wholly inappropriate areas of social life. There was of course a close connection between this morality and the official ethos of the socialist period, with its parallels in pre-socialist peasant Hungary, all of which emphasised mistrust of the market-place and sought to erect value systems outside it (compare Stewart 1990). There was, however, no question of hackneyed socialist rhetoric against the private sector and 'speculators' being trotted out in the old style. The moralising was all the more effective because it was not made in the old political terms. In any case, by this time all the leading Hungarian political parties (including the ex-Communist Party) were basically agreed on the need to encourage the growth of a 'real market economy'.

13.3 PROPERTY AND MARKET IN TÁZLÁR

The village of Tázlár lies on the Great Hungarian Plain, about eighty miles south east of Budapest. It has no regular market-place, and very few foreigners are seen here. It was a significant event in 1990 when a Polish car (apparently containing tourists rather than traders) had a breakdown on the main road which passes through the scattered farms of this community. Over the last few decades Tázlár has had a dynamic agricultural economy. In common with most of the communities of this region its poor quality, sandy soils are compatible with some high-value branches of production, particularly vineyards. Many of these communities have been allowed to develop distinct forms of collective farm which I call 'specialist co-operative' (Hungarian: *szakszövetkezet*), but before considering these it is important to outline the pre-collectivisation history of this area.

The community took shape on previously uninhabited *puszta* towards the end of the nineteenth century (for further detail on this period see Hann 1979). It was remote from major market centres, and comparatively few farmers produced any significant surplus. Tázlár remained poor and there were pronounced inequalities, for example some of the poorest families sent their children to work as servants (*cseléd*) on the farms of the rich landowners, and others worked as day labourers on large estates further afield. During this period many other Hungarian villages experienced similar tendencies, as inequalities in property-holding increased and lands formerly held and used on a communal basis were 'fragmented into exactly measured and independently used parcels of private property' (Fél and Hofer 1969:52). Tázlár was unusual in that, as a late settlement, its lands were from the outset held and used as private property, and there was therefore a more active market in land here than in more traditional communities. Whatever the legal details, I suspect that the diverse immigrant groups which made up the new population managed their farms in traditional family-centred ways. I attribute their move to Tázlár to the uneven impact of capitalist development which forced many other peasants in Hungary at the same period to seek their fortune in Budapest, or some other city, or abroad. But it would be wrong to imply – as I fear I did in early formulations – that the settlers were all equally in flight from capitalism. Late in the nineteenth century, for example, Ferenc Nacsa bought and farmed a large tract of land on a promising site in Tázlár, whilst retaining a perfectly adequate patrimony in his natal community sixty miles away. This enterprising family emerged as one of the prosperous upper stratum in the first half of the twentieth century, with strong links to traders in nearby market centres.

Using the shorthand of the substantivist tradition in economic anthropology I might have claimed that Tázlár owed its modern genesis to the impact of the 'market principle' upon Hungary, where the phrase 'market principle' stands for the onset of limited industrialisation, intensified participation in national and international division of labour, and the increased commodification of land and labour in the rural sector. Clearly many people were uprooted ('disembedded') from their earlier communities. Their new settlement probably lacked the old cohesion of villages with a long history of continuous settlement, and was slow to develop any alternative. Yet they were remote from major market centres and it is hardly likely that the inhabitants of Tázlár would have perceived any connection between the market-place at the neighbouring village of Soltvadkert, their main point of articulation with the national economy, and some abstract 'market principle'.

In a period which lasted almost two decades, between the end of the 1940s and the mid-1960s, this abstraction was ideologically condemned and markets were systematically repressed, though never entirely extinguished. In agriculture a system of compulsory deliveries was imposed, there were formidable campaigns against the so-called rich peasants (*kuláks*) to strip them of their holdings (the decendants of Ferenc Nacsa experienced exactly this fate), and mass agitation to persuade peasantry as a whole to enter new co-operatives. After very poor results with such policies in the early 1950s the Kádár government after 1956 set about renewing the mass collectivisation programme in a less dogmatic spirit. In Tázlár the impact of collectivisation was felt at the level of ideology and property arrangements rather than at the level of technique and farm management. Let us now consider the distinctive features of this specialist co-operative.[9]

The essence of the *szakszövetkezet* is that in practice the co-operative did not take the bulk of the land into collective cultivation (as was the norm for the Soviet *kolkhoz*) but left the member and his family to carry on in the customary way. The farmer obtained remuneration in cash for the produce which he generated, subject to a 10 per cent deduction for sales made through the co-operative. There was no recourse to a collectivist payments system (such as the Soviet 'work-points' scheme). Indeed although the co-operative farmed significant areas of collectively used land (much of which had formerly belonged to the richer private owners) there was no obligation upon co-operative members to *work* for the collective at all. Most farmers remained independent, though they maintained significant links with the co-operative for marketing, fodder supplies, tractor services, transportation and the like.

The origins of this variant of co-operative, which falls in certain respects closer to western agricultural co-operatives than to the *kolkhoz*, are not at all clear. It may have been an appreciation of the economic losses which would follow from adherence to the standard model in an area of scattered vineyards which led to the decision to allow family farming to continue here. Other accounts, including some related in Tázlár itself, suggest that certain Communist Party officials who were natives of the region played a key role in arguing for concessions. This seems plausible to me, and in any case the economic arguments would still have had to be made politically.[10] Whatever its precise origins, for the next quarter of a century this type of co-operative remained suspect ideologically. It was periodically asserted that they were 'lower forms' of property, which would need to progress steadily towards the more 'progressive' forms. In fact they never did this at all consistently, and in the 1980s the gap widened further. This is why I see this form of co-operative as containing the germ of a new system of property rights, one that is still capable of further development in the spirit of 'market socialism', if it is not destroyed in the present wave of reaction. (See Hann 1992.)

The economic success of this type of co-operative has been widely attested and a number of villages very close to Tázlár have become well known throughout the country for their high levels of income and accumulation. Tázlár itself is not quite in this league, but a lot of new wealth was evident in the mid-1970s: for example in housebuilding in the village centre, and in the purchase of cars and other status symbols. This is the period in which Hungary acquired its reputation as a 'consumerist' island in Eastern Europe, and there was much in this village to justify this image. I emphasise that this did not entail active market-places within the village. For the citizens of a small community like Tázlár this consumer culture was built around shopping trips which took them as far as Budapest or Yugoslavia, and it involved the usual sort of networking skills as well as much patience (particularly in the queue for private cars).

Relatively few Tázlár farmers participated regularly in agricultural markets, finding it more convenient to sell most of their produce through the co-operative, which typically engaged in large contracts with a few state enterprises. The prices were effectively determined by the state. Part of my research in the 1970s was devoted to showing that farmers responded elastically to these 'price signals', contrary to conventional models of the 'peasant economy'. Thus when prices were briefly cut in the mid- 1970s, in a phase of hard-line socialist propaganda which highlighted concern over increasing wealth differentials, there was a drop in production by the small-farm sector. Since the entire edifice of Kádár's Hungary rested upon a compromise in which abundant cheap food supplies were a crucial component, policies were quickly altered and farmers responded well to increased prices for their products.

In this limited sense one may therefore identify a market mechanism at work in Hungary in the mid-1970s. Prices were controlled by the government, and when supplies fell the price had to be increased in order to provide small farmers with effective incentives to supply the commodities the country needed. This pattern contrasted sharply with other collectivised countries. In later work I made much of the contrast with Poland, where in spite of the persistence of private property rights in a *formal* sense, peasants were much worse off because in the absence of an effective mechanism they lacked *substantive* rights (Hann 1985). Perhaps it would be more accurate to say that Hungarian farmers constituted an effective pressure group on the basis of a certain market power. In this way it is possible to detect a covert pluralism behind the ostensibly totalitarian politics of Hungarian rural life in this period.

Of course I had carried out my fieldwork at a comparatively favourable moment: the social compromise of the Kádár era required that small farmers be encouraged, and prosperity continued until well into the 1980s. By 1990 that era was over, however, and I found that many farmers were gravely worried about stagnant price levels for their products (while costs had risen massively) and *insecure* markets.

Soon after my arrival back in the village in mid-August 1990 I called at the headquarters of the 'Peace' specialist co-operative (unlike many others that year, with names like 'Lenin' or 'Red Star', it was not expected to change its name). The chairman seemed pleased to enter into a discussion about the progress of the farm since his assuming the main leadership role in 1984. He came from a peasant family in the neighbouring village and despite his professional training as an agronomist and reaching a very senior position when still in his thirties he had always managed to avoid joining the Communist Party. His strategy for the co-operative was eclectic. At the Thatcherite extreme he had been responsible for the privatisation of virtually all the co-operative's machinery (the tractors had been sold 'for a song', according to critics, to their drivers) and for shedding surplus labour in other divisions too. Land was readily available to those who wanted it, on a basis of long leases. The chairman had consciously sought new ways to generate joint investment and production schemes between the co-operative and its members, all within a fully democratic framework. He was particularly proud of collaborative schemes for establishing new vineyards, which involved many of the productive tasks being carried out by the families of the members in the traditional labour-intensive ways. He was therefore reluctant to countenance the demise of the co-operative, though he knew only too well that this was the target of some villagers, particularly those associated with the Independent Smallholders Party. He argued too that the co-operative was needed to provide basic resources at low cost to weaker members, not to mention its organisation of various sideline activities which provided the main source of wage-labour for females in the village.

In sum, the Tázlár specialist co-operative had an honourable record, claimed the chairman, and he had particularly enjoyed the irony in 1990 of *kolkhoz* chairmen coming to the village from other parts of the country on fact-finding missions: the lower form of socialist property was now seen as worthy of emulation by the so-called higher forms! Survival could not be taken for granted. For many co-operatives, including some of *kolkhoz* type, everything would depend above all upon the persistence of a special subsidy paid to those considered to be farming in unfavourable ecological conditions. Unexpectedly and without warning these subsidies had been drastically cut by the new government, with its commitment to *piacgazdaság*. The chairman likened this move in his end-of-the-year report to a 'natural disaster' (*természeti csapás*). He knew that such subsidies contradicted the logic of a pure-market economy, but could I name anywhere else in Europe, he asked me, where governments deal with agriculture according to 'pure-market relations'?

I heard other points of view from co-operative members during the next few days. The leaders of the Smallholders Party favoured moving within a few years to the abolition of the co-operative and the redistribution of all its lands. They were committed to their party's national manifesto, which promised full restitution of property rights on the basis of the 1947 situation (that is after the Land Reform and before the impact of socialist levelling and collectivisation). This platform had strong emotive appeal, but the practical problems with it in this region were numerous. Even the local Smallholders could see an injustice in reallocating a vineyard planted and worked by one family for a generation to some city-dweller or even foreign emigrant, just because the latter's father or grandfather had owned that land in 1947. It was suggested that in such cases, that is when the land had been improved and was in use as part of a family farm, the original owners should be offered compensation elsewhere. A few owners were not satisfied with this proposed compromise and were only interested in reclaiming their original fields.

When the new political activists in the Smallholders Party talk about adopting the principles of a western market economy, as they frequently do, what they actually have in mind is not the removal of state subsidies through the application of a pure 'market principle', but a vision of private property rights as substantiated in bourgeois political theory through the ages. Even the co-operative chairman agreed that it might be desirable to strengthen these private property rights, and the worst scenario of all, he told me, would be a long period of uncertainty in which no one had good incentives to improve and invest. However, I suspect that the majority of active farmers take a much less ideological stance. They are interested not so much in freehold possession as in good prices (and expectations remain comparatively high after the prosperity which they knew in the 1970s) and above all in a secure market for their products. Unfortunately the former stability in the wine trade in this region of Hungary was founded on large orders from undiscriminating buyers in East Germany and the USSR (where the Tázlár product had socialist value added to emerge as champagne!). These markets were near collapse by 1990, and with prices declining in real terms over the preceding five years many farmers were bitter. Some complained that they wanted to dispose of the vineyard plots which they had established jointly with the co-operative, but could not find a buyer at any price. These people were not impressed by the campaign for restoration of private property rights, and certainly not before they knew what their new tax liabilities on such land would be. Few were willing to gamble on the classical embourgeoisement recipe in the prevailing conditions; and perhaps some perceived clearly that one of the consequences of the elimination of the co-operative and the revival of a 'pure' land market would be pre-war patterns of polarisation on the labour market.

Such is my interpretation of certain events in the village which had taken place earlier in 1990, which I was not present to observe. It seems that the leading Smallholder activist (not himself a farmer, but a private motor mechanic) had canvassed support throughout the village for an attack on the co-operative leadership before its annual general meeting. In ones and twos he had amassed what he thought would be an unstoppable force, but when it came to the meeting no one was willing to join him in his public denunciation of the co-operative and the *status quo* was not significantly altered. He was chastened by this experience, attributing it to Tázlár's lack of cohesion in the past and an irrational resentment that any villager should assume a prominent leadership role. But it is also possible that this public reticence on the part of the villagers was based on a shrewd perception of where the unconditional endorsement of private property rights and a *piacgazdaság* would leave the greater part of the local population, and on a value system which was very different from that of Kornai and the new intellectual elites.

13.4 ETHNOGRAPHIC FRAGMENTS IN LIEU OF A CONCLUSION

Perhaps the most salient 'market' in contemporary rural Hungary concerns not the land but housing construction. In contrast to the cities, where the redistributive state played a significant (though never monopolistic) role for most of the socialist period, in the countryside this was always a key area for private enterprise (as well as diffuse networks of reciprocity). Small building firms flourished in the 1970s and 1980s and Tázlár possessed several. Size (some employed large numbers of labourers, others very few) and a reputation for quality tended to be inversely related, but I think the elements of competition and choice were widely appreciated throughout the community. I was therefore interested to hear criticisms of this market in 1990, particularly from some well-established entrepreneurs. Their reasons were set out as follows in an article in a Soltvadkert newspaper entitled 'The Small Businessman's Situation':

> In our large community at present 133 small businessmen are operating; in 98 cases it is their main occupation, whilst 25 are active alongside a waged-labour job, and 10 are officially pensioners… The number of licensed small builders is 25, among them 8 qualified bricklayers. These respectable tax-paying small businessmen are justifiably incensed by the fact that at least 25–30 'cowboys' [*kontár*] have been working for years on a full-time basis without authorisation. Because demand is dropping these are all the time representing stiffer competition and the established businesses are unable to compete effectively. Whilst an illegal operator rakes in profits, the honest businessman has to pay rates, national insurance, tax etc. and after all this he's lucky if 15 – 20 per cent is left

of his takings. The small businessmen can only campaign against this phenomenon through the organisation which has represented them collectively in the
past, with the aid and effective action of the tax inspectors...

Today it is open to everyone to become an entrepreneur, but for market
competition it is also essential to make sure they are subject to fair, equal
conditions... .[11]

There is clearly no shortage of entrepreneurial talent in rural Hungary. The phenomenon later analysed by Szelényi (1988) was obvious enough in Tázlár in the mid-1970s
and has remained conspicuous since. A good example is Jani (b.1949), great-grandson
of one of the first settlers in the nineteenth century. He had inherited some land, but
only in the form of vineyards since his family's large holdings had all been appropriated in the 1950s. In any case Jani was more interested in machines than in the soil.
After completing secondary education he took a vocational course and within a few
years (and still in his twenties) he was the proud owner of a private tractor. When I
first met him in 1976 he was competing efficiently with the co-operative in the
provision of mechanical services to farmers, and the additional purchase of a combine
harvester a few years later enabled him to offer a full range of services. He himself
preferred to work mainly on the maintenance side (the machines were usually old
models, scrapped from some state farm or *kolkhoz*, and parts were always a problem)
whilst assistants carried out the work in the fields. Without any significant advantage
in terms of inherited land (but with the very significant assistance of his wife, who
generated substantial income through small-scale farming in addition to holding a
wage-labour job in the village and bringing up the children) Jani succeeded within a
few years in re-establishing his family at a level of material superiority comparable to
that enjoyed previously by his forefathers. Perhaps I should stress that at no stage did
he have anything to do with the Communist Party.

This new wealth was not achieved without some cost. Both Jani and his wife
worked extremely hard, especially in the summer months. A few years ago he was
briefly hospitalised and he tries now to work less and to follow a healthier diet. He has
also had to put up with a certain amount of mockery and teasing precisely because he
has done so well financially: he has a nickname which suggests a person who is
excessively calculating, always with an eye on material advantage, with some connotations of deviousness and lack of normal sociability.

By 1990 Jani and his family had moved into an imposing new dwelling on the
outskirts of the village, where in the yard he had added a fodder supply shop to his
machine park. Business was satisfactory, he had retail outlets in neighbouring villages
as well, and was looking ahead to the possibility of establishing the community's very
first petrol station. He himself was now driving a brand new BMW – paid for in
forints handed over to a Hungarian émigré who returns frequently to the region, who
then dispatched the vehicle to Jani from Switzerland as a 'gift'.

Conversation was not easy on my first visit in 1990, mainly because the phone kept
ringing throughout the evening with news of important potential deals (mostly
agricultural equipment and the motor trade). Later we were entertained when two
drunks staggered into the fodder shop. Only one of these dishevelled characters was in

any state to talk at all, which he did with very limited vocabulary and what I took to be an alcohol-induced slur. The other occupied himself in front of a miror, moaning gently as he prodded his mouth with a number of small implements. I deduced that whatever he had consumed that evening it has not been enough to deaden the pain of ferocious toothache.

As I listened to a stream of banter over the next hour or so the reason for this visitation became clear. These men were Soviet Army officers, stationed at the barracks of Kiskunhalas about seven miles away. They had run up a very large bill at a restaurant in the town that afternoon, whilst bidding farewell to a colleague. Now they needed cash to pay their bill. To my surprise, when he had finally tired of teasing them, Jani took out his cash box and handed over the sum required. I caught only an oblique reference to goods in return as the Soviets drove off back to their restaurant.

In the next few days I saw soldiers in the village on a number of occasions – all in civilian dress, though sometimes travelling in military vehicles. In the 1970s I had never seen a soldier in Tázlár – only the tracks of tanks in the forests. Occasionally I had been woken by the rumble of a convoy on a night exercise, but there was little else to remind villagers of the proximity of a large Soviet base. Uniformed soldiers had been an occasional forlorn sight on the streets and in the coffee-bars of Kiskunhalas. I recall hearing rumours in the 1970s that some astute local traders had bartered alcohol for Soviet diesel fuel, but I had never found evidence for this. In short I ignored the presence of the Soviet military in my monograph because they seemed to have no detectable impact on village life.

By summer 1990 it had been decided that these soldiers were to return to the USSR, most of them before the year's end. The villagers seemed rather sorry for them, for it was commonly thought that they would have to survive the Soviet winter in tents. Meanwhile, of course, there were substantial material assets at bases all over Hungary, many of which could not be transported home. Hence the scope for an entrepreneur such as Jani, and it turned out that his dealings with the Soviets were already well known in the village. The joke was that sooner or later he would purchase a tank. (I heard from a number of sources, in all seriousness, that small arms had indeed been acquired in large numbers.) Jani had already acquired a military jeep, but that particular deal had almost ended in disaster. Apparently higher ranking officers for once refused to accept the fiction that a piece of equipment had been written off in an accident. When the jeep was discovered on the outlying family homestead (where Jani's father still resided) some substantial bribes had to be paid very quickly to avoid trouble.

On a more mundane level, Jani had managed to furnish his new holiday-home at a nearby beauty spot drawing on the unwanted stocks of the officers' mess in the Soviet base. Through his contacts he had also recruited private soldiers to work as day-labourers in his vineyards. Apparently they were only too keen to work, a change from their routine. They did not need to be paid as much as Hungarian day-labourers, the main thing for the hirer was to ensure a good alcohol supply. The ordinary soldiers drew little more benefit than booze from the arrangements, but for the officers contact with Jani offered them a chance to accumulate wealth (for example enough forints to purchase a second-hand Volga car) that might really make a difference after the return home to the USSR. Marrying a Hungarian girl was their main alternative strategy, but this was rare.

In the course of just a few days it was not possible for me to assess the strength of Jani's links with his Soviet suppliers, and I can hardly present this as a paradigmatic 'market' situation. I am not aware of any other Tázlár people with similar contacts. But I am quite sure that, whatever Jani's image in the community as a somewhat devious character who never looks beyond the immediate and short-term benefits of the transactions in which he is engaged, he had established a very solid basis of trust with his Soviet partners. This had already widened into a network that extended to other bases across the county. I think some enduring friendships had been formed, and I was told that Jani had taken his whole family as tourists to the Ukraine in the previous year, where they had been guests of the comrade with the toothache.

I did, of course, tackle Jani about the rockets story which I had heard on television and read about in the press, since it was allegedly at the Kiskunhalas barracks that this particular violation of moral propriety had been committed. He said that in his view the whole story was a fabrication, a myth put about in the media to discredit the Soviets. I think he wanted to imply that if anyone had put up some rockets for sale, he would certainly have known and been offered first option! Perhaps Jani's market information was not as good as he supposed. In any case it is plausible to suggest that this and other stories received the publicity they did in Hungary in summer 1990 because powerful interests wished to alter public perceptions of 'market' exchange. Although the direct impact of the anthropology of Polanyi on his native country has been negligible, his moral sensibility remains directly relevant to the present transition if only because a similar concept of the 'market principle' has been pushed so hard over the last few years by those dedicated to the rejection of the compromises of 'market socialism'. Thus the campaigns against foreigners who sell off unsuitable, inalienable objects can be seen as further skirmishes forming part of a gigantic political struggle throughout Eastern Europe. At least in the case of Hungary I suspect that for many years to come, and long after the Soviet troops have gone home, it will not be difficult to incite public opinion against 'the market'.

NOTES

1. See LeGrand and Elstrin (1989) for a stimulating recent collection and some guidance concerning the general literature. On market socialism in Hungary see Swain 1992.
2. For a comprehensive history of economic reform in socialist Hungary see Berend 1990.
3. It may be added that Kornai is by no means the most extreme or unrealistic commentator, and he has spoken out against a rapid privatisation which would dispose of state assets too cheaply. He favours what he calls an 'organic' transition in which the ratio of private property will be gradually increased. For a discussion of property relations in Hungary which aims to move beyond a simplistic public-private dichotomy see Hann 1992.
   The simplest and crudest representation of 'market economy' which I· found in the Hungarian press in 1990 came in an interview in a mass-circulation daily with a distinguished academic economist from my own institution:

D. M. Newbery, Head of Department, Cambridge University:

'Professor, what would you teach us East Europeans?'

'It's as clear as two times two: the most important thing is to be competitive... In order to create the market an entirely new way of thinking is needed. It is not enough to encourage market economy in the abstract, whilst holding back from risk-taking. It is not possible to liberalise an economy in half measures, just as it's not possible to make love and retain one's virginity...I tell you again, basic modes of thought have to be adjusted towards the market economy.' (*Népszabadság*, 5.5.1990, p.6)

4. On Polanyi see Polanyi-Levitt (1990); also Hann, forthcoming.

5. Thus she sums up recent changes in Eastern Europe as including 'the intention to decentralise economic and political decision-making, as well as to allow a much increased integrative role to the market' (1991:432).

6. I made most frequent use of two established media, *Népszabadság* ('People's Freedom'), the former Communist Party daily, which was transformed into a limited company in 1990 and actually succeeded in expanding its circulation; and *Heti Világgazdaság*, ('World Economy Weekly'), a lively news magazine specialising in economic affairs both at home and abroad, and likewise free of sectarian affiliation.

7. The etymology and associations of this expression may be of interest. The word *piac*, meaning market, is derived from the Italian *piazza*. *Gazdaság* can refer not only to a national economy but to a single farm; it is derived from *gazda*, which can also mean 'owner' and is the standard Hungarian term (though of Slav origin) for farmer.

8. Newspapers admitted that Hungarian citizens also benefited from the trading opportunities created by the opening of this Soviet border in 1990. The queues to cross were many miles long on both sides, and the days of waiting produced many ugly scenes (as elsewhere on East European borders in 1990). When the Soviet authorities moved to restrict traffic across this border they justified their action with reference to adverse economic effects; but there were complaints in the Hungarian press that restricting cross-border movements by Hungarian and Soviet citizens would simply strengthen the trading power of the Poles throughout the area.

9. Strictly speaking the specialist co-operatives were not formally constituted in Tázlár until 1968. Between 1960 and 1968 villagers joined 'production co-operative groups' but these in practice functioned just as the specialist co-operatives. Fertő et al. (1988) suggest that the delayed institutional emergence of these co-operatives in Tázlár was a factor in the village's relative backwardness when compared with neighbouring communities, where farmers were able to join a specialist co-operative from the beginning.

10. See Simó (ed.) 1987.

11. *Vadkerti Újság*, 1990, 2(5): 7–8. The word *kontár*, which I have translated as 'cowboy' in this passage, is given in the dictionary as 'amateur' – usually in the sense of 'bungler'. It is possibly related to the English counterfeit, and it was formerly used in Hungary to identify craftsmen who worked outside the framework of the guild. (Compare *Magyar Történelmi és Etimológiai Szótár*, Vol. 2 1970 Budapest: Akadémiai. pp.553–4.)

REFERENCES

Berend, I. T. 1990. *The Hungarian Economic Reforms, 1953-1988.* Cambridge: Cambridge University Press.

Bohannan, P. and G. Dalton (eds.), 1961 *Markets in Africa.* Evanstone: Northwestern University Press.

Fél, E. and T. Hofer, 1969. *Proper Peasants: Traditional Life in a Hungarian Village.* Chicago: Aldine.

Fertő, I. et al., 1988. 'Egy Forma Lehetőségei' [The Possibilities of A Form], *Gazdálkodás,* 32 (12):41–9.

Hann, C. M. 1979. 'A Frontier Community on the Great Plain', *New Hungarian Quarterly,* 20 (74): 116–22.

Hann, C. M. 1980. *Tázlár: a Village in Hungary.* Cambridge: Cambridge University Press.

Hann, C. M. 1985. *A Village Without Solidarity: Polish Peasants in Years of Crisis.* New Haven: Yale University Press.

Hann, C. M. 1992. 'Property Relations in the New Eastern Europe' in M. DeSoto and D. G. Anderson (eds.), *The Curtain Rises: Rethinking Culture, Ideology and the State in Eastern Europe.* New York: Humanities Press.

Hann, C. M. forthcoming, 'Radical Functionalism: the life and work of Karl Polanyi', *Dialectical Anthropology.*

Hann, C. M. (ed.), 1990. *Market Economy and Civil Society in Hungary.* London: Frank Cass.

Konrád, G. and I. Szelenyi, 1979. *The Intellectuals on the Road to Class Power.* Brighton: Harvester Press.

Kornai, J. 1990. *The Road to a Free Economy.* New York: W.W. Norton.

LeGrand, J. and S. Elstrin (eds.), 1989. *Market Socialism.* Oxford: Oxford University Press.

Polanyi, K. 1944. *The Great Transformation.* Boston: Beacon Books.

Polanyi, K. *et al.* (eds.), 1957. *Trade and Markets in the Early Empires.* New York: Free Press.

Polanyi-Levitt, K. (ed.), 1990. *The Life and Work of Karl Polanyi.* Montreal: Black Rose Books.

Potter, S. H. and J. M. Potter, 1990. *China's Peasants.* Cambridge: Cambridge University Press.

Simó, T. (ed.), 1987. *Szakszövetkezetek Bács-Kiskun Megyében* [Specialist Co-operatives in Bács-Kiskun County]. Kecskemét: Kiskunsági Mezőgazdasági Szövetkezetek Területi Szövetsége.

Stewart, M. 1990. 'Gypsies, Work and Civil Society', in C. M. Hann (ed.), *op.cit* 140–62.

Swain, N. 1992. *Hungary: The Rise and Fall of Feasible Socialism.* London: Verso.

Szelényi, I. 1988. *Socialist Entrepreneurs; Embourgeoisement in Rural Hungary.* Cambridge: Polity.

Verdery, K. 1991. 'Theorizing Socialism: A Prologue to the Transition', *American Ethnologist,* 18 (3): 419–39.

Market, Plan and Structured Social Inequality in China

NORMAN STOCKMAN

14.1 VISIONS OF ECONOMIC CO-ORDINATION IN SOCIALIST SOCIETIES

Just as in all other complex societies, in all socialist societies, whether really existing or merely imagined, the problem of the co-ordination of economic action has to be addressed, even if not explicitly. Since socialism may be minimally delimited from capitalism by its rejection of reliance on the 'blind' working of the market mechanism, the problem of co-ordination is, or could be, raised at a higher level of societal self-consciousness than would be the case in any reasonably close approximation to an ideal-typical capitalist society, were any such society to exist. Possible answers to the problem of co-ordination could be advanced and debated with reference to desired societal goals or conceptions of a good society. Institutions of co-ordination, once established, could be assessed or judged as adequate or inadequate in terms of the degree to which they were conducive to the attainment of such goals. Furthermore, if such institutions of co-ordination were to fall below that level of societal self-consciousness, to become themselves 'blindly' working mechanisms operating on internally generated criteria and withdrawn from the possibility of social criticism, this fact in itself would be a signal that the project of socialism had become distorted, abandoned or forgotten. Whether such an enlightenment ideal of a transparent or 'rational' society is socially possible remains an open question.

Really existing socialist societies have developed institutions of co-ordination which can be analysed as variations or combinations of two types: the institutions of state-directed central planning and the institutions of market socialism. Neither of these sets of institutions has as yet turned out to be particularly satisfactory, when judged against a variety of societal goals or images of a good society. (It remains to be seen whether the institutions of economic co-ordination developed in certain 'no-longer-really-existing-socialist' societies prove to be any more satisfactory in these respects.) In particular, as will be the primary concern of this chapter, neither institutional form has fully measured up to the socialist goal of the radical reduction of the degree of structured social inequality that existed in pre-socialist societies. It is generally recognised that structured social inequality of various kinds continues to be a prominent feature of the social structure of socialist societies. It may also be suggested that different aspects of structured social inequality are brought to the fore, depending at least in part on which institutions of economic co-ordination are more in evidence in a given society at a given time. Thus, to put it crudely, in market socialist societies, structured inequalities of wealth and income derived from differential market positions are more accentuated, while in centrally planned economies, inequalities of positional power derived from differential hierarchical rank in the organs of the party and of state administration are particularly significant. [1] This is of course not to say that both such forms of inequality are not found in both types of socialist economy, nor is it to deny that convertibility of societal resources allows for the transfer of advantages from one sphere to another; the contrast is a matter of degree, but no less significant for all that. Nor, it hardly needs to be said, does this imply that yet other aspects of structured social inequality do not remain prominent.

In China, since 1949, both types of institution of co-ordination, those of central planning and of market socialism, have been on the agenda both in theoretical discussions and in practical policies. After the immediate post-liberation period of 'new democracy', institutions of central planning were established under the influence and advice of Soviet comrades, while continually subjected to criticism from more market-oriented Chinese economists and politicians; such critics were rewarded for their thoughtful suggestions by being branded as 'rightists' from 1957 onwards, pushed into obscurity and even jailed. In the period since the Third Plenum of the Eleventh Central Committee in 1978, those market-oriented critics have been rehabilitated and have come to prominence, their critical writings of the 1950s and 1960s have been published and widely discussed (Halpern 1987; Hsu 1985), and institutions of market socialism have begun to be introduced. None the less, much of the formal apparatus of central planning has been retained (White 1988a). The consequences of these different emphases in the institutions of co-ordination for the structure of social inequalities (rather than their economic feasibility [Nove 1983]) will be one theme to be explored in this chapter.

As the contributors to the volume edited by Dorothy Solinger (Solinger 1984; see also Van Ness 1989) convincingly argue, however, these two visions of socialist society have not been the only ones that have coexisted in China in the last half-century. There has been a third image, that promoted by Mao Zedong and his associates, in which criticism and suspicion of both central planning and of any kind of markets, socialist or otherwise, has been expressed, and an alternative, in some ways more radical, conception of the problem of economic co-ordination and its relation to structured social inequality has been formulated. The second theme of this chapter will be an attempt to interpret in sociological terms this third, 'Maoist' alternative, and its relation to the two more 'orthodox' conceptions of socialism. The question of continuity from pre-socialist times in indigenous Chinese cultural interpretations of markets and marketing will be raised towards the end of the chapter. Suspicion of markets has a long history in official Chinese thinking, and there are echoes of that official thinking in Maoist social imagery, and to some extent also in that of proponents of state planning.

These three 'visions of socialism', which some writers refer to with the shorthand (and no doubt misleading) terms of 'Stalinism', 'Titoism' and 'Maoism' (Friedman

1982) must be thought of as just that, as 'visions' or images of a socialist society, or, sociologically speaking, as conceptually pure types; they have never been realised in their purity, certainly not in China, and presumably nowhere else either. They cannot therefore be interpreted as 'phases' in the history of China since 1949, as if there had been, for example, a 'Stalinist' phase from 1955 to 1958, a 'Maoist' phase from 1959 to 1976 (or 'Maoist' phases from 1959 to 1961 and from 1966 to 1976) and a 'Titoist' phase since 1978, however tempting and pedagogically useful such a simplified device might be. Even though one of these three visions might be dominant at a given time, even though one vision might form the 'official line' in terms of propaganda output, the actual institutions of economic co-ordination have, for the whole post-liberation period, been constituted by a complex interweaving of different tendencies, from which Solinger et al.'s 'three visions' can only be extracted analytically. The two-line conflict of the 'socialist road' and the 'capitalist road' did take place, of course (Gray 1973), but it was always a polemical simplification, and its conversion into a 'three line' struggle goes only a short way to capture the underlying complexities. The upshot of these reflections is that it is sociologically illegitimate to use differences in the pattern of structured social inequality at different times since 1949 as direct and conclusive evidence of the social structural effects of pursuing different 'lines' of policy. The data can be illustrative of such variation, but no more than that.

14.2 PLANNED ECONOMY AND PLANNED INEQUALITIES

The planning mechanism in China was establised in the early 1950s on lines initially borrowed from the Soviet Union. It formed part of a general centralised system of state administration operating on the branch principle of organisation, with administrative units linked hierarchically according to functional principles (Schurmann 1968:175), though this branch hierarchy was soon modified by various measures of decentralisation. This complex hierarchical system of organisation formed a hierarchy of roles, whose occupants were supplied with varying degrees of positional power, which we may conceive of as the right to issue commands, or to relay commands emanating from higher levels, with a chance that these commands would be carried out. Especially after early moves towards decentralisation to the regional level, when regional party committees took on the role of co-ordinating the policies of numerous ministries as they affected the particular regions, the hierarchy of state administration became intertwined with that of the Communist Party, and the party organs took over from functionally specific control systems the role of ensuring conformity at local levels to centrally generated state plans.

Associated with the planning mechanism in the early years was an attempt to introduce the Soviet system of industrial organisation known as 'one-man management'. According to this system, managers are given specific production targets to meet, together with the authority over workers to ensure that work is carried out in such a way that targets are met. Articles from 1953 stress the necessity for hierarchical systems of managerial authority peaking at the single factory manager in order to ensure efficient implementation of the plan (Schurmann 1968:253ff). The management hierarchy, again a hierarchy of roles furnished with different levels of positional power, would be staffed by people with different degrees of technical expertise. One-man management was seen as functionally related to the system of central planning.

The hierarchical structure of positional power was paralleled by a planned structure of income differentiation. In 1955 a wage structure for all state workers and staffs was introduced: government cadres were divided into twenty-six grades, technicians into seventeen grades, and workers into eight grades (Riskin 1987:64; Parish 1984:87). The span of income differentiation ranged from Y30 to Y560 among government cadres; an official guideline for top and bottom wages in an enterprise set a ratio of 6:1 or 7:1 (Howe 1973:36). Piece-rate systems were also used in the early years of planned industrialisation.

In the countryside, land reform had redistributed large areas of land, eliminating landlordism, but retaining considerable inequalities between 'rich' and 'poor' peasants: the average farm size of the former was nearly three times that of the latter in 1954 (Riskin 1987:67). Rich peasants were intially seen as the best potential for agricultural development and the source of investment funds for industrial development, and the distribution of agricultural produce was initially left to the market. Early results of this policy were held to be disappointing, however, and peasants came increasingly under the authority of state administration. They were encouraged to form mutual-aid teams and then agricultural producer co-operatives, and this encouragement came to take on elements of pressure and coercion (Shue 1980). Since the proportion of produce marketed by peasants was falling, a system of compulsory state purchase quotas was set up in 1953. I am not so much concerned here with the economic success of these developments (which was not impressive), as with the incorporation of the peasantry into a hierarchical structure of power which increasingly constrained the life chances of rural inhabitants. This was accentuated by collectivisation, which 'for the first time subjected virtually the entire peasantry to direct control of productive activities by the government' (Riskin 1987:91), and by the system of residence registration combined with controls, through the mechanism of rationing of basic necessities, over geographical mobility (Potter 1983).

The planning mechanism also reinforced material inequalities between rural and urban inhabitants, despite official pronouncements on the priority to be given to agriculture. This can be seen in the proportion of national investment directed into agriculture, which remained comparatively low except in periods of agricultural crisis (Riskin 1987:238), and also in the 'scissors gap' in the structure of relative prices of agricultural and industrial products, by which administered prices were used by the state as a means to withdraw resources from agriculture to support industrialisation (Riskin 1987:242). The consequences of these planning policies are evident in the discrepancies between rural and urban incomes and levels of consumption, although it must always be stressed that highly aggregated data conceal wide variations between and within regions.

This extremely abbreviated sketch of the structure of inequality built in to the mechanism of the centrally planned economy, and thus backed by the institutionalised power of the state, does not, of course, even in principle exhaust the forms of inequality generated by the plan. One aspect of inequality of especial interest here concerns the convertibility of resources, and particularly the use of positional power to gain material advantages. The relatively narrow spans of income differentiation associated with organisational hierarchy resulted in cadres having official salaries, consumption patterns and housing provision which did not markedly diverge from that of workers; but the possibility of using hierarchical power to gain advantages through illegal and semi-legal methods was ever-present, even if it does not show up in official statistics. As Hinton put it: 'Anything created by a peasant who lives in the administrative sphere of a higher official, if it will enhance the latter's career, can be moved, removed, manipulated, or expropriated by that official just as if he were the lord of a feudal fief' (Hinton 1982:114). Higher officials in China also had various privileges, such as access to special shops; but such privileges may be distinguished from previously mentioned opportunities to the extent that they were less likely to be defined as illegal and subjected to control in, for example, a campaign to clear up corruption. It is sociologically important to distinguish between those advantages of positional power that are given backing by the institutionalised power of the state, and those that are arrogated despite not being given that backing.

Finally, it is also imperative to refer to another form of structured social inequality whose existence is known to everyone but which is most difficult to capture through research, namely inequalities generated through the differential distribution of those resources which Bourdieu calls 'social capital' and which Kreckel terms 'selective association'. In any society, advantages may be conferred and disadvantages incurred by individuals' and groups' location within patterns of private social interaction. In centrally planned economies, it has been argued, such patterns of interaction take on a particular significance, since they form the basis for getting things done within the interstices of the plan, in the absence of the possibility of making market transactions. Thus factory managers will use 'connections' to get access to materials not allocated to their factories through the plan; and individuals will use 'connections' to gain access to foods or consumer goods which the planned distribution system would otherwise make scarce or unobtainable; and so on. In China in particular, such patterns of interaction are given a specific cultural flavour by the fact that particularistic orientations to social interaction, which legitimate the use of connections (or what in Chinese are called 'guanxi') to gain advantages for individuals or, more especially, for groups such as families, have never been eroded by 'modern' universalism. Thus, in China, people are even more likely than elsewhere to think in terms of mobilising connections when in search of some improvement to their life-chances or of some means to defend themselves against a worsening of them. It follows that those best placed to operate in this way, those with the greatest stock of 'social capital' (whether inherited or acquired), will best be able to convert those resources into other advantages, whether material or relational. I will come back to this point later in this chapter.

14.3 MARKET MECHANISM AND UNPLANNED INEQUALITIES

Since 1978, market mechanisms, so long rejected as inappropriate to a socialist society, have been introduced in various sectors of the Chinese economy. In the urban-industrial economy, moves have been made to bring in market criteria in the allocation of capital, in the recruitment and circulation of labour, and in the exchange of commodities; in all these areas, resistance to and obstacles in the way of the establishment of markets are strong, and much of the planning mechanism remains intact (White 1988a). In the rural economy, the contract responsibility system and the partial dismantling of the state compulsory grain purchase system have also gone some way towards the 'marketisation' of agricultural activity, though here again the implementation of markets is only partial, and peasants and cadres find themselves operating in an uncertain and fluctuating situation 'between plan and market' (Oi 1986a, 1986b, 1989; Prybyla 1986).

Apart from considerations of macro-economic dynamism and micro-economic efficiency, the economic reforms were envisaged by political leaders to have consequences for the structure of social inequality in Chinese society. These envisaged consequences were, however, complex, and it is necessary to distinguish between consequences in the sphere of material inequalities and those in the sphere of positional power and hierarchy. The slogans which are used to refer to reform objectives in relation to inequality already make this distinction clear: among the proclaimed aims of reform have been the abolition of 'commandism' and 'egalitarianism'. However, in the case of the former at least, the situation is by no means clear cut.

As far as the distribution of material resources is concerned, the explicit intention is to widen the span between low and high incomes. Deng Xiaoping has spoken of the objective of creating 200 million wealthy Chinese; the clear implication is that the other four-fifths of the population would be relatively less wealthy, though of course the suggestion is that the economic dynamism led by the activities of the most innovative and talented people (for which they must be given due incentives and due reward) will eventually have beneficial consequences for the absolute level of well-being of the whole population. At least four categories of people were to be given the opportunity to become rich first: peasants who are most successful in taking advantage of the contract responsibility system, by contracting for more land and efficiently producing high-value produce for sale on the market, especially by specialising in particular lines of production; private entrepreneurs who are most successful in establishing industrial or commercial businesses, hiring labour and making profits; managers of efficient and successful state-owned enterprises; and workers whose skills are scarce or whose work-intensity is high, who would benefit from wider income-differentials in industrial enterprises. Initial experience of the implementation of the reforms have proved that these accentuated inequalities of income have indeed been forthcoming, although it must also be stressed that urban–rural inequalities have, at least at the aggregate level of average incomes, been narrowed by the effects of the reforms (Trescott 1985, Ghose 1987; Nolan and Paine 1987, Nolan and Dong 1990). The pages of Chinese newspapers and foreign language magazines such as *Beijing*

Review came to be full of stories of successful businessmen and of enterprising rural households, references to millionaires became not uncommon, and Chinese sociologists began to debate the emergence of a new capitalist class (He Jianzhang et al. 1988), before the events of 1989 placed severe contraints on independent critical social analysis.

The situation as far as positional power is concerned is more complex. The attack on 'commandism' referred in particular to the positional power of local cadres to determine the economic activity of producers. This can be seen most clearly in the case of rural labour. Before the reforms, the individual peasant's labour was managed by the production team leader; in addition, labour (and other production team resources) could be commandeered by higher levels of the commune organisation to carry out brigade or commune work. The reforms first increased the autonomy of production teams in dealing with brigade or commune authorities, and then increased the autonomy of each individual household to determine the nature of its economic activity. Thus 'hierarchical relations within the communes have been replaced by contractual relations' (Ghose 1987:63). Cadres have lost a considerable amount of their formal positional power.

As Oi has argued, however, cadres have not completely lost the advantages they gain from their position. While they may no longer be able to exercise powers of command over the peasants in their areas, the fact that they are tied in to networks of association derived from their location in the former structure of power means they are well placed to secure benefits from this. Thus some cadres have themselves used their positions to become heads of successful specialist households; while others use their connections to gain privileged access to farm inputs which they can then make available to farmers to their own advantage (Oi 1986b, 1989). This is just one example of the continued importance of selective association as a source of social inequalities in China.

In urban industry, however, the consequences of market reforms for the structure of positional power are different. Here, the reformers believe that increased microeconomic efficiency requires greater managerial power in enterprises; enterprise managers need to be able to choose which workers to employ, to be able to fire workers whose work may be poor or who become surplus to the enterprise's requirements, and to be able to dispose labour within the enterprise in any way that may be technically most effective. Even though trends in these directions are not proceeding as fast as some reformers or managers may wish, it none the less seems that an increase in the positional power of enterprise managers is likely to prove a concomitant to the extension of the market mechanism in the co-ordination of Chinese industry (White 1988b:196f).

14.4 THE MAOIST VISION AND THE VICISSITUDES OF EGALITARIANISM

In the preceding two sections, I have lightly sketched out some of the forms of structured social inequality associated with central planning and the market mechanism, respectively. The time has come to cast a glance at the third 'vision' of socialism in China, the Maoist, or 'radical' vision.

In relation to central planning and market mechanisms, the essence of the Maoist vision has been negative, subjecting both forms of economic co-ordination to critique. The critique of central planning, often directed against Stalinist practice in the Soviet Union and as a warning against its emulation in China, centred on the growth of an all-powerful and all-pervasive bureaucracy of planners and administrators. The organisational hierarchy of bureaucratic positions, the hierarchy of work-grades and its associated hierarchy of salaries and privileges, created new vested interest groups whose power derived from their control over the means of production as well as from their occupancy of positions of state power. Combined with a concern for the transmission of the privileges of cadres to their children, this critique of the arrogation of power easily became a theory of the emergence of a new class (Esherick 1979:62ff; Kraus 1981:143ff).

The critique of the market, even of markets within socialism, centred on their promotion of attitudes of selfishness and profit-seeking, and their engendering of material inequalities. The market 'was considered to be the embodiment of capitalism and the antithesis of socialism; even minor rural market activities and peasant sideline production for local markets were criticised as the "tails of capitalism"' (Hsu 1985:437). In the early and mid-1970s, when radicals were at their most influential, local agricultural markets were placed under severe restrictions or even closed altogether (Chan and Unger 1982:459). Maoists opposed reliance on material incentives that would be encouraged by market mechanisms (even more so than by centrally planned wage scales) as distracting from political consciousness and collective interest which were thought to motivate socialist development (Esherick 1979:59). Markets would do nothing to lessen the inequalities in Chinese society, especially those referred to as the 'three great differences' (between city and countryside, worker and peasant, and mental and manual labour); in fact, the free play of market forces would increase those differences, channelling resources towards urban areas and industry, and increasing the relative wages of skilled workers.

Although Maoist radicalism runs as a thread of social and economic thought throughout the whole post-1949 period, and although it is clearly not yet dead despite official condemnation after 1978, there was no time at which this third vision held sufficient sway to eclipse any other conception of socialist society, especially the view of the central planners. Thus, as mentioned earlier, it is difficult to take any phase in China's recent history as a source of evidence for the consequences of the Maoist vision for the structure of social inequality, not even the highpoint of the Cultural Revolution. In fact, if some commentators are to be believed, the Maoists actually had no answer to the question of economic co-ordination and developed no specific institutions to fill the gap that would have been left had there been neither central planning nor markets (Riskin 1987:203). The Maoist vision was embodied in two slogans, both deriving from the Yan'an revolutionary era: 'self-reliance' and 'egalitarianism'. The former was the very antithesis of economic co-ordination, enjoining localities and regions to follow their own development strategies, drawing on their local resources, raw materials and human labour, to raise production by the sheer exercise of will. It is now generally thought to have generated considerable disorganisation, and to have repeatedly required the renewed corrective of centralised planning (Riskin 1987:203f). Egalitarianism, especially the attack on the three great differences, did produce consequences for the distribution of income, although ones that are difficult to disentangle from those attributable to the planning system. Measures of the distribution of per capita household income in the 1970s show China to have achieved a degree of social equality at the more equal end of the scale among other socialist societies (Parish 1984:89ff), and much more equal than comparable low-income countries (Riskin 1987:248ff); these measures are reinforced by data on access to housing and levels of consumption. However, as Riskin (among others) argues, in some respects the values of self-reliance and egalitarianism run counter to each other, for the weakening of central mechanisms for redistributing resources between localities and regions made it difficult for the state to redress regional inequalities and urban-rural inequalities, which remained high (Riskin 1987:236ff).

Even if Maoism had succeeded in having greater impact on the formal structures of inequality that comprised the three great differences, and reduced the hierarchically organised positional power of cadres and bureaucrats, two other sources of social inequality would have remained significant, as indeed they did so remain in the actual conditions of China during the Cultural Revolution. The first of these has already been discussed: the informal, private, unofficial sources of inequality deriving from asymmetries in the structures of selective association. It can indeed be argued that in the absence of viable institutions of economic co-ordination, informal mechanisms become even more significant and, it might be said, functionally necessary for co-ordinating different spheres of economic activity;[2] and in these circumstances those who have greater resources in the form of location in social networks, connections and *guanxi* will be best placed to benefit from the situation (Chan and Unger 1982: Oi 1985, 1989; Walder 1986; Zafanolli 1988; Yang 1989). Second, the radical vision, by 'putting politics in command' and stressing moral and political incentives rather than material ones, places a high premium on politico-moral judgements of personal worth. Life chances will be differentially distributed not on the basis of technical skills or intellectual abilities (this is what radicals rejected as the survival of 'bourgeois right' [Esherick 1979:60ff]), but on the basis of political and moral 'virtue'. Shirk has coined the term 'virtuocracy' to refer to a society where life chances are allocated according to judgements of virtue, and has analysed the dynamics of contests for virtue during the Cultural Revolution (Shirk 1982,1984). The state, especially during the period when radicals had most influence, but also during the earlier post-revolutionary years, generated forms of discrimination which were supposed to be legitimate by allocating people and families to 'class status' and other categories on the basis of their revolutionary virtue. Even during the 1980s, elements of virtuocratic principles can be seen, for example, in the list of criteria used to allocate housing in a Beijing factory (Yang 1989:29). In this list, categories of the morally deserving, such as 'Those old cadres who participated in the Revolution before the establishment of the country', or 'Those who have been chosen municipal model workers', appear as accruing points for determining priority in housing allocation.

14.5 THE IMMORALITY OF MARKETS: CULTURAL CONTINUITIES

It is clear that both advocates of central planning and Maoists were concerned to restrict severely or even to eliminate the role of markets in the Chinese economy and society. It would be easy to read this as a purely Marxist orientation, as a rejection of the 'anarchic', unplanned character of capitalist markets. And, of course, that is in part what it was. But only in part. For, as was hinted earlier in this chapter, it is also possible to see a cultural continuity in Chinese suspicion of markets, which has a long historical pedigree.

Chinese society has long been a relatively highly commoditised society. Money has been used for a wide range of transactions, including symbolic transactions with ancestors. Many monetary instruments were first developed in China. Many people were perfectly accustomed to using money to supply some of their needs. There was a complex network of local markets, periodical markets, temple fairs, and so on (Skinner 1964–5).

Despite this, commerce was stigmatised in traditional China. In the Confucian social hierarchical classification of the 'four peoples'(*simin*), merchants were ranked last, below scholars, farmers and craftsmen. Whatever their need to encourage marketing activity as a basis for taxation, imperial governments were inclined to see markets as sources of disorder and immorality (Mann 1987). Markets were places where merchants made money, and they could possibly make so much money that they were significantly wealthier than their social superiors, thus introducing a disturbing element of status inconsistency into the social hierarchy. The inequalities that marketing activity could generate might also be felt by farmers and craftsmen to be illegitimate, and might be an occasion for social disturbance and conflict. The profits of marketing might be perceived as deriving from immoral practices, such as speculation, adulteration of goods or price-fixing.

Thus, from the point of view of Confucian-trained scholar-officials, marketing could easily offend against two of the highest social values: order and morality. The greatest social evil in the Confucian canon was disorder or chaos (*luan*), and to the extent that markets were a possible source of disorder, they were suspect. It was therefore necessary to control them, and this is exactly what imperial authorities attempted to do, although often with inadequate resources. For centuries, Chinese governments had laid down regulations governing market transactions, and it has been argued that the primary function of legislation concerning marketing was to ensure the orderly conduct of their proceedings (Gernet 1957; MacCormack 1990). Markets were to be registered, traders were supposed to be licensed, prices were controlled, inspectors guarded against adulteration and deceitful weighing of goods. As Susan Mann shows, since the Qing state was mostly unable to afford to staff such an apparatus of control, it relied instead on 'liturgical' methods by which market control and even taxation was entrusted to merchant organisations (Mann 1987).

From the point of view of farmers and other villagers, on the other hand, markets had a different, though corresponding value, namely as a source of excitement. Markets were sought out for their noise, bustle, sociability, fun – all the characteristics evoked by the Chinese term *renao*. Anthropological accounts of marketing activity in twentieth-century Taiwan have stressed this aspect of markets, and appealed to such 'deviations' from the model of 'rational economic man' to explain why an apparently ideal site for a standard marketing town was not actually very popular.

> There is no question about the fact that central towns with their gaudy streets, bustling crowds, blaring moviehouse sound tracks, and the even chance they afford to witness a funeral, a fight, or the girls in a teahouse, are eminently more appealing to the Taiwanese than the dusty streets, tawdry shops, and sleeping dogs that typify standard towns. (Crissman 1972:243)

The reference to the opportunity to watch (or take part in?) a fight is evidence of exactly that which officials and local figures of authority were worried about: the potential for disorder inherent in the social occasion of marketing. It has also been suggested that market towns formed the basis for lineage and inter-lineage organisation of militias and of revolt, such as in the case of resistance to the British occupation of the Hong Kong New Territories in 1899 (Groves 1969).

It is clear that traditional cultural orientations to marketing, especially on the part of the apparatus of authority, make available to modern Chinese communist leaders a rhetoric which justifies severe control and restriction of marketing activity. It is the imagery of marketing as disorderly and immoral that is easily given a Marxist gloss by Chinese Stalinists and Maoists alike, and provides them with a powerful rhetoric against proponents of markets, socialist or otherwise (Solinger 1983, 1984). It is not difficult to show that there is an elective affinity between aspects of Chinese traditional culture and the anti-market stance of western Marxism. Whereas in the case of the party bureaucrats who took over from Soviet planners the models and procedures of economic planning, this elective affinity shows itself more in the rhetoric of the market as disorder and anarchy, in the case of Maoists this imagery is overlaid by a vision of the market as amoral, encouraging selfish and self-seeking behaviour. The answer is to encourage a commitment to 'serve the people'.

14.6 SYSTEM AND LIFEWORLD: AN INTERPRETATION
OF MAOIST EGALITARIANISM

In the final section of this chapter, I want briefly to suggest a more abstract sociological interpretation of the third, Maoist, vision of socialism, its relation to the other two, and its implications for structured social inequality. In this section, I draw on Jürgen Habermas's distinction between 'system' and 'lifeworld' developed as key concepts of his 'theory of communicative action' (Habermas 1987).

According to Habermas, it is fruitful to distinguish between two levels of the co-ordination of social action. In the lifeworld, 'social integration' is achieved by the co-ordination of action-orientations, in which participants in interaction draw upon the taken-for-granted stock of culture to achieve mutual understanding. Small-scale, localised, traditional societies can be integrated in this way. In the course of social evolution, however, more differentiated and larger-scale societies come into existence which require co-ordination of action at a level beyond that of the locality. Mechanisms of 'system integration' are required, which co-ordinate action-systems through the delinguistified steering media of money and power. Although these systems must remain anchored in the lifeworld (and sociological access to them, as Habermas has long argued, remains bound to the hermeneutic conditions of communication), the action-systems of the economy and the state (steered by the media of money and power) must also be 'uncoupled' from the lifeworld. Action ceases to be solely governed by the traditional norms of the local community, but becomes increasingly purposive-rational, responding to institutionalised system-imperatives whose mechanisms are not understandable within the terms of the lifeworld.

From this point, Habermas can reformulate the Marxist critique of reification. As the systems of the economy and the state become uncoupled from the lifeworld, they also increasingly penetrate the lifeworld. Instead of associating the problem of reification with rationalisation as such, 'reification should be connected to ways in which the "functional conditions of system reproduction" in modern societies impinge upon and undermine the rational foundation of communicative action in the lifeworld' (Giddens 1985:106). The task of critical theory is then to rescue the lifeworld from the pathological conquest of it by system imperatives, or at least to defend it against further colonisation, a task which Habermas associates with the 'new social movements' of western societies.

My suggestion is that there is an underlying correspondence between Habermas's critique of the conquest of the lifeworld by the imperatives of the economy and the state, and Maoist criticisms of both market socialism ('the capitalist road') and central planning. The language of Maoist social theory is superficially quite different from Habermas's, being tied to a rather crude version of 'positivistic' Marxism. But the distinctive Chinese context in which Marxism was appropriated and 'sinified' may well have been favourable to a similar kind of theoretical endeavour, and to attempts to realise it in practice.

It has often been argued that a distinctive feature of traditional Chinese society was its relatively low level of structural differentiation. Commonly, as in Parsons's account of social evolution, this has been seen in terms of a relative lack of differentiation of societal sub-systems (Parsons 1966:71ff). Now, using Habermas's alternative evolutionary framework, it can be suggested that what was peculiar to traditional Chinese society was a relatively low degree of the uncoupling of system and lifeworld. Despite the large size of China's territory, and despite the networks of markets referred to above, economic activity to a considerable extent remained confined to the environment of the village; China's economy was a 'cellular' one, made up of very large numbers of similar villages whose inhabitants are mainly concerned with subsistence production and consumption (Donnithorne 1972; Shue 1988). Such economic activity can, to some considerable degree, be co-ordinated within the lifeworld, drawing on a shared stock of cultural orientations with interaction based on mutual understanding. Chinese peasants have, until relatively recently, not been drawn to any great extent into a market economy, nor was the local texture of their lives penetrated by the authoritative command of state bureaucracy (Huang 1985:219 and *passim*). Or, using Habermas's framework, one could say that peasants have not been greatly incorporated into systems steered by the delinguistified media of money and power.

This is of course not to deny that the Chinese economy had become increasingly commodified, especially since the Song dynasty; nor is it to deny that the Chinese had rather precociously developed complex bureaucratic state institutions, especially since the establishment of the civil service examination system during the Tang. But these 'systems' were only partially uncoupled from the 'lifeworld'. An indication of this is the extent to which Chinese social theory remained caught in essentially moral categories. There was indeed a tradition of state theory, namely 'Legalism', which operated at a purely strategic, non-normative level, and which advocated the ruler's use of stratagems of power to maintain his dominance over his rivals and subordinates. But this tradition, founded before the unification of the empire in the third century BC, came to be associated with the dictatorial rule of the first Qin emperor, and its prescriptions were much softened in later years. More typical of Chinese social theory was the tradition of Confucius, in which ethical considerations, enjoining the correct way of life of the 'gentleman', were at the heart of the theory of society, and in which the empire was conceived very much as the family writ large. Until Chinese intellectuals of a reformist persuasion began to import western economic, political and social theory at the turn of the century, social theorising about 'systems' was not highly developed, which I take as a symptom of the relative lack of 'uncoupling' of system and lifeworld in Chinese society.

In the twentieth century all this began to change. In the closing years of the empire and in the republican period, market relationships increasingly penetrated into the countryside, enforcing the calculus of money on social relationships to a greater extent than had ever hitherto been known. Often this brought foreign competition to traditional products and encouraged further differentiation and stratification. The reach of the state also began to become wider and deeper, although the republican state did not have the resources, either allocative or authoritative, to make its presence fully felt. During the early years of the People's Republic, the new state did, to a greater extent, develop the resources to enforce its commands, and peasants found themselves more and more subject to systems of power uncoupled from their taken-for-granted lifeworlds. And again, these systems were essentially characterised by asymmetries and inequalities which had no place within the existing categories of the lifeworld.

Mao's reaction to this increasing level of 'systemness' in Chinese society can, I want to suggest, be seen as a reassertion of the need for the co-ordination of economic action to be rooted in the principles of the lifeworld. Briefly, three aspects of Mao's thought suggest such an interpretation. First, the slogan of 'putting politics in command' can be seen as an attack on a society steered by blindly working mechanisms, whether of the market or of the administrative state. No aspect of social organisation should be governed by principles withdrawn from the possibility of political discussion and criticism. Second, Mao's interpretation of the 'mass line' emphasises the crucial role of communication between the leadership and the masses in the building of a socialist society. In a way that can be read as a sinified version of the early critique by Lukács of Leninism (always one of the basic spurs to Habermas's theorising), Mao sees social organisation in terms of a continual dialogue between the party and the people, in which the aim is to reach mutual understanding and agreement (Starr 1979:147ff). Third, Mao's emphasis on the need to build socialism on the ethical principles of selflessness, self-reliance, persistence, honesty and faith (Starr 1979:224ff) is evidence of a social theory which, true to Confucian traditions, prefers to operate at the level of the lifeworld rather than that of systems.

A social theory which remains bound to the communicative categories of the lifeworld does, however, face difficulties in grasping the complexities of large-scale differentiated societies. Mao's critiques of central planning and market socialism, more true to the Marx of *The German Ideology* than were most other Marxists of his generation, thus appear in the form of a critique of social differentiation as such. Rejecting system integration either through the medium of money or that of power, and the structured social inequality that would thereby be generated, and unable to imagine any other form of integration of large-scale societies, he is forced back, under the slogan of 'self-reliance', to conceptions of undifferentiated and self-sufficient local societies, socially integrated through 'new' patterns of mutual understanding. This feature of Mao's social thought has not gone unremarked, though Habermas's distinction between system and lifeworld has not previously been available to provide a theoretical interpretation. Thus Brantly Womack uses conventional structural–functional language to suggest that Mao's '"uninterrupted revolution" can be viewed as a rejection of the structural prerequisites of a complex society, a rejection nostalgically based on a successful experience of an undifferentiated revolutionary community' (Womack 1984:420), and he goes on to argue that Mao's successors distinguish themselves by their acknowledgement of social and economic complexity. Bienkowski uses a different language to make a similar point:

> Thanks to the revolution, China reverted to the road carved out by its traditions and cleared it of alien accretions; it is restoring, or perhaps it is only now that it wants to realise consistently, a natural form of classless society. (A classless society in the marxist sense is the end product of class society; 'natural' classlessness results from the checking of processes of social differentiation and a reversion to primitive classlessness.);

in this society, social integration could only be achieved by 'complete uniformity of thought' (Bienkowski 1981:243). The language of Habermas's communicative theory of society could, as I have suggested, provide a potentially more theoretically elaborated framework for understanding Mao's view of Chinese society. However we interpret it, Mao's vision of socialism was of an egalitarian society integrated neither by market nor by plan, and it will continue to be worthy of examination by those disenchanted by the results to date of either.

NOTES

1. The argument of this chapter draws on, without elaborating, the conceptual framework of a multi-dimensional approach to structured social inequality advanced by Kreckel (1982) and further developed in an unpublished paper of my own (Stockman 1988). This framework distinguishes four dimensions, or resources, of social inequality: wealth, knowledge, hierarchical organisation and selective association. Of these, three will mainly figure in this chapter: for reasons of space,

consideration of inequalities of 'knowledge', especially educational inequalities, will be left to one side, though not because they are thought to be unimportant.

2. For an interesting discussion of this thesis in the context of Hungarian industry, see Czako and Sik (1987)

REFERENCES

Bienkowski, W. 1981. *Theory and Reality: The Development of Society Systems.* London: Allison and Busby.

Chan, A. and J. Unger, 1982. 'Grey and Black: the Hidden Economy of Rural China', *Pacific Affairs*, 55 (3): 452–71.

Crissman, L. W. 1972. 'Marketing in the Changhua Plain, Taiwan', in W. E. Willmot (ed.), *Economic Organization in Chinese Society.* Stanford: Stanford University Press. pp. 215–60.

Czako, A. and E. Sik, 1987. 'Managers' reciprocal transactions', in G. Lengyel (ed.), *Education, Mobility and Network of Leaders in a Planned Economy,* Sociological Working Papers No.4. Budapest: Karl Marx University of Economic Sciences.

Donnithorne, A. 1972. 'China's cellular economy: some economic trends since the cultural revolution', *The China Quarterly,* 52: 605–19.

Esherick, J. W. 1979. 'On the "restoration of capitalism": Mao and Marxist theory', *Modern China,* 5 (1): 41–78.

Feuchtwang, S., A. Hussain and T. Pairault, (eds), 1988. *Transforming China's Economy in the Eighties Vol. I: The Rural Sector, Welfare and Employment; Vol. II: Management, Industry and the Urban Economy.* London: Zed Books.

Friedman, E. 1982. 'Maoism, Titoism, Stalinism', in M. Selden and V. Lippit (eds.), *op. cit.*

Gernet, J. 1957. 'La vente en Chine d'après les contrats de Touen-Houang' (ixe-xe siècles)', *T'oung Pao,* XLV: 295–391.

Giddens, A. 1985. 'Reason without revolution? Habermas's Theorie des kommunikativen Handelns', in R. J. Bernstein (ed.), *Habermas and Modernity.* Cambridge: Polity Press.

Ghose, A. K. 1987. 'The people's commune, responsibility systems and rural development in China 1965-1984', in A. Saith (ed.), *op. cit.*

Gray, J. 1973. 'The two roads: alternative strategies of social change and economic growth in China', in S. R. Schram (ed.), *Authority Participation and Cultural Change in China.* Cambridge: Cambridge University Press.

Groves, R. G. 1969. 'Militia, market and lineage: Chinese resistance to the occupation of Hong Kong's New Territories in 1899', *Journal of the Hong Kong Branch of the Royal Asiatic Society,* 9: 31-64.

Habermas, J. 1987. *The Theory of Communicative Action. Volume 2: Lifeworld and System: A Critique of Functionalist Reason.* Cambridge: Polity Press.

Halpern, N. 1987. 'Economists and economic policy-making in the early 1960s', in Merle Goldman *et al.* (eds.), *China's Intellectuals and the State: In Search of a New Relationship.* Cambridge, Mass.: The Council on East Asian Studies / Harvard University Press.

He Jianzhang *et al.* 1988. '"Woguo xianjieduan jieji jieceng jiegou taolunhui" bufen lunwen zhaibian (Digest of articles delivered at the symposium on the structure of classes and strata during the present stage in China)', *Shehuixue Yanjiu (Sociological Studies),* 5: 67-86.

Hinton, W. 1982. 'Village in transition', in M. Selden and V. Lippit, (eds.), *op. cit.*

Howe, C. 1973. *Wage Patterns and Wage Policy in Modern China 1919-1972.* Cambridge: Cambridge University Press.

Hsu, R. C. 1985. 'Conceptions of the market in post-Mao China: an interpretive essay', *Modern China,* 11 (4): 436–60.

Huang, P. C. C. 1985. *The Peasant Economy and Social Change in North China.* Stanford: Stanford University Press.

Kraus, R. C. 1981. *Class Conflict in Chinese Socialism.* New York: Columbia University Press.

Kreckel, R. 1982. 'Class, status and power? Begriffliche Grundlagen für eine politische Soziologie der sozialen Ungleichheit', *Kölner Zeitschrift für Soziologie und Sozialpsychologie,* 34: 617–648.

MacCormack, G. 1990. *Traditional Chinese Penal Law.* Edinburgh: Edinburgh University Press.

Mann, S. 1987. *Local Merchants and the Chinese Bureaucacy, 1750–1950,* Stanford: Stanford University Press.

Nolan, P. and S. Paine, 1987. 'Towards an Appraisal of the Impact of Rural Reform in China, 1978-1985', in A. Saith (ed.), *op. cit.*

Nolan, P. and D. Fureng (eds.), 1990. *Market Forces in China.* London: Zed Books.

Nove, A. 1983. *The Economics of Feasible Socialism.* London: George Allen and Unwin.

Oi, J. C. 1985. 'Communism and Clientelism: Rural Politics in China', *World Politics,* 37 (2): 238–66.

Oi, J. C. 1986a. 'Peasant Households between Plan and Market: Cadre Control over Agricultural Inputs', *Modern China,* 12 (2): 230–51.

Oi, J. C. 1986b. 'Commercializing China's Rural Cadres', *Problems of Communism,* 35 (5): 1–15.

Oi, J. C. 1989. *State and Peasant in Contemporary China: the Political Economy of Village Government.* Berkeley, California: University of California Press.

Parish, W. L. 1984. 'Destratification in China', in J. L. Watson (ed.), *Class and Social Stratification in Post-Revolution China.* Cambridge: Cambridge University Press.

Parsons, T. 1966. *Societies: Evolutionary and Comparative Perspectives.* Englewood Cliffs, N.J.: Prentice-Hall.

Potter, S. H. 1983. 'The Position of Peasants in Modern China's Social Order', *Modern China,* 9 (4): 465–500.

Prybyla, J. S. 1986. 'China's Economic Experiment: from Mao to Market', *Problems of Communism,* 35 (1): 21–38.

Riskin, C. 1984. 'Introduction', in D. Solinger, (ed.), *op. cit.*

Riskin, C. 1987. *China's Political Economy: The Quest for Development since 1949.* Oxford: Oxford University Press.

Saith, A. (ed.), 1987. *The Re-emergence of the Chinese Peasantry.* London: Croom Helm.

Schurmann, F. 1968. *Ideology and Organization in Communist China.* Berkeley: University of California Press.

Selden, M. and V. Lippit (eds.), 1982. *The Transition to Socialism in China.* Armonk, New York: M. E. Sharpe.

Shirk, S. L. 1982. *Competitive Comrades: Career Incentives and Student Strategies in China.* Berkeley: University of California Press.

Shirk, S. L. 1984. 'The decline of virtuocracy in China', in J. L. Watson (ed.), *op. cit.*

Shue, V. 1980. *Peasant China in Transition.* Berkeley, California: University of California Press.

Shue, V. 1988. *The Reach of the State: Sketches of the Chinese Body Politic.* Stanford: Stanford University Press.

Skinner, W. G. 1964–5. 'Marketing and Social Structure in Rural China, Parts 1-3', *Journal of Asian Studies,* 24 (1–3).

Solinger, D. J. 1983. 'Marxism and the Market in Socialist China: the Reforms of 1979-80 in Context', in V. Nee and D. Mozingo (eds.), *State and Society in Contemporary China.* Ithaca: Cornell University Press. pp 194–222.

Solinger, D. J. 1984. 'Commerce: the Petty Private Sector and the Three Lines in the early 1980s', in D. J. Solinger (ed.), *op. cit.*

Solinger, D. J. (ed.), 1984. *Three Visions of Chinese Socialism.* Boulder, Colorado: Westview Press.

Starr, J. B. 1979. *Continuing the Revolution: The Political Thought of Mao.* Princeton: Princeton University Press.

Stockman, N. 1988. 'Preliminary notes on conceptual foundations of a political sociology of the revolutionary transformation of social inequality in China'. Paper presented at the Third Annual Conference on Stratification and Mobility in Comparative Perspectives, Inter-university Centre of Postgraduate Studies, Dubrovnik.

Trescott, P. B. 1985. 'Incentives versus Equality: What does China's Recent Experience Show?', *World Development,* 13 (2): 205–17.

Van Ness, P. and S. Raichur, 1989. 'Dilemmas of Socialist Development: an Analysis of Strategic Lines in China, 1949-1981', in P. Van Ness (ed.), *Market Reforms in Socialist Societies: comparing China and Hungary.* Boulder: Lynne Rienner.

Walder, A. G. 1986. *Communist Neo-traditionalism: Work and Authority in Chinese Industry.* Berkeley: University of California Press.

Watson, J. L. (ed.), 1984. *Class and Social Stratification in Post-revolution China.* Cambridge: Cambridge University Press.

White, G. 1988a. 'Evolving Relations between State and Markets in the Reform of China's Urban-Industrial Economy', in S. Feuchtwang et al. (eds.), *op. cit.* (Vol. II).

White, G. 1988b. 'State and Market in China's Labour Reforms', *Journal of Development Studies,* 24 (4): 180–202.

Womack, B. 1984. 'Modernization and Democratic Reform in China', *Journal of Asian Studies,* 43 (3): 417–39.

Yang, M. M. 1989. 'The Gift Economy and State Power in China', *Comparative Studies in Society and History,* 31 (1) 25–54.

Zafanolli, W. 1988. 'A Brief Outline of China's Second Economy', in S. Feuchtwang et al. (eds.), *op. cit.* (Vol. I).

Part VI

Overview and Conclusions

15

Markets, Models and Morality

The Power of Practices

STEPHEN GUDEMAN

Markets have long been of interest to economists, for according to most arguments only through the competitive transactions that take place in markets can allocative efficiency in production and distribution be reached. Markets allow choice to be exercised, rationality to be displayed and personal goals to be optimised. But markets not only possess attributes worthy of theoretical speculation, they are important in material life and have provided a host of metaphors affirming the importance of political freedom. Anthopologists, however, have been wary, if not ambivalent, about the study of markets. Some apply market models in the belief that this illuminates ethnographic data everywhere (Plattner 1989a, 1989b); others, such as Marxists, avoid focusing on markets for theoretical reasons; a number of anthropologists stay clear of the subject out of respect for the technical proficiency of economists. Only rarely have anthropologists used their own techniques and theories in the analysis of markets (Bohannan and Dalton 1965; Geertz 1979; Gell 1982; Malinowski and de la Fuente 1982). The essays of this volume, by starting with ethnographic observations and human practices, mark a fresh step in research on markets: they reinsert anthropology into the study of one of the world's central institutions and offer valuable insights into market-place behaviour.

Many of the essays' themes revolve about models of the market, and I shall explore three of the issues that are raised – specifically, the form of models, the link between models and morality, and the connection between rationality and practices. Elsewhere I have suggested that two model types might be distinguished: the universal and the local (Gudeman 1986; Gudeman and Penn 1982). This polarity, however, may be viewed epistemologically, for the model types are linked to different ways of putting knowledge into practice and practice into knowledge. For its part, universal knowledge is axiomatic and deductive (Euclidean theorems being a good example); it features central assumptions, modes of deduction and inferences. Universal knowledge is said to be timeless, because it reaches towards the fundamentals of human thought and behaviour, and is claimed to be global in reach. Yet, it is open to correction and amplification through procedures of verification or falsification. Universal knowledge is closely linked to rational thought, defined either as the use of consistent criteria in choice or the considered selection of means to reach established ends. This way of putting knowledge into practice might be called Cartesian, though I shall also link it to use of the Benthamite calculus and utilitarianism. Universal models, which characterise much of modern economics, draw upon this epistemology and form of behaviour.

Local models are built out of practice knowledge. I think this way of knowing might be characterised as artisanship, using the term in its fullest sense. It is also pragmatic in that the act itself, in its engagement, alters its own finality. Local knowledge is learned in context, through trial and error, apprenticeship and exemplification. This type of knowledge offers no claim to holism or consistency and is limited in scope; yet, it can be permutated and metaphorically extended. Practical knowledge changes – having no claim to timelessness – and is often the locale of creativeness and innovations. Local models are constructed and changed through this way of knowing, and in my view they characterise a great deal of 'the economy' in other societies as well as our own. Some practitioners of economic anthropology, however, insist upon using their universal models in all contexts so that the existence of local models is suppressed. The essays in this volume demonstrate that behaviour in real markets and market-places is often a mix of the two model forms.

Other model types might also be distinguished. Economists and anthropologists often begin with the idea that a market is 'perfectly competitive'. In the perfect market, with its multitude of buyers and sellers and fully shared information, the resource endowments of transactors have no effect on pricing. Although few, if any, perfectly competitive markets exist, this is the image against which most real markets are assessed and understood. But only the persuasive power of our own texts leads us to think of this as the 'ideal market' and as having special claims to verisimilitude. Other market forms have been modelled, and these too have rightful call on our attention, especially the monopoly (one seller) or monopsony (one buyer) market type (Chamberlin 1933, Robinson 1933). I suggest that we think of markets in terms of a continuum: at one end are perfectly competitive markets, at the other are 'imperfect' markets with many buyers and one seller or one buyer and many sellers. In practice, most markets are a mix of the two: a very small number are perfectly competitive, most markets exhibit a degree of oligopoly control, while a few are truly monopolistic or monopsonistic. Visualising markets in terms of this continuum not only helps us to break with the image of a single market form but also undermines the notion that the economy is a separate sector of life immune to the exercise of power, for it is through oligopolies, cartels and monopolies, through the differential withholding power which they embody, that power comes to be exercised in the economy. The intertwining of power and social life has become a central theme in anthropology, especially after the influence of Foucault, but there are different ways of considering how power permeates the economy. Certainly, as most political scientists would argue, the polity and economy as institutions are 'articulated'; and as post-Marxists might claim, the impact that the 'world system' has upon a local area must always be considered. But these perspectives do not capture all the connections between power and material practices. In competitive transactions, the differential control of assets lends economic power which in a market context is bodied forth and implemented as monopolies and oligopolies. In turn, these have an effect on prices, profits and the distribution of income.

Just as power penetrates material practice, so does morality. But this is often denied by the oppositions we deploy. Several distinctions have been used in and outside anthropology that would separate rational practice from morality. The descriptive, social scientists have told us, should be distinguished from the prescriptive; philosophers have argued that fact should not be conflated with value; and in anthropology Geertz (1973) has distinguished between 'models of' and 'models for'. Of course, a critic might turn the several oppositions to a use for which they were not intended by arguing that rationality is actually a prescriptive and not a descriptive model of behaviour; after all, while rational figuring can provide helpful advice – from the size of inventory to hold to selecting a stock portfolio – not everyone employs it. I question the opposition for a different reason, however: in most practical situations the 'ought' and the 'is' are mixed together, and morality permeates economic models. For example, in his analysis of Adam Smith's invisible hand metaphor, Heinz Lubasz shows how for Smith the distributive good of society should and would emerge from individual choice since morally right natural law underwrote personal behaviour. This was the invisible hand, but the metaphor has been dramatically altered by modern economists who have dropped the moral and natural law assumptions, replacing them with perfect competition and impersonal communication. As many of the other essays suggest, the concept of morality also returns the study of economy to a Durkheimian conception of society and to a consideration of obligations that are not rationally and individually constructed. Against those formulations of market behaviour that draw only upon the western notion of individual rationality, I would pose both practice models and art as well as the social rules and morality that provide a context for all rational calculations.[1] At the essay's conclusion, in fact, I shall propose the seeming paradox that only through non-rational practices can the modern market's central project – making a profit – be achieved.

But there are other reasons for anthropologists to employ the concept of models in their work; above all, they can claim back some of the high ground from economists! According to an accepted view among economists, and the rest of us too, only economists truly model the economy. The assumption is that economists, by using their sophisticated disciplinary apparatus, can offer a firmer grasp on what is happening in material life than anything a participating folk or anthropologist can say; thus, economics occupies a position of prestige in the academy that is not shared by its social science rivals. Chris Hann's ethnographic report from Hungary illustrates the importance of this link between control of formal knowledge and social persuasion. A Hungarian economist, well recognised for his modelling acumen, has had immense influence in warranting that country's change-over to a free market system, though very few are acquainted with the technical works which have found him prestige.[2]

In addition to countering the influence of economists and elevating the importance of practical knowledge, a different mode of understanding becomes available once the focus shifts to ethnographic models. The role of anthropology, I think, is not simply to interpret others, to engage in comparison or to seek cross-cultural generalities (if that is possible), but to see ourselves as others see us or to view our models through the prism of others' models. This is the reflexive and critical office of anthropology that is not available to other disciplines, even to history which can never explore practice models themselves.

The idea of attaining a critical and moral appreciation of one's own behaviour by adopting the apperception of others did not originate in anthropology. In fact, Adam Smith offered a subtle discussion of the point, an appreciation of which might have led economics in a very different direction. Throughout the world, *The Wealth of Nations* (1976 [1776]) has become an important charter for establishing and maintaining a free market economy and a democratic polity. But this book did not represent the entirety of Adam Smith's thought nor can it always be reconciled with his prior effort, *The Theory of Moral Sentiments* (1976 [1759]). Lubasz explores several links between the two works in relation to Smith's market model. But a different connection of the texts has other implications. In *The Theory of Moral Sentiments*, Smith focused on the bonds of social life and the sources of 'our fellow-feeling' (1976 [1759]:10).[3] Upon turning to 'our first moral criticisms', he then explained that these are

> exercised upon the characters and conduct of other people; and we are all very forward to observe how each of these affects us. But we soon learn, that other people are equally frank with regard to our own... We begin, upon this account, to examine our own passions and conduct, and to consider how these must appear to them, by considering how they would appear to us if in their situation. We suppose ourselves the spectators of our own behaviour, and endeavour to imagine what effect it would, in this light, produce upon us. This is the only looking-glass by which we can, in some measure, with the eyes of other people, scrutinize the propriety of our own conduct. (1976 [1759]: 112)

Adam Smith's brilliantly formulated moral apperception, exercised through the imagined looking-glass of the way we would respond to ourselves if in the place of others, constructs this capacity as an individual's emerging awareness and expression of mutual connections within a community. Smith's moral apperception is a form of social reflexivity; yet his sociological sense was never incorporated into market models which are inevitably atomistic, individualistic and competitive in their assumptions.

In his critical examination of the presuppositions of neo-classical economics, Peter Preston practises a form of social reflexivity. Preston appraises many of the accepted premises of neo-classical economics, such as the doctrine of perpetual scarcity, by drawing upon sceptical western voices. But this type of critical appraisal, which uses one part of western experience to reflect on another, has limitations. Let me explain. Preston briefly refers to development theory and to the impact that the World Bank and International Monetary Fund have had on economic policy in less developed countries. This is an area that is ripe for fresh reflection. For example, one objection sometimes expressed to comparing 'our' models with 'others' is that we have developed formal, written models while theirs, signed in behaviour and often unverbalised, are practice models. In fact, our models are also involved in practices; development agencies are a key example. Jock Stirrat provides observations on some development models that emerged in political oratory and have had considerable impact on behaviour. A common development discourse, as Stirrat shows, is based on a complex of views drawn from the accepted wisdom, such as: the individual is the seat of natural propensities and the sole economic actor; social and cultural obligations are a constraint to economic efficiency; and economic efficiency, as the means for achieving the greatest satisfaction of individual wants, constitutes a laudable end itself. The several metaphors of transparency, accountability and visibility to which Stirrat also draws our attention bespeak an unconstrained utilitarianism, to which even John Stuart Mill might have objected, and bring to mind a comparison between the development process, as powerful institutions of the world would have it, and Bentham's Panopticon or prison which under the 'rule of economy' needs only one governor to carry out the wishes of a committee of trustees. Just as the prisoners in the Panopticon are to be controlled and changed by being made perpetually visible in a world not of their making, and just as the prison manager must publish for public scrutiny his monetary accounts (Bentham 1791:31), so a recipient nation is held accountable for meeting the model of the donor, is required to undertake 'structural adjustments', and must visually demonstrate its will and progress by pounding 'squishy' numbers into an appropriate economic model (Klitgaard 1990:235). This type of development practice conveys a morality, and it is powerful, being capable of producing on the ground what it represents as reality, because the allocation of financial assets is tied to the consent to be modelled. Above all, the process is based on the application of the power-holder's knowledge, as in Bentham's Panopticon, leaving no room for art, for local knowledge or for the making of culture in the changing practices. (Does this help account for the uneven success of many development projects?)

Thus, I agree with Preston's and Stirrat's attempts to listen to and use our own 'other' voices to criticise neo-classical and development economics. But we need to rethink modern theory more comprehensively. Anthropology offers the possibility of 'escaping' the social reflexivity involved when offering a critique from within the same culture. Ethnographic models multiply the possible perspectives. With good reason did Thorstein Veblen complain that economics was limited in its appreciation of human behaviour: 'helplessly behind the times' as compared to 'modern anthropology, ethnology, and psychology' (1942 [1898]:56). His critical perception of American society, as expressed in *The Theory of the Leisure Class* (1953 [1899]) and one of his less appreciated works, *The Instinct of Workmanship* (1914), was often founded on the use of ethnography from other societies.

Critical and reflexive comparisons of this second sort are undertaken by Paul Alexander and Joanna Overing, though to different ends. Alexander examines the models of Javanese traders and uses the findings to raise doubts about our own market assumptions. For example, according to theory, market efficiency is enhanced by bargaining over price; but in fact prices on many goods in Javanese and western markets are posted or set by large suppliers. Thus, 'economies of scale', which are said to provide greater efficiency as well as lower prices, may do the reverse: they enable larger traders to set higher prices, secure bigger profits and remain unresponsive to changing conditions! The implication is that the image of 'economies of scale' is partly a myth of our own system (see Marglin 1974). Size simply enhances oligopolistic control in one or another market. Alexander also questions the assumption that the core of economic behaviour is rational calculation. The premise is central to arguments against state interference; it also has important anthropological implications, for according to its proponents – universal modellers – customary or cultural behaviour that cannot be fitted to the mould of rational calculation is to be interpreted as a constraint on productive or allocative efficiency.[4]

Overing's critical comparison has a different focus. She uses her ethnography from the Piaroa to question the anthropological distinction, drawn by Lévi-Strauss and others, between 'primitive' exchange that enhances moral solidarity and market exchange that effaces such bonds. For her, this anthropological distinction is a reflexive projection of western experience, produced by the social violence of our market mentality. I would add, however, that the anthropological opposition itself has a history; it is part of a 'long conversation' in the west (Gudeman and Rivera 1990), as suggested by the split between Smith's *The Theory of Moral Sentiments* (1976 [1759]) and *The Wealth of Nations* (1976 [1776]): on the one side lies altruism and the morality of sharing; on the other lies self-interested exchange. What anthropologists have 'found' in other societies is one side of a distinction already implied by our economic theories. In fact, I would extend Overing's critique. According to the well-known tripartite model of Sahlins (1972), exchange form can be mapped onto social distance in a precise way: among intimates in a social group, altruism, the free gift or generalised exchange obtains; at the next social distance, such as between affines, reciprocity or give-and-take holds; finally, bargaining and trade are found between those who have no social ties. The Piaroa disrupt this layout in an interesting way: gifts are given only between more socially distant affines, while strict reciprocity is observed between the most intimate. The ethnography brings the western influenced model into doubt. If we then ask why this Piaroa pattern obtains, rational deduction from first principles offers little aid; the design is part of a larger model that Overing displays. The composition is a product of 'art', a conclusion that is underscored by the Piaroa way of modelling the market-place. Overing shows how hunting, an aspect of production, is used to model shopping, which is considered to be a facet of exchange. To place the new event, the Piaroa have metaphorically extended a received construction; and this formulation of the new experience in terms of the old has more to do with the practice of art than with rationality. Overall, the elucidation of such other models is the stuff – in my terms – of 'cultural economics' (Gudeman 1986).

If the Piaroa afford a glimpse of the way existent conversations are 'thinly' extended to fashion new contexts, Michael Stewart's study of Gypsies demonstrates how 'thick' conversations may characterise long-running, mixed situations. Gypsies seem to be avid horse traders in Hungarian markets; they show little personal caution and celebrate exchanges with peasants as gains for themselves. But connected to these transactions is another, serious one among Gypsy men themselves. They swap horses, one for one; yet, the horses stand in place of women who cannot be swapped;

ultimately, Gypsy men do with horses what they cannot with females! But finally women raise piglets to sell and pay for the horses that the men trade and then swap in lieu of themselves! This raises the possibility that by a complex web of exchanges the uncosted work of Gypsy females helps support Hungarian peasant markets. More broadly, Stewart shows how a moral model of social relationships among Gypsies is connected to a market model shared by Gypsies and peasants; very different models are mixed together here. Tristan Platt's material on Bolivia, as well as Peter Geschiere's on Cameroonian societies, illustrates much the same.

In other cases, very distinct models may be brought into confrontation within a single context. This is well illustrated by Norman Stockman's study of the several visions of socialism in China. Three models of the economy have been deployed. First, there is the central planning model; it contains moral and monetary inequities deriving from the exercise of positional power. In the second model, market social-ism, inequities arise within the economic structure itself. The radical (Maoist) vision, with its critique of the market, and of selfishness and profit-seeking, comprises the third model. In this one, with its emphasis on self reliance and egalitarianism, moral and political judgements are to be made solely on the basis of personal worth. Stockman explains how these models have been put to use in China, but each contains contradictions and in practice has been usually interwoven with another. The models cannot be separated in terms of temporal succession, and though each has achieved dominance at a time, usually it has provoked another voice in response. The picture is one of process and change or of historically thick conversations.

This is not the whole story, however, for Mao's third model was itself a mixture of western and Chinese traditions. Mao emphasised the importance of manifesting personal worth and virtue, or moral behaviour, within the economy. This view has a long history in western culture. It was implicit in Aristotle's model (1926, 1946) of the household economy and its various exchanges. In his analysis of trade, Aristotle grappled with the different ways a rate or price between parties might be set. How could an ethically proper price be established? As Aristotle noted, the market offered opportunities for monopolistic practices and for avaricious individuals to benefit at the expense of others. Aristotle's quest for a right rate of exchange became known as the 'just price' theory, and in variant form the broad question of how morally right behaviour was to be established in the market-place occupied an important part of the literature right up to Adam Smith. With *The Wealth of Nations* (1976 [1776]), the concept of the just price was dropped (replaced by the natural price), and the market model was installed. This hardly quelled the moral issue, however. Marx, for example, provided one formulation of a just price theory. In my view, his claim that value is created only by labour was a moral or prescriptive model of what ought to happen in the market; it was not a scientific or technical observation. The well-known 'transfor-mation problem' in Marxist economics is actually a problem about morality and models, and not about how surplus as a quantity of labour can or cannot be mathematically transformed to profit as a quantity of money. Marx wanted to show that labour value, extracted in production, is transformed to commodity price in market exchange; he wanted to establish that price as measured in money is really a transformation of value as measured in labour. If he had been able to demonstrate that money price can be perfectly reduced to labour value, he would have been justified in criticising contemporary economics for basing itself on the false appearance of price and obscuring the fact that all profit comes from the exploitation of labour. But the 'transformation problem' has never been mathematically solved. Yet, I am arguing that this is not even a problem for mathematics. It concerns models and morals, or whether a prescriptive model about the value of labour can be transformed into a descriptive model about market price. Philosophers have long argued that the 'is' is not logically derivable from the 'ought'. But in human society local models often conflate the two, and so did Marx in his attempt to transform value into price.

My larger argument is that Mao – fully conversant with Marx – was a part of this moral discussion that began with Aristotle and continued through Marx; but Mao merged it with a Confucian vision that brought into play such ideals as selflessness, persistence, honesty and personal virtue. Mao presented a combined model that merged nineteenth century and earlier western thought with Chinese conceptions. This thick model was then brought into confrontation with the two other cultural models ('Titoism' and 'Stalinism'). I surmise that such 'thick' conversations, with their contradictions and oppositions, are characteristic of economic practices in many if not all societies. But they escape the scrutiny of Cartesian economists.

Ladislav Holy's study of economic reform in Czechoslovakia shows how the descriptive and prescriptive dimensions of models may be welded together, and it suggests how moral valorisations shift. In Czechoslovakia, socialism and communism traditionally were considered to be honourable reactions to the social atomism and unfettered individualism that is characteristic of capitalism. This has now been reversed, and the market is modelled as the civilised, natural and normal, while socialism represents the artificial. The assumption is that the authentic individual as an autonomous moral agent can most fully emerge within a market system. This claim for the market's morality finds its foundation in natural law theory and the concept of possessive individualism, in which respect the Czechoslovak model is at one with many of the development models. This same Czechoslovak view, however, justifies national opposition to the infusion of foreign capital with its potential control of domestic property and production; in the Czechoslovak perspective, market behaviour represents a frightening loss of control.

The connection between market expansion and loss of control has been an important theme in anthropology, but several processes are said to be occurring. The market increases personal choice yet dissolves socially governed behaviour. This troubled observers such as Polanyi while it is applauded by utilitarians for whom culture is a constraint. The utilitarian argument, however, has then to be reconciled with the Weberian view that a market economy leads to increased rationalisation and bureaucratic domination. Whatever the outcome – increased choice or increased bureaucratic rules – the individual seems to experience a morally shifting and confusing world. But why? If rational behaviour has the greatest opportunity of being expressed in a market system, then social life should be more predictable in a market economy, and the sense of rational control should be robust. Clearly, this is not the experiential inference. I shall argue that the notions of practice and of culture-making help explain both the sense of loss of control and how profit is made in the market. Several of the studies explore these alternate directions.

The informal economy, Keith Hart proposes, is dialectically produced by the market economy; it does not represent a momentary transition from traditional community to urban life. The dialectic has its source in the modern state bureaucracy and the corporation, where the state – with its centralisation of political power – has come to represent both social and moral obligations. State institutions attend primarily to corporate organisations, and this leaves to one side a vast number of people who, to sustain themselves, must undertake 'informal' activities. The informal economy is a market-organised system that lies outside the margins of state morality as encoded in rules and institutions, hence its liminal and sometimes illegal status.

As Hart asks, when the informal economy emerges, what relations of trust grow within it so that economic practices can be undertaken? What past models can people draw upon to formulate these obligations? Asking this question is not to reduce moral obligations to the rational calculation of actors, for if people reasoned and acted in that manner, it would undermine the bindingness of the relations that they do establish, by continually subjecting them to new calculations. If a relation is socially binding, then it is not subject to transient choice. But what is the connection between the two? This returns us again to the broad puzzle that Aristotle posed: what is the link between social morality, made continuously evident in sharing, distribution and co-operation, and exchanges that are directed to personal maximisation?

As a reaction to the rule-governed rationalisation of life, the informal economy is a zone of individual practices and activities. It grows around the establishment of new ways for making a living, and these 'new combinations' often break accepted moralities and expectations. Part of the informal economy's 'amorality' lies in the combinations it fosters outside the accepted expectations of a community. But to a degree this is true of all new behaviour in markets.

The discomfiture produced by new market behaviour is exemplified by the ethnographic material from Eastern Europe. Chris Hann tells of the shock experienced in Hungary when market activities began, and in effect he provides examples of folk tales in the making. Initially, people feared that markets would be undermined by the activities of foreigners: Gypsies were selling their children, Yugoslavs and Bulgarians had formed gangs to circulate counterfeit currency, the Soviets were selling off army equipment, and Poles were accused of everything! In Czechoslovakia, Holy recounts, it was feared that the new entrepreneurs would not sell the basic commodities, would overcharge for what they did sell, and would undermine 'just prices'. Similar fears of exchange were recorded, on Tristan Platt's account, in nineteenth century Bolivia; the focus there was on whether or not protectionist trade policies, prohibiting a certain range of imports, should be maintained. Such moral outrage is not a once-and-for-all event that occurs only when a market is first established, for a market-place is a living region in which new commodities are continually being brought to the bar of exchange. This ceaseless change is unsettling. I am suggesting that entrepreneurial activities, whether indexed by the informal economy, the intrusion of foreigners and the activity of traders, or defended against by tariffs and trade barriers, often become the focus of unease and outrage for the disruption they represent. The entrepreneur, by changing old relations and invoking new ones, epitomises the moral shifts that are occurring in a market.

The essay on South and West Cameroon, by Peter Geschiere, illuminates how these frightening features of entrepreneurial activity may come to be symbolised. He describes, for a series of neighbouring societies, a set of overlapping models that concern money-making activity. They all revolve about stealing the bodies of witch-craft victims in order to put them to work. In some areas the secret practice is condemned but not in others. The image of bodies being put to work, of extracting labour from lifeless people, is a rather Marxist picture of the way profit is made. But is the construction a folk reaction to the inception of wage labour or has it a broader implication about making gains in the market? Note that where capital equipment is relatively scarce, and land is sometimes in short supply, then labour indeed is the crucial productive resource, as suggested in the model. Geschiere also shows how this new metaphor about money making was pieced together from traditional materials; it is part of a thick, historical conversation. More important, he describes the material inventions and borrowings that are going on amongst the people, and the many combinations of the old and new. Some of these, such as haggling over sums paid at a funeral, are shocking to folk and observer alike when first tried. Above all, entrepreneurial success, based on market innovations, is attributed to, explained by, and modelled as 'spirit' control. The imagery is about entrepreneurial accumulations and the opaque practices that create wealth. This local model has now spread throughout the country!

The Cameroon model of innovation and profit certainly looks irrational – at least from our perspective. After all, markets are not run by controlling spirit labour! But perhaps the Cameroon model suggests that we should consider again our own models of profit. When these are seen in terms of real practices do they, too, have a non-rational component?

Summarily argued, we recognise in text and voice two types of profit. One, arising in conditions of perfect competition, is the return for making new products, new processes, new organisations or new markets. This is the return to entrepreneurs and organisations for innovations, and it is sometimes called 'normal profit'. This competitive profit is short-term, for in the absence of a patent or another protection system, the innovation will be copied by others and the profit will come to be shared with other corporations, labourers and consumers. Innovations in this 'perfect' sense are shared in the community over time through partitioning of the gain among higher wages, lower prices and increased quality of goods.

A 'supernormal' profit is found where monopolies, oligopolies or cartels prevail. Such a profit may originate in innovation, but the gain is held and perpetuated through monopoly power. Monopoly gain is linked to a financial, legal or other capacity for withholding a past innovation from others. It bespeaks the existence of a market in which pecuniary assets or information are asymmetrically held. For example, the Zuwaya traders and truckers in Libya, described by John Davis, provide an interesting case of market control and monopoly profit. In times past, Zuwaya controlled oases and operated a kind of 'protection racket'. But this was contested by other groups; now Zuwaya hold unusual advantages in trade. The Zuwaya 'cartel' consists of sharing information; maintaining common prices; and offering mutual assistance in obtaining supplies and trucks, and in cases of vehicle breakdown. Being Zuwaya is not itself a rational choice but a moral identity that establishes trust, an identity which was strengthened in opposition to Ottoman control and the state; however, this moral identity now has important economic implications, for it helps secure for Zuwaya a supernormal profit in the market. Davis's claim that Zuwaya are risk averse, and avoid uncertainty and speculation, seems apt, for they can reap a monopoly profit simply by sustaining their network control of the market.

The Java market study by Alexander also suggests how monopoly power of traders, embodied in financial and information control, yields a supernormal profit. But the case is complex, for these traders couple market power with price testing to secure gains. The traders achieve a combined gain, manifested through their use of both posted and bargained or tested prices.

My argument is that these two types of profit – the normal and the supernormal – are linked to two different kinds of activity (Gudeman 1992). Monopoly profit, which avoids uncertainty, is directed to the longer term. Larger firms endeavour to achieve monopoly profit as do cartels and trading organisations; it allows for the routinisation of activities and the establishment of rule-governed behaviour or – in Weber's terms – the rationalisation of action. Ultimately, this is the purpose of the Benthamite project, to establish efficient and certain control over a set of activities, whether in the prison or the market. In the context of market action, Benthamite utilitarianism fuses easily with Cartesianism rationalism.

But another type of activity is also at play in markets as suggested by the ethnography from Eastern Europe, China, Cameroon, Java, Libya and Latin America. It is linked to the fact that rational practice does not cover the entirety of financial activity. In Spanish, this other form of behaviour is partly captured by the term *tantear* which means to grope, feel one's way or test out a situation. For example, Platt tells how the expression, 'tax-testing', (*tasa tanteo*) was used in Bolivia for the collection of those taxes whose amounts could not be determined in advance and were established by the various persuasions of individual collectors. My claim is that the dominant texts of the west have largely adopted Cartesian and Benthamite models of economic action, but the ethnography from real and newly developing markets asks us to consider whether practice models of economic behaviour must be added to them. In fact, in the western conversation, practice models have been voiced, but they are often silenced by the hegemonic texts.

Consider Diderot, central Enlightenment figure and author as well as editor and inspiration behind the great French *Encyclopédie* that was published in the latter half of the eighteenth century. One of the *Encyclopédie*'s first entries, written by Diderot himself, was on 'Art'. The selection was circulated in advance of the *Encyclopédie*'s publication as an advertisement of Diderot's intention and theory of knowledge that would inform what was to follow. In this foundational statement, Diderot first contrasted the sciences and the arts. Focusing on the arts, he then argued that every art has both a speculative and a practical dimension; some arts have been created by the mind, others by the hands. Diderot urged that it was time to accord attention and honour to the practical arts; observing that the sciences and the liberal arts had long been praised, although the mechanical arts had brought humans more benefits and happiness, Diderot concluded: 'How strangely we judge!' His emphasis on practical achievements and his frequent citations of Bacon were surely intended as a correction to the Cartesianism so prevalent at the time. The article also announced a central focus of the *Encyclopédie* which told in detail about the developing mechanical arts in France and was copiously illustrated with etchings of processes and workshops. This epistemological shift from rationalism to empiricism and in the kind of knowledge presented in the *Encyclopédie* had radical social implications, for it meant that unknown folk of the past and practising artisans of the present as opposed to landowners, royalty, clergy and writers were foregrounded as the makers of economy and culture.

Central to Diderot's thought was his construction of artisanship. The artisan, Diderot claimed, 'brought together' (*rapprocher*) or 'separated' (*éloigner*) the substances with which he was working. Everything depended upon the activity of combining or conjoining, and removing or putting into absentia. Practical and concrete, this was Diderot's trope of production – and of the species ability itself. The image was not innocent of the ideational capacity either, for it has another reading, as a trope of modelling. For Diderot, the artisan engaged in making by drawing together and separating or by finding similarities and dissimilarities. But these are not always sequential activities. Likeness stands out only when difference can also be drawn, while separating is a critique of what previously was linked: it draws upon analytical processes, invokes disbelief in what has been presented, loosens an object for reconsideration and shifts the context of similarity. Within artisanship, combining and separating are distinct and sequential but also copresent. Artisanship involves two activities, in tension: the synthetic and the analytic. Diderot was discussing artisanship as a material practice and central activity in the economy, but ultimately he was describing human practical activity and modelling that have a non-Cartesian form.

Diderot's work was soon eclipsed by Bentham's utilitarianism which was given great dissemination by John Stuart Mill. Mill did not thoroughly apply utilitarianism in his own economic text (1929[1848]), but it became the cornerstone of neo-classical economics which arose in the latter part of the nineteenth century; on Sahlins's (1976) reading it was implicit in Marx as well. Artisanship and modelling – combining, separating, seeing similarities, finding differences and criticising – have no place in the pre-eminent texts of economics.

A countervoice is heard once again, however, in Joseph Schumpeter's work on the entrepreneur. Like the artisan for Diderot, the entrepreneur is the principal trope for Schumpeter. Writing more than 150 years after Diderot, Schumpeter (1934) lauded the entrepreneur as the architect and engine of economic progress.[5] On Schumpeter's view, economic *growth* occurs by expanding existing technologies and resources;

development, which is crucial for capitalism and any other economic system, is different. Development takes place when new products are made, new resources are found, new processes are invented, new markets are opened or new forms of productive organisation are devised. These achievements are the result of entrepreneurial practices. Schumpeter's summary of the process was telling. Entrepreneurs, he often repeated, make 'new combinations' by uniting materials and forces (1934:65). Diderot's artisan – belonging to a lower class and occupied with useful but menial tasks – becomes the central figure of the economy for Schumpeter. And the success and failure of this figure determines the progress of the economy: as Schumpeter once emphasised, the entrepreneur 'triumphed for others ... and created a model for them which they can copy' (1934:133). When replicated by others, however, entrepreneurial innovations lose their differential value and become common coin within a culture. Schumpeter was interested in the entrepreneur because new combinations, in his view, are the sole source of development in society; and innovations, when successfully carried out and accepted in the market, are rewarded by profit. But the profit is short term, for the innovations may quickly be replicated; and the size of profit is unpredictable, for the entrepreneur operates in a context of uncertainty. Innovations achieve a short-cycle profit; only a monopoly can preserve the gain, as a 'supernormal' profit.

In his early writing (1934), Schumpeter argued that entrepreneurial activity was comprised of making 'new combinations'. He did briefly observe that it 'consists precisely in breaking up old, and creating new, traditions' (1934:92), but the emphasis was upon the creative side. Several decades later (1976[1942]), Schumpeter still fancied this view but now referred to it as a process of 'creative destruction'. Some may link this more negative formulation to Schumpeter's pessimistic prognosis for capitalism; others may see similarities to the dialectical idea of breaking the fetters and revolutionising the forces of production; still others may draw a parallel between Schumpeter's view and the ethnographic materials in which innovations represent a morally destructive impulse. But Schumpeter's oxymoron, 'creative destruction', can also be appreciated in light of the fact that the entrepreneur draws upon synthetic and analytic capacities. In Schumpeter's developed argument the transient and reflexive quality of market activities is underlined, for the entrepreneur not only critiques the past but subjects current making to critical appreciation. Schumpeter perhaps did not sufficiently emphasise that the entrepreneur operates within a changing context and that as the context changes, similarities and dissimilarities may be sharpened, and this alone may stimulate innovations. A successful innovation also shifts the context for which it is made, and this too may open the way for change. Still, we might say that Schumpeter offered a 'punctuated development' theory of history. In his model, there is no necessary connection between the before and the after in time; this emphasis on disconnection and unpredictable shifts in human making, on the kaleidoscope and collage at the centre of capitalism, surely ranks Schumpeter as an early voice of postmodernism or as a mixed voice of modernism and post-modernism. His later pessimistic view of capitalism was connected to his forecast that entrepreneurial practices would wither as accumulation occurred, motivation decreased and the processes of production became routinised. The creativeness of entrepreneurship would be overwhelmed by the regularity of monopolies, and this would spell the end of development. Nevertheless, on Schumpeter's argument, innovations make for development in the economy; at their inception they return a monetary profit to the entrepreneur, and this profit is central to the successful working of capitalism.

Schumpeter's account of the entrepreneur is attractive and persuasive, yet it has a final implication for standard economics that must be considered ironic; indeed, it makes Schumpeter a fellow traveller of Diderot and anthropologists. The doctrine of rational behaviour in the economy is threatened by Schumpeter's view because of the uncertainty, non-deductibility and lack of predictable connection it suggests between the inception and the end of a profit-making activity. The entrepreneur as artisan (and bricoleur) is engaged in non-rational practices. To be certain, after the fact a successful practice can be assessed as having been rational, for it makes a profit. But before it is started or completed, the results are unknowable: the means can hardly be arranged to best fit the ends since the entirety is a test, an experiment, a matter of groping (*al tanteo*). The contingent and serendipitous nature of development was apparent also to Diderot, although his explanation for technology's 'progress' was different.

He spoke of the origins of the mechanical arts as being 'fortuitous' events, and though he cited no actual cases, he offered as typical a hypothetical account of the birth of paper-making:

> A piece of cloth had accidentally fallen into a container filled with water and had remained in it long enough to dissolve, so that when the container was emptied it was found to have in it, instead of a piece of cloth, only a kind of sediment. (Diderot 1965:7)

Diderot's artisan ultimately appears as a rather passive maker when compared to Schumpeter's entrepreneur who initiates changes. In advanced economies today, planned innovations within corporations represent an even more active attempt to influence the future, and advertising is surely an effort to persuade others of an innovation's worth. The rationalisation of innovation has almost hidden the 'making process' from view. Like a mirror, however, the examples in this volume reveal the degree to which profit-making and development have a non-rational basis. Max Weber long ago suggested that the act of belief in the legitimacy of rational behaviour could not itself be justified as a rational act; in this (paradoxical) sense, rationality had a non-rational basis. Based on the ethnography here presented we might offer a different paradox: profit-making, as a competitive gain for innovations, is a non-rational act; but profit-making, as a monopolistic gain for control of a market, is a rational one. Could the lack of a currently accepted theory of profit, about which Joan Robinson once complained, be a sign of the impossibility of developing a rational account for those unpredictable, creative acts that result in profit for their maker? Are the many ethnographic images, from feeling one's way, to controlling spirit labour, to the fear of outsiders' controlling a market, variant attempts to model the non-rational basis of profit-making? Conversely, does the cultural assertion of Zuwaya identity and of moral ties among Gypsies actually promote rational control of a market? Or is it – and I would conclude this way – that most market behaviour is a dialectical mix of the two, just as most markets are a blend of competition and monopoly. Alexander's study of Javanese markets, in which profits are made both by posting prices and by testing the waters, might persuade one of this last conclusion.

NOTES

1. In his more recent studies even John Elster has become disillusioned with the 'power of reason' and has turned to the relation between rational choice and independently given social obligations. See, for example, *The Cement of Society* (1989).
2. See, for example, Kornai, *Anti-equilibrium* (1972).
3. For example, the book begins, 'How selfish soever man may be supposed, there are evidently some principles in his nature, which interest him in the fortune of others, and render their happiness necessary to him though he derives nothing from it except the pleasure of seeing it' (Smith 1976[1759]:9). This principle of human altruism is exactly the reverse of Smith's now famous dictum that we secure our food and drink not from the benevolence but from the self-interest of the baker, the butcher and the brewer (Smith 1976[1776]:18).
4. The imperialism of economists is well known, and though it seems to be an odd position for anthropologists to adopt, it has been a dominant feature of formalist writings in economic anthropology (Nash 1961; Plattner 1989a).
5. The English version of *The Theory of Economic Development* was published in 1934, but Schumpeter traced the beginnings of the work to 1907; the first German edition was published in 1911.

REFERENCES

Aristotle. 1926. *The Nicomachean Ethics*, (trans. H. Rackham). London: Heinemann.

Aristotle. 1942. *The Politics*, (trans. Ernest Barker). London: Oxford University Press.

Bentham, J. 1791. *Panopticon*. London: T. Payne.

Bohannan, P. and G. Dalton, (eds), 1965. *Markets in Africa*. Garden City: Anchor Books.

Chamberlin, E. H. 1933. *The Theory of Monopolistic Competition*. Cambridge: Harvard University Press.

Diderot, D. 1751. 'Art', *Encyclopédie, ou Dictionnaire Raisonné des Sciences, des Artes et des Métiers*, (ed. Diderot and D'Alembert). 1:713–17. Paris: Briasson, David, Le Breton, Durand.

Diderot, D. 1965. 'Art', *Encyclopedia: selections*, (trans. Nelly S. Hoyt and T. Cassirer). Indianapolis: Bobbs-Merrill.

Elster, J. 1989. *The Cement of Society*. Cambridge: Cambridge University Press.

Encyclopédie, ou Dictionnaire Raisonné des Sciences, des Artes et des Métiers, (ed. Diderot and D'Alembert). Paris: Briasson, David, Le Breton, Durand.

Geertz, C. 1973. *The Interpretation of Cultures*. New York: Basic Books.

Geertz, C. 1979. *Meaning and Order in Moroccan Society* (C. Geertz, H. Geertz and L Rosen). Cambridge: Cambridge University Press.

Gell, A. 1982. 'The Market Wheel: Symbolic Aspects of an Indian Tribal Market', *Man*, 17(3): 470–91.

Gudeman, S. 1986. *Economics as Culture: models and metaphors of livelihood*. London: Routledge and Kegan Paul.

Gudeman, S. 1992. 'Remodeling the House of Economics: culture and innovation', *American Ethnologist*, 19(1): 139–52.

Gudeman, S. and M. Penn. 1982. 'Models, meanings and reflexivity', in D. Parkin (ed.), *Semantic Anthropology*. London: Academic Press. pp. 89–106.

Gudeman, S. and A. Rivera. 1990. *Conversations in Colombia*. Cambridge: Cambridge University Press.

Klitgaard, R. 1990. *Tropical Gangsters*. Basic Books.

Kornai, J. 1972. *Anti-equilibrium*. Amsterdam: North-Holland Publishing.

Malinowski, B. and J. de la Fuente. 1982. *Malinowski in Mexico*. London: Routledge & Kegan Paul.

Marglin, S. 1974. 'What do bosses do?', *Review of Radical Political Economics*, 6(2): 60–112.

Mill, J. S. 1929 [1848]. *Principles of Political Economy*, (ed. W. J. Ashley). London: Longmans, Green.

Nash, M. 1961. 'The Social Context of Economic Choice in a Small Society', *Man*, 219: 186–91.

Plattner, S. 1989a. 'Economic behavior in markets', in S. Plattner (ed.), *Economic Anthropology*. Stanford: Stanford University Press, pp. 209–21.

Plattner, S. 1989b. 'Markets and marketplaces', in S. Plattner (ed.), *Economic Anthropology*. Stanford: Stanford University Press. pp. 171–208.

Robinson, J. 1933. *The Economics of Imperfect Competition*. London: Macmillan.

Sahlins, M. 1972. *Stone Age Economics*. Chicago: Aldine.

Sahlins, M. 1976. *Culture and Practical Reason*. Chicago: University of Chicago Press.

Schumpeter, J. 1934. *The Theory of Economic Development*. Cambridge: Harvard University Press.

Schumpeter, J. 1976 [1942]. *Capitalism, Socialism and Democracy*. New York: Harper and Row.

Smith, A. 1976[1759]. *The Theory of Moral Sentiments*. Oxford: Oxford University Press.

Smith, A. 1976 [1776]. *The Wealth of Nations*. Chicago: University of Chicago Press.

Veblen, T. 1914. *The Instinct of Workmanship*. New York: Macmillan.

Veblen, T. 1942 [1898]. 'Why is Economics not an Evolutionary Science?', *The Place of Science in Modern Civilisation*. New York: Viking Press. pp. 56–81.

Veblen, T. 1953 [1899]. *The Theory of the Leisure Class*. New York: Mentor Books.

Index